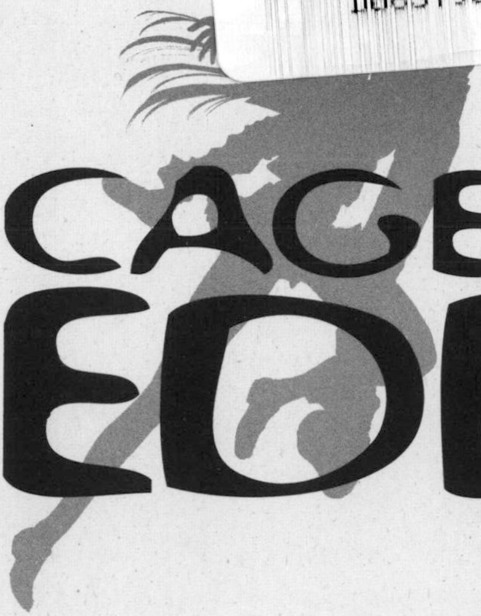

CAGE of EDEN

VOLUME 2

Yoshinobu Yamada

Translated and Adapted by Mari Morimoto

Lettered by Bobby Timony

KC
KODANSHA COMICS

Cage of Eden volume 2 is a work of fiction. Names, characters, places, and incidents are the products of the author's imagination or are used fictitiously. Any resemblance to actual events, locales, or persons, living or dead, is entirely coincidental.

A Kodansha Comics Trade Paperback Original

Published in the United States by Kodansha Comics, an imprint of Kodansha USA Publishing, LLC, New York.

Publication rights for this English edition arranged through Kodansha Ltd., Tokyo.

First published in Japan in 2009 by Kodansha Ltd., Tokyo, as *Eden no Ori,* volume 2.

ISBN 978-1-935429-26-5

Printed in the United States of America

www.kodanshacomics.com

9 8 7 6 5 4 3 2 1

Translator: Mari Morimoto
Lettering: Bobby Timony

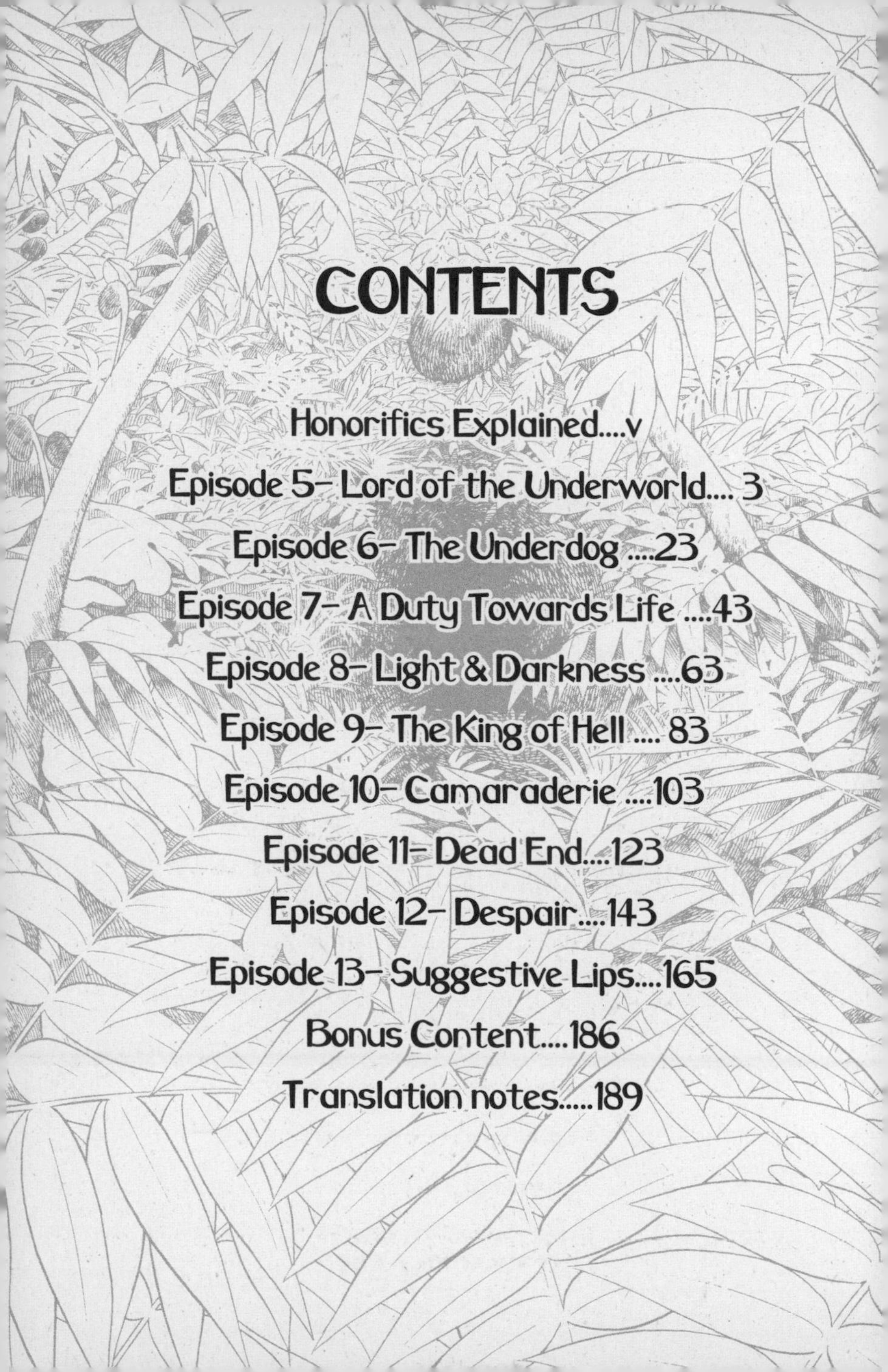

CONTENTS

HONORIFICS EXPLAINED

Throughout the Kodansha Comics books, you will find Japanese honorifics left intact in the translations. For those not familiar with how the Japanese use honorifics and, more important, how they differ from American honorifics, we present this brief overview.

Politeness has always been a critical facet of Japanese culture. Ever since the feudal era, when Japan was a highly stratified society, use of honorifics—which can be defined as polite speech that indicates relationship or status—has played an essential role in the Japanese language. When addressing someone in Japanese, an honorific usually takes the form of a suffix attached to one's name (example: "Asuna-san"), is used as a title at the end of one's name, or appears in place of the name itself (example: "Negi-sensei," or simply "Sensei!").

Honorifics can be expressions of respect or endearment. In the context of manga and anime, honorifics give insight into the nature of the relationship between characters. Many English translations leave out these important honorifics and therefore distort the feel of the original Japanese. Because Japanese honorifics contain nuances that English honorifics lack, it is our policy at Kodansha Comics not to translate them. Here, instead, is a guide to some of the honorifics you may encounter in Kodansha Comics.

-san: This is the most common honorific and is equivalent to Mr., Miss, Ms., or Mrs. It is the all-purpose honorific and can be used in any situation where politeness is required.

-sama: This is one level higher than "-san" and is used to confer great respect.

-dono: This comes from the word "tono," which means "lord." It is an even higher level than "-sama" and confers utmost respect.

-kun: This suffix is used at the end of boys' names to express familiarity or endearment. It is also sometimes used by men among friends, or when addressing someone younger or of a lower station.

-chan: This is used to express endearment, mostly toward girls. It is also used for little boys, pets, and even among lovers. It gives a sense of childish cuteness.

Bozu: This is an informal way to refer to a boy, similar to the English terms "kid" and "squirt."

Sempai/
Senpai: This title suggests that the addressee is one's senior in a group or organization. It is most often used in a school setting, where underclassmen refer to their upperclassmen as "sempai." It can also be used in the workplace, such as when a newer employee addresses an employee who has seniority in the company.

Kohai: This is the opposite of "sempai" and is used toward underclassmen in school or newcomers in the workplace. It connotes that the addressee is of a lower station.

Sensei: Literally meaning "one who has come before," this title is used for teachers, doctors, or masters of any profession or art.

-[blank]: This is usually forgotten in these lists, but it is perhaps the most significant difference between Japanese and English. The lack of honorific means that the speaker has permission to address the person in a very intimate way. Usually, only family, spouses, or very close friends have this kind of permission. Known as yobisute, it can be gratifying when someone who has earned the intimacy starts to call one by one's name without an honorific. But when that intimacy hasn't been earned, it can be very insulting.

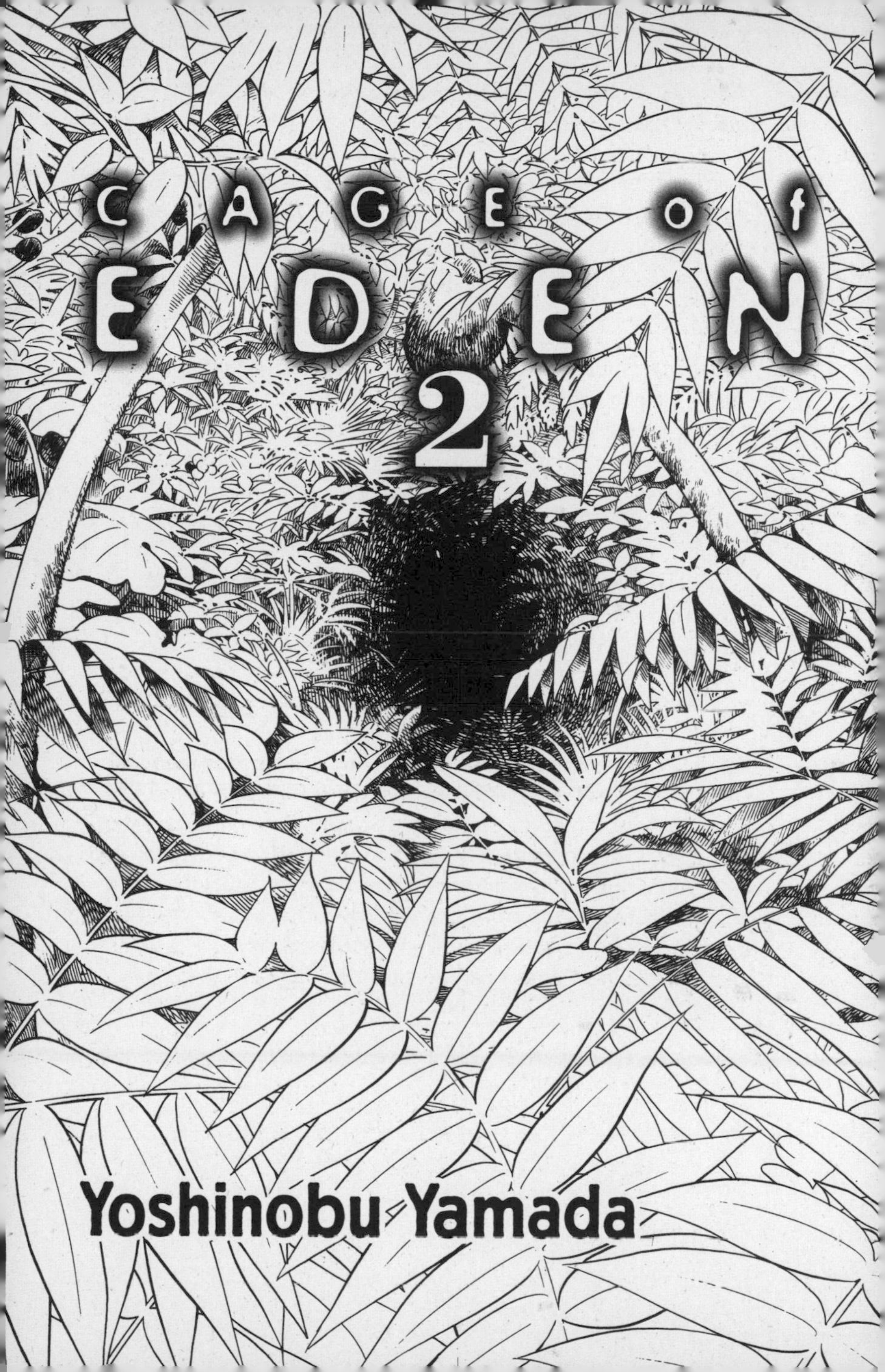
CAGE of
EDEN
2
Yoshinobu Yamada

CAGE of EDEN

Episode 5
Lord of the Underworld

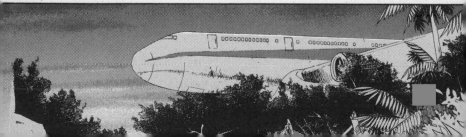

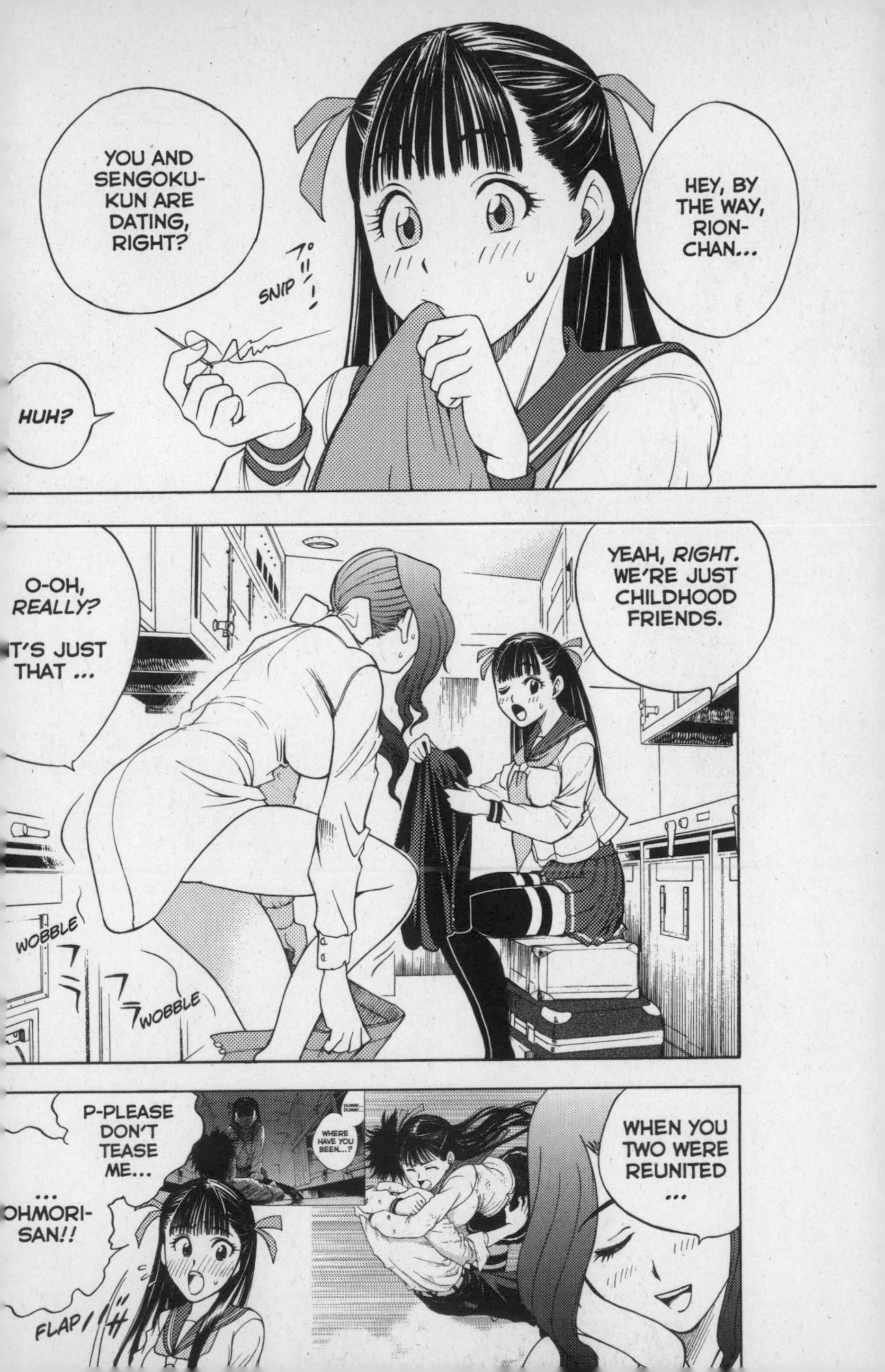
HEY, BY THE WAY, RION-CHAN...
YOU AND SENGOKU-KUN ARE DATING, RIGHT?
SNIP
HUH?
YEAH, *RIGHT*. WE'RE JUST CHILDHOOD FRIENDS.
O-OH, *REALLY?*
IT'S JUST THAT ...
WOBBLE
WOBBLE
WHEN YOU TWO WERE REUNITED ...
WHERE HAVE YOU BEEN...?
P-PLEASE DON'T TEASE ME...
... OHMORI-SAN!!
FLAP!

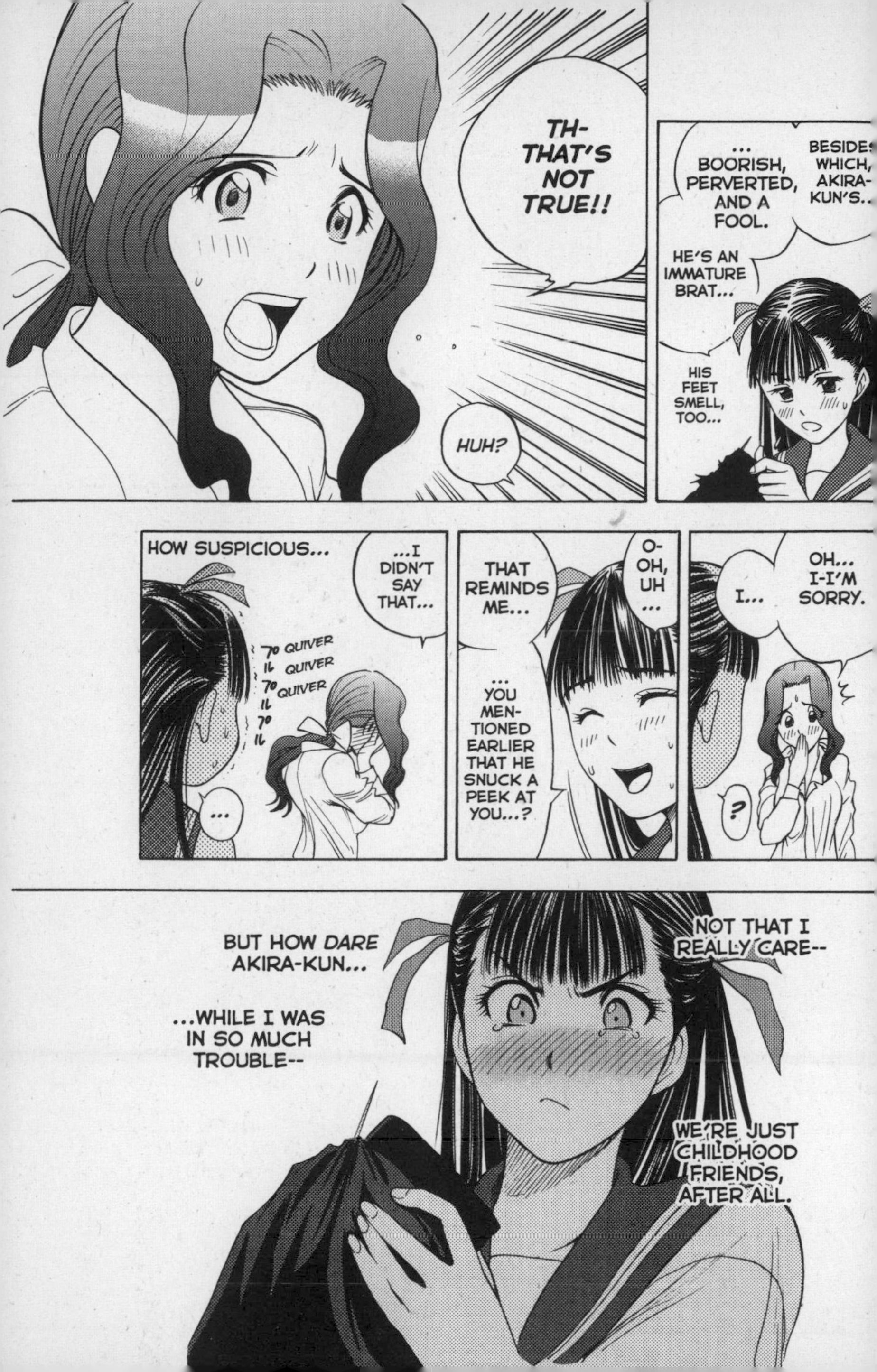
BESIDES WHICH, AKIRA-KUN'S..
... BOORISH, PERVERTED, AND A FOOL.
HE'S AN IMMATURE BRAT...
HIS FEET SMELL, TOO...
TH-THAT'S NOT TRUE!!
HUH?
OH... I-I'M SORRY.
I...
?
O-OH, UH ...
THAT REMINDS ME...
... YOU MENTIONED EARLIER THAT HE SNUCK A PEEK AT YOU...?
...I DIDN'T SAY THAT...
HOW SUSPICIOUS...
QUIVER
QUIVER
QUIVER
...
NOT THAT I REALLY CARE--
BUT HOW *DARE* AKIRA-KUN...
...WHILE I WAS IN SO MUCH TROUBLE--
WE'RE JUST CHILDHOOD FRIENDS, AFTER ALL.

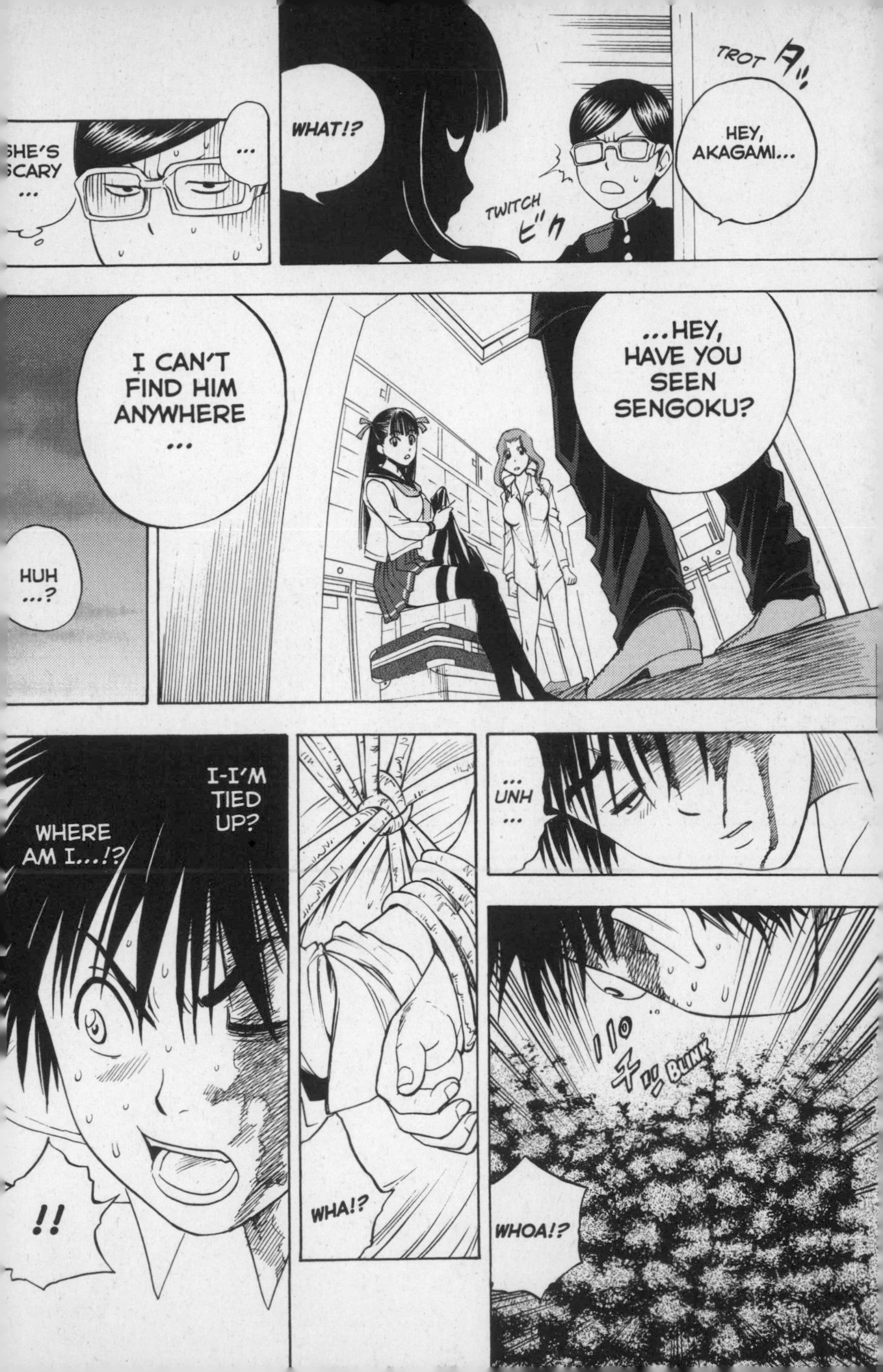
TROT
HEY, AKAGAMI...
TWITCH
WHAT!?
...
SHE'S SCARY ...
...HEY, HAVE YOU SEEN SENGOKU?
I CAN'T FIND HIM ANYWHERE ...
HUH ...?
... UNH ...
BLINK
WHOA!?
WHA!?
I-I'M TIED UP?
WHERE AM I...!?
!!

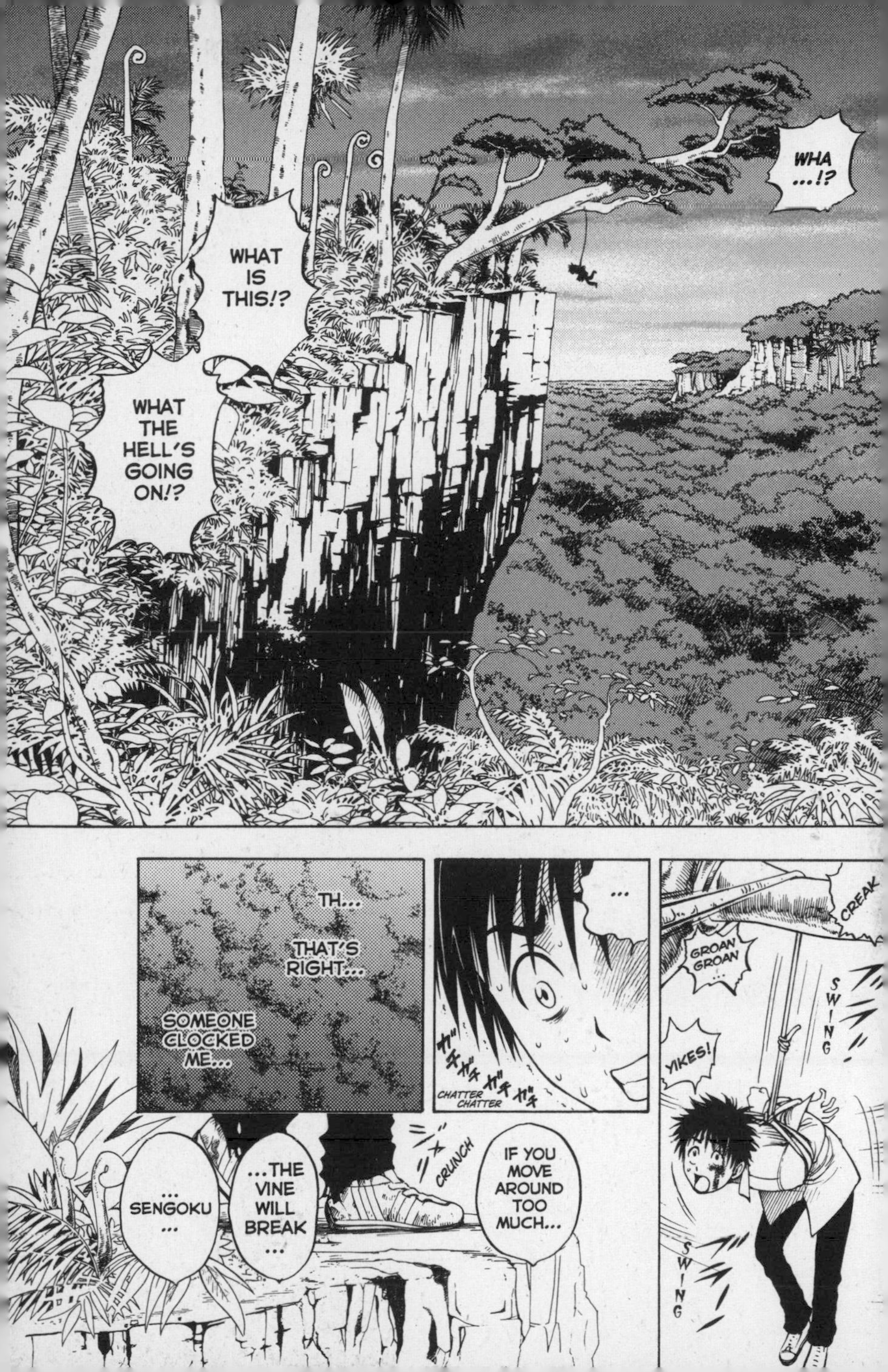
WHA ...!?
WHAT IS THIS!?
WHAT THE HELL'S GOING ON!?
CREAK
GROAN GROAN ...
SWING
YIKES!
SWING
...
CHATTER CHATTER
TH...
THAT'S RIGHT...
SOMEONE CLOCKED ME...
IF YOU MOVE AROUND TOO MUCH...
CRUNCH
...THE VINE WILL BREAK ...
... SENGOKU ...

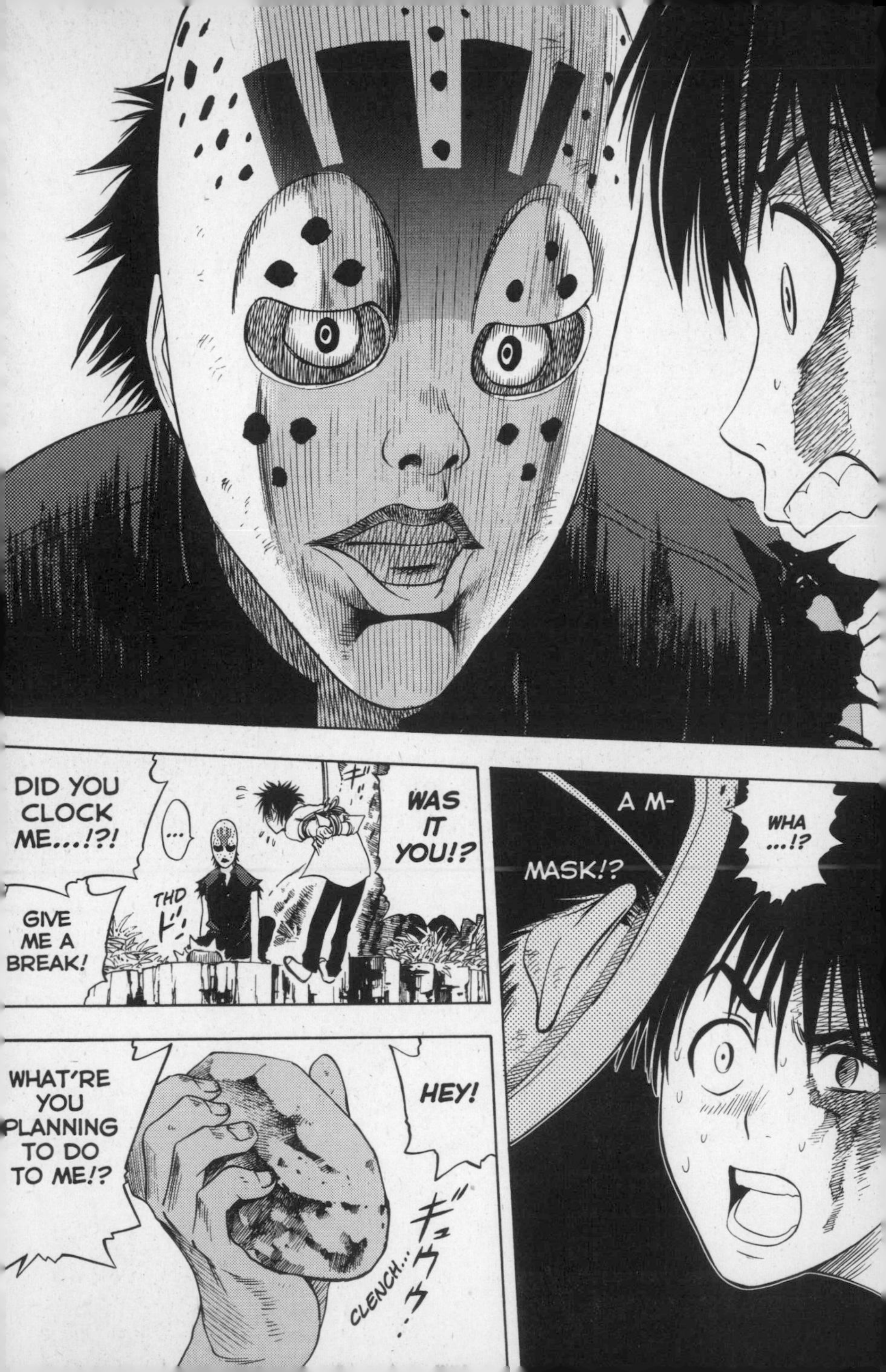
WHA ...!?
A M-
MASK!?
WAS IT YOU!?
...
DID YOU CLOCK ME...!?!
THD
GIVE ME A BREAK!
HEY!
CLENCH...
WHAT'RE YOU PLANNING TO DO TO ME!?

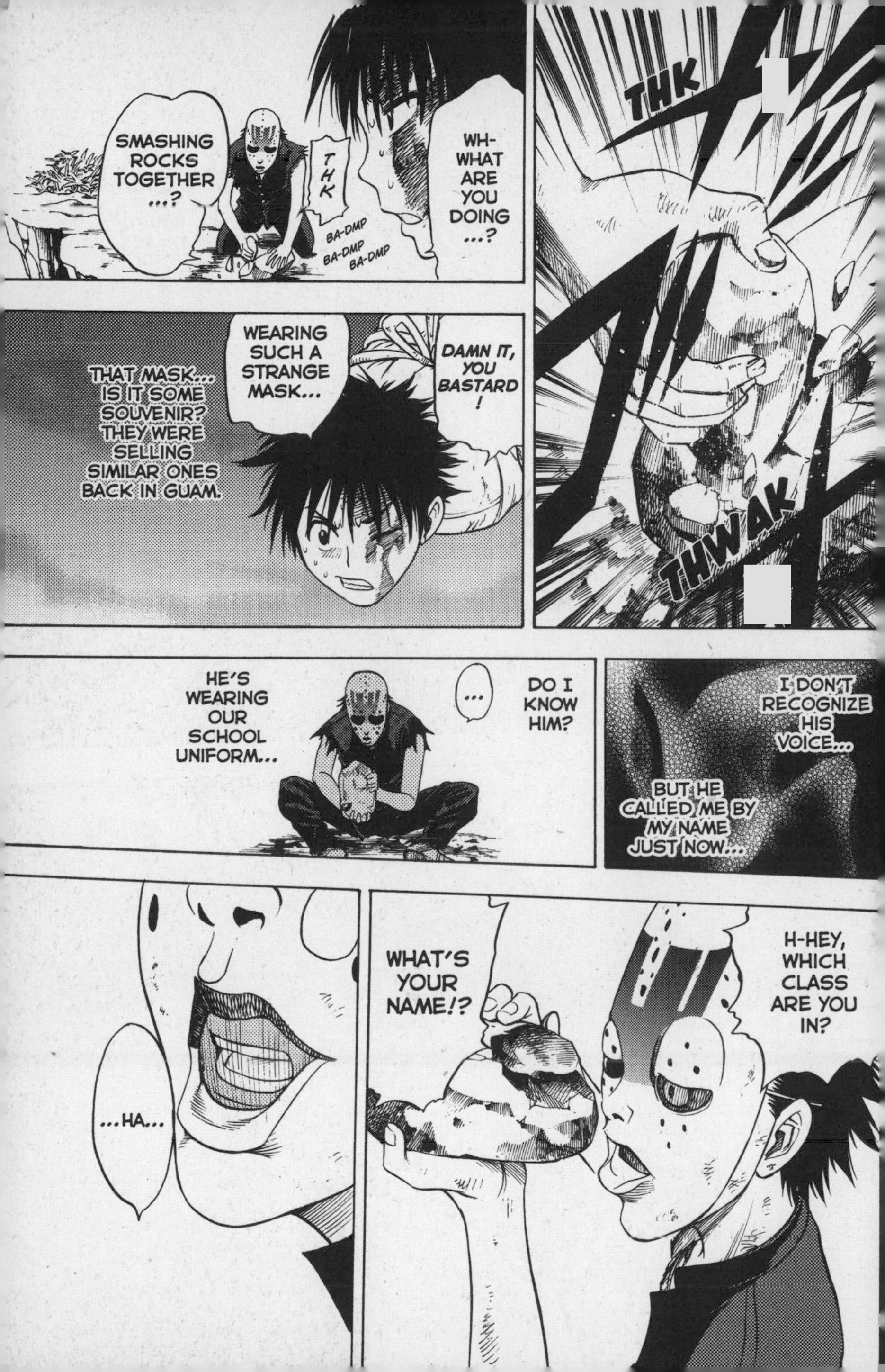
THK
THWAK
WH- WHAT ARE YOU DOING ...?
THK
BA-DMP BA-DMP BA-DMP
SMASHING ROCKS TOGETHER ...?
DAMN IT, YOU BASTARD!
WEARING SUCH A STRANGE MASK...
THAT MASK... IS IT SOME SOUVENIR? THEY WERE SELLING SIMILAR ONES BACK IN GUAM.
I DON'T RECOGNIZE HIS VOICE...
BUT HE CALLED ME BY MY NAME JUST NOW...
DO I KNOW HIM?
...
HE'S WEARING OUR SCHOOL UNIFORM...
H-HEY, WHICH CLASS ARE YOU IN?
WHAT'S YOUR NAME!?
...HA...

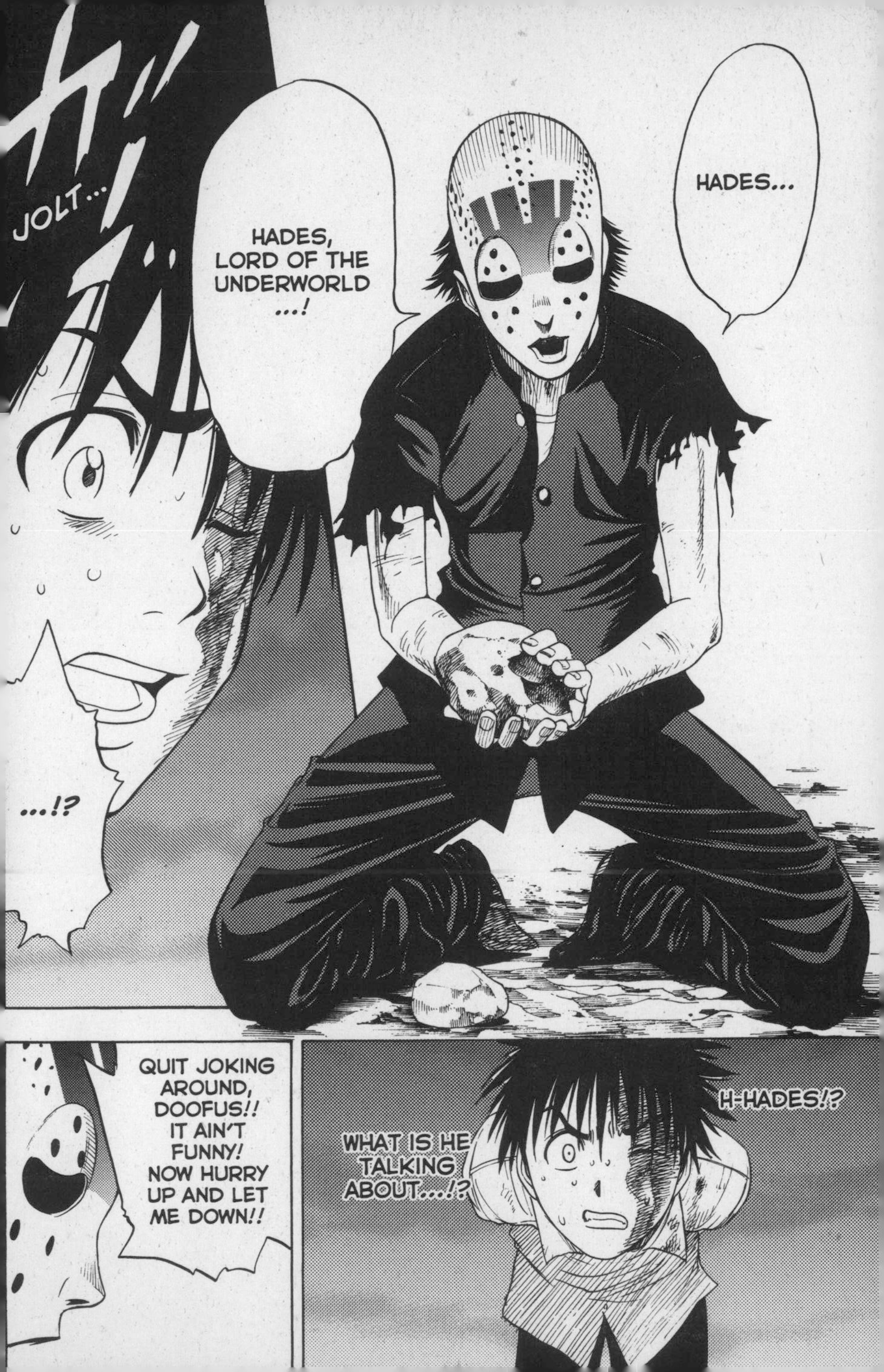
HADES...
HADES, LORD OF THE UNDERWORLD ...!
JOLT...
...!?
H-HADES!?
WHAT IS HE TALKING ABOUT...!?
QUIT JOKING AROUND, DOOFUS!! IT AIN'T FUNNY! NOW HURRY UP AND LET ME DOWN!!

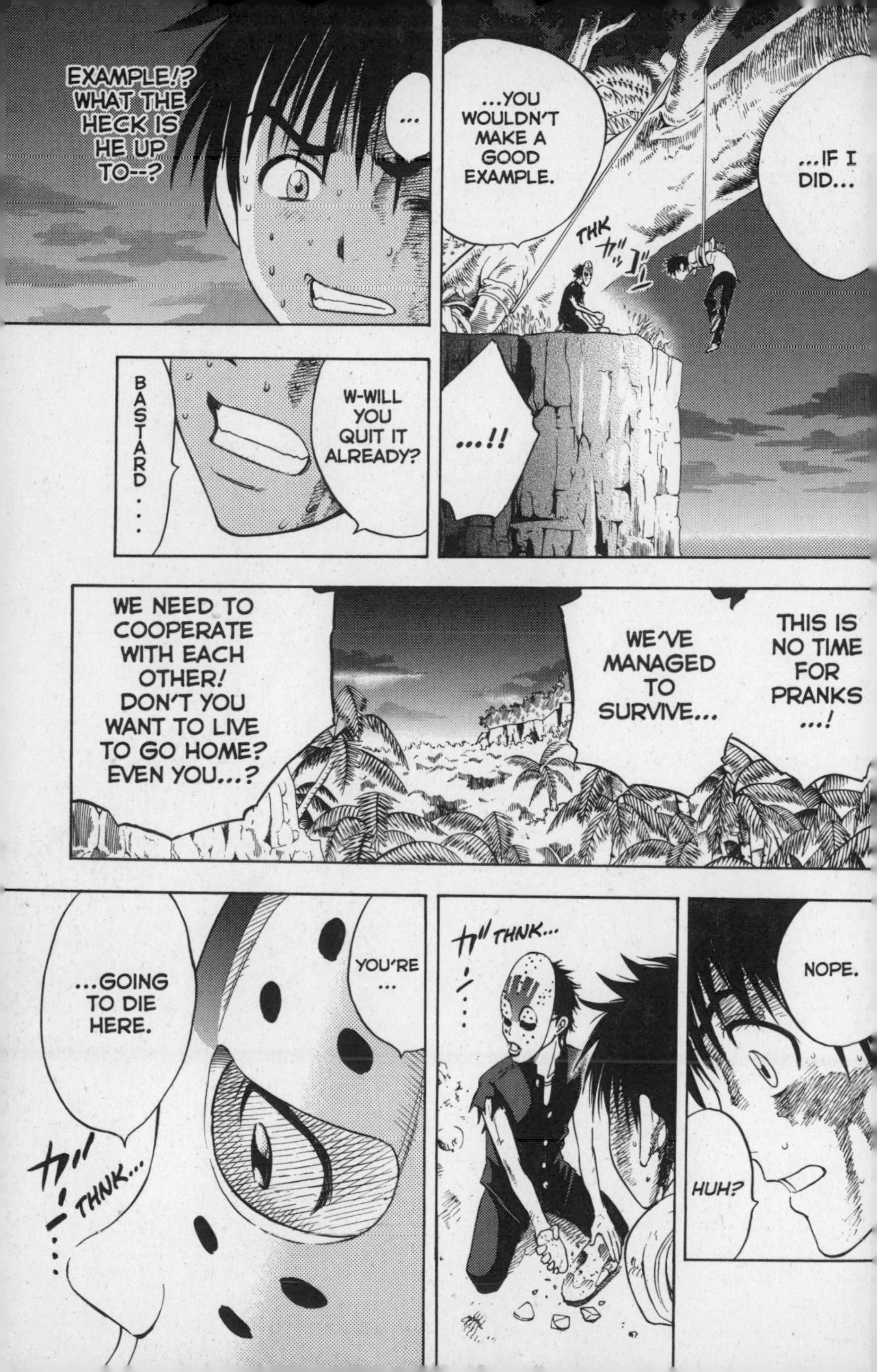
...IF I DID...
...YOU WOULDN'T MAKE A GOOD EXAMPLE.
THK
...!!
...
EXAMPLE!? WHAT THE HECK IS HE UP TO--?
W-WILL YOU QUIT IT ALREADY?
BASTARD...
THIS IS NO TIME FOR PRANKS...!
WE'VE MANAGED TO SURVIVE...
WE NEED TO COOPERATE WITH EACH OTHER! DON'T YOU WANT TO LIVE TO GO HOME? EVEN YOU...?
NOPE.
HUH?
THNK...
YOU'RE...
...GOING TO DIE HERE.
THNK...

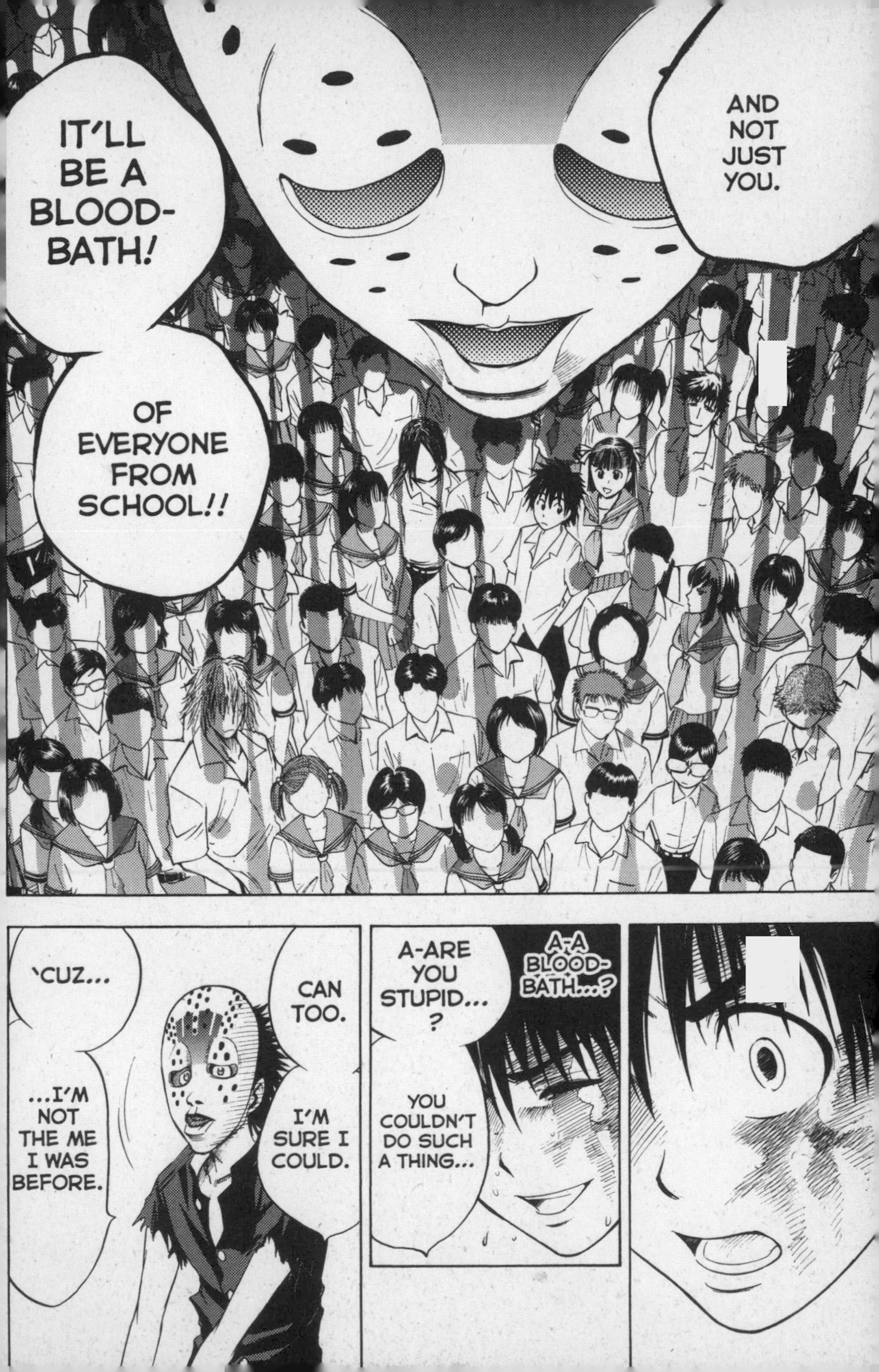
AND NOT JUST YOU.
IT'LL BE A BLOOD-BATH!
OF EVERYONE FROM SCHOOL!!
A-A BLOOD-BATH...?
A-ARE YOU STUPID...?
YOU COULDN'T DO SUCH A THING...
CAN TOO.
I'M SURE I COULD.
'CUZ...
...I'M NOT THE ME I WAS BEFORE.

HEH. HEH HEH. A-HA HA!
I'M STRONG NOW!
I CAN DO WHATEVER I WANT... HOWEVER MUCH I WANT!!

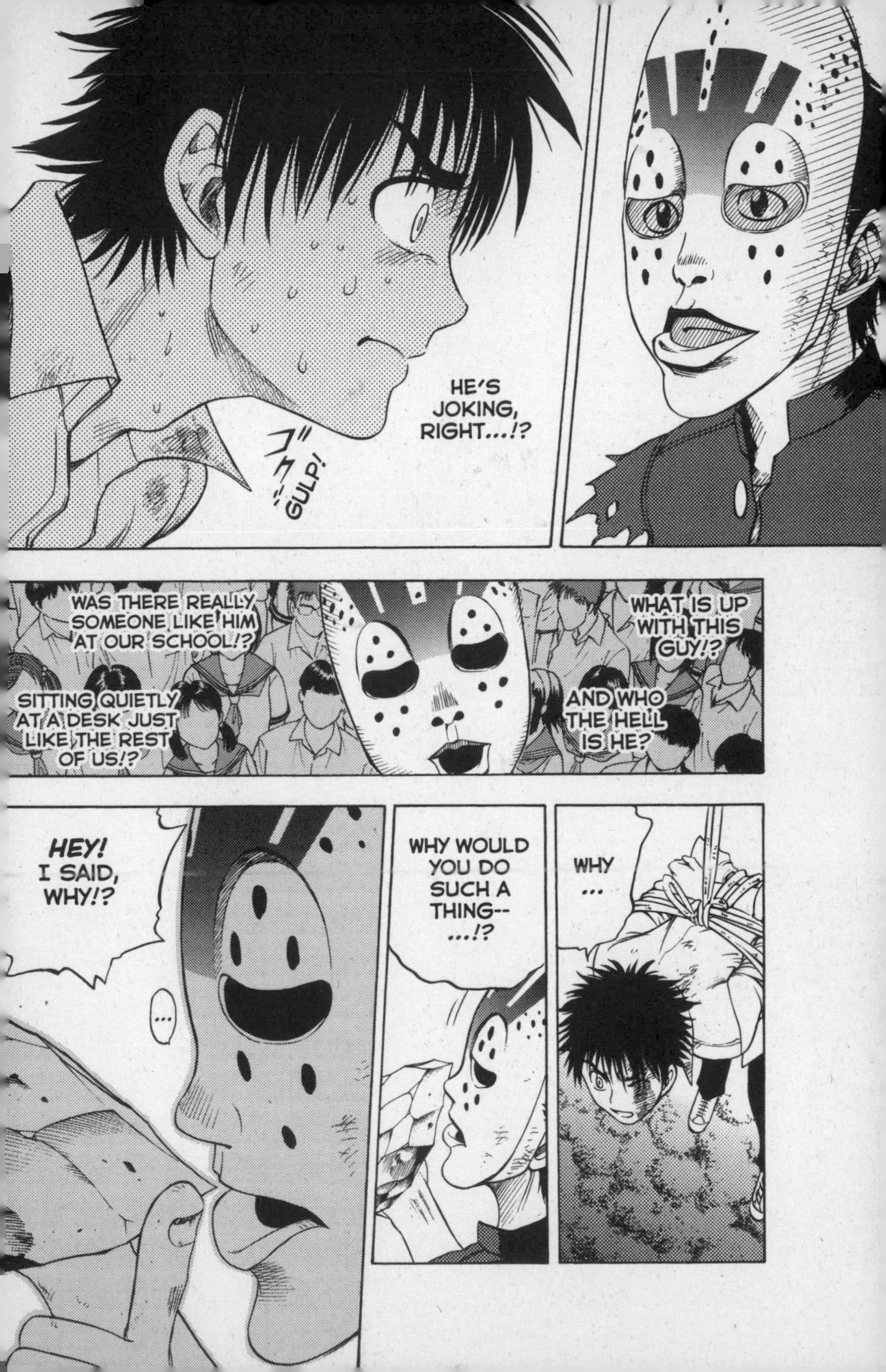
HE'S JOKING, RIGHT...!?
GULP!
WHAT IS UP WITH THIS GUY!?
AND WHO THE HELL IS HE?
WAS THERE REALLY SOMEONE LIKE HIM AT OUR SCHOOL!?
SITTING QUIETLY AT A DESK JUST LIKE THE REST OF US!?
WHY ...
WHY WOULD YOU DO SUCH A THING-- ...!?
HEY! I SAID, WHY!?
...

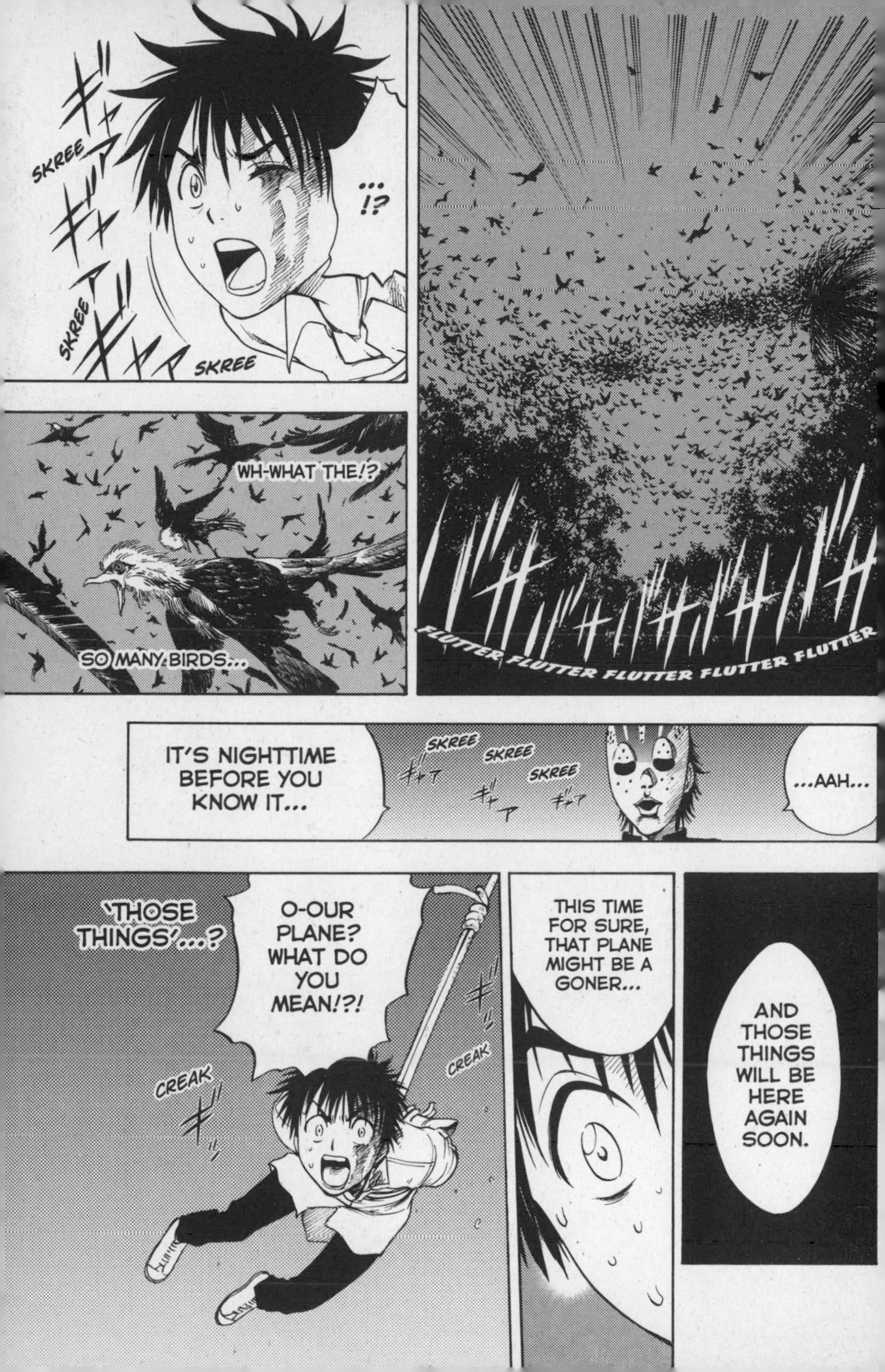
FLUTTER FLUTTER FLUTTER FLUTTER FLUTTER
SKREE
SKREE
SKREE
...!?
WH-WHAT THE!?
SO MANY BIRDS...
...AAH...
SKREE
SKREE
SKREE
IT'S NIGHTTIME BEFORE YOU KNOW IT...
AND THOSE THINGS WILL BE HERE AGAIN SOON.
THIS TIME FOR SURE, THAT PLANE MIGHT BE A GONER...
O-OUR PLANE? WHAT DO YOU MEAN!?!
CREAK
'THOSE THINGS'...?
CREAK

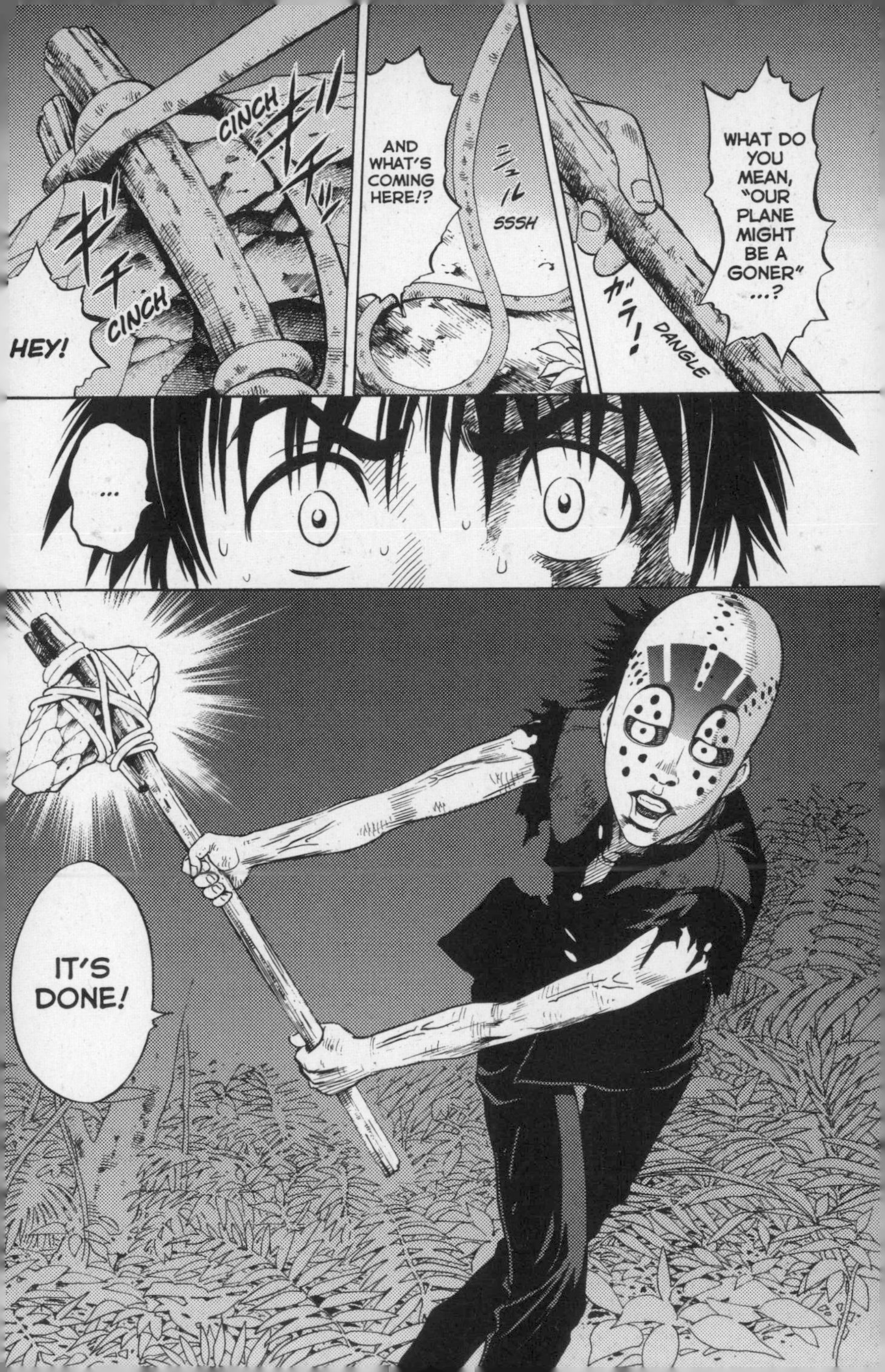
WHAT DO YOU MEAN, "OUR PLANE MIGHT BE A GONER"...?
DANGLE
AND WHAT'S COMING HERE!?
SSSH
CINCH
CINCH
HEY!
...
IT'S DONE!

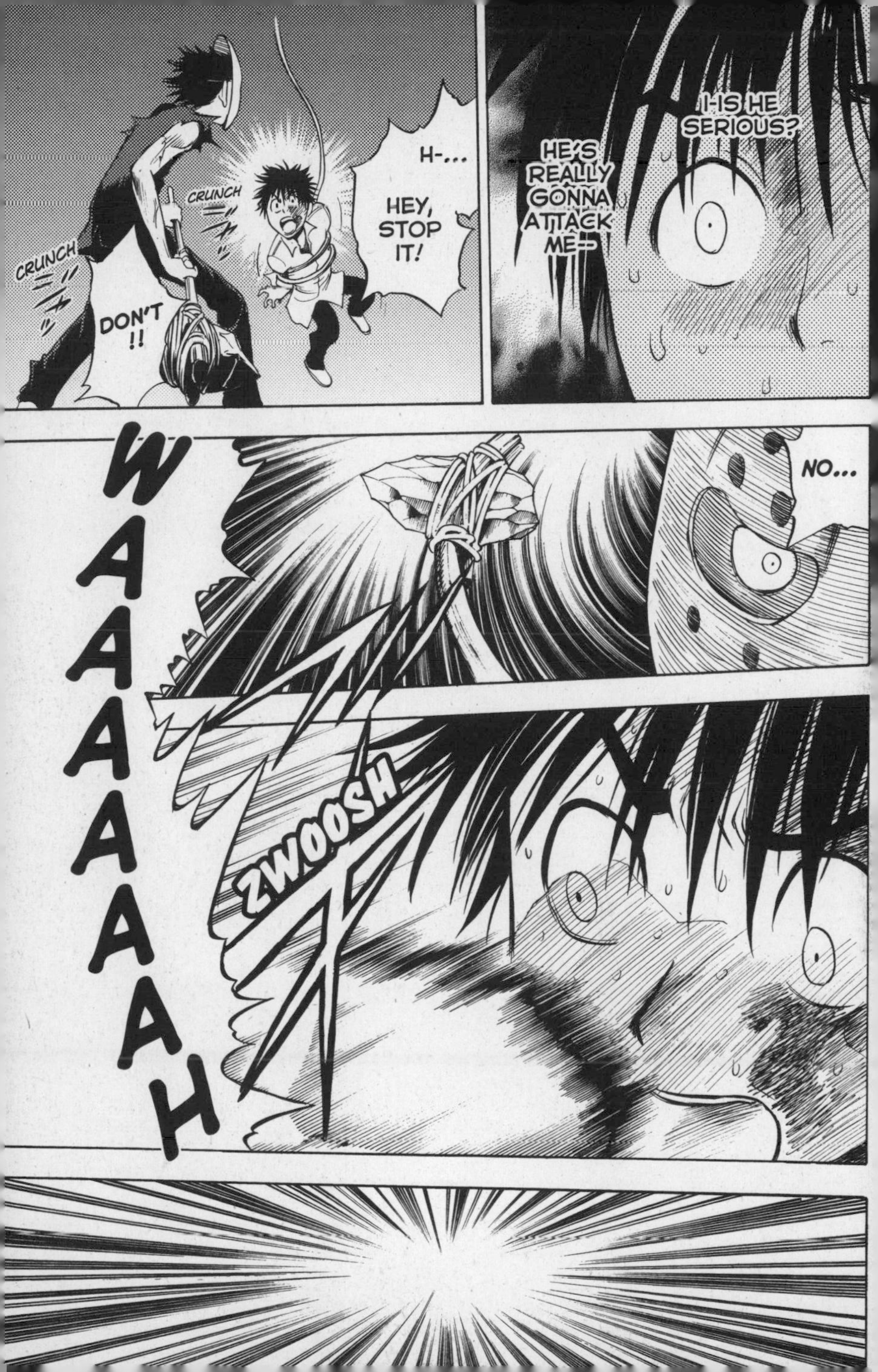
I-IS HE SERIOUS?
HE'S REALLY GONNA ATTACK ME--
H-...
HEY, STOP IT!
CRUNCH
CRUNCH
DON'T !!
NO...
WAAAAAAH
ZWOOSH

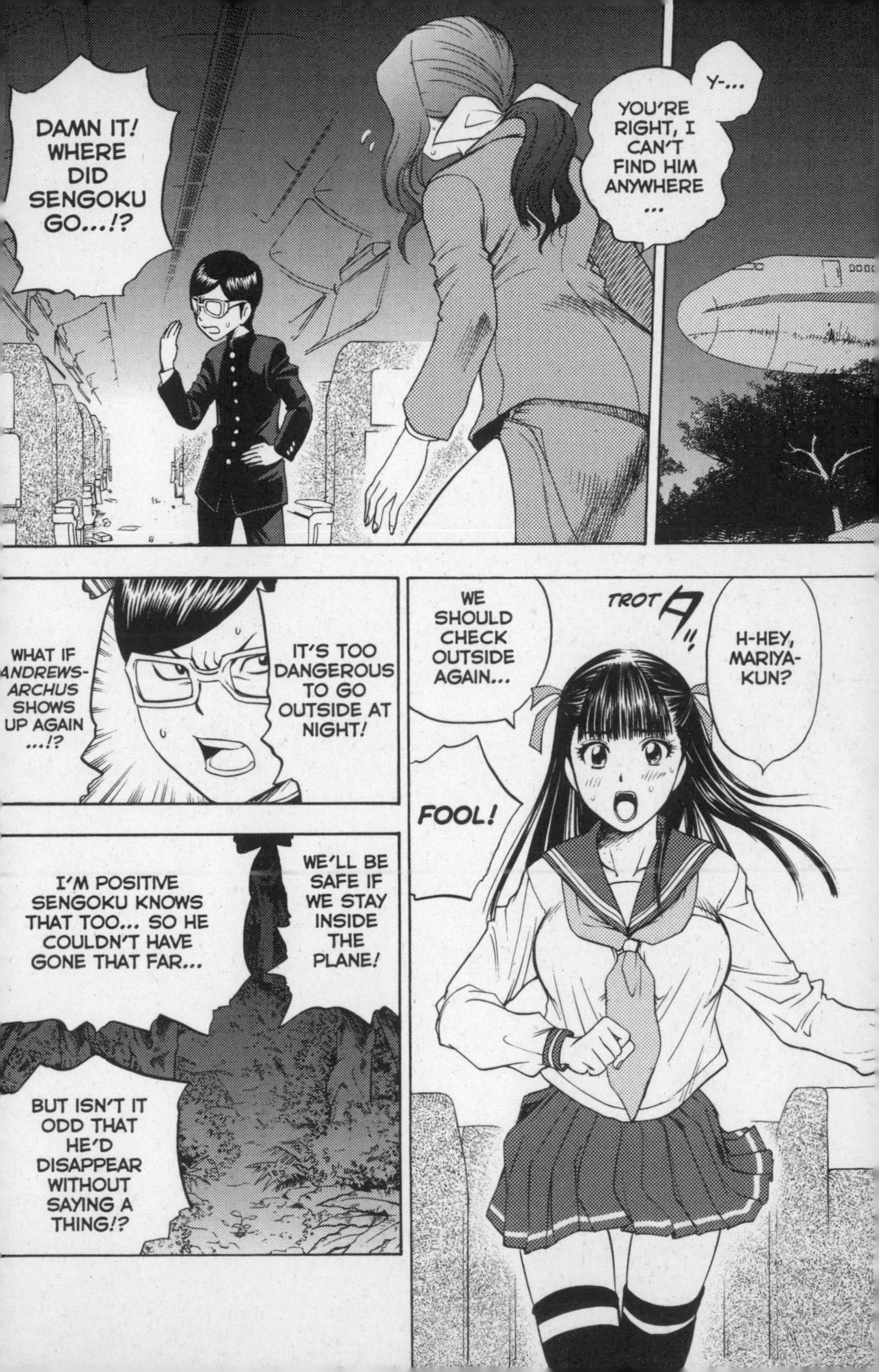
Y-... YOU'RE RIGHT, I CAN'T FIND HIM ANYWHERE ...
DAMN IT! WHERE DID SENGOKU GO...!?
H-HEY, MARIYA-KUN?
TROT
WE SHOULD CHECK OUTSIDE AGAIN...
FOOL!
IT'S TOO DANGEROUS TO GO OUTSIDE AT NIGHT!
WHAT IF ANDREWS-ARCHUS SHOWS UP AGAIN ...!?
WE'LL BE SAFE IF WE STAY INSIDE THE PLANE!
I'M POSITIVE SENGOKU KNOWS THAT TOO... SO HE COULDN'T HAVE GONE THAT FAR...
BUT ISN'T IT ODD THAT HE'D DISAPPEAR WITHOUT SAYING A THING!?

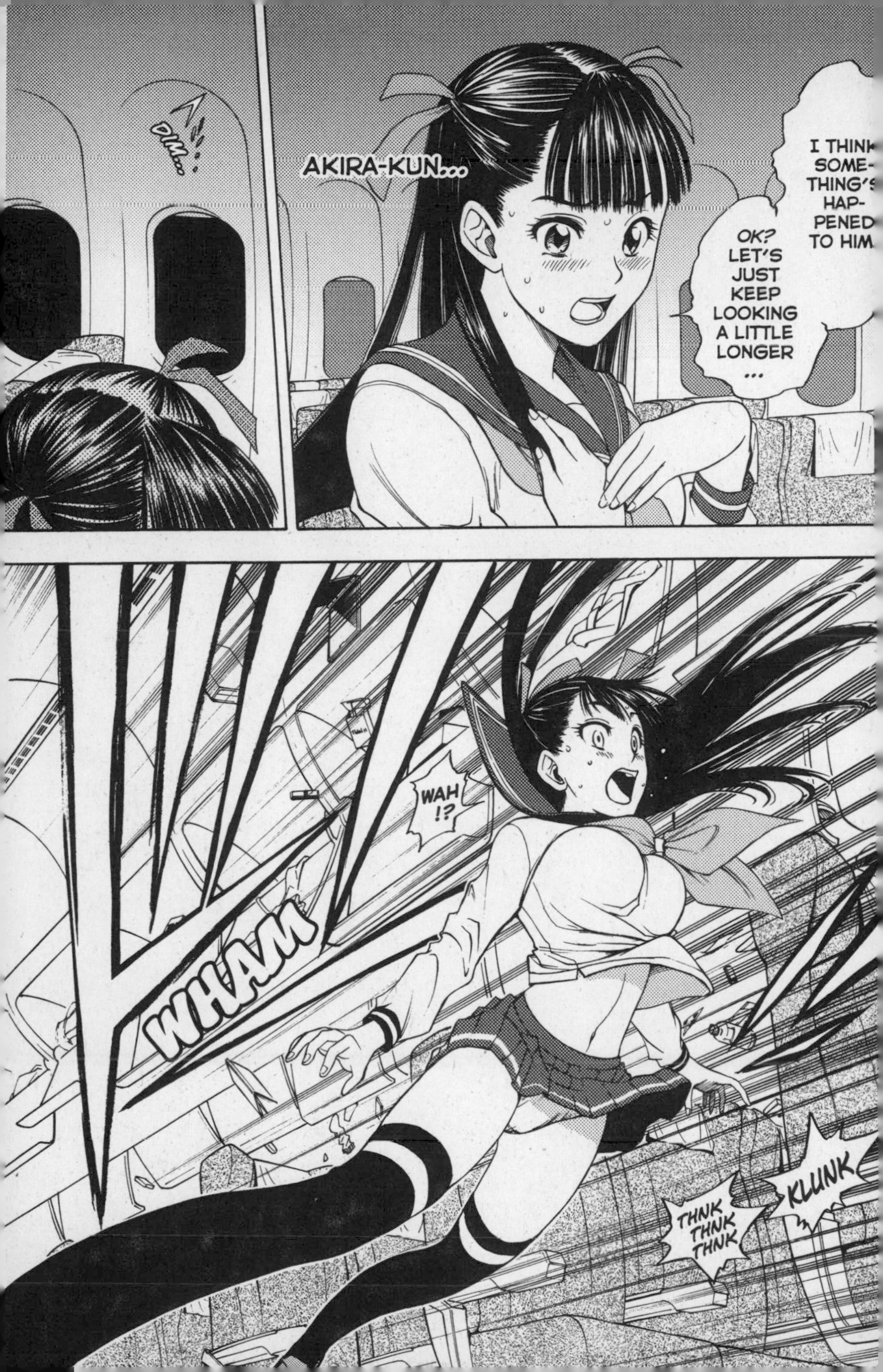
I THINK SOMETHING'S HAPPENED TO HIM.
OK? LET'S JUST KEEP LOOKING A LITTLE LONGER ...
AKIRA-KUN...
DIM...
WAH !?
WHAM
KLUNK
THNK THNK THNK

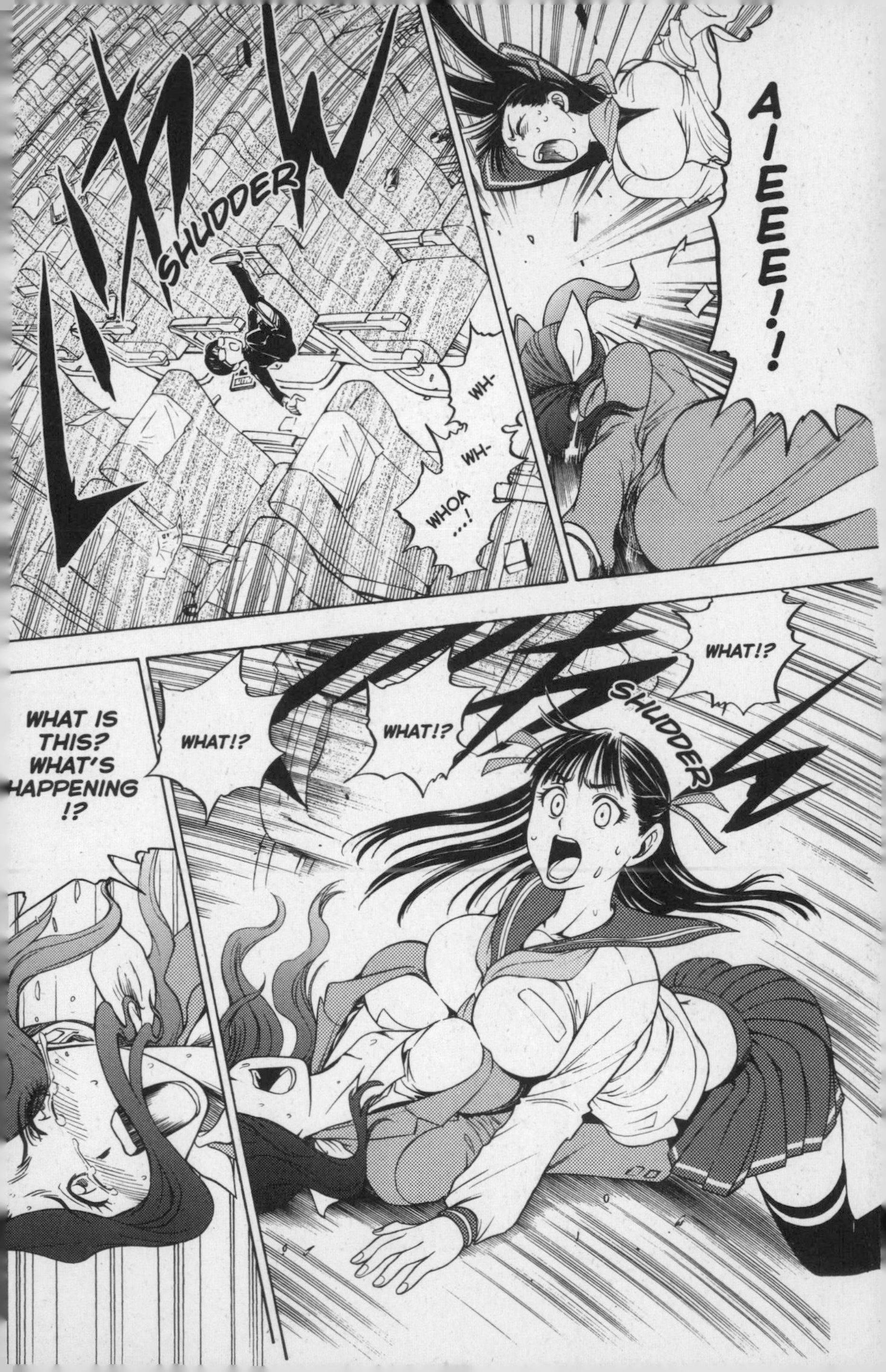
AIEEE!!
SHUDDER
WH-
WH-
WHOA ...!
WHAT!?
SHUDDER
WHAT!?
WHAT!?
WHAT IS THIS? WHAT'S HAPPENING !?

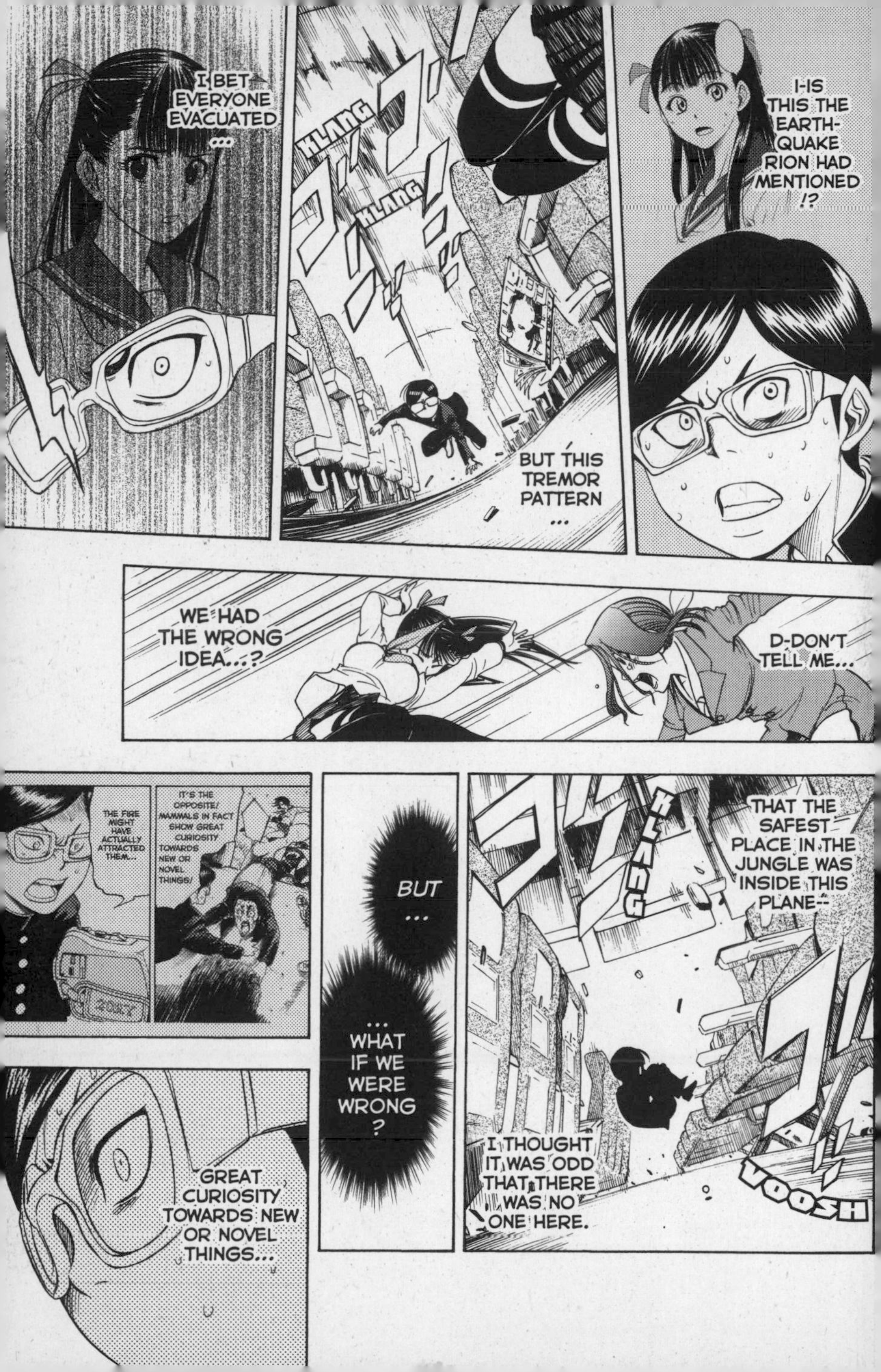
I-IS THIS THE EARTH-QUAKE RION HAD MENTIONED!?
KLANG
KLANG
BUT THIS TREMOR PATTERN...
I BET EVERYONE EVACUATED...
D-DON'T TELL ME...
WE HAD THE WRONG IDEA...?
THAT THE SAFEST PLACE IN THE JUNGLE WAS INSIDE THIS PLANE--
KLANG
VOOSH
I THOUGHT IT WAS ODD THAT THERE WAS NO ONE HERE.
BUT...
...WHAT IF WE WERE WRONG?
IT'S THE OPPOSITE! MAMMALS IN FACT SHOW GREAT CURIOSITY TOWARDS NEW OR NOVEL THINGS!
THE FIRE MIGHT HAVE ACTUALLY ATTRACTED THEM...
GREAT CURIOSITY TOWARDS NEW OR NOVEL THINGS...

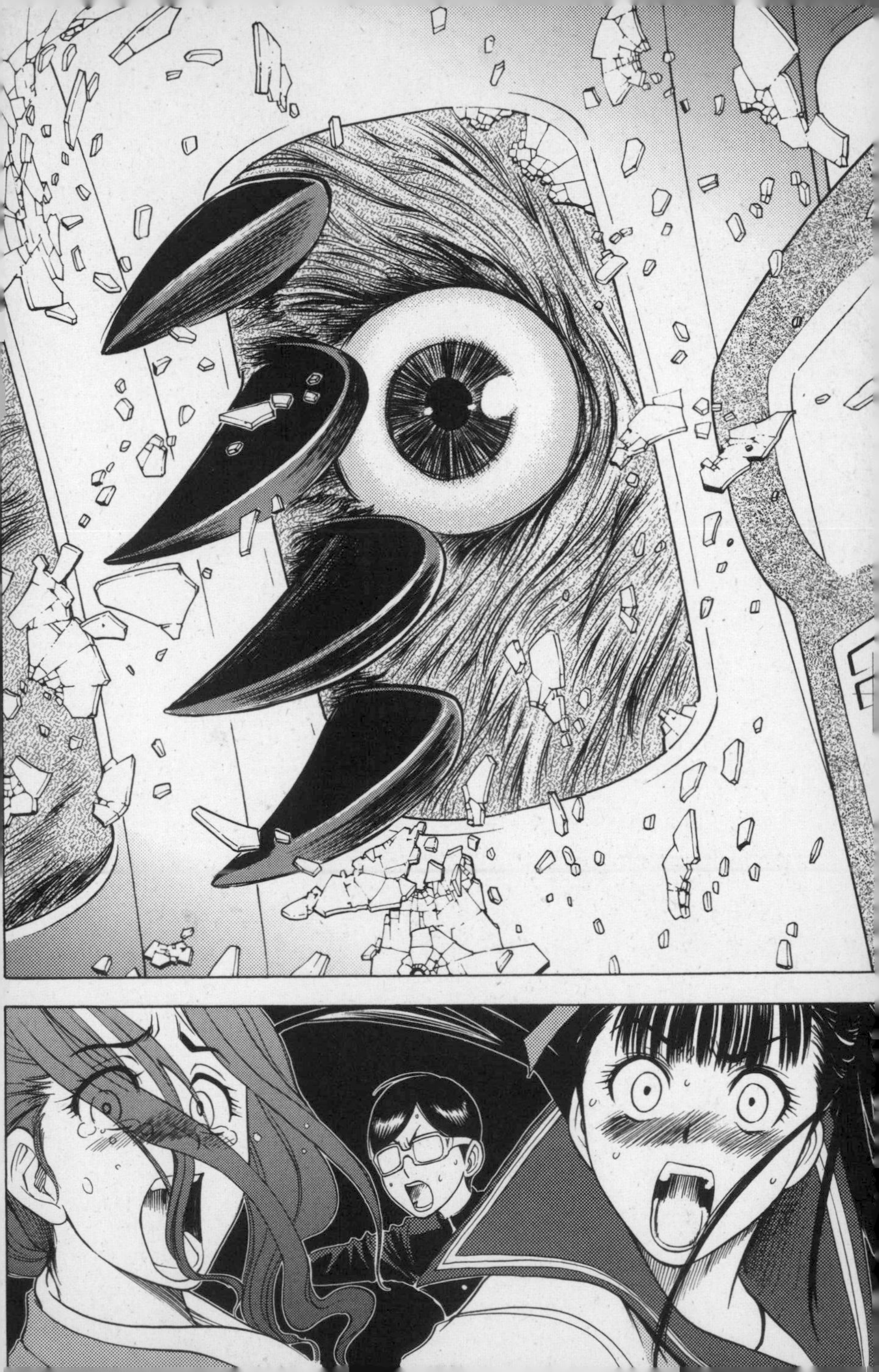

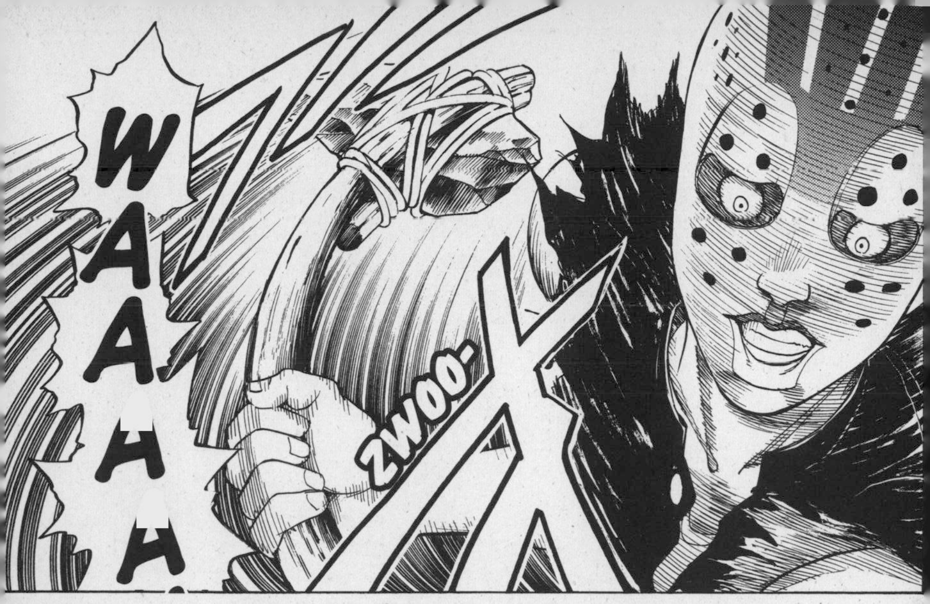
WAAAAA
ZWOO-

Episode 6 The Underdog

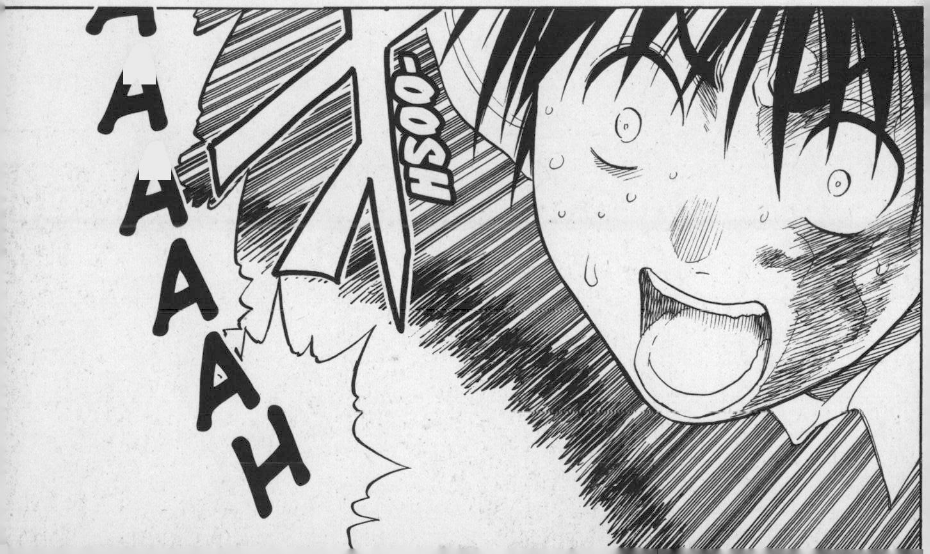
-OOSH
AAAAAAH

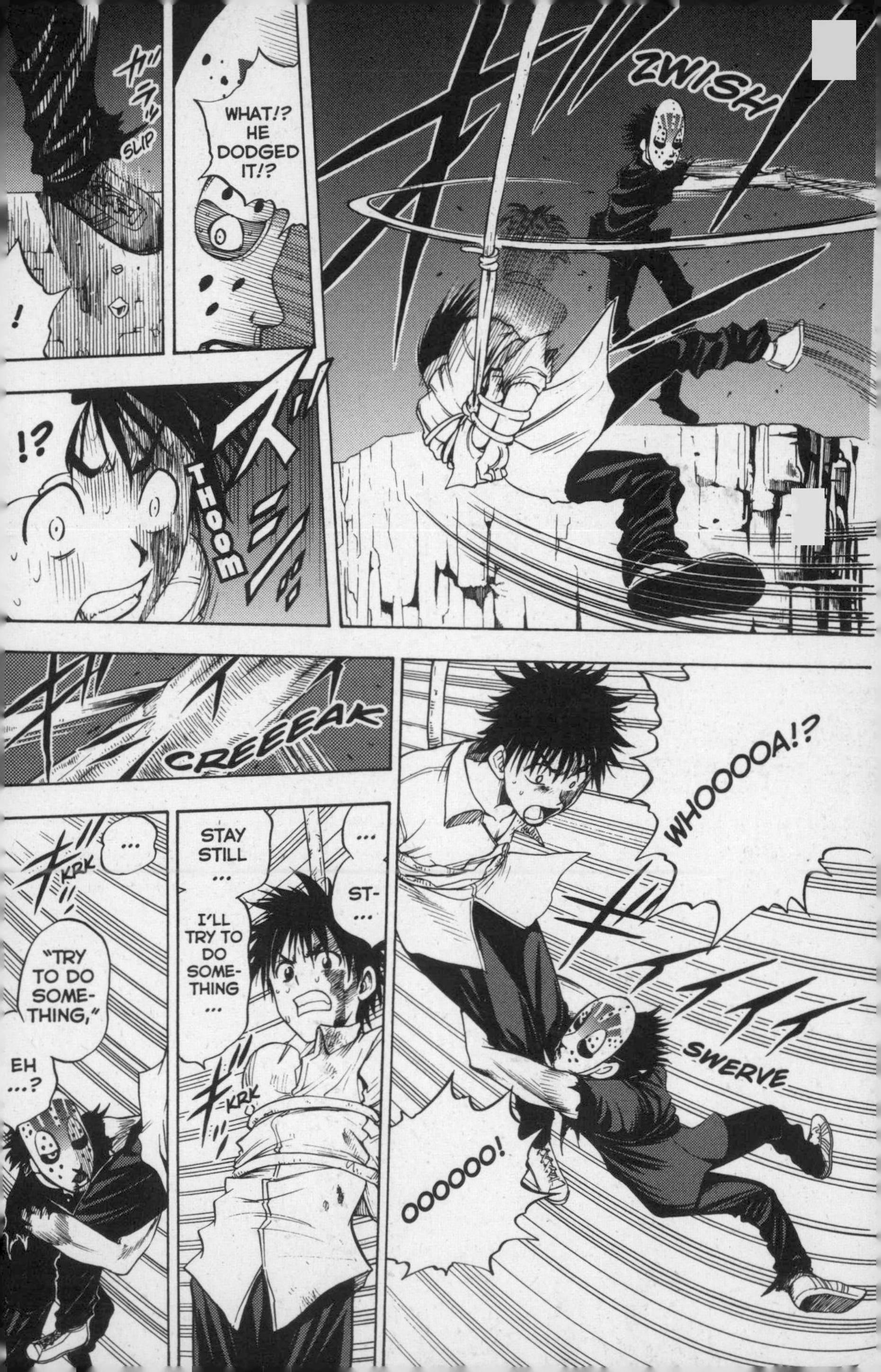
ZWISH
WHAT!? HE DODGED IT!?
SLIP
!
!?
THOOM
WHOOOOA!?
SWERVE
OOOOOO!
CREEEEAK
... ST- ...
STAY STILL ...
I'LL TRY TO DO SOME-THING ...
KRK
...
KRK
"TRY TO DO SOME-THING,"
EH ...?

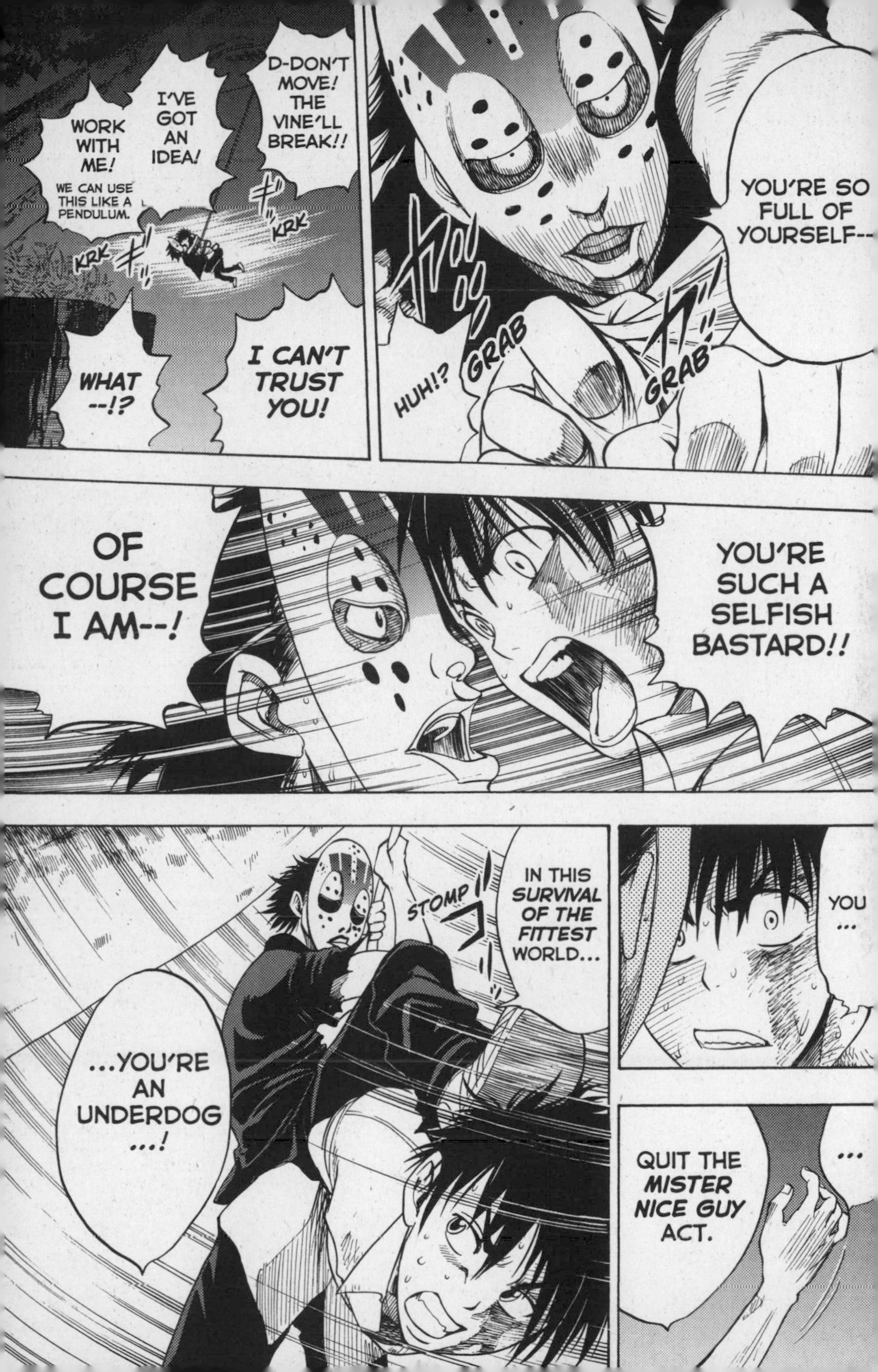
YOU'RE SO FULL OF YOURSELF--
HUH!?
GRAB
GRAB
D-DON'T MOVE! THE VINE'LL BREAK!!
I'VE GOT AN IDEA!
WORK WITH ME!
WE CAN USE THIS LIKE A PENDULUM.
KRK
KRK
I CAN'T TRUST YOU!
WHAT --!?
YOU'RE SUCH A SELFISH BASTARD!!
OF COURSE I AM--!
YOU ...
...
QUIT THE MISTER NICE GUY ACT.
IN THIS SURVIVAL OF THE FITTEST WORLD...
STOMP
...YOU'RE AN UNDERDOG ...!

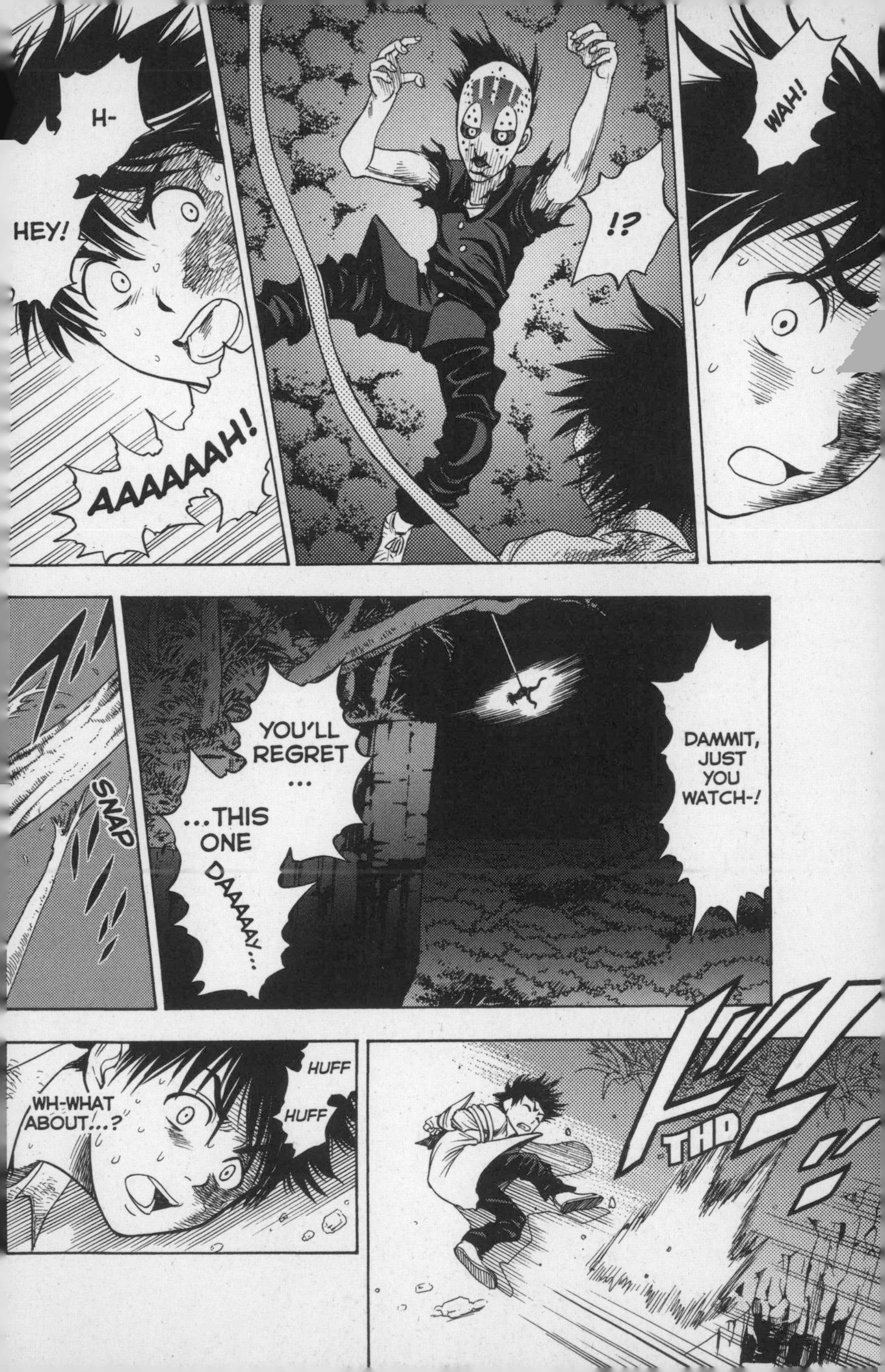
WAH!
!?
H-
HEY!
AAAAAAH!
DAMMIT, JUST YOU WATCH-!
YOU'LL REGRET ...
...THIS ONE DAAAAAY...
SNAP
THD
HUFF
HUFF
WH-WHAT ABOUT...?

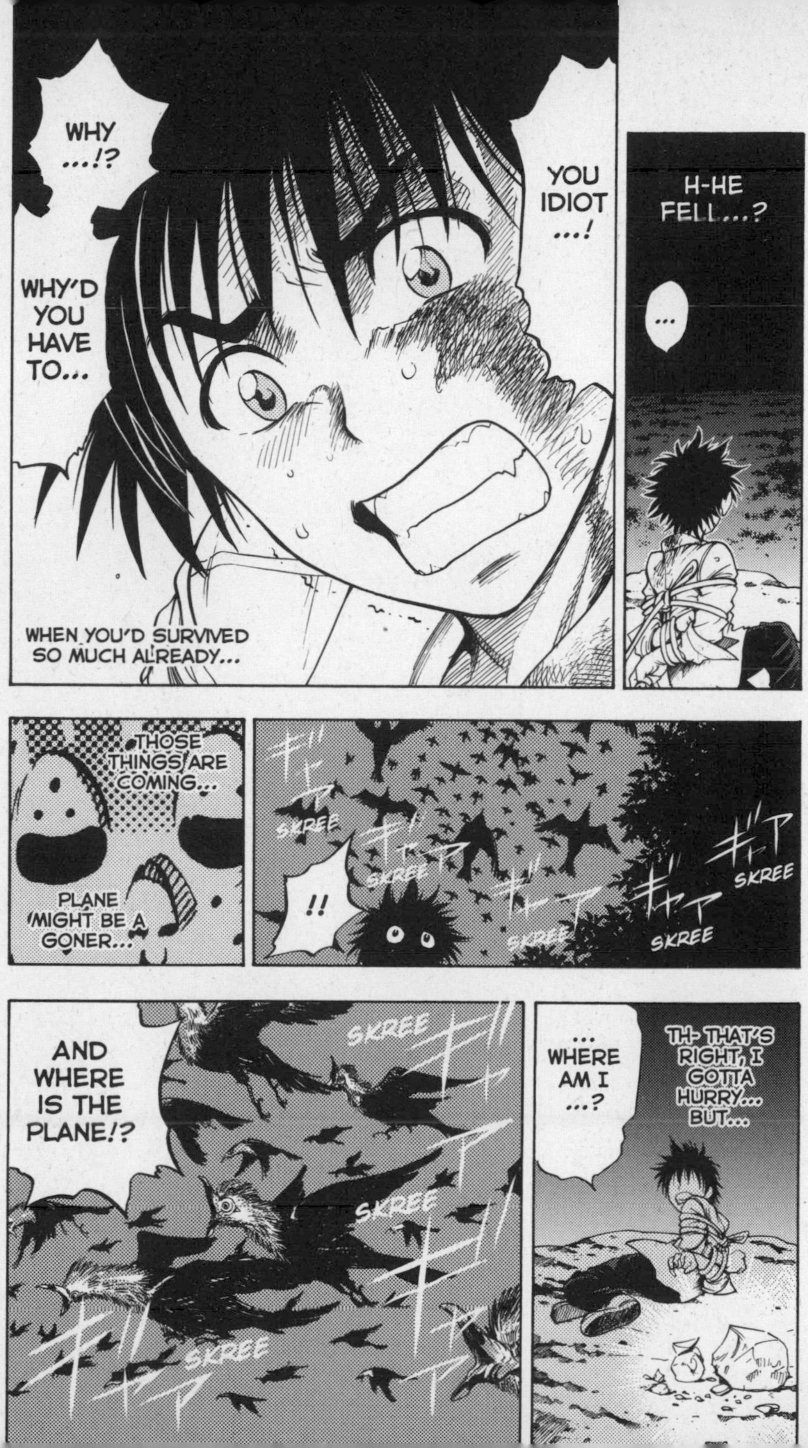
H-HE FELL...?
...
YOU IDIOT ...!
WHY ...!?
WHY'D YOU HAVE TO...
WHEN YOU'D SURVIVED SO MUCH ALREADY...
SKREE
SKREE
!!
SKREE
SKREE
SKREE
SKREE
THOSE THINGS ARE COMING...
PLANE MIGHT BE A GONER...
TH- THAT'S RIGHT, I GOTTA HURRY... BUT...
... WHERE AM I ...?
SKREE
AND WHERE IS THE PLANE!?
SKREE
SKREE

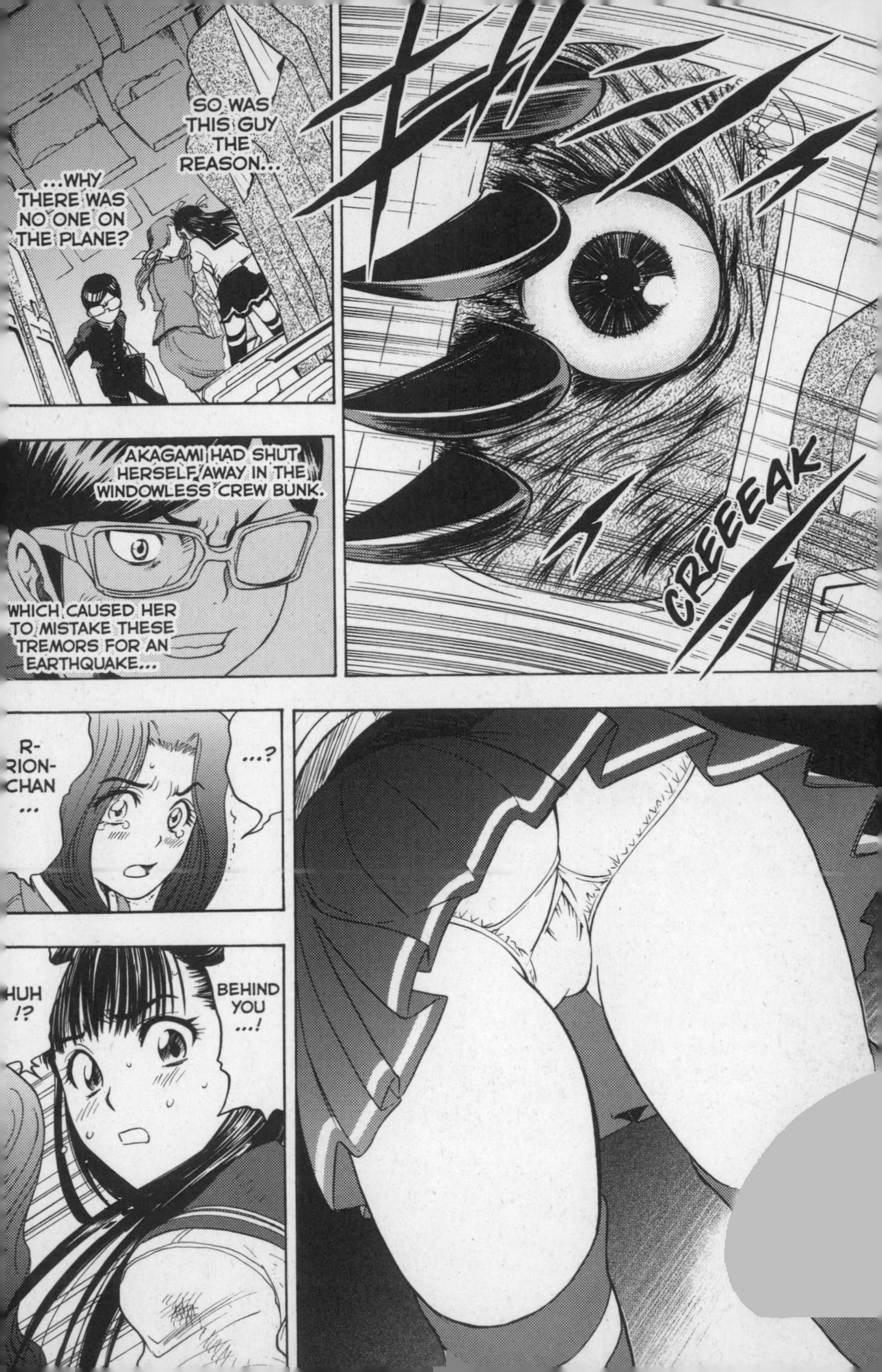
CREEEAK
SO WAS THIS GUY THE REASON...
...WHY THERE WAS NO ONE ON THE PLANE?
AKAGAMI HAD SHUT HERSELF AWAY IN THE WINDOWLESS CREW BUNK.
WHICH CAUSED HER TO MISTAKE THESE TREMORS FOR AN EARTHQUAKE...
...?
R-RION-CHAN...
BEHIND YOU...!
HUH!?

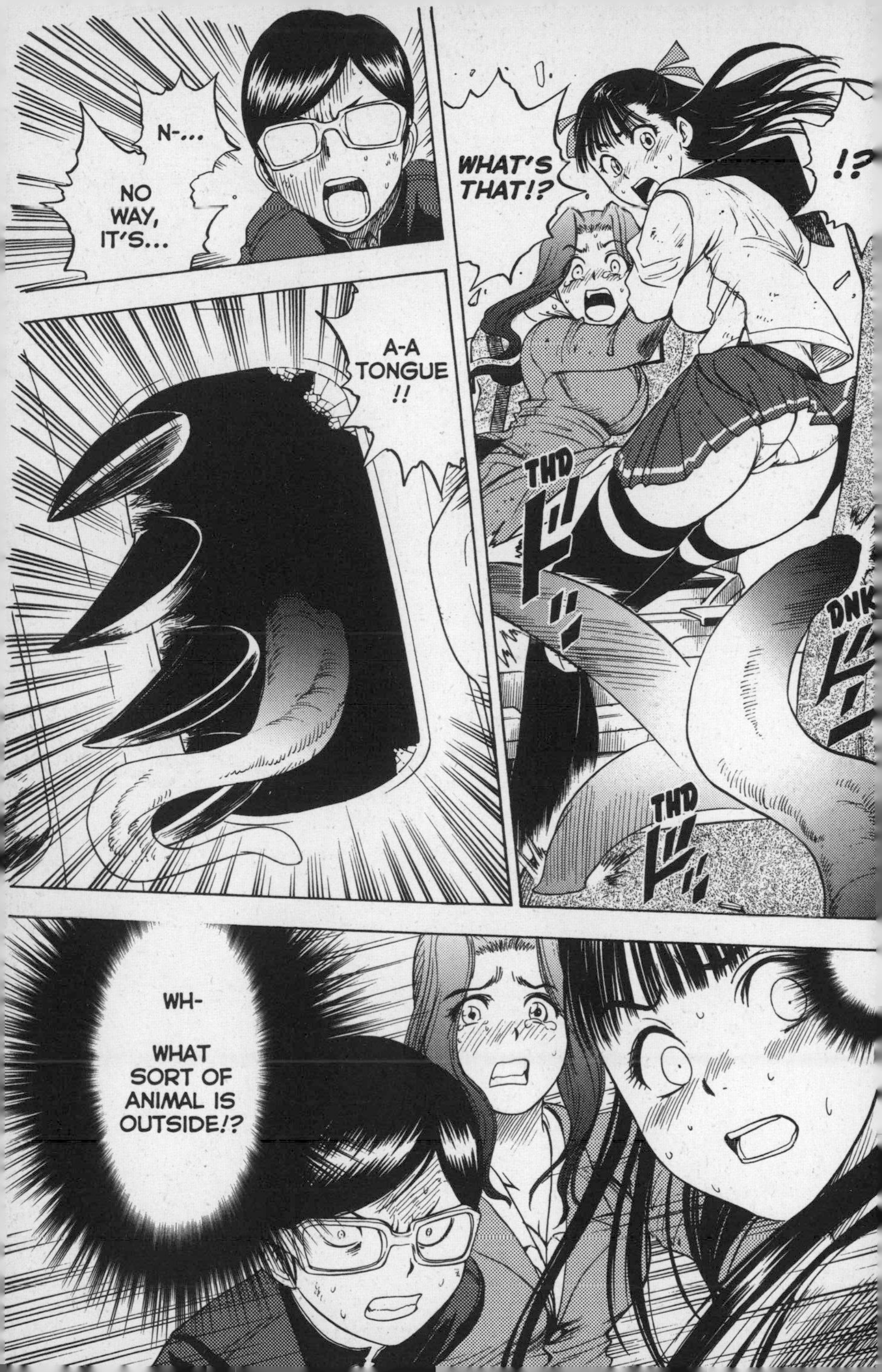
WHAT'S THAT!?
!?
THD
DNK
THD
N-...
NO WAY, IT'S...
A-A TONGUE !!
WH-
WHAT SORT OF ANIMAL IS OUTSIDE!?

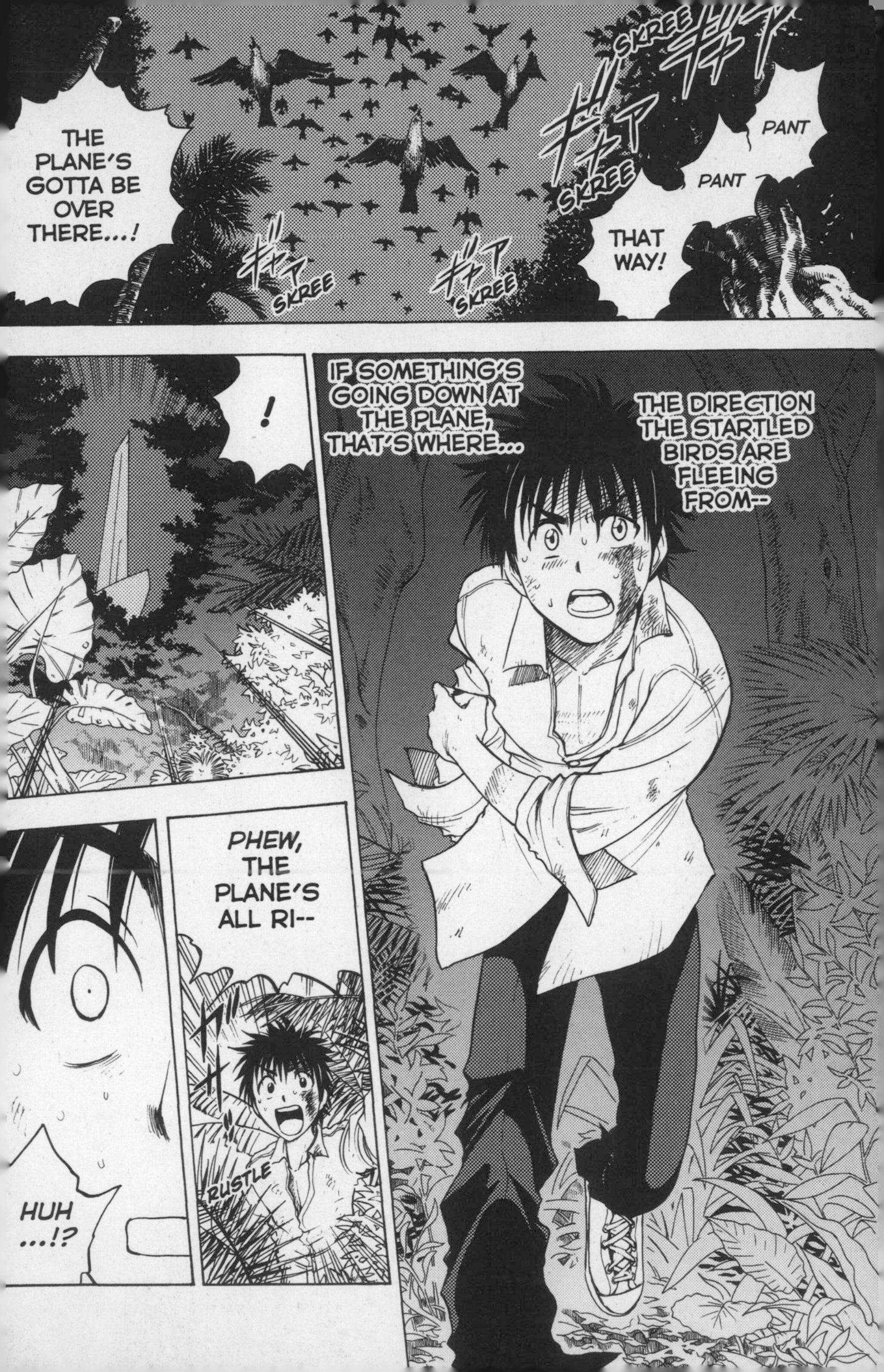
SKREE
SKREE
PANT
PANT
THAT WAY!
SKREE
SKREE
THE PLANE'S GOTTA BE OVER THERE...!
THE DIRECTION THE STARTLED BIRDS ARE FLEEING FROM--
IF SOMETHING'S GOING DOWN AT THE PLANE, THAT'S WHERE...
!
PHEW, THE PLANE'S ALL RI--
RUSTLE
HUH ...!?

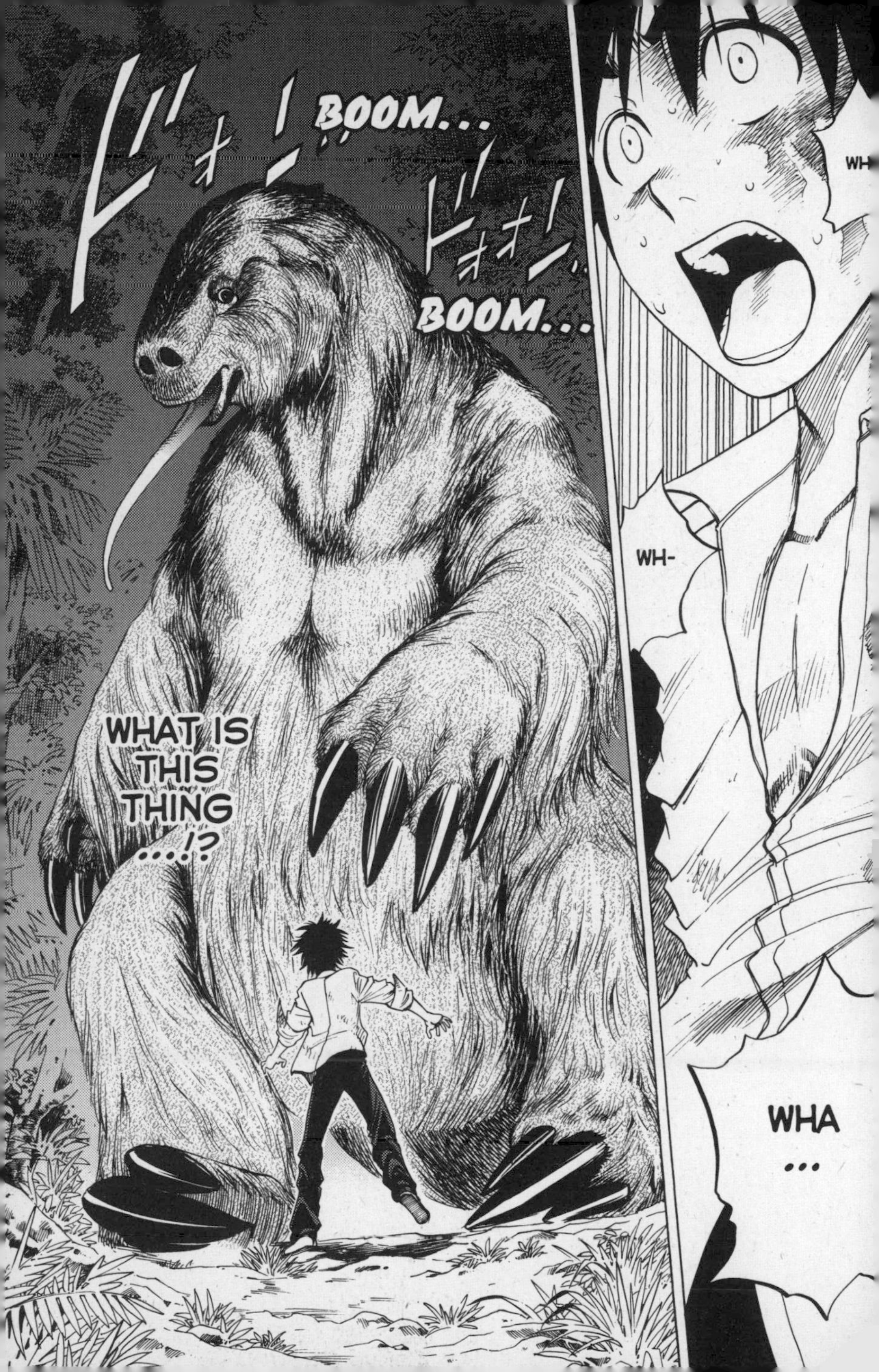
WH
WH-
WHA ...
ドォ!
BOOM...
ドォオン!
BOOM...
WHAT IS THIS THING ...!?

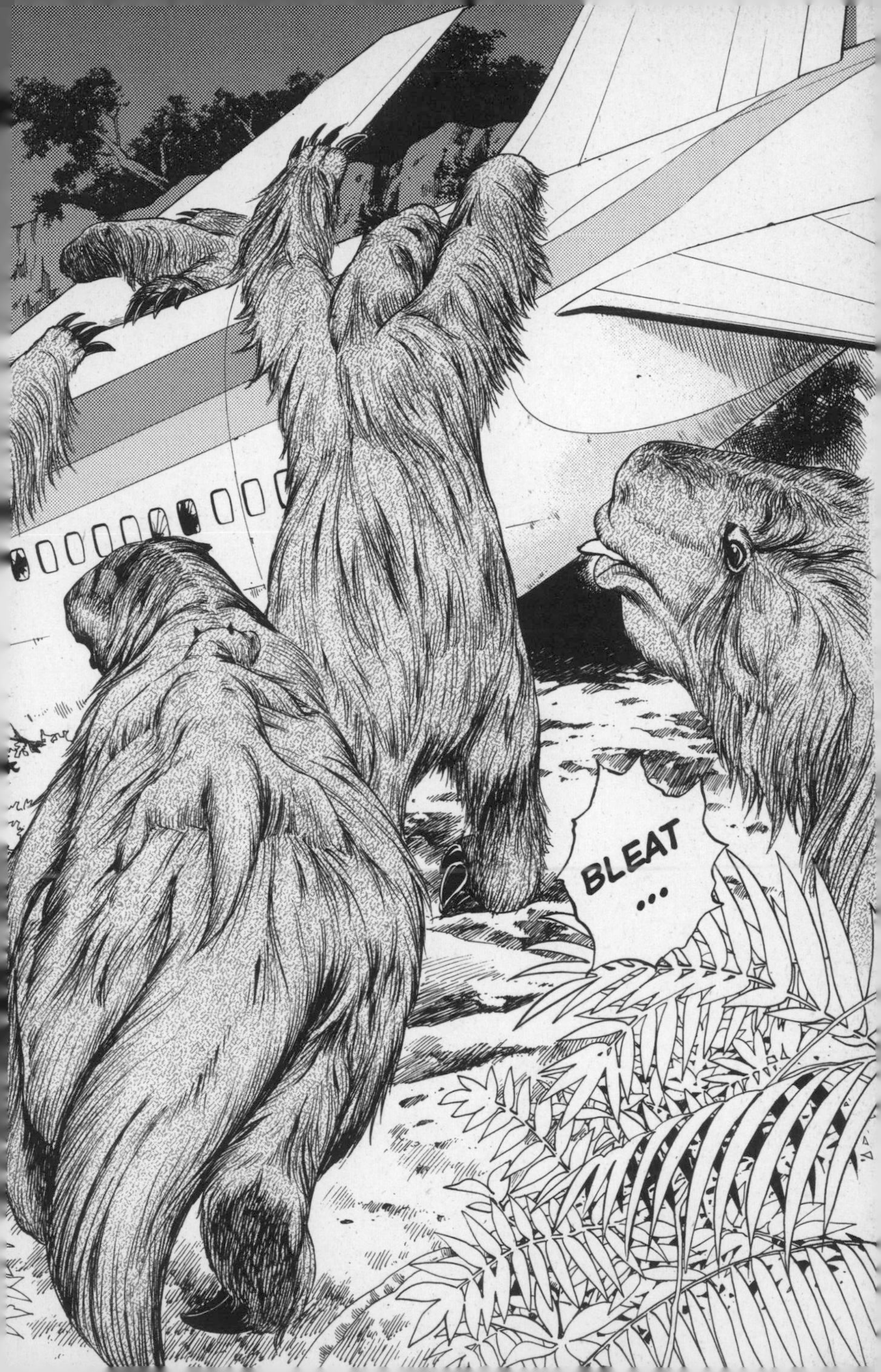
BLEAT ...

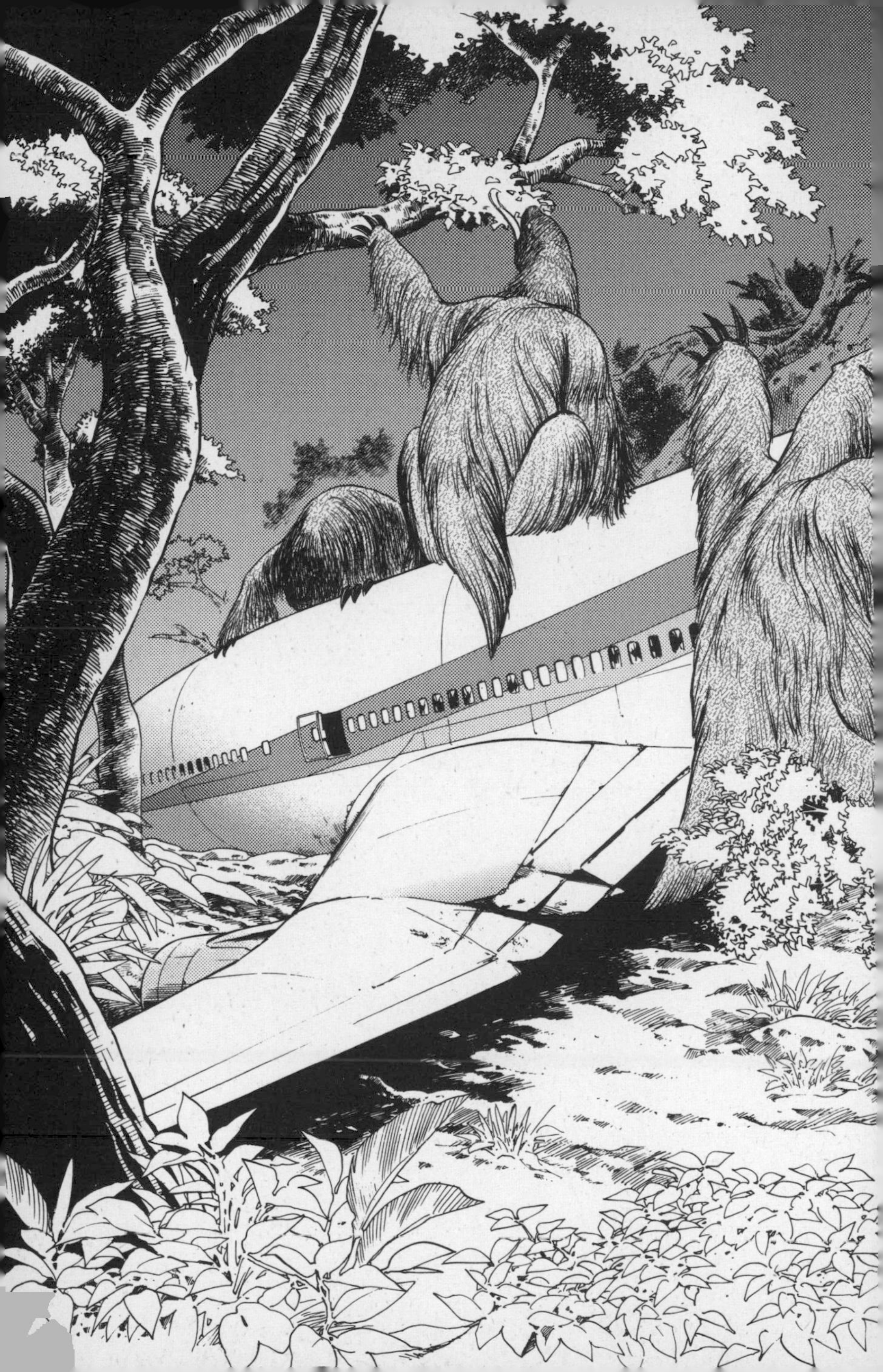

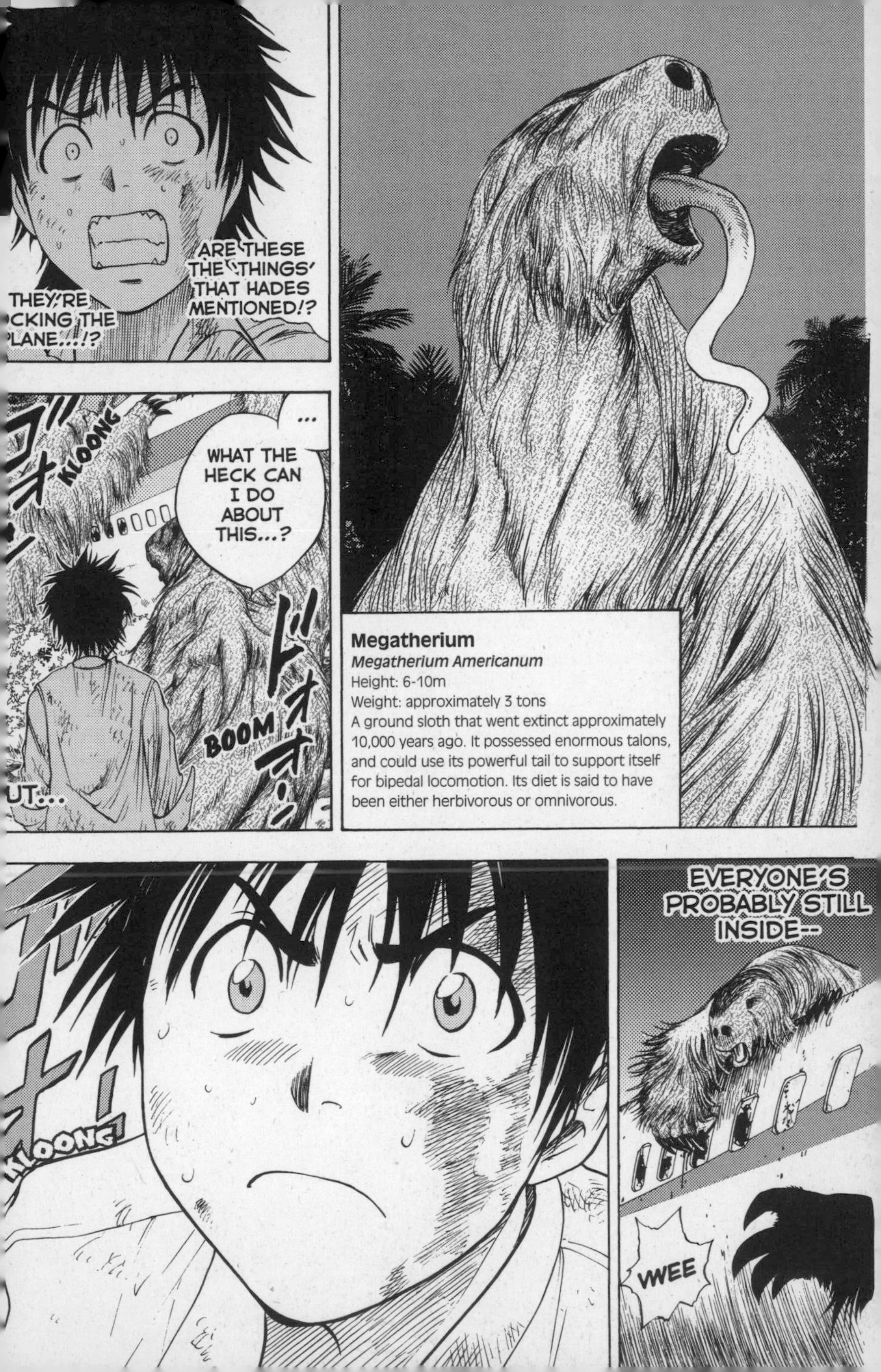
Megatherium
Megatherium Americanum
Height: 6-10m
Weight: approximately 3 tons
A ground sloth that went extinct approximately 10,000 years ago. It possessed enormous talons, and could use its powerful tail to support itself for bipedal locomotion. Its diet is said to have been either herbivorous or omnivorous.
ARE THESE THE 'THINGS' THAT HADES MENTIONED!?
THEY'RE CKING THE LANE...!?
KLOONG
...
WHAT THE HECK CAN I DO ABOUT THIS...?
BOOM
UT...
EVERYONE'S PROBABLY STILL INSIDE--
VWEE
KLOONG!

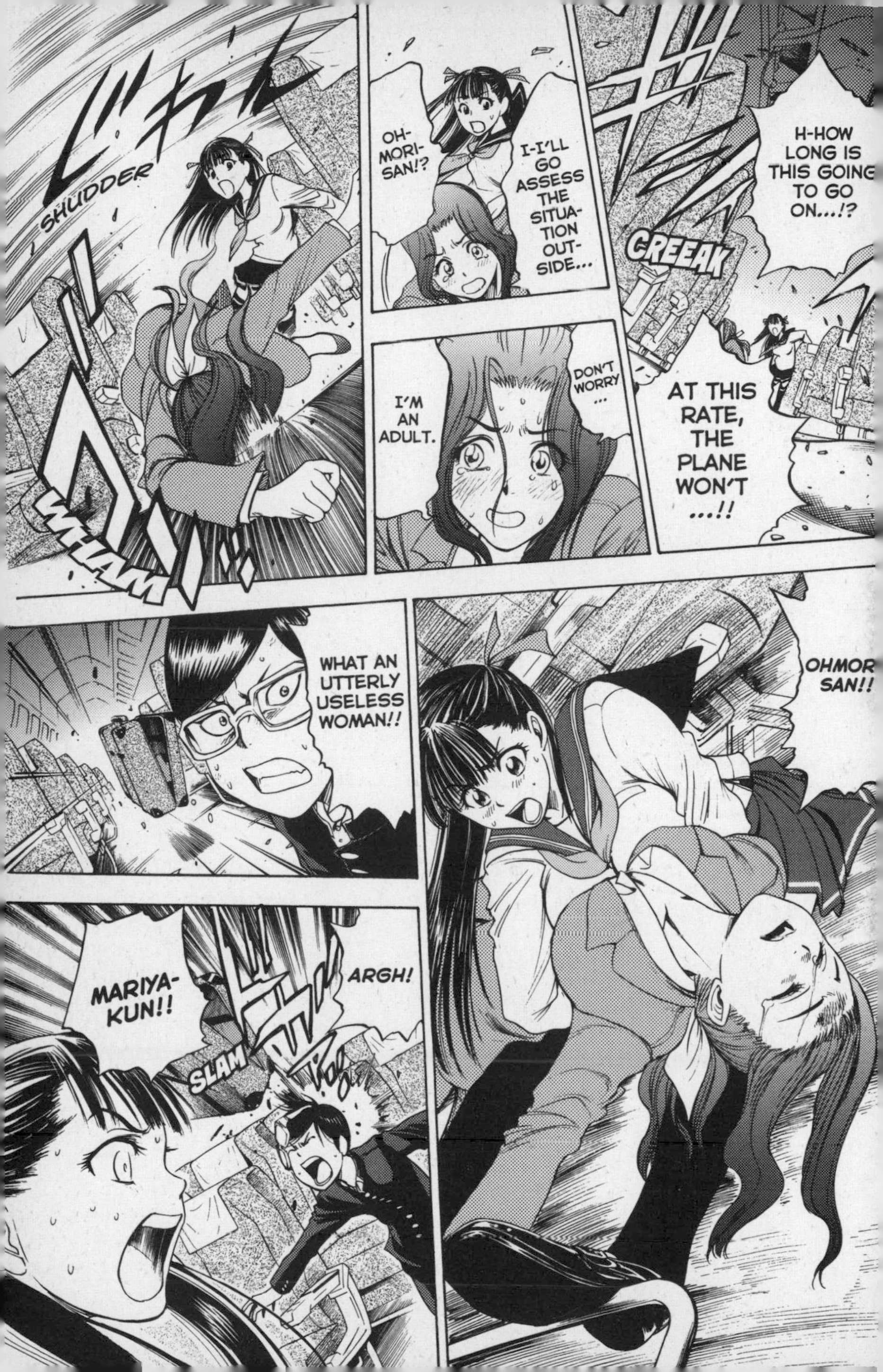
H-HOW LONG IS THIS GOING TO GO ON...!?
CREEAK
AT THIS RATE, THE PLANE WON'T ...!!
I-I'LL GO ASSESS THE SITUA-TION OUT-SIDE...
OH-MORI-SAN!?
DON'T WORRY ...
I'M AN ADULT.
SHUDDER
WHAM
OHMOR SAN!!
WHAT AN UTTERLY USELESS WOMAN!!
ARGH!
MARIYA-KUN!!
SLAM

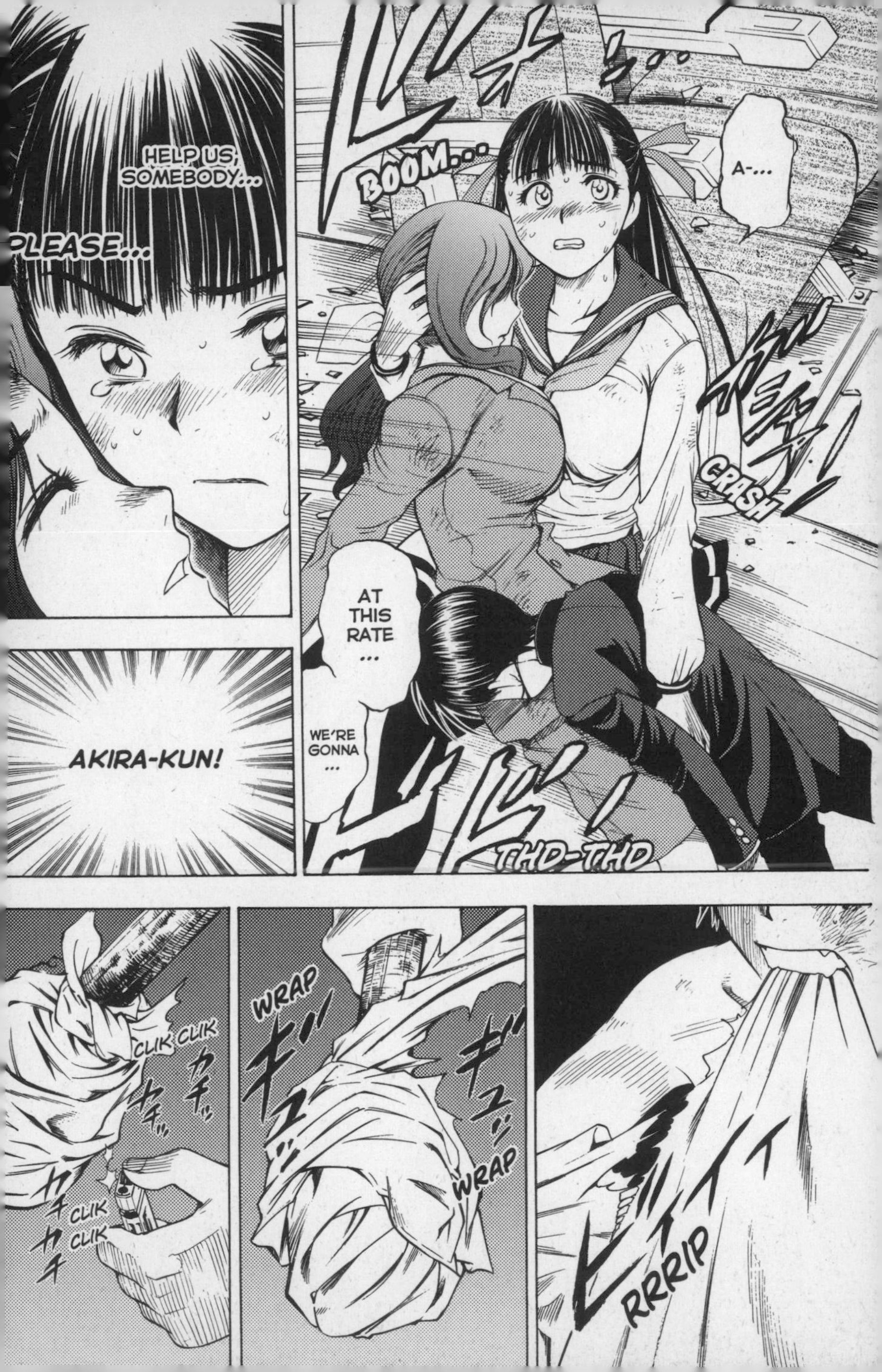
A-...
BOOM...
CRASH
AT THIS RATE...
WE'RE GONNA...
THD-THD
HELP US, SOMEBODY...
PLEASE...
AKIRA-KUN!
RRRIP
WRAP
WRAP
CLIK CLIK
CLIK CLIK

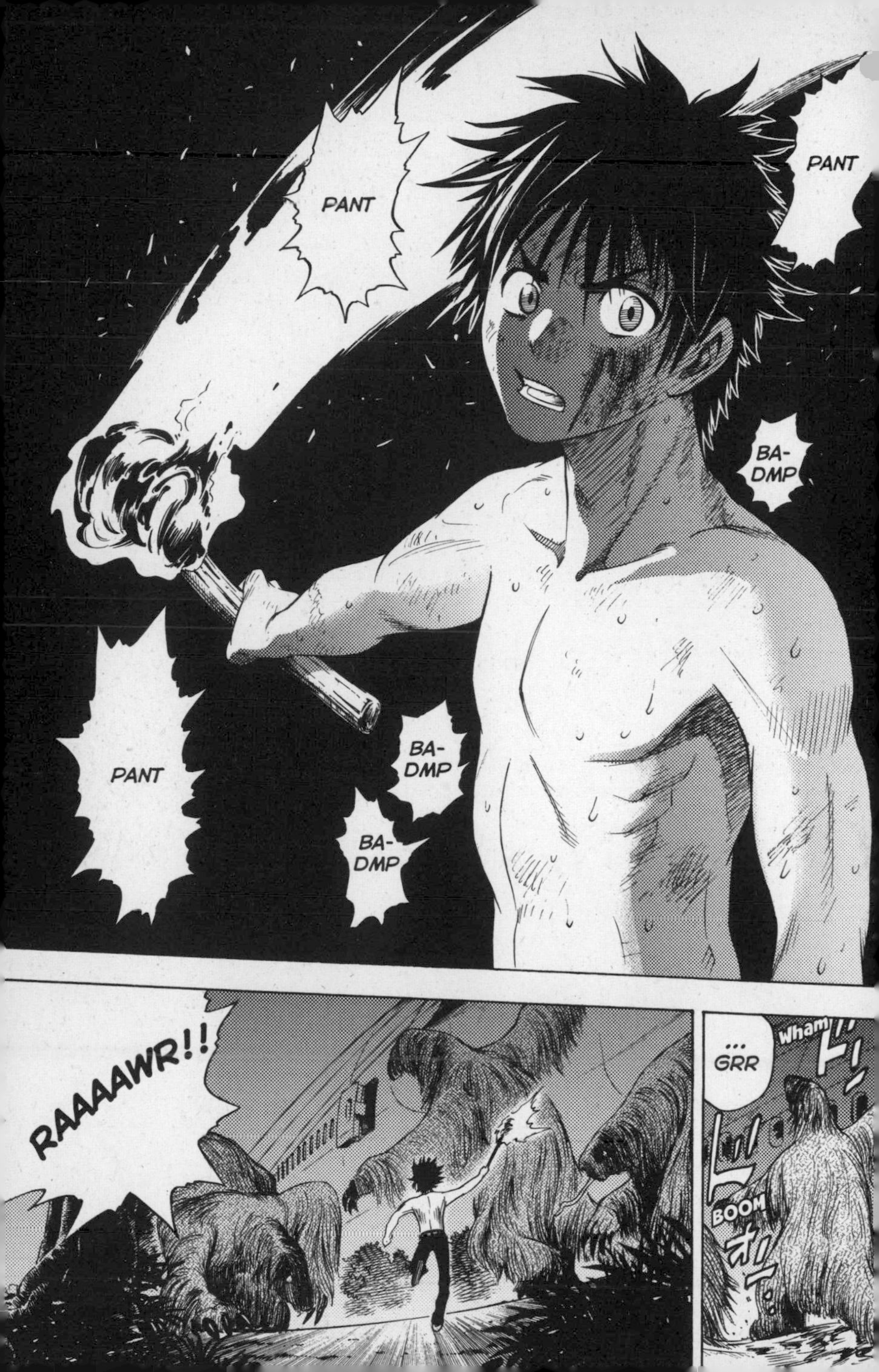
PANT
PANT
BA-DMP
BA-DMP
PANT
BA-DMP
Wham
... GRR
BOOM
RAAAAWR!!

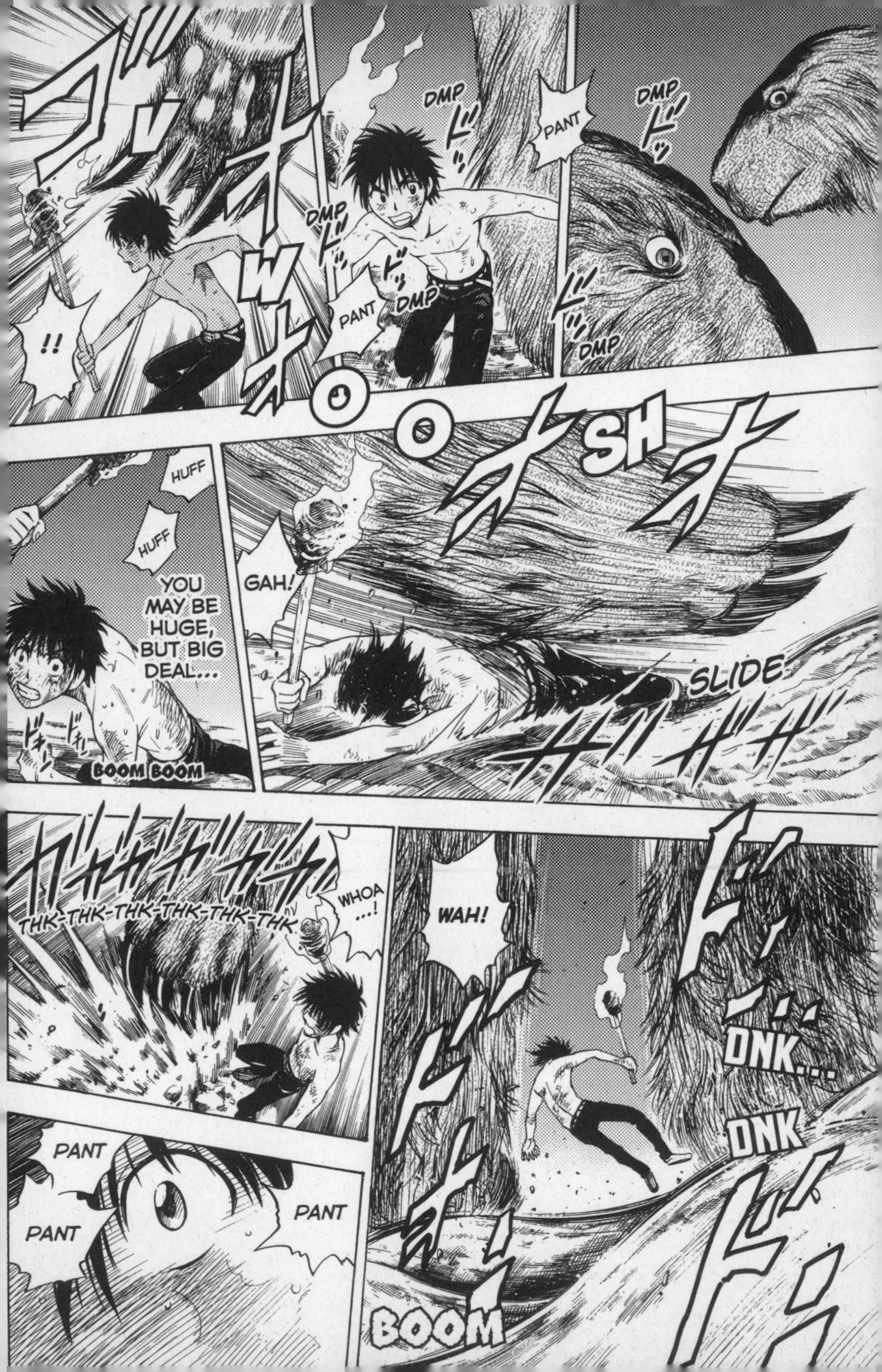
DMP
PANT
DMP
DMP
DMP
PANT
DMP
WOOSH
!!
GAH!
SLIDE
HUFF
HUFF
YOU MAY BE HUGE, BUT BIG DEAL...
BOOM BOOM
WAH!
ONK...
ONK
BOOM
THK-THK-THK-THK-THK-THK
WHOA ...!
PANT
PANT
PANT

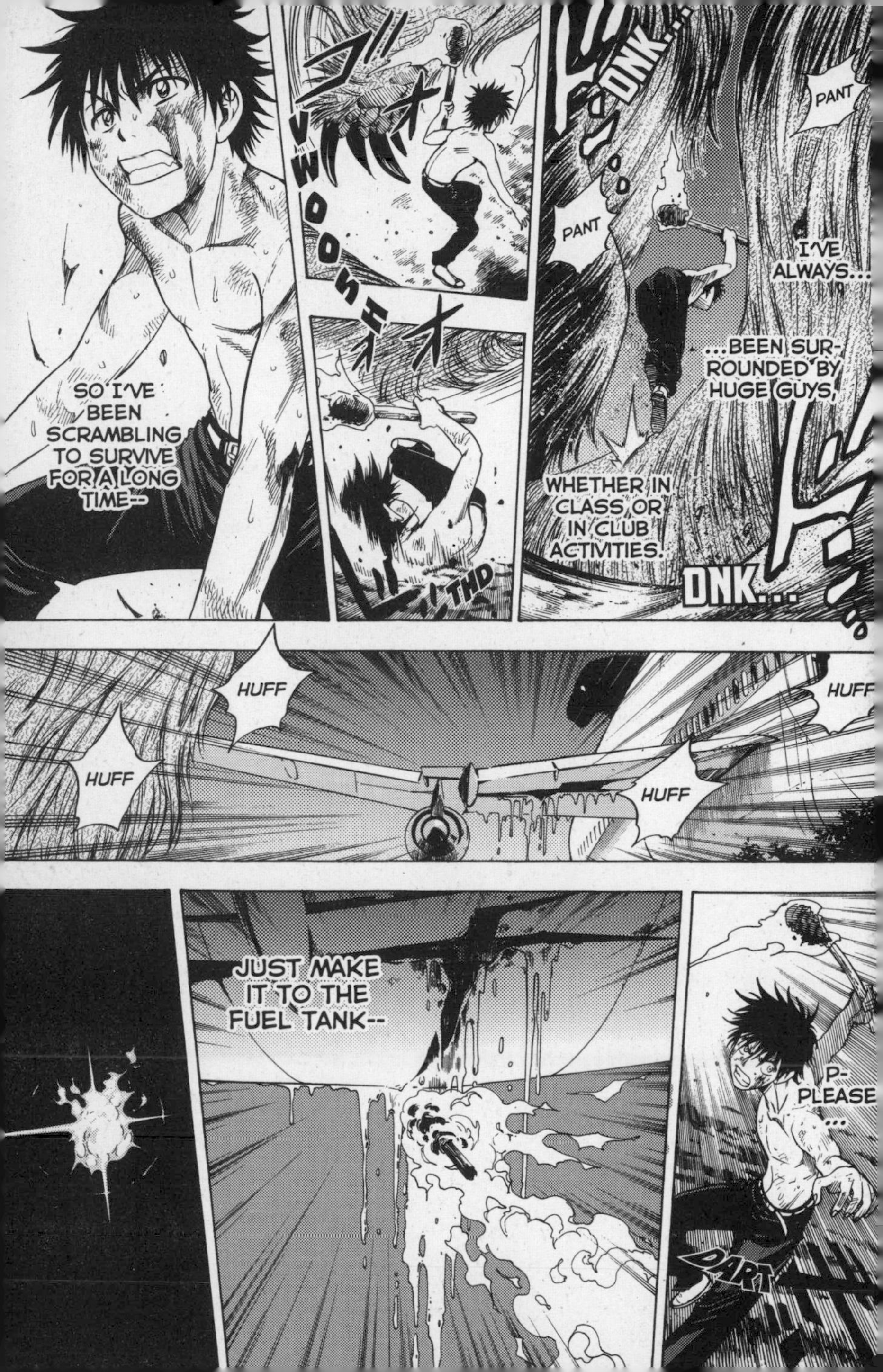
DNK...
PANT
PANT
I'VE ALWAYS...
...BEEN SUR-ROUNDED BY HUGE GUYS,
WHETHER IN CLASS OR IN CLUB ACTIVITIES.
DNK...
VWOOSH
THD
SO I'VE BEEN SCRAMBLING TO SURVIVE FOR A LONG TIME--
HUFF
HUFF
HUFF
HUFF
P-PLEASE...
DART
JUST MAKE IT TO THE FUEL TANK--

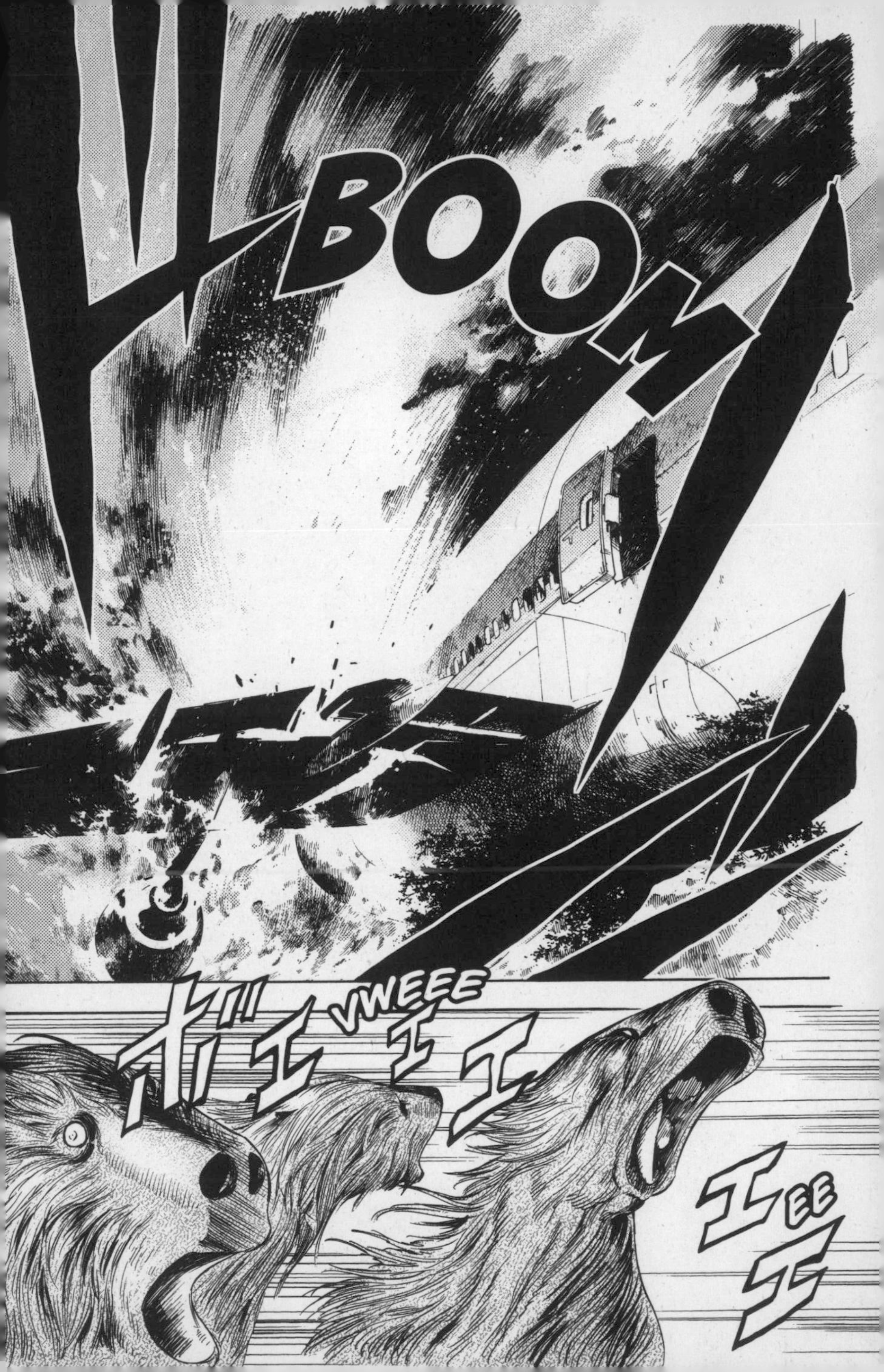
BOOM
VWEEE
EE

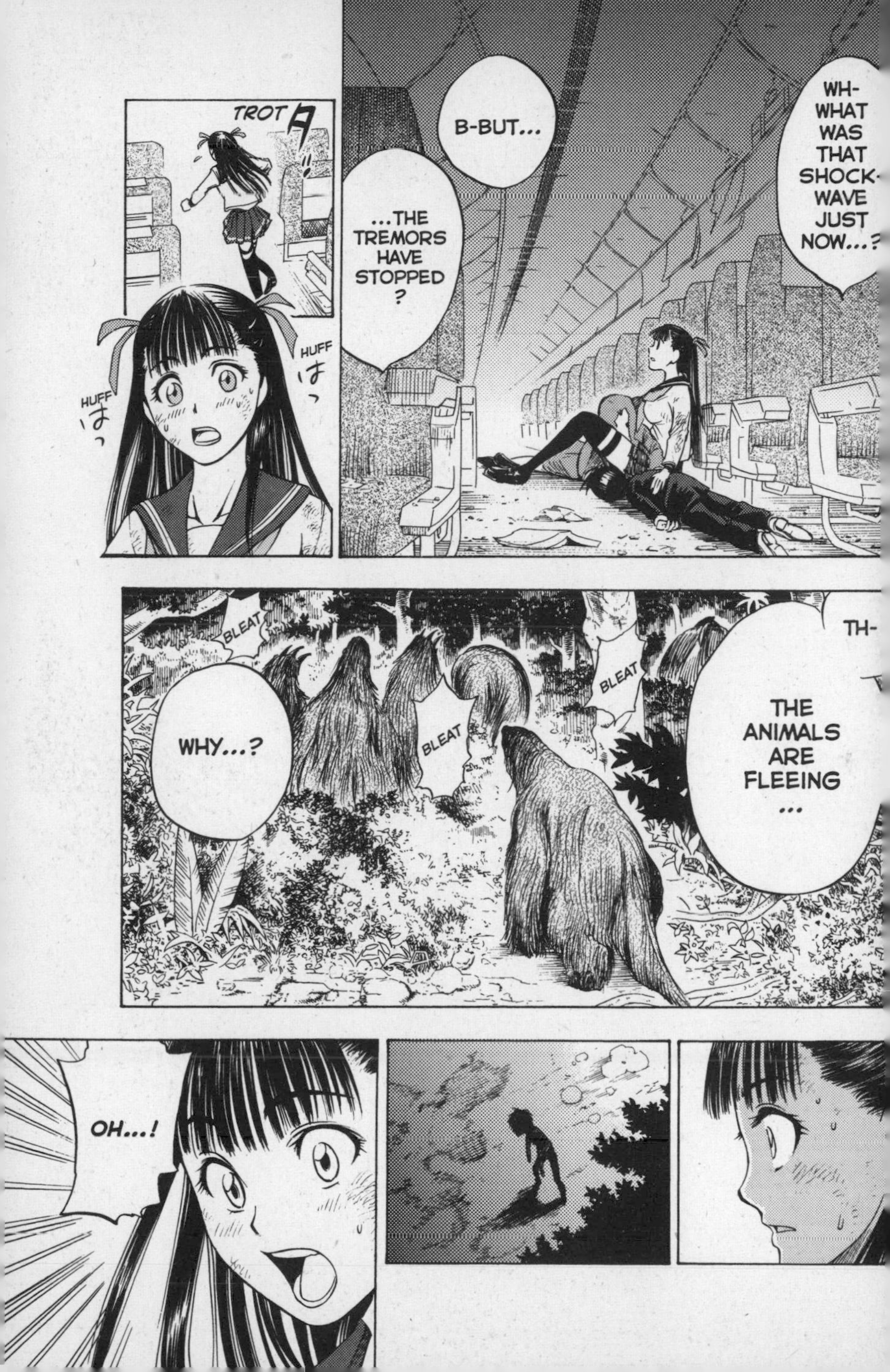
WH- WHAT WAS THAT SHOCK-WAVE JUST NOW...?
B-BUT...
...THE TREMORS HAVE STOPPED?
TROT
HUFF
HUFF
TH- THE ANIMALS ARE FLEEING...
BLEAT
BLEAT
BLEAT
WHY...?
OH...!

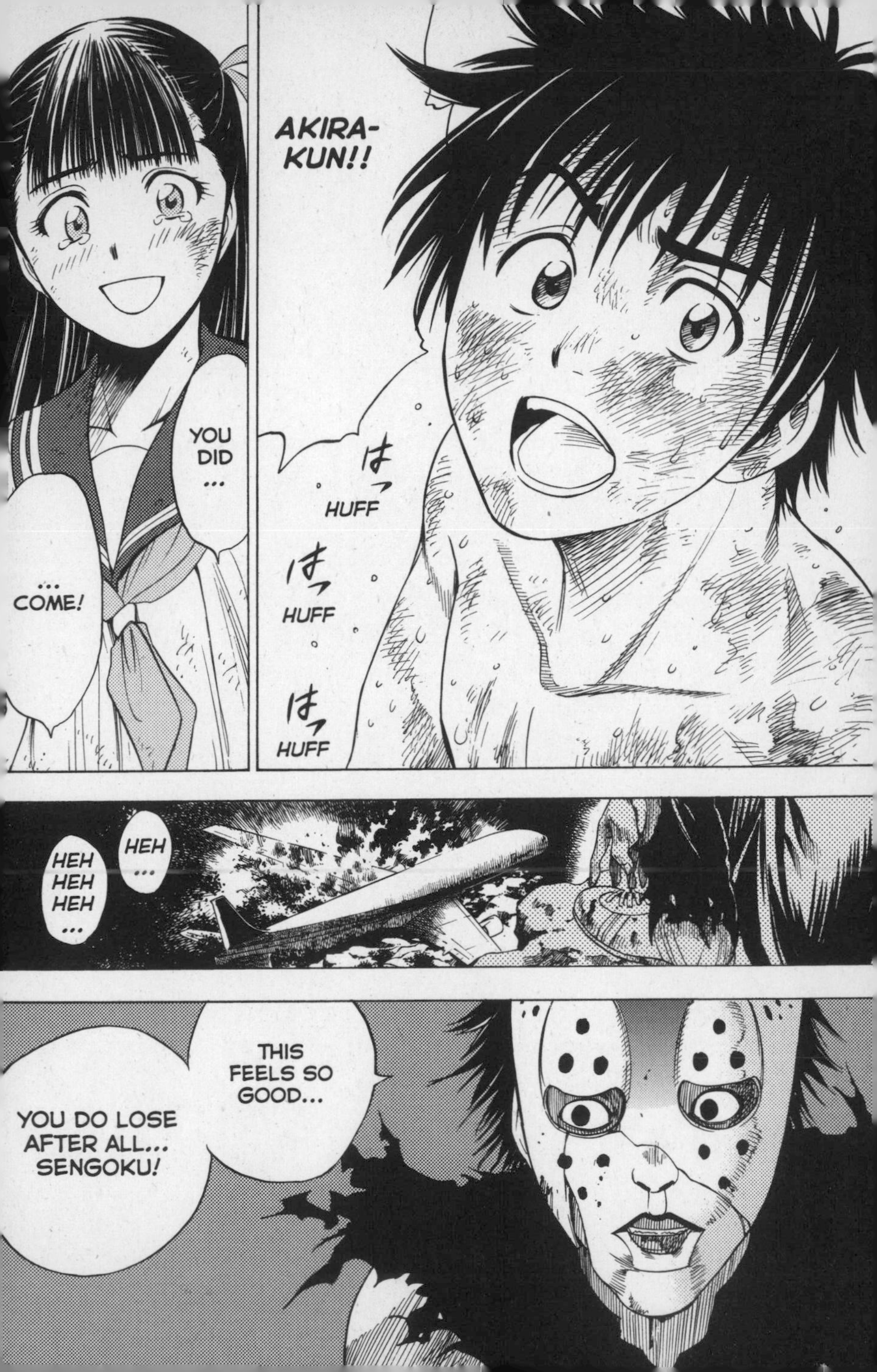
AKIRA-KUN!!
はっ HUFF
はっ HUFF
はっ HUFF
YOU DID ...
... COME!
HEH ...
HEH HEH HEH ...
THIS FEELS SO GOOD...
YOU DO LOSE AFTER ALL... SENGOKU!

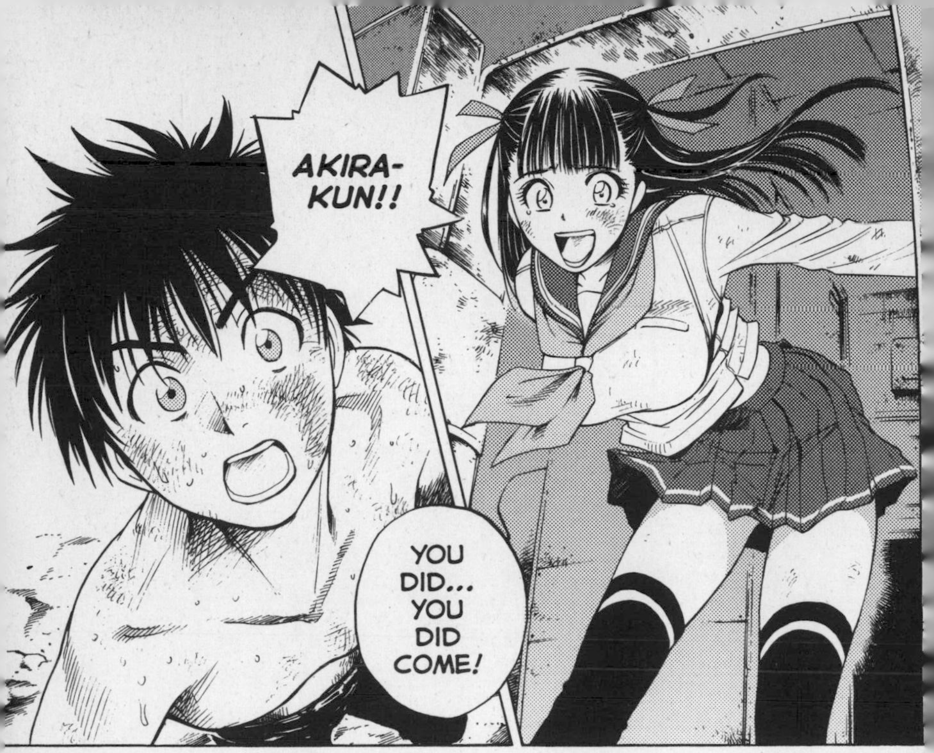
AKIRA-KUN!!
YOU DID... YOU DID COME!

Episode 7 A Duty Towards Life

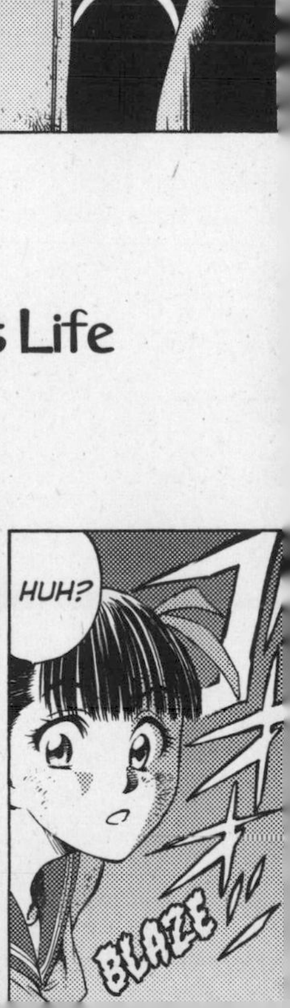
HUH?
BLAZE

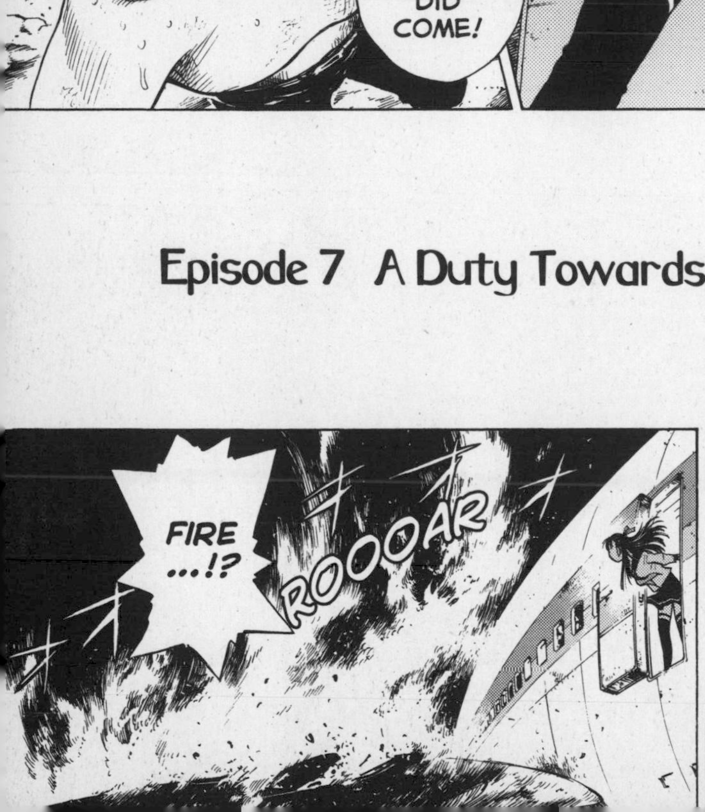
FIRE ...!?
ROOOAR

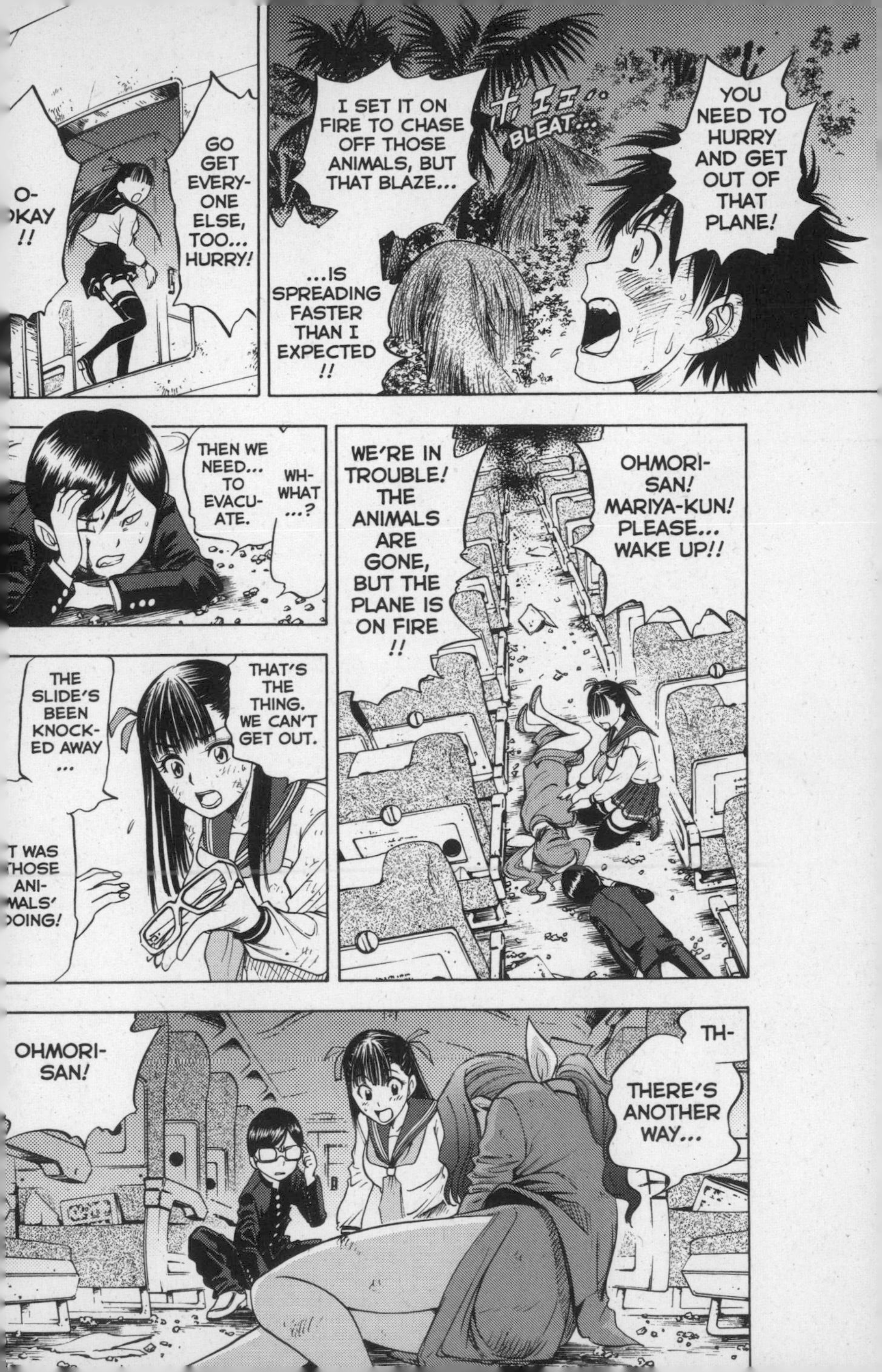
YOU NEED TO HURRY AND GET OUT OF THAT PLANE!
BLEAT...
I SET IT ON FIRE TO CHASE OFF THOSE ANIMALS, BUT THAT BLAZE...
...IS SPREADING FASTER THAN I EXPECTED!!
GO GET EVERYONE ELSE, TOO... HURRY!
O-OKAY!!
OHMORI-SAN! MARIYA-KUN! PLEASE... WAKE UP!!
WE'RE IN TROUBLE! THE ANIMALS ARE GONE, BUT THE PLANE IS ON FIRE!!
WH-WHAT...?
THEN WE NEED... TO EVACUATE.
THAT'S THE THING. WE CAN'T GET OUT.
THE SLIDE'S BEEN KNOCKED AWAY...
T WAS HOSE ANIMALS' OING!
TH-
THERE'S ANOTHER WAY...
OHMORI-SAN!

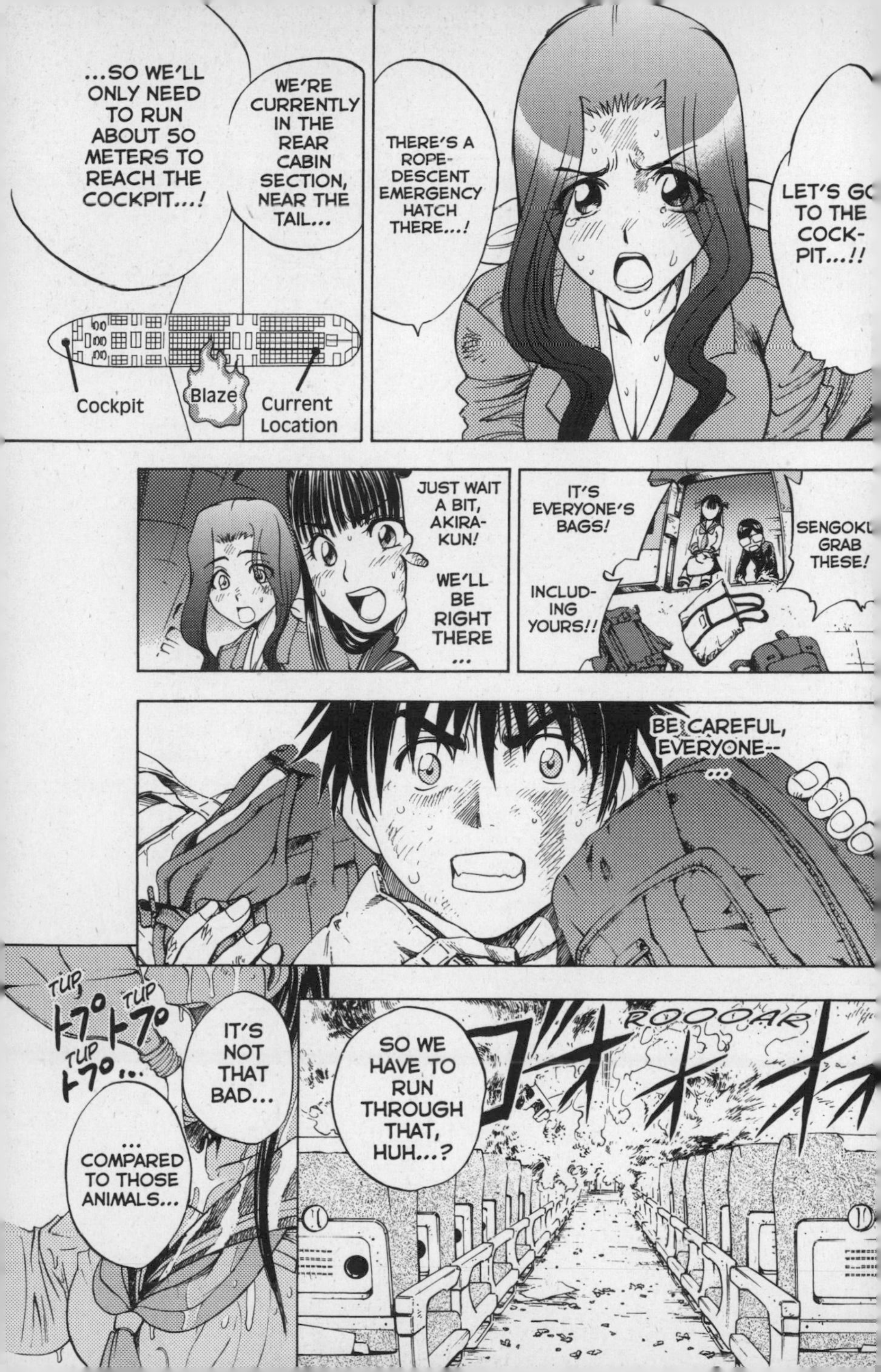
LET'S G
TO THE COCK-PIT...!!
THERE'S A ROPE-DESCENT EMERGENCY HATCH THERE...!
WE'RE CURRENTLY IN THE REAR CABIN SECTION, NEAR THE TAIL...
...SO WE'LL ONLY NEED TO RUN ABOUT 50 METERS TO REACH THE COCKPIT...!
Current Location
Blaze
Cockpit
SENGOKU GRAB THESE!
IT'S EVERYONE'S BAGS!
INCLUDING YOURS!!
JUST WAIT A BIT, AKIRA-KUN!
WE'LL BE RIGHT THERE ...
BE CAREFUL, EVERYONE-- ...
ROOOAR
SO WE HAVE TO RUN THROUGH THAT, HUH...?
IT'S NOT THAT BAD...
... COMPARED TO THOSE ANIMALS...
TUP
TUP
TUP

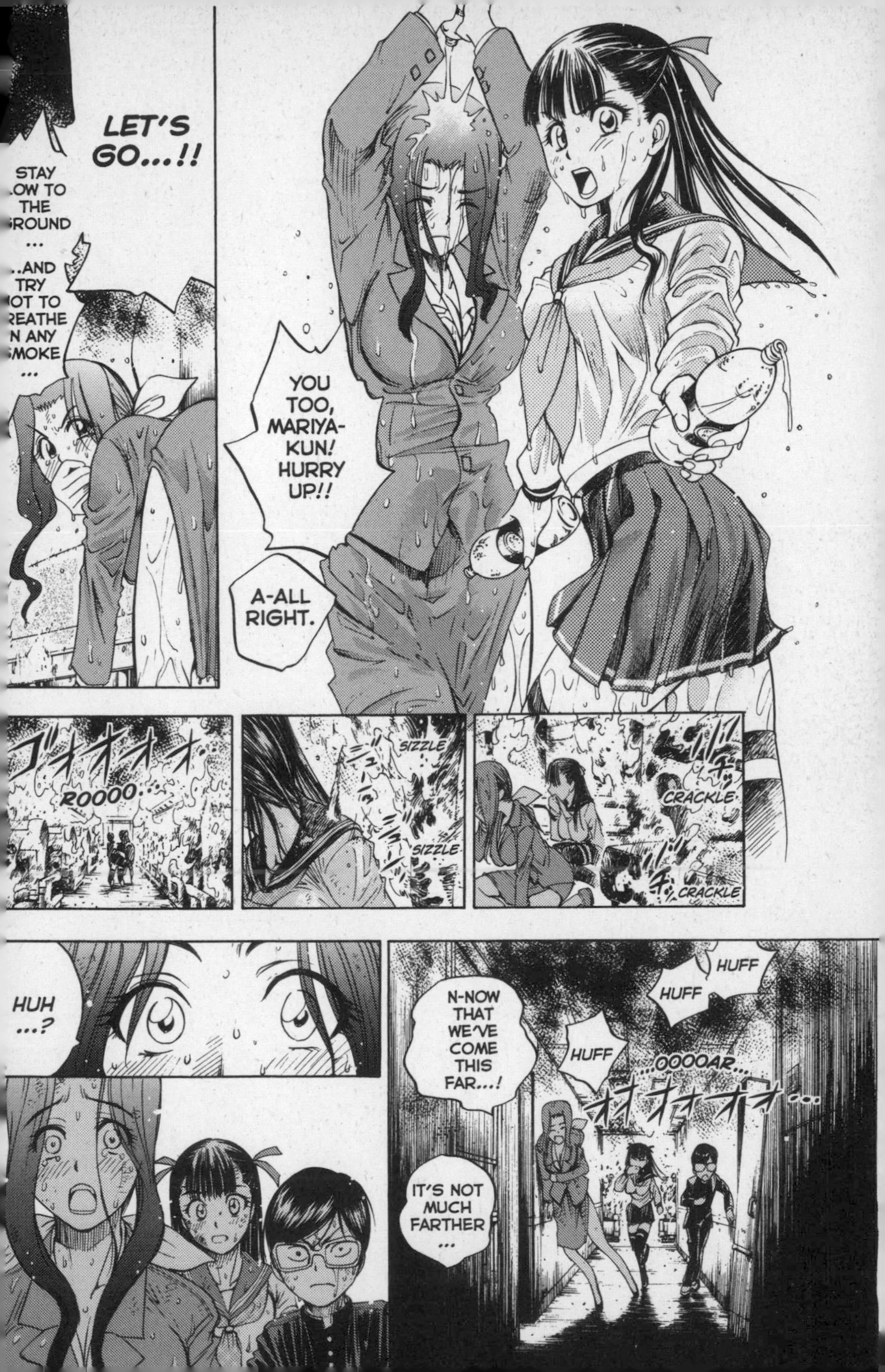
YOU TOO, MARIYA-KUN! HURRY UP!!
A-ALL RIGHT.
LET'S GO...!!
STAY OW TO THE ROUND ...
..AND TRY OT TO REATHE N ANY MOKE ...
CRACKLE
CRACKLE
SIZZLE
SIZZLE
ゴオオオオ
ROOOO...
HUFF
HUFF
N-NOW THAT WE'VE COME THIS FAR...!
HUFF
...OOOOAR...
IT'S NOT MUCH FARTHER ...
HUH ...?

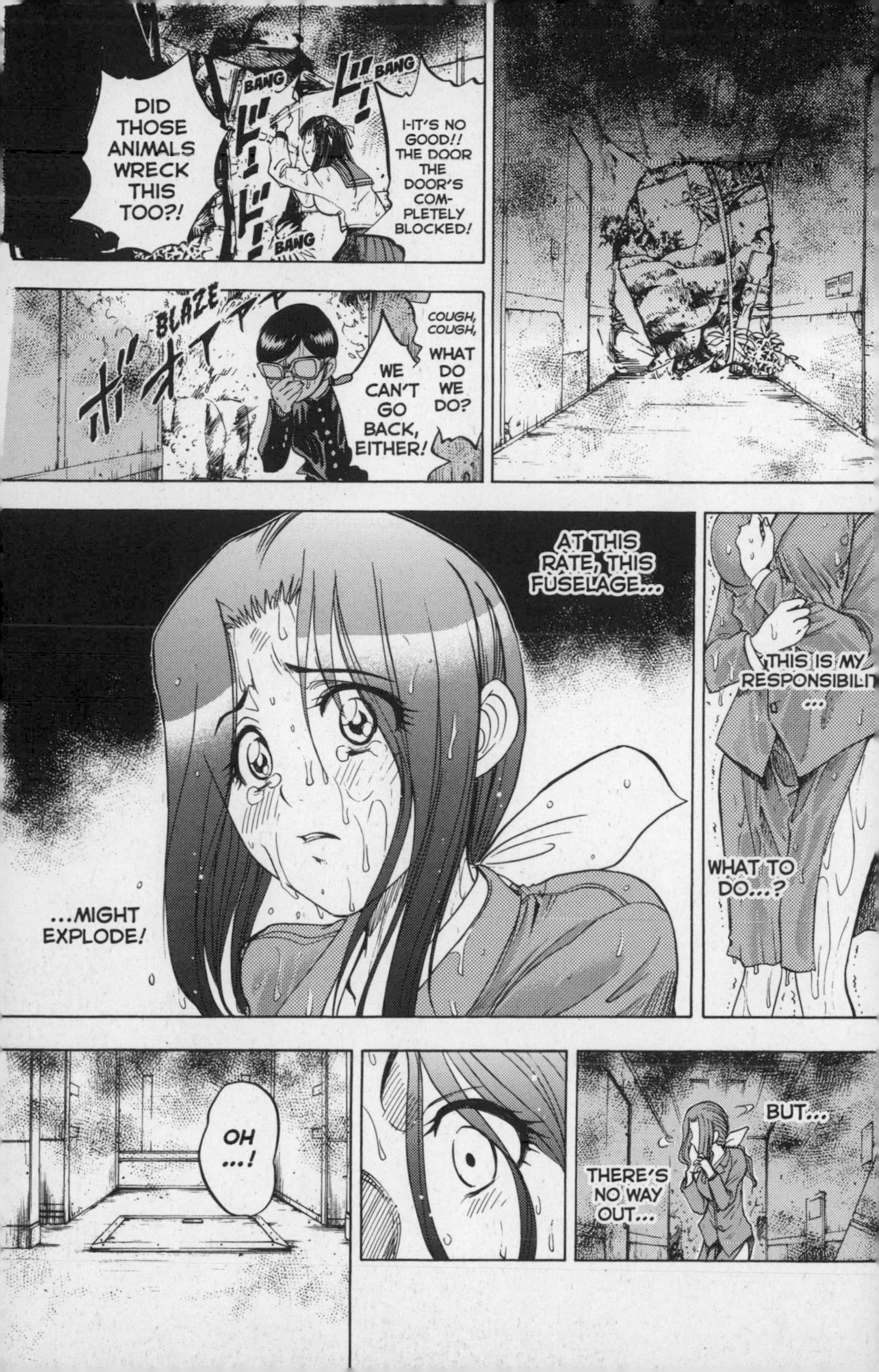
BANG
I-IT'S NO GOOD!! THE DOOR THE DOOR'S COM- PLETELY BLOCKED!
DID THOSE ANIMALS WRECK THIS TOO?!
BANG
BANG
COUGH, COUGH,
WHAT DO WE DO?
WE CAN'T GO BACK, EITHER!
BLAZE
THIS IS MY RESPONSIBILIT ...
WHAT TO DO...?
AT THIS RATE, THIS FUSELAGE...
...MIGHT EXPLODE!
BUT...
THERE'S NO WAY OUT...
OH ...!

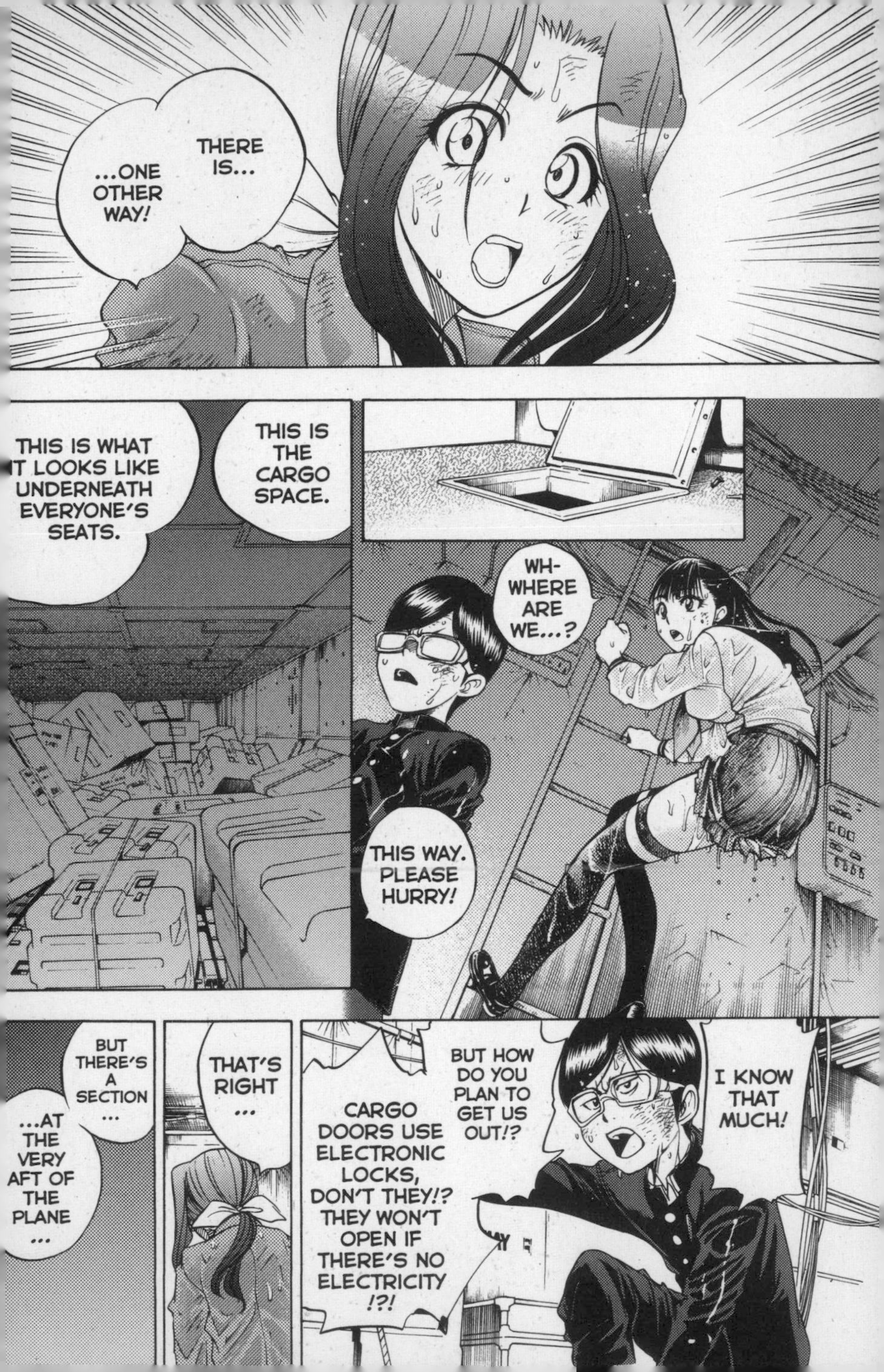
THERE IS...
...ONE OTHER WAY!
WH- WHERE ARE WE...?
THIS WAY. PLEASE HURRY!
THIS IS THE CARGO SPACE.
THIS IS WHAT IT LOOKS LIKE UNDERNEATH EVERYONE'S SEATS.
I KNOW THAT MUCH!
BUT HOW DO YOU PLAN TO GET US OUT!?
CARGO DOORS USE ELECTRONIC LOCKS, DON'T THEY!? THEY WON'T OPEN IF THERE'S NO ELECTRICITY!?!
THAT'S RIGHT ...
BUT THERE'S A SECTION ...
...AT THE VERY AFT OF THE PLANE ...

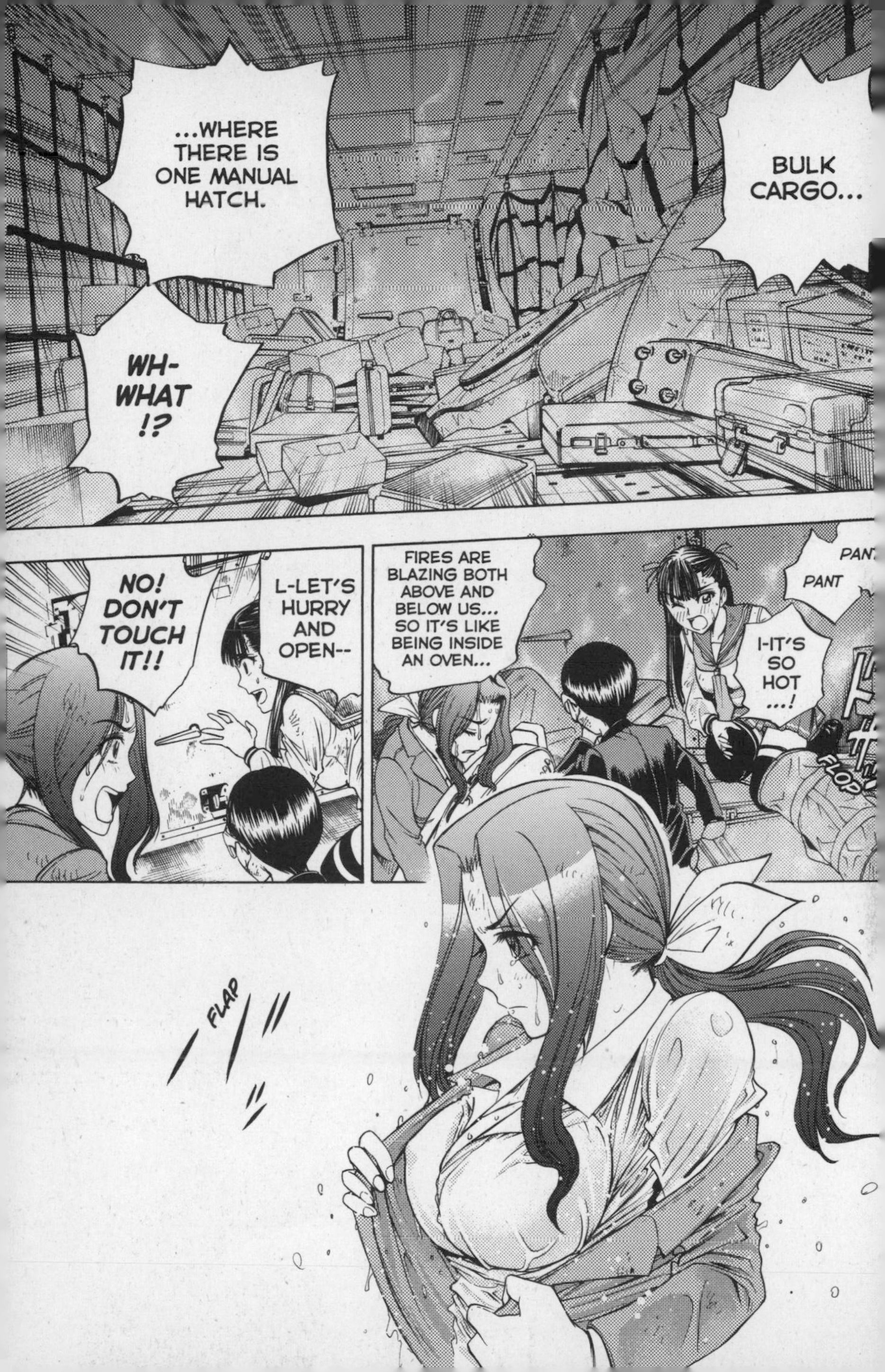
BULK CARGO...
...WHERE THERE IS ONE MANUAL HATCH.
WH-WHAT!?
PANT PANT
I-IT'S SO HOT ...!
FIRES ARE BLAZING BOTH ABOVE AND BELOW US... SO IT'S LIKE BEING INSIDE AN OVEN...
FLOP
L-LET'S HURRY AND OPEN--
NO! DON'T TOUCH IT!!
FLAP

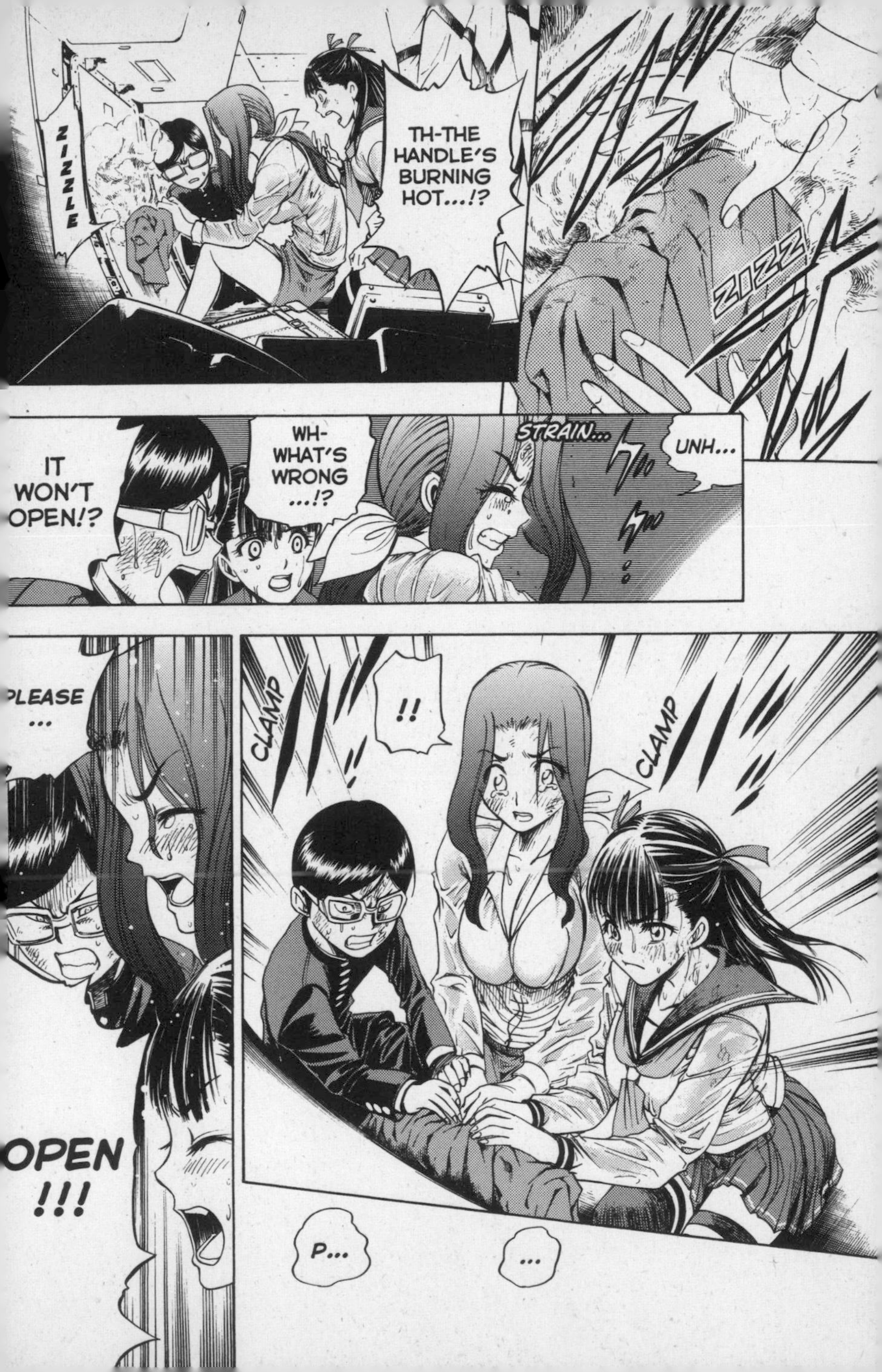
ZIZZ
TH-THE HANDLE'S BURNING HOT...!?
ZIZZLE
UNH...
STRAIN...
WH-WHAT'S WRONG ...!?
IT WON'T OPEN!?
CLAMP
!!
CLAMP
...
P...
PLEASE ...
OPEN !!!

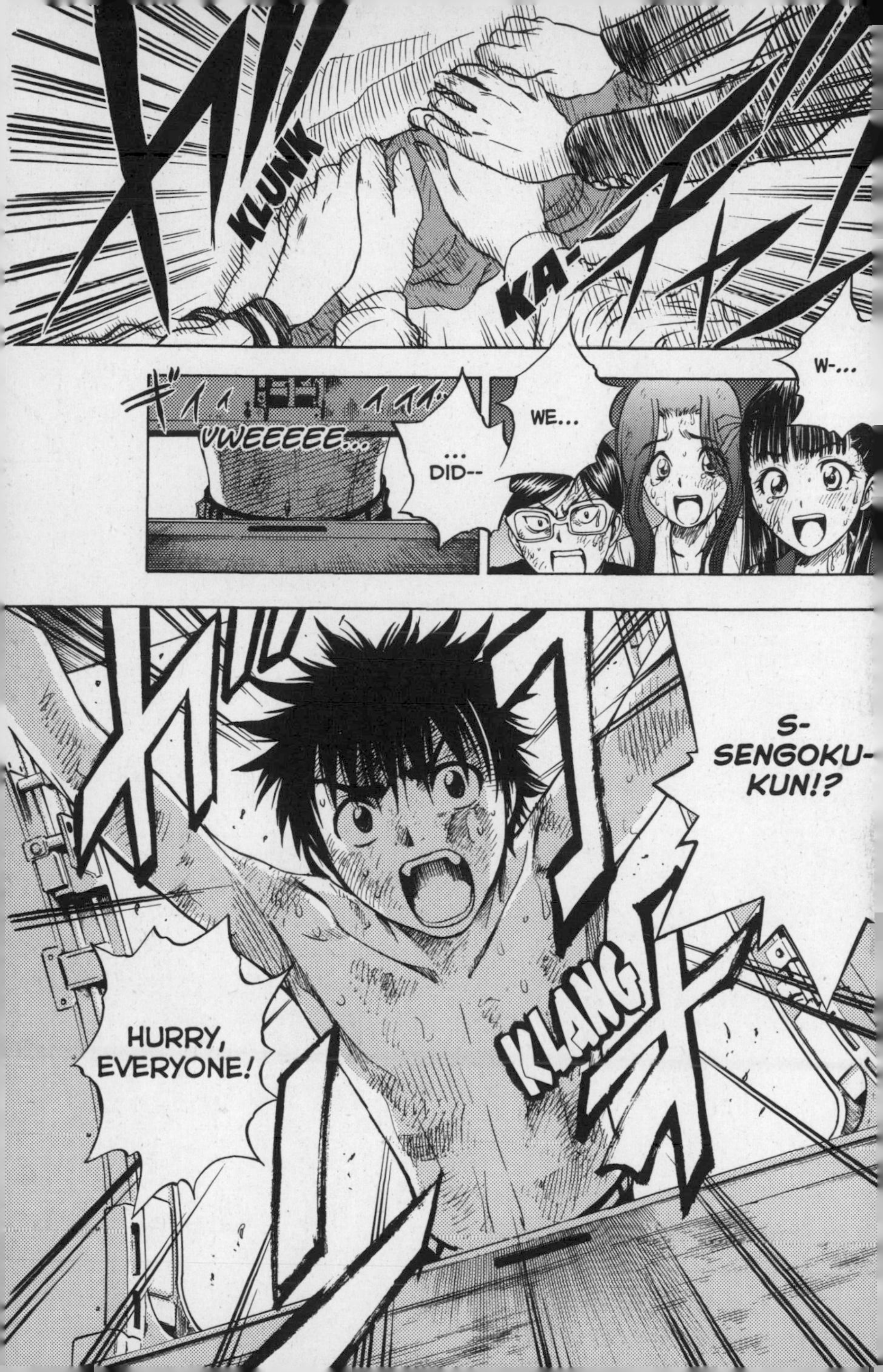
KA-
KLUNK
W-...
WE...
... DID--
VWEEEEE...
S-SENGOKU-KUN!?
KLANG
HURRY, EVERYONE!

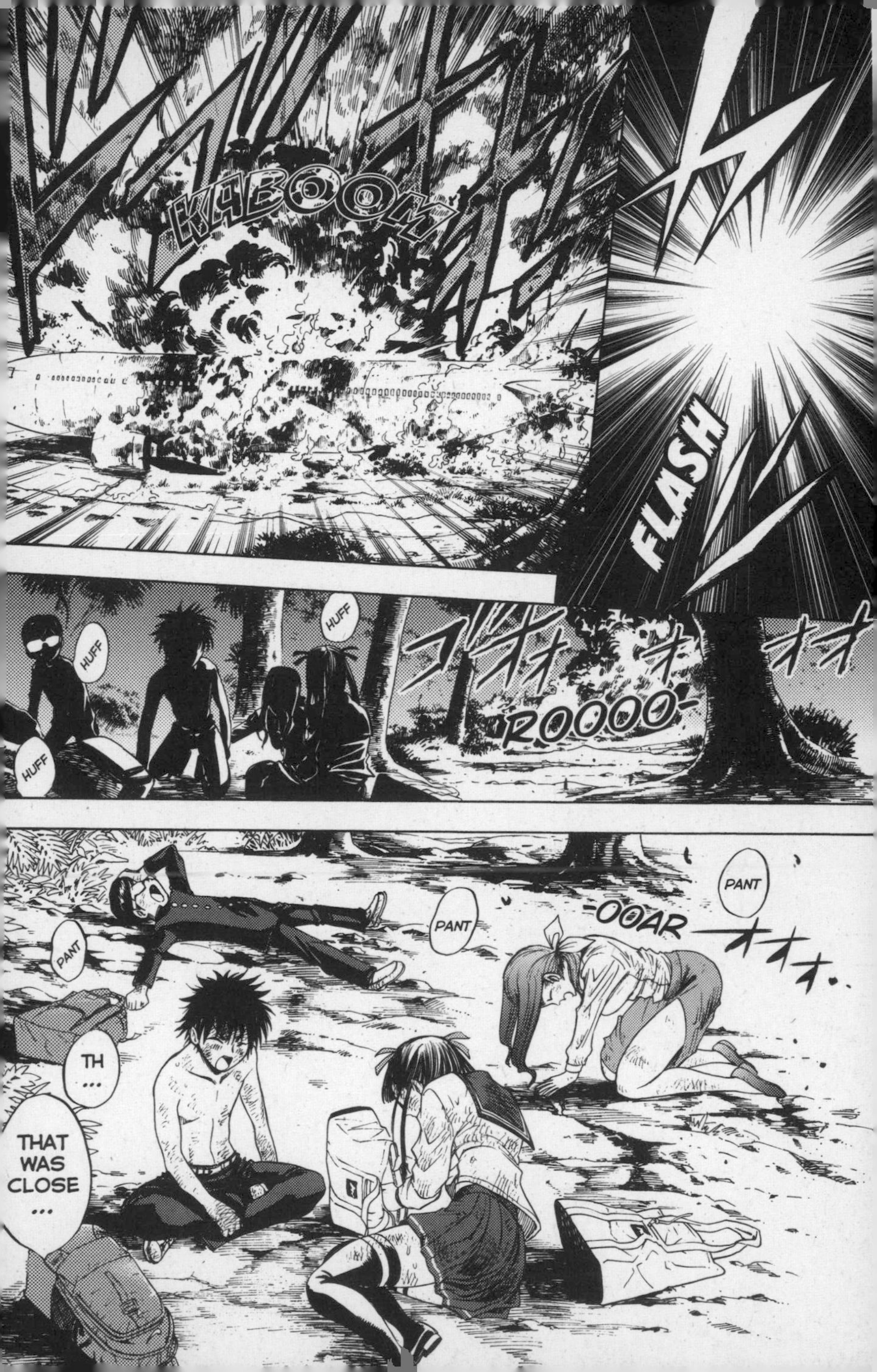

FLASH
KABOOM
HUFF
HUFF
HUFF
ROOOO-
PANT
-OOAR
PANT
PANT
TH ...
THAT WAS CLOSE ...

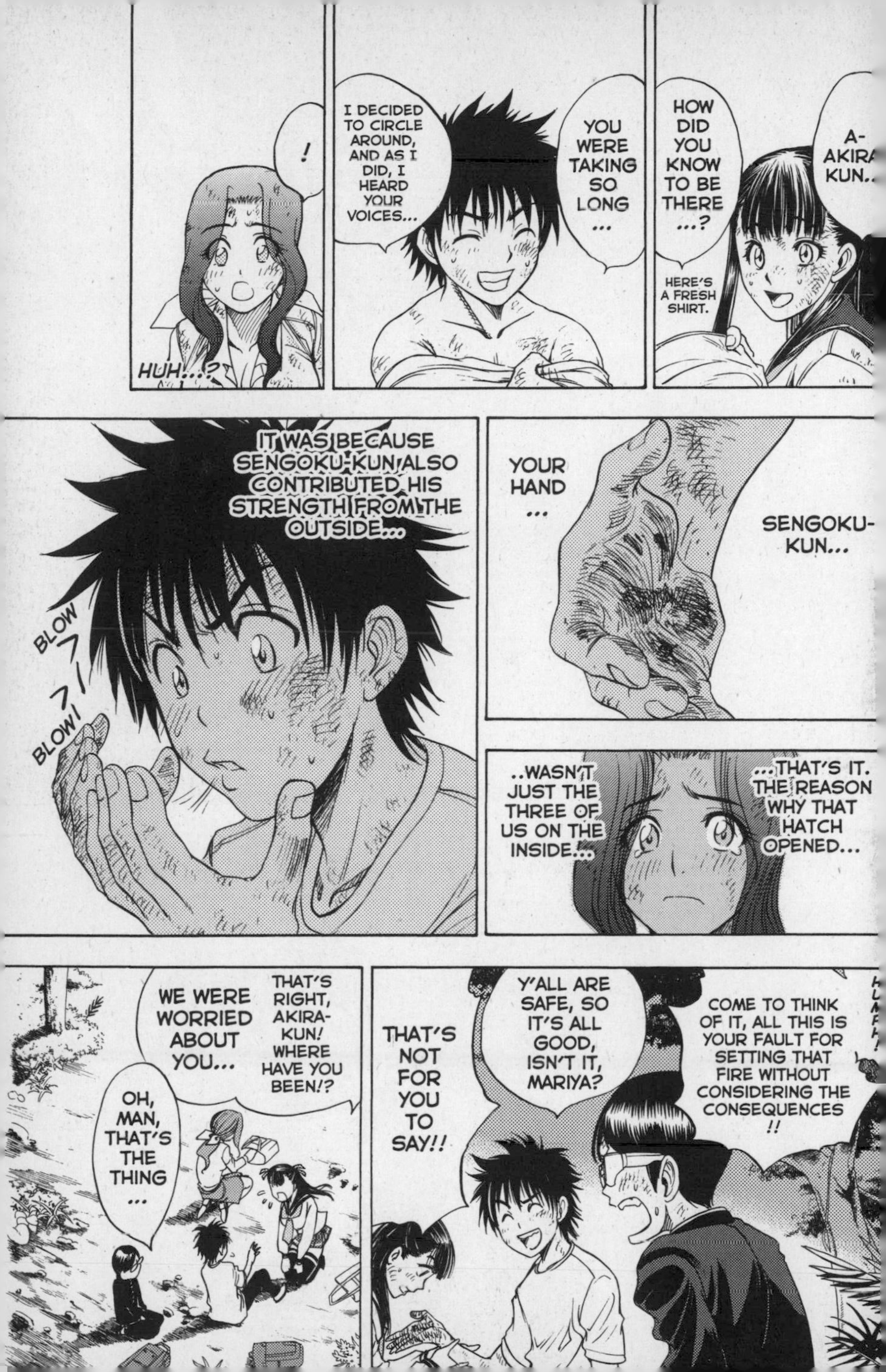
A- AKIRA KUN...
HOW DID YOU KNOW TO BE THERE ...?
HERE'S A FRESH SHIRT.
YOU WERE TAKING SO LONG ...
I DECIDED TO CIRCLE AROUND, AND AS I DID, I HEARD YOUR VOICES...
!
HUH...?
SENGOKU-KUN...
YOUR HAND ...
...THAT'S IT. THE REASON WHY THAT HATCH OPENED...
..WASN'T JUST THE THREE OF US ON THE INSIDE...
IT WAS BECAUSE SENGOKU-KUN ALSO CONTRIBUTED HIS STRENGTH FROM THE OUTSIDE...
BLOW~
BLOW!
HUMPH!
COME TO THINK OF IT, ALL THIS IS YOUR FAULT FOR SETTING THAT FIRE WITHOUT CONSIDERING THE CONSEQUENCES !!
Y'ALL ARE SAFE, SO IT'S ALL GOOD, ISN'T IT, MARIYA?
THAT'S NOT FOR YOU TO SAY!!
THAT'S RIGHT, AKIRA-KUN! WHERE HAVE YOU BEEN!?
WE WERE WORRIED ABOUT YOU...
OH, MAN, THAT'S THE THING ...

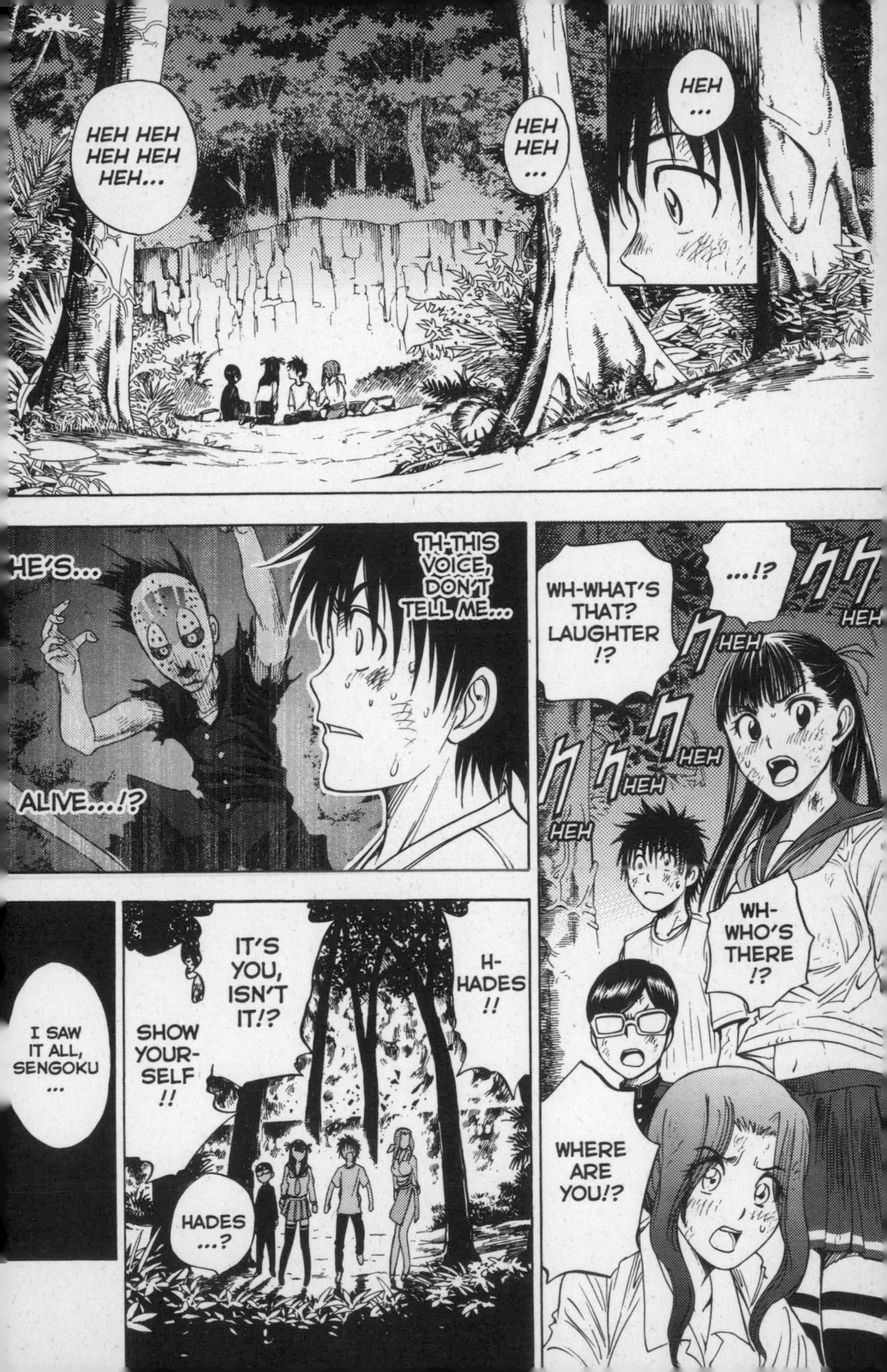
HEH ...
HEH HEH ...
HEH HEH HEH HEH HEH...
...!?
WH-WHAT'S THAT? LAUGHTER !?
HEH
HEH
HEH
HEH
HEH
WH- WHO'S THERE !?
WHERE ARE YOU!?
TH-THIS VOICE, DON'T TELL ME...
HE'S...
ALIVE...!?
H- HADES !!
IT'S YOU, ISN'T IT!?
SHOW YOUR- SELF !!
HADES ...?
I SAW IT ALL, SENGOKU ...

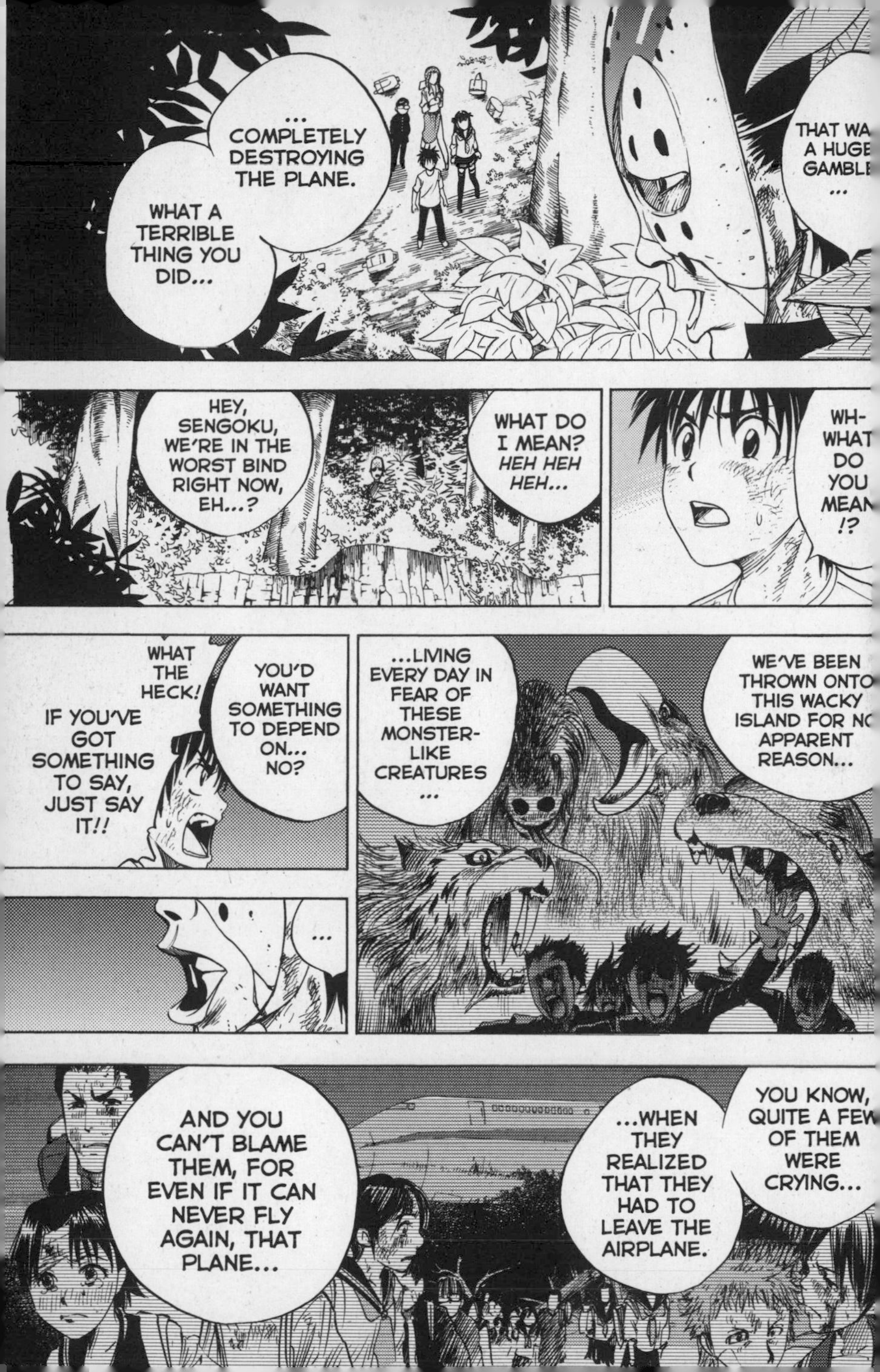
THAT WA A HUGE GAMBLE ...
... COMPLETELY DESTROYING THE PLANE.
WHAT A TERRIBLE THING YOU DID...
WH- WHAT DO YOU MEAN !?
WHAT DO I MEAN? HEH HEH HEH...
HEY, SENGOKU, WE'RE IN THE WORST BIND RIGHT NOW, EH...?
WE'VE BEEN THROWN ONTO THIS WACKY ISLAND FOR NO APPARENT REASON...
...LIVING EVERY DAY IN FEAR OF THESE MONSTER-LIKE CREATURES ...
YOU'D WANT SOMETHING TO DEPEND ON... NO?
WHAT THE HECK!
IF YOU'VE GOT SOMETHING TO SAY, JUST SAY IT!!
...
YOU KNOW, QUITE A FEW OF THEM WERE CRYING...
...WHEN THEY REALIZED THAT THEY HAD TO LEAVE THE AIRPLANE.
AND YOU CAN'T BLAME THEM, FOR EVEN IF IT CAN NEVER FLY AGAIN, THAT PLANE...

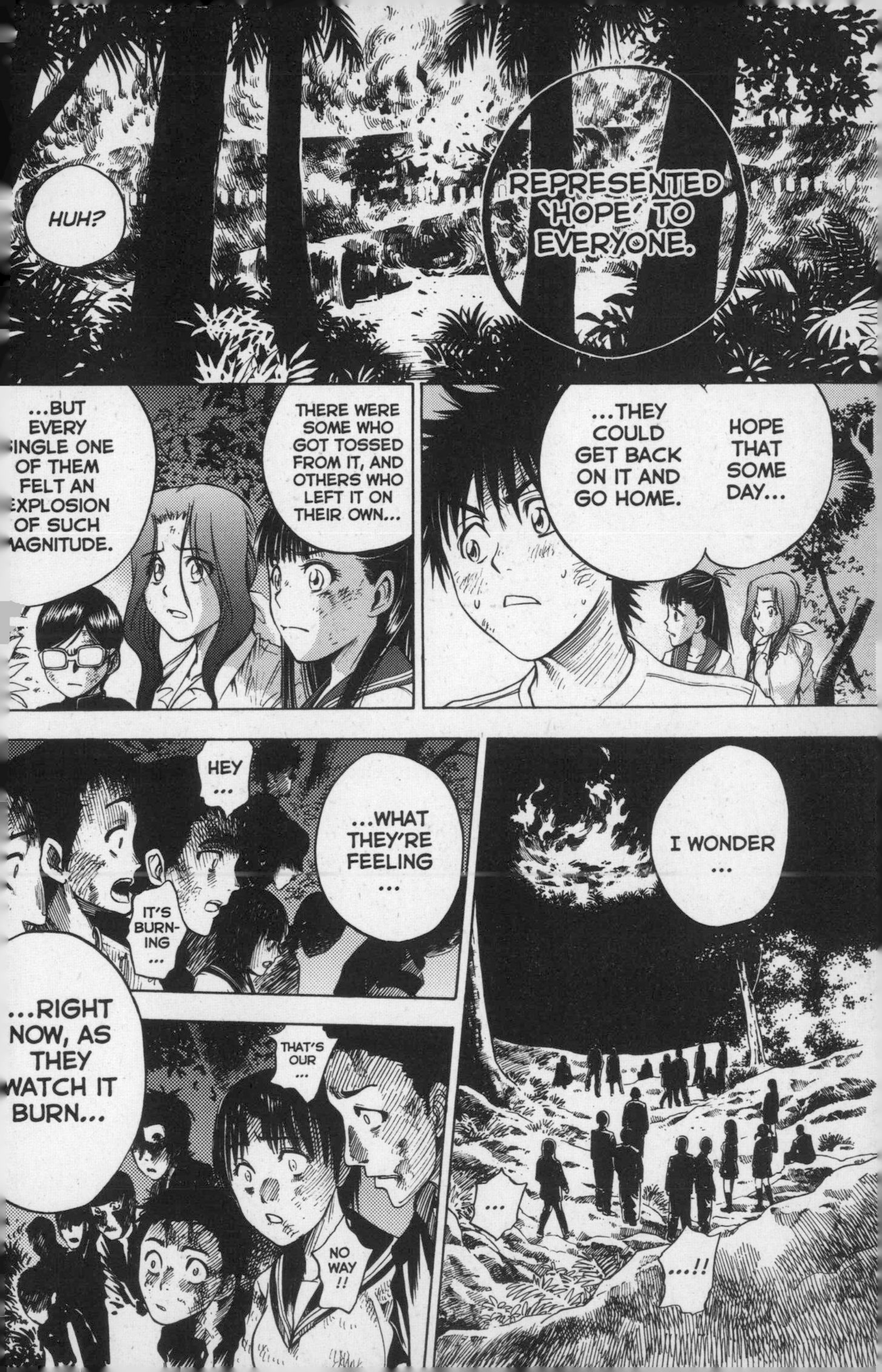
REPRESENTED 'HOPE' TO EVERYONE.
HUH?
HOPE THAT SOME DAY...
...THEY COULD GET BACK ON IT AND GO HOME.
THERE WERE SOME WHO GOT TOSSED FROM IT, AND OTHERS WHO LEFT IT ON THEIR OWN...
...BUT EVERY SINGLE ONE OF THEM FELT AN EXPLOSION OF SUCH MAGNITUDE.
I WONDER ...
...
...!!
...WHAT THEY'RE FEELING ...
HEY ...
IT'S BURN-ING ...
...RIGHT NOW, AS THEY WATCH IT BURN...
THAT'S OUR ...
NO WAY !!

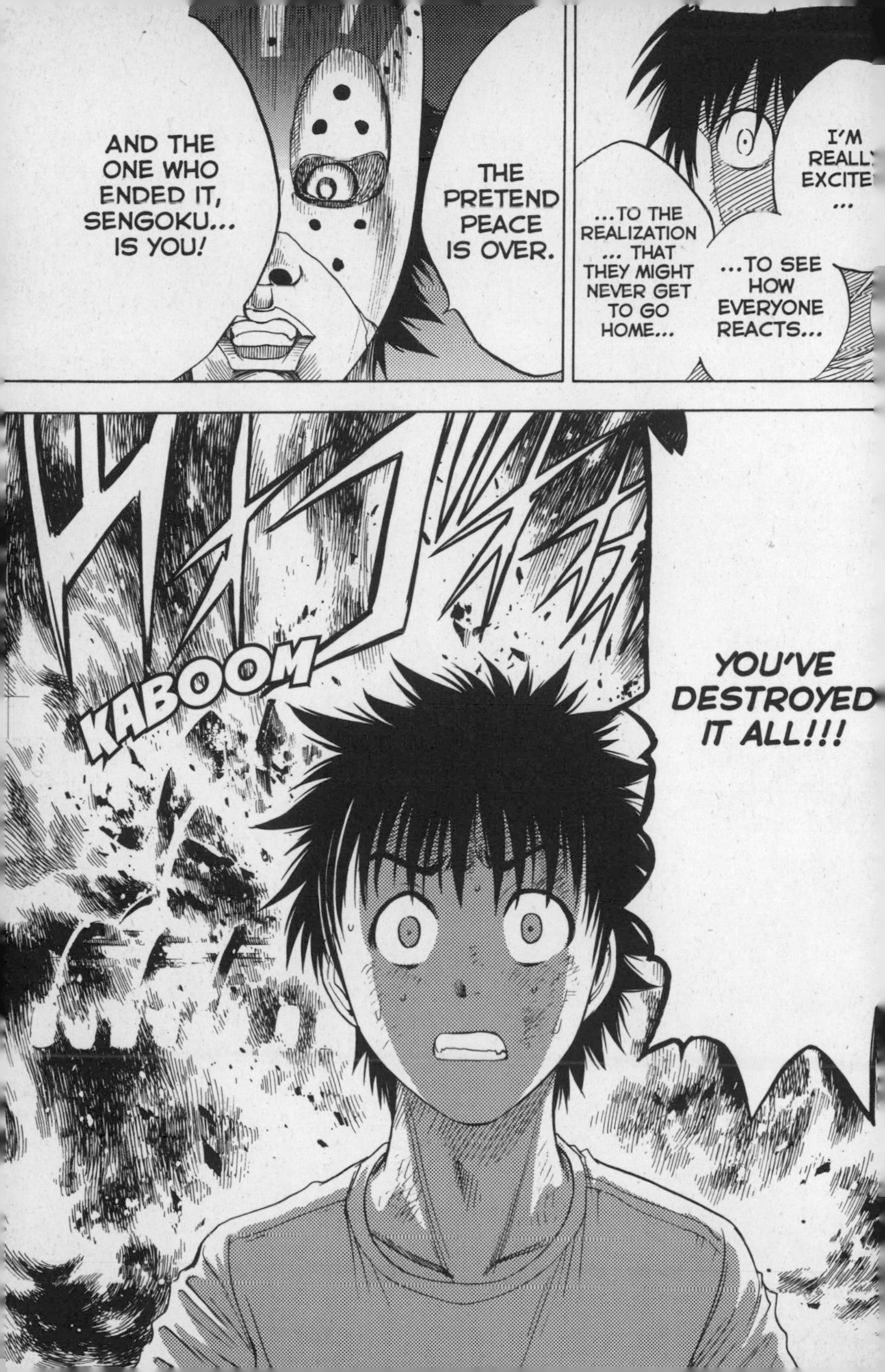
I'M REALL EXCITE ...
...TO SEE HOW EVERYONE REACTS...
...TO THE REALIZATION ... THAT THEY MIGHT NEVER GET TO GO HOME...
THE PRETEND PEACE IS OVER.
AND THE ONE WHO ENDED IT, SENGOKU... IS YOU!
YOU'VE DESTROYED IT ALL!!!
KABOOM

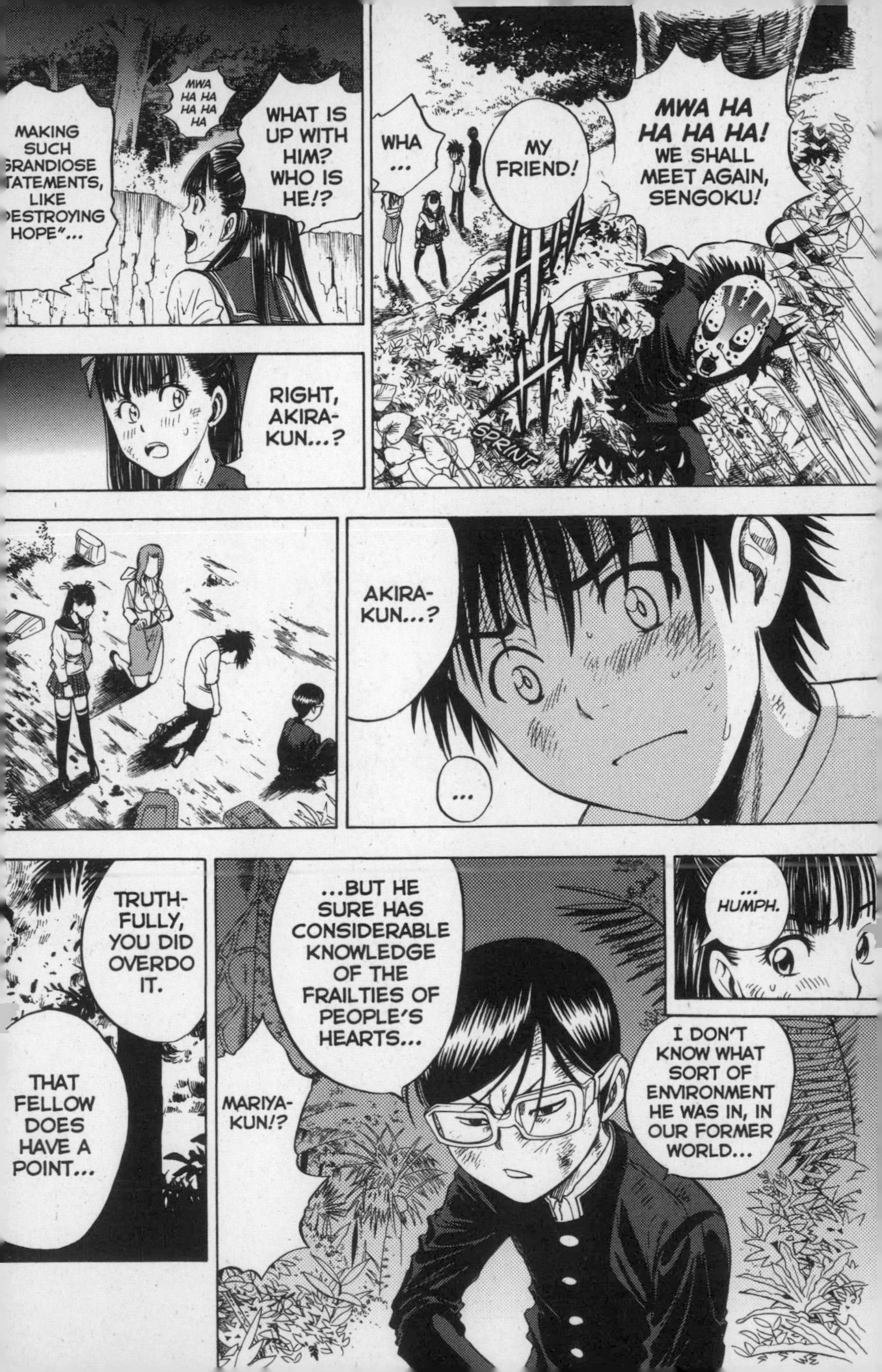
MWA HA HA HA HA HA! WE SHALL MEET AGAIN, SENGOKU!
MY FRIEND!
WHA ...
SPRINT
WHAT IS UP WITH HIM? WHO IS HE!?
MWA HA HA HA HA HA
MAKING SUCH GRANDIOSE TATEMENTS, LIKE ESTROYING HOPE"...
RIGHT, AKIRA-KUN...?
AKIRA-KUN...?
...
... HUMPH.
I DON'T KNOW WHAT SORT OF ENVIRONMENT HE WAS IN, IN OUR FORMER WORLD...
...BUT HE SURE HAS CONSIDERABLE KNOWLEDGE OF THE FRAILTIES OF PEOPLE'S HEARTS...
MARIYA-KUN!?
TRUTH-FULLY, YOU DID OVERDO IT.
THAT FELLOW DOES HAVE A POINT...

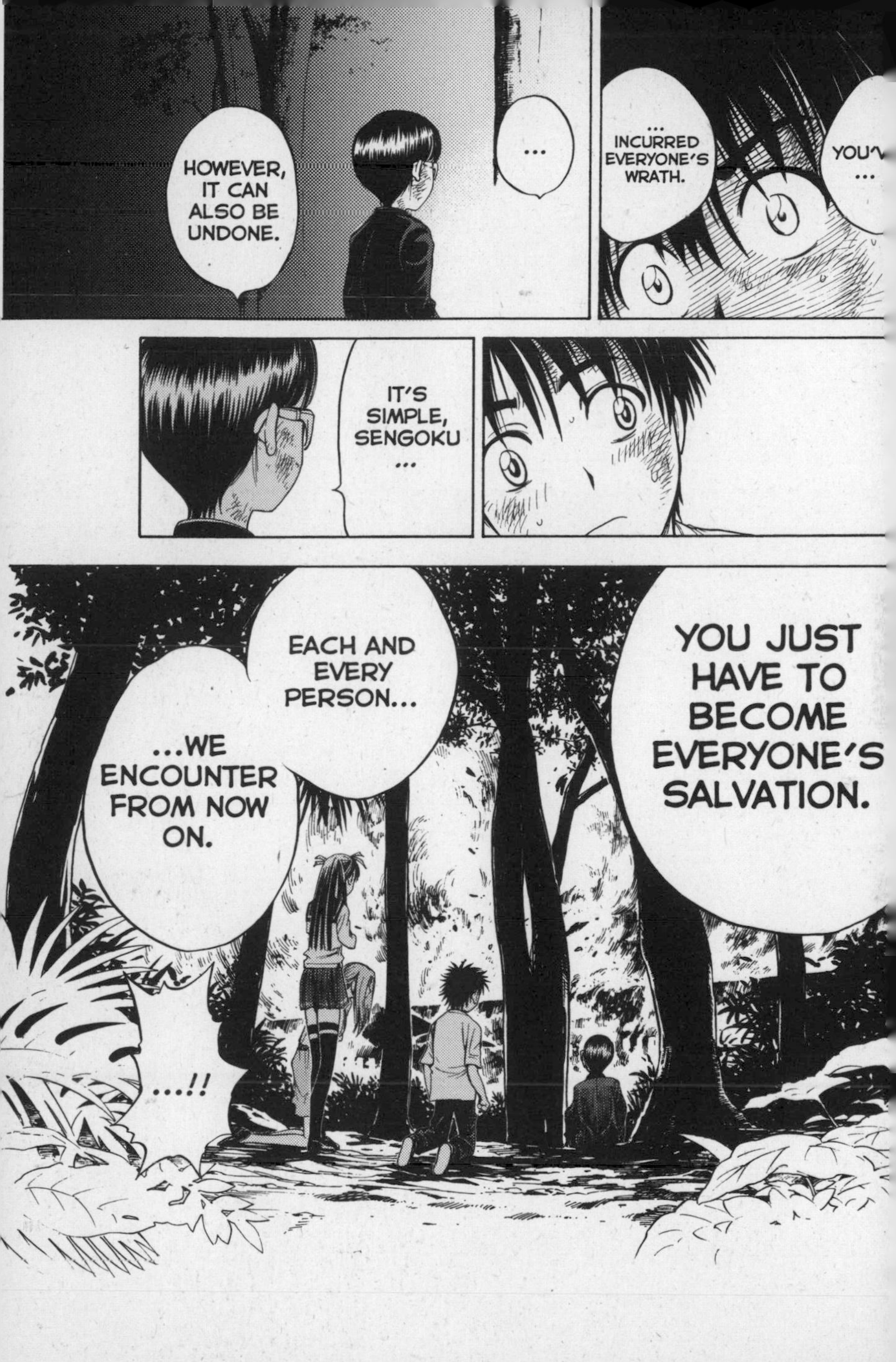
YOU'V ...
... INCURRED EVERYONE'S WRATH.
...
HOWEVER, IT CAN ALSO BE UNDONE.
IT'S SIMPLE, SENGOKU ...
YOU JUST HAVE TO BECOME EVERYONE'S SALVATION.
EACH AND EVERY PERSON...
...WE ENCOUNTER FROM NOW ON.
...!!

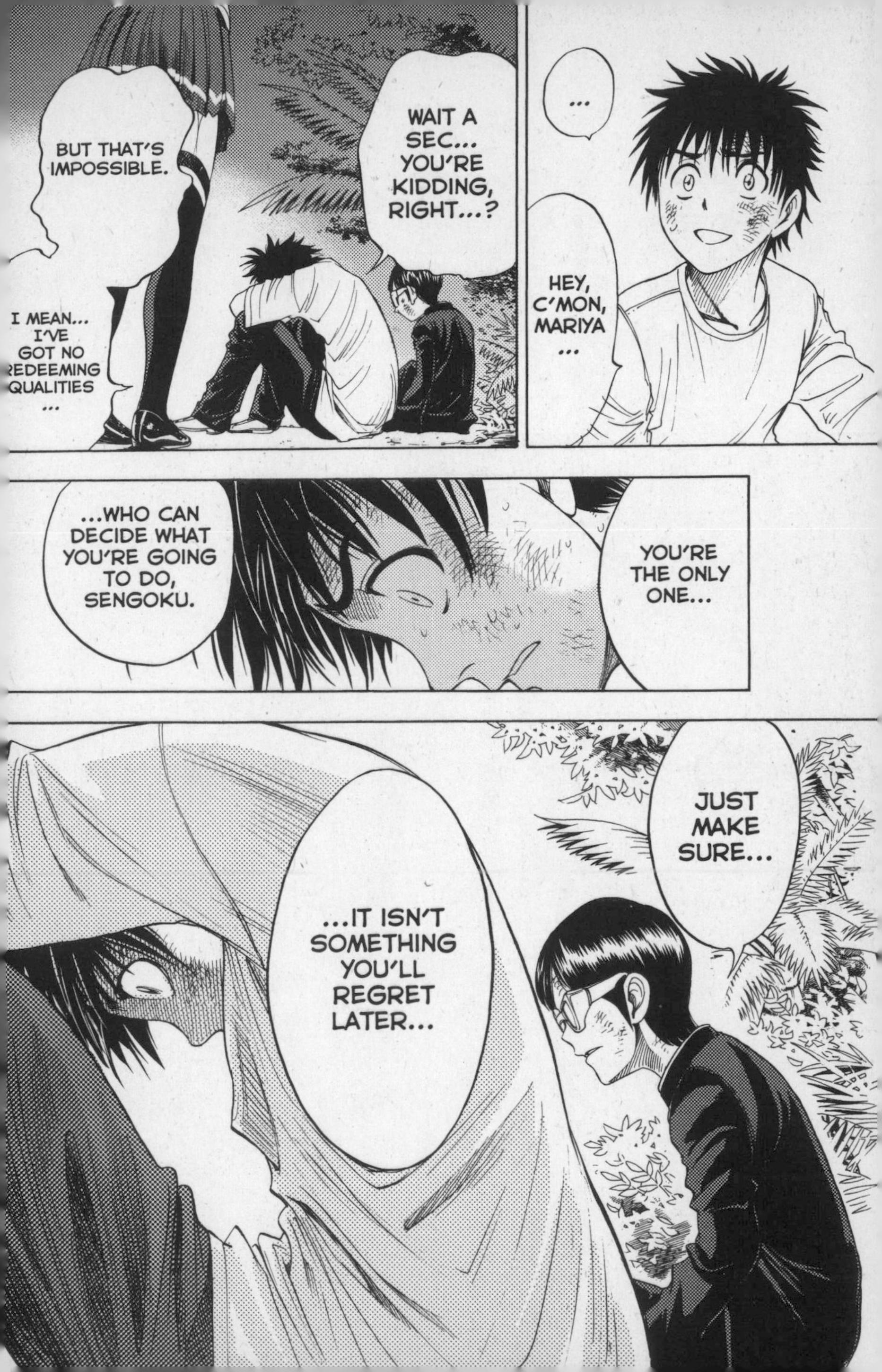
...
HEY, C'MON, MARIYA...
WAIT A SEC... YOU'RE KIDDING, RIGHT...?
BUT THAT'S IMPOSSIBLE.
I MEAN... I'VE GOT NO REDEEMING QUALITIES...
YOU'RE THE ONLY ONE...
...WHO CAN DECIDE WHAT YOU'RE GOING TO DO, SENGOKU.
JUST MAKE SURE...
...IT ISN'T SOMETHING YOU'LL REGRET LATER...

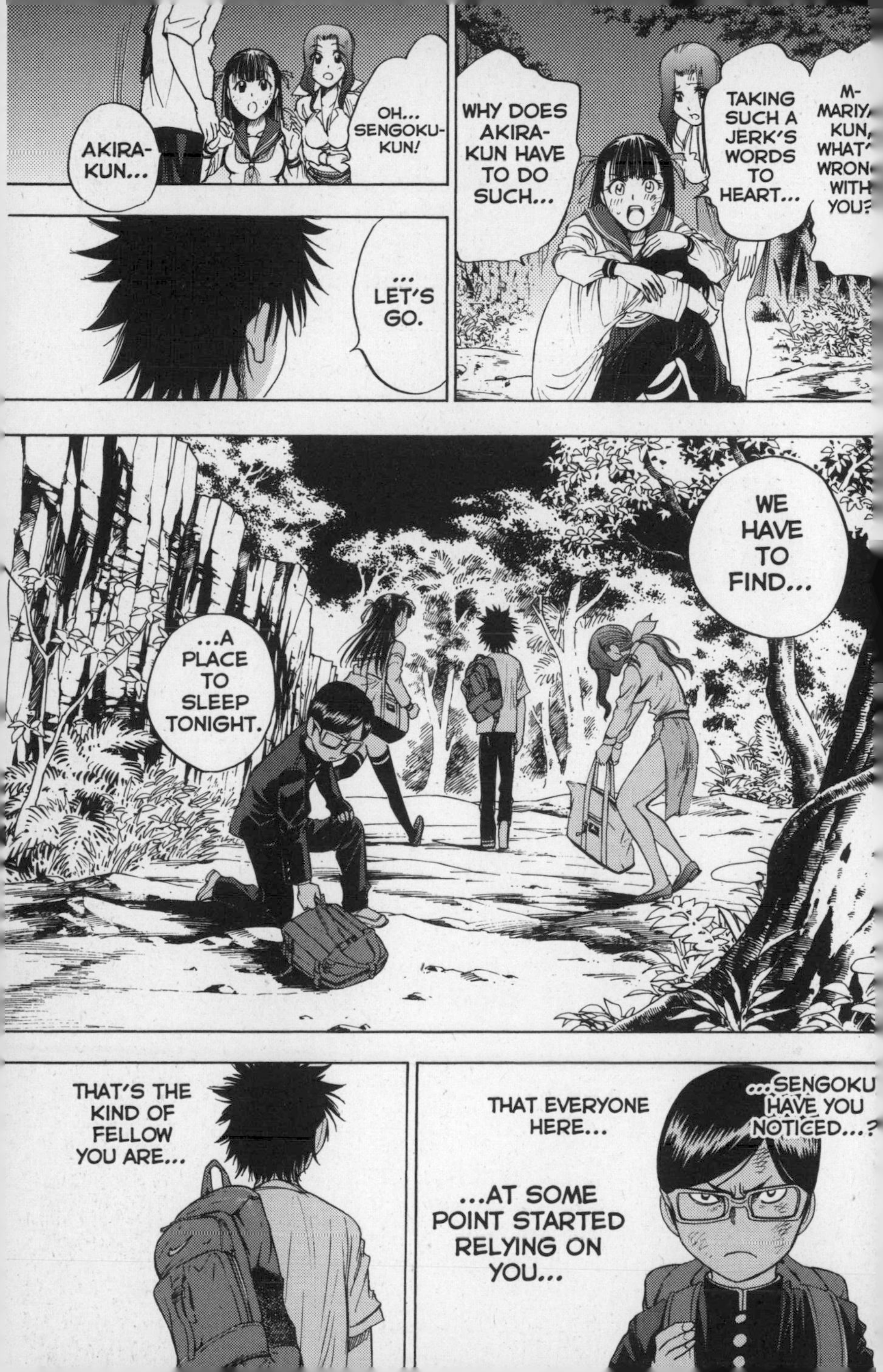
M-MARIY KUN, WHAT WRON WITH YOU?
TAKING SUCH A JERK'S WORDS TO HEART...
WHY DOES AKIRA-KUN HAVE TO DO SUCH...
OH... SENGOKU-KUN!
AKIRA-KUN...
...LET'S GO.
WE HAVE TO FIND...
...A PLACE TO SLEEP TONIGHT.
...SENGOKU HAVE YOU NOTICED...?
THAT EVERYONE HERE...
...AT SOME POINT STARTED RELYING ON YOU...
THAT'S THE KIND OF FELLOW YOU ARE...

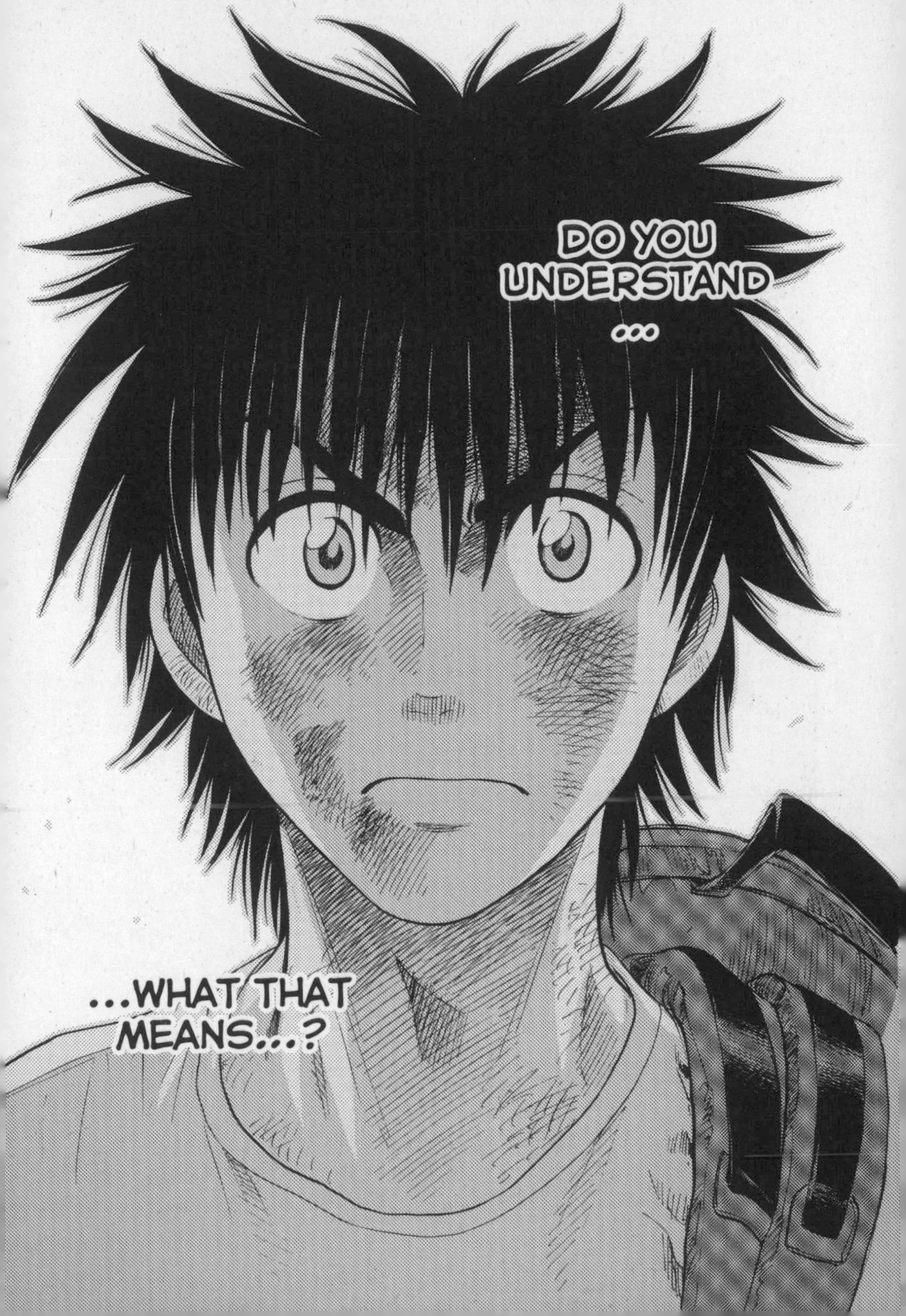
DO YOU UNDERSTAND ...
...WHAT THAT MEANS...?

Episode 8 Light & Darkness

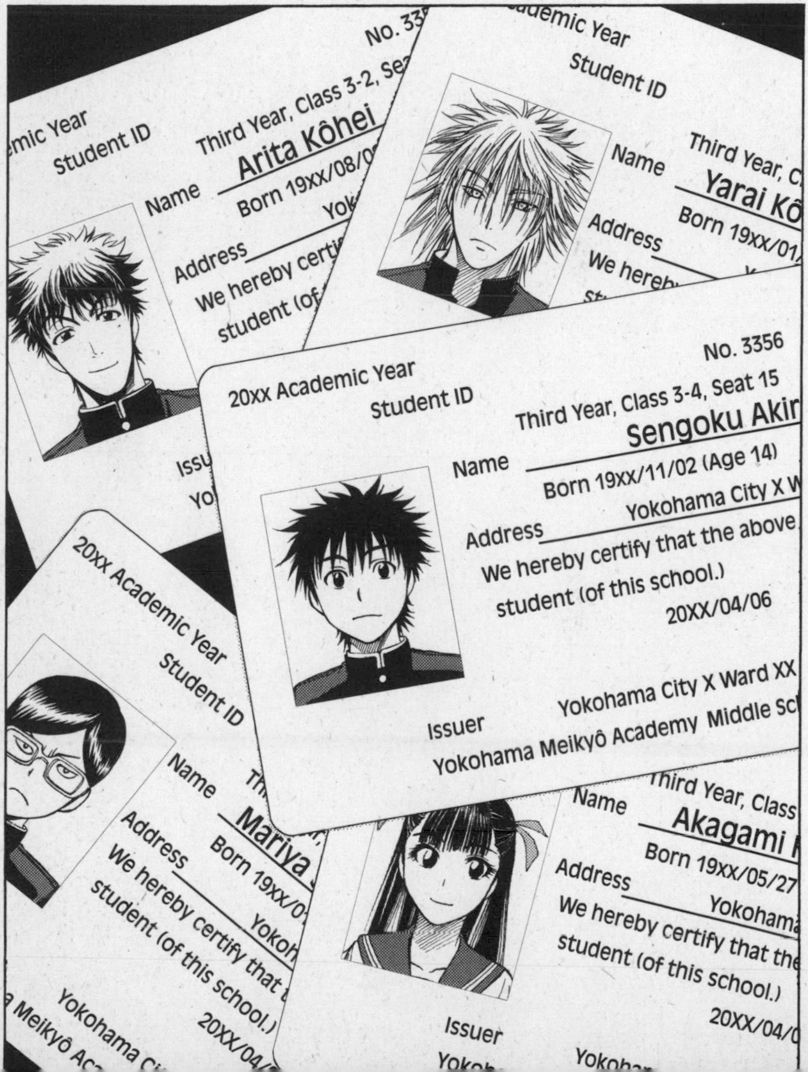

Academic Year
Student ID
Name
Third Year, C
Yarai Kô
Born 19xx/01
Address
We hereb
No. 33
mic Year
Student ID
Third Year, Class 3-2, Sea
Name
Arita Kôhei
Born 19xx/08/0
Address
We hereby certi
student (of
No. 3356
20xx Academic Year
Student ID
Third Year, Class 3-4, Seat 15
Name
Sengoku Akir
Born 19xx/11/02 (Age 14)
Address
Yokohama City X W
We hereby certify that the above
student (of this school.)
20XX/04/06
Issuer
Yokohama City X Ward XX
Yokohama Meikyô Academy Middle Sc
Third Year, Class
Name
Akagami
Born 19xx/05/27
Address
Yokohama
We hereby certify that the
student (of this school.)
20XX/04/0
Issuer
20xx Academic Year
Student ID
Name
Mariya
Born 19xx/0
Address
We hereby certify that
student (of this school.)
20XX/04/
Yokohama Ci
Meikyô Ac

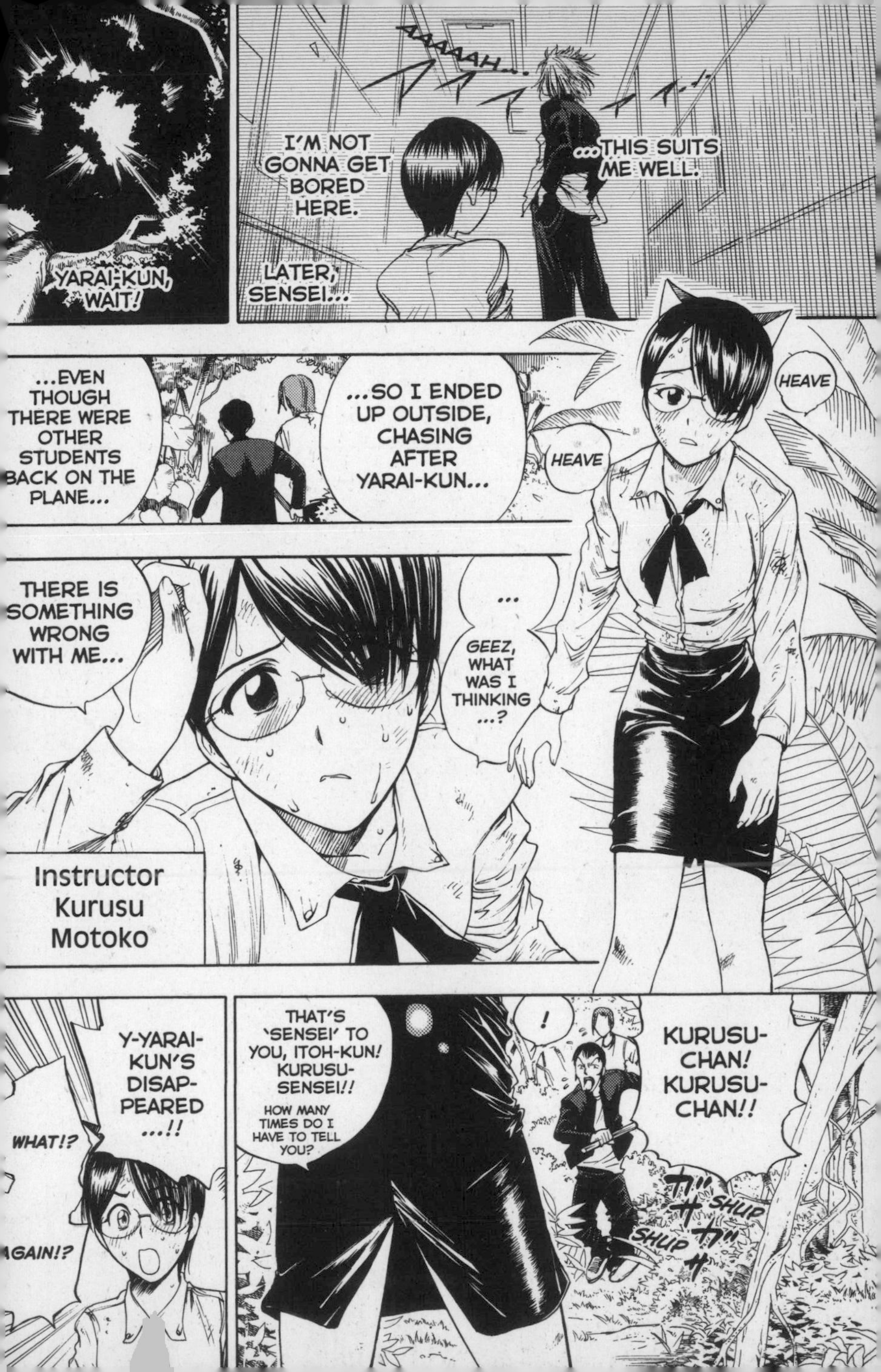
AAAAAAH...
...THIS SUITS ME WELL.
I'M NOT GONNA GET BORED HERE.
LATER, SENSEI...
YARAI-KUN, WAIT!
HEAVE
HEAVE
...SO I ENDED UP OUTSIDE, CHASING AFTER YARAI-KUN...
...EVEN THOUGH THERE WERE OTHER STUDENTS BACK ON THE PLANE...
...
GEEZ, WHAT WAS I THINKING ...?
THERE IS SOMETHING WRONG WITH ME...
Instructor Kurusu Motoko
KURUSU-CHAN! KURUSU-CHAN!!
!
THAT'S 'SENSEI' TO YOU, ITOH-KUN! KURUSU-SENSEI!!
HOW MANY TIMES DO I HAVE TO TELL YOU?
SHUP
SHUP
Y-YARAI-KUN'S DISAPPEARED ...!!
WHAT!?
AGAIN!?

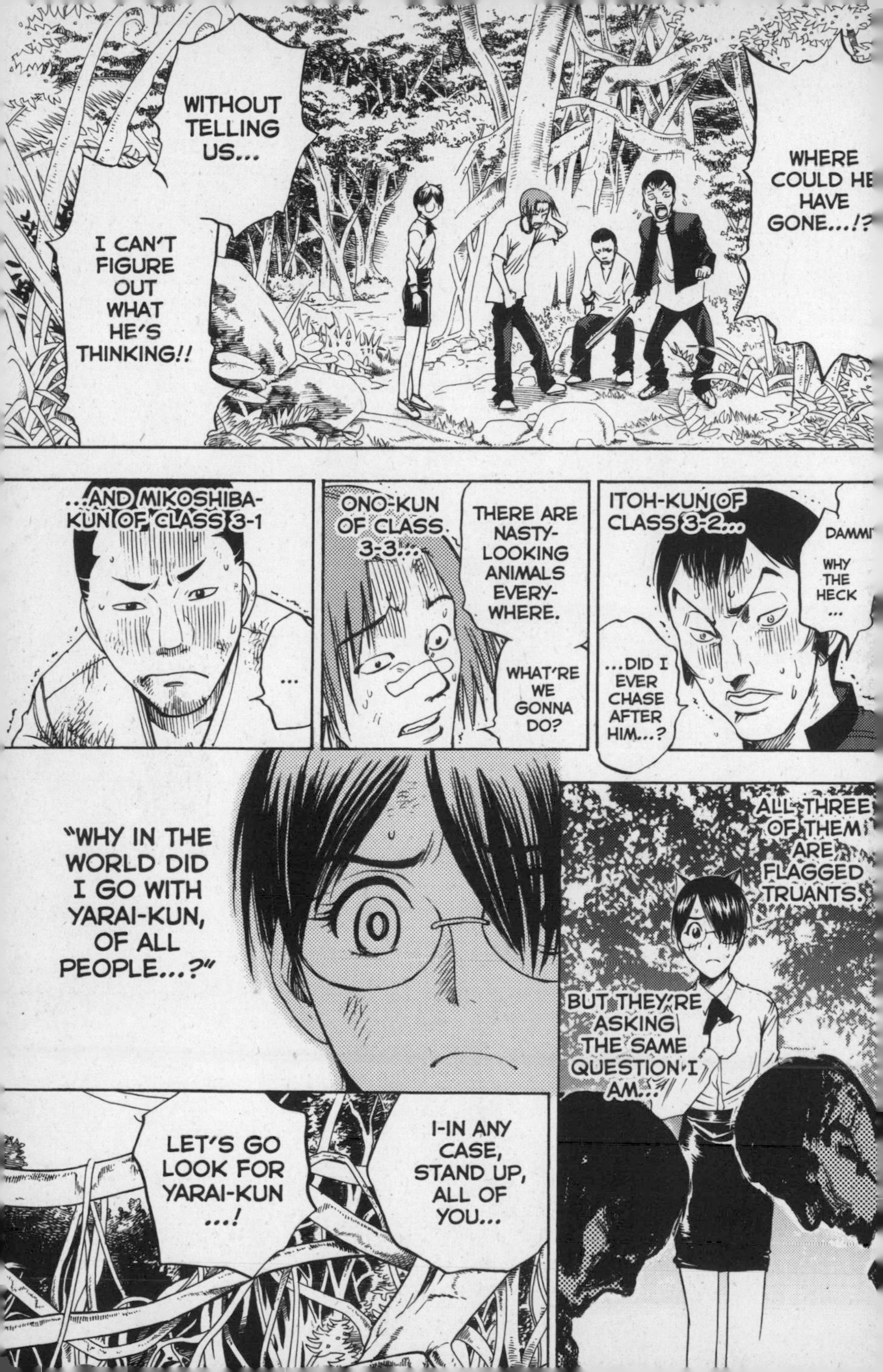
WHERE COULD HE HAVE GONE...!?
WITHOUT TELLING US...
I CAN'T FIGURE OUT WHAT HE'S THINKING!!
ITOH-KUN OF CLASS 3-2...
DAMMI
WHY THE HECK ...
...DID I EVER CHASE AFTER HIM...?
ONO-KUN OF CLASS 3-3...
THERE ARE NASTY-LOOKING ANIMALS EVERY-WHERE.
WHAT'RE WE GONNA DO?
...AND MIKOSHIBA-KUN OF CLASS 3-1
...
ALL THREE OF THEM ARE FLAGGED TRUANTS.
BUT THEY'RE ASKING THE SAME QUESTION I AM...
"WHY IN THE WORLD DID I GO WITH YARAI-KUN, OF ALL PEOPLE...?"
I-IN ANY CASE, STAND UP, ALL OF YOU...
LET'S GO LOOK FOR YARAI-KUN ...!

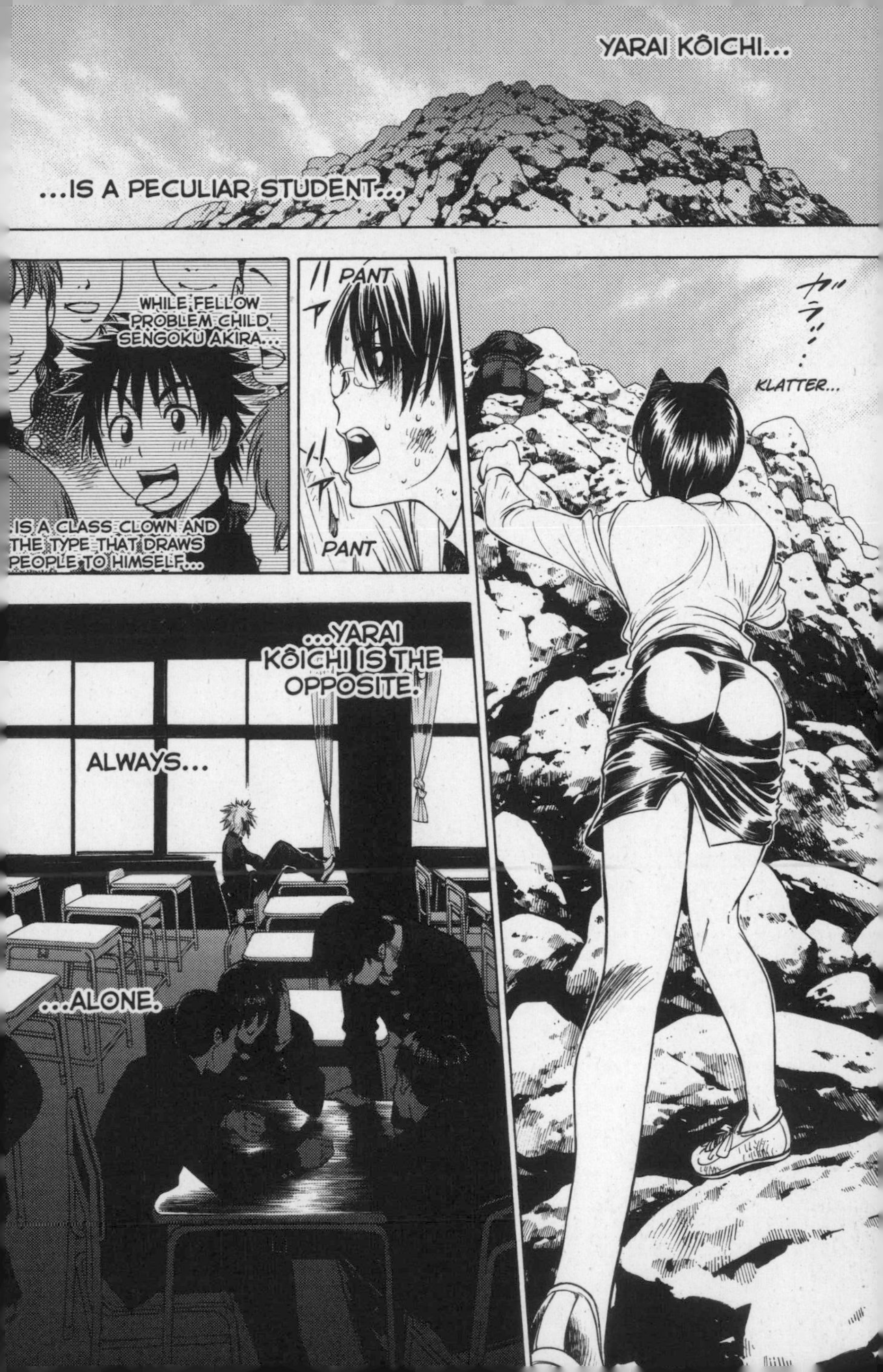
YARAI KÔICHI...
...IS A PECULIAR STUDENT...
KLATTER...
PANT
PANT
WHILE FELLOW PROBLEM CHILD SENGOKU AKIRA...
IS A CLASS CLOWN AND THE TYPE THAT DRAWS PEOPLE TO HIMSELF...
...YARAI KÔICHI IS THE OPPOSITE.
ALWAYS...
...ALONE.

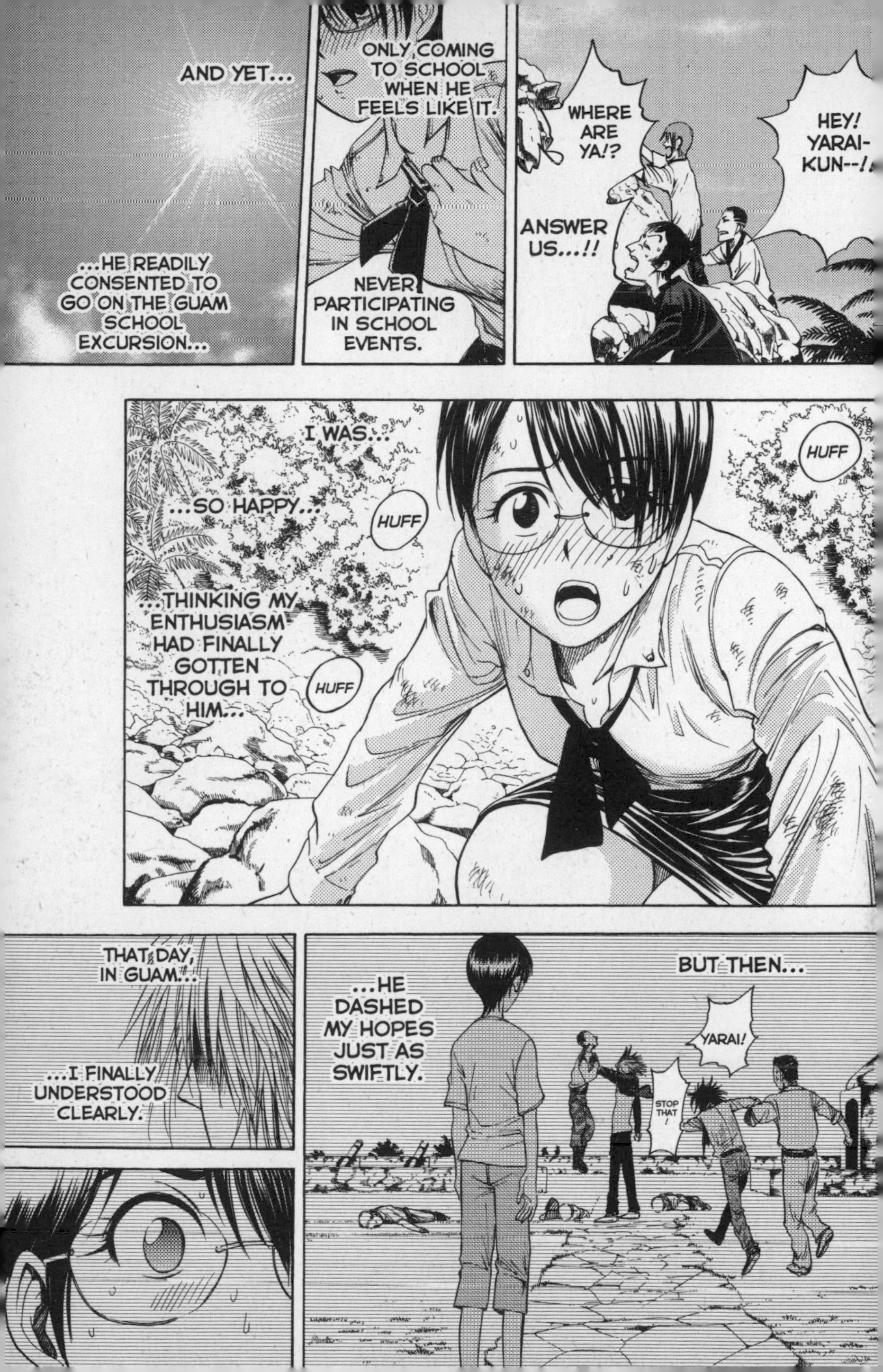
HEY! YARAI-KUN--!!
WHERE ARE YA!?
ANSWER US...!!
ONLY COMING TO SCHOOL WHEN HE FEELS LIKE IT.
NEVER PARTICIPATING IN SCHOOL EVENTS.
AND YET...
...HE READILY CONSENTED TO GO ON THE GUAM SCHOOL EXCURSION...
HUFF
I WAS...
...SO HAPPY...
HUFF
...THINKING MY ENTHUSIASM HAD FINALLY GOTTEN THROUGH TO HIM...
HUFF
BUT THEN...
...HE DASHED MY HOPES JUST AS SWIFTLY.
YARAI!
STOP THAT!
THAT DAY, IN GUAM...
...I FINALLY UNDERSTOOD CLEARLY.

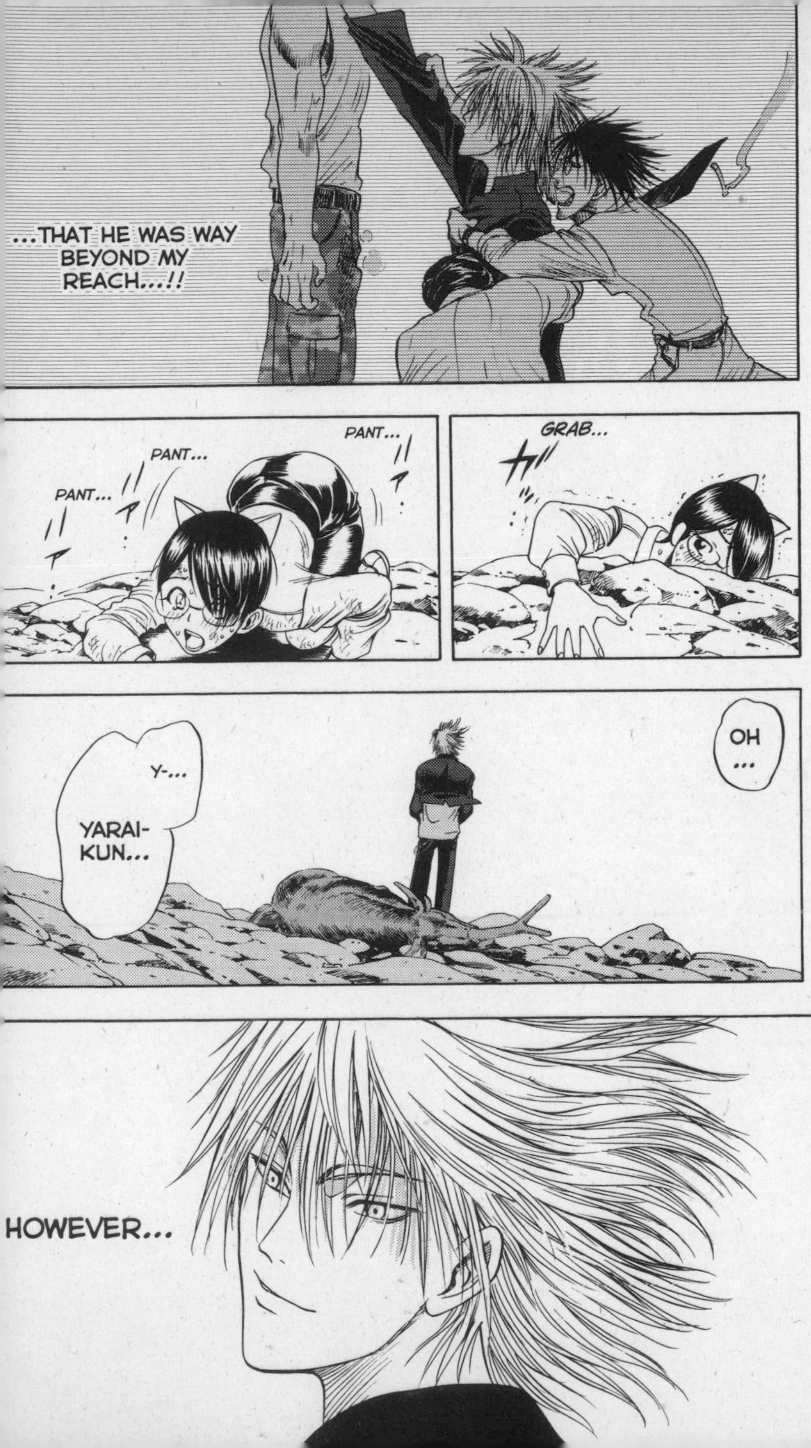

...THAT HE WAS WAY BEYOND MY REACH...!!
GRAB...
PANT...
PANT...
PANT...
OH ...
Y-...
YARAI-KUN...
HOWEVER...

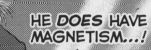

HE *DOES* HAVE MAGNETISM...!

A POWERFUL MAGNETISM THAT DRAWS PEOPLE TO HIM AND DOESN'T LET THEM GO...!!

THAT'S THE KIND OF STUDENT YARAI KÔICHI IS--

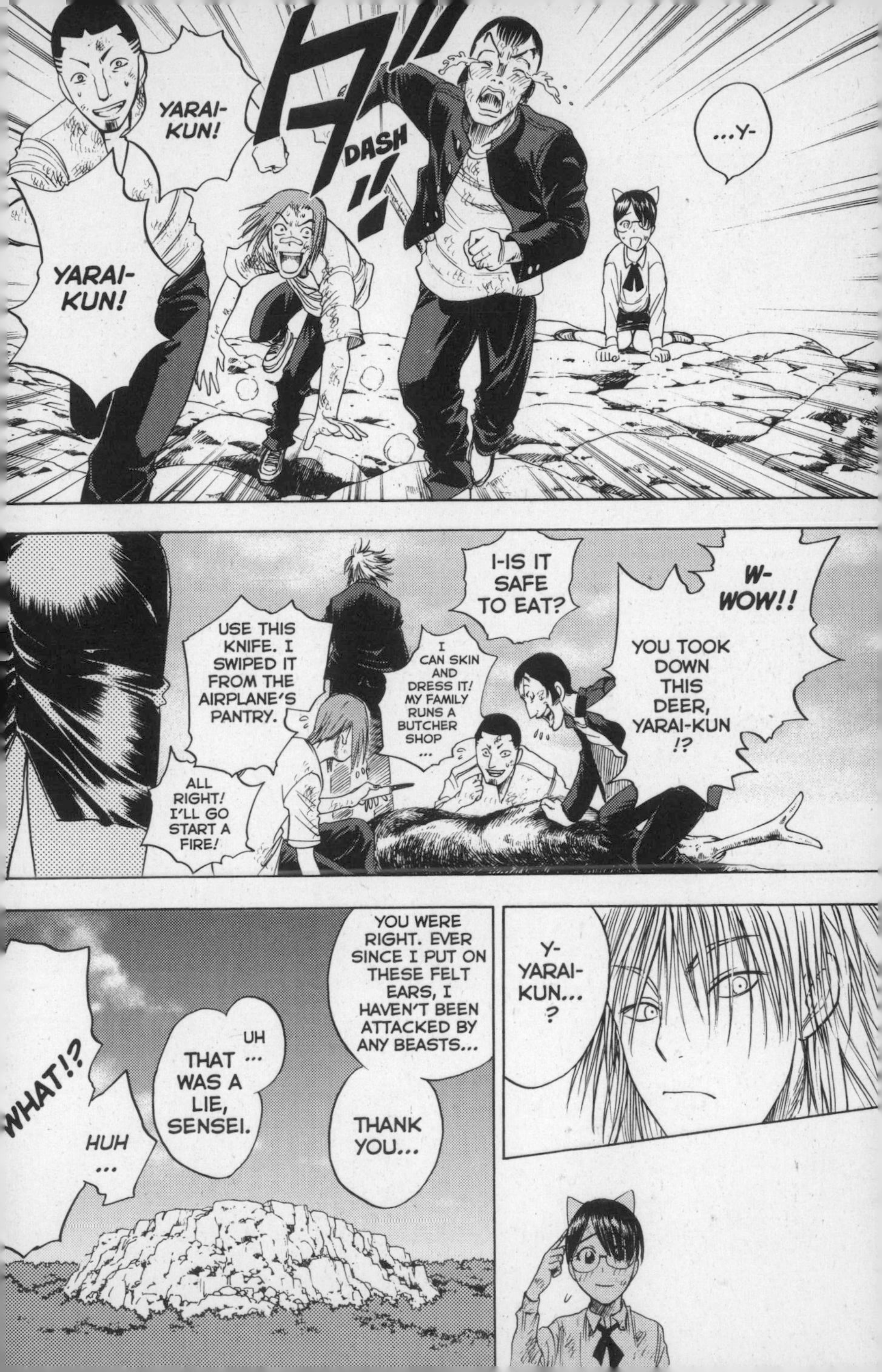
...Y-
DASH!!
YARAI-KUN!
YARAI-KUN!
W-WOW!!
YOU TOOK DOWN THIS DEER, YARAI-KUN!?
I-IS IT SAFE TO EAT?
I CAN SKIN AND DRESS IT! MY FAMILY RUNS A BUTCHER SHOP ...
USE THIS KNIFE. I SWIPED IT FROM THE AIRPLANE'S PANTRY.
ALL RIGHT! I'LL GO START A FIRE!
Y-YARAI-KUN...?
YOU WERE RIGHT. EVER SINCE I PUT ON THESE FELT EARS, I HAVEN'T BEEN ATTACKED BY ANY BEASTS...
THANK YOU...
UH ...
THAT WAS A LIE, SENSEI.
WHAT!?
HUH ...

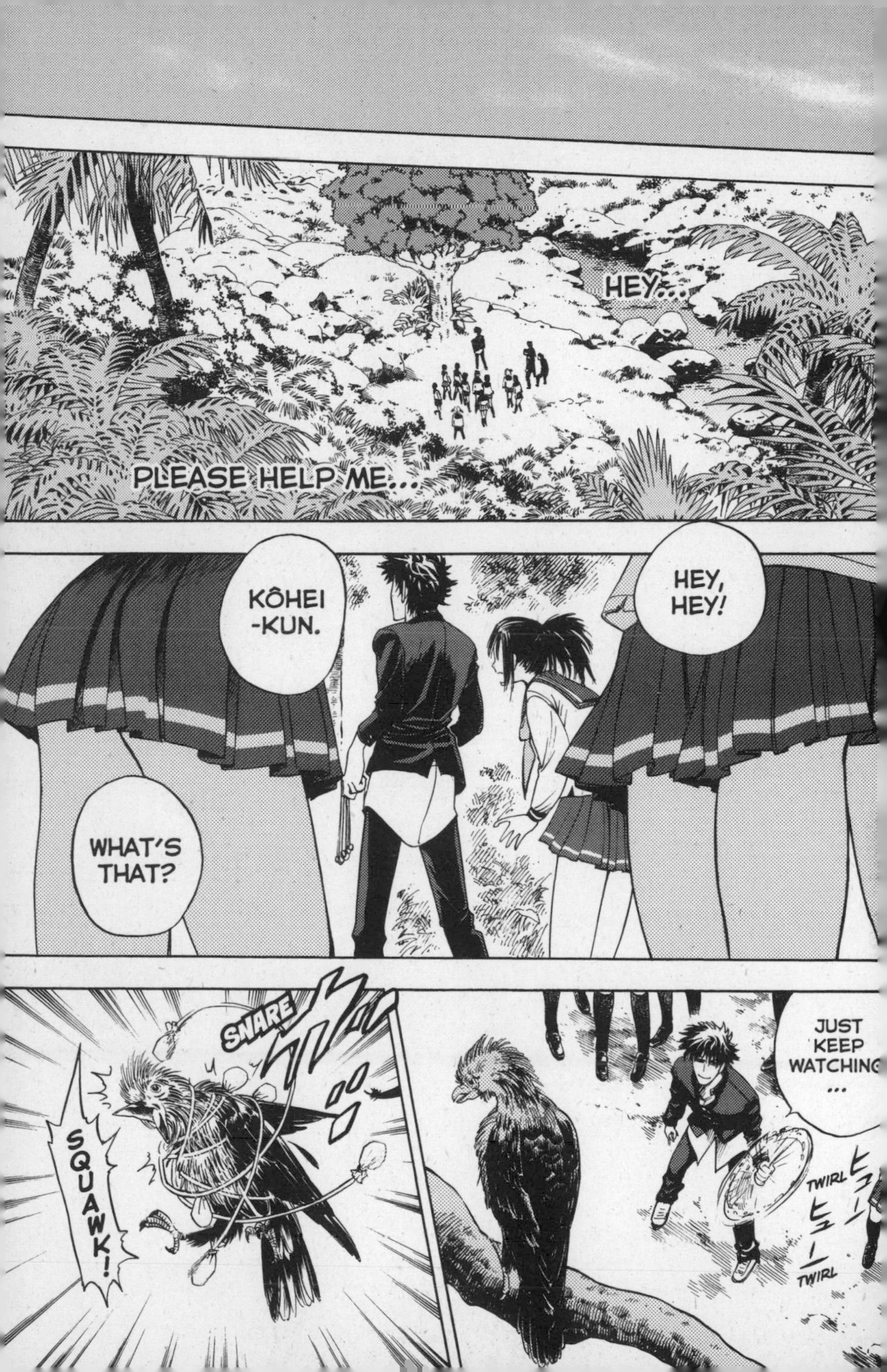
HEY...
PLEASE HELP ME...
HEY, HEY!
KÔHEI -KUN.
WHAT'S THAT?
JUST KEEP WATCHING...
TWIRL
TWIRL
SNARE
SQUAWK!

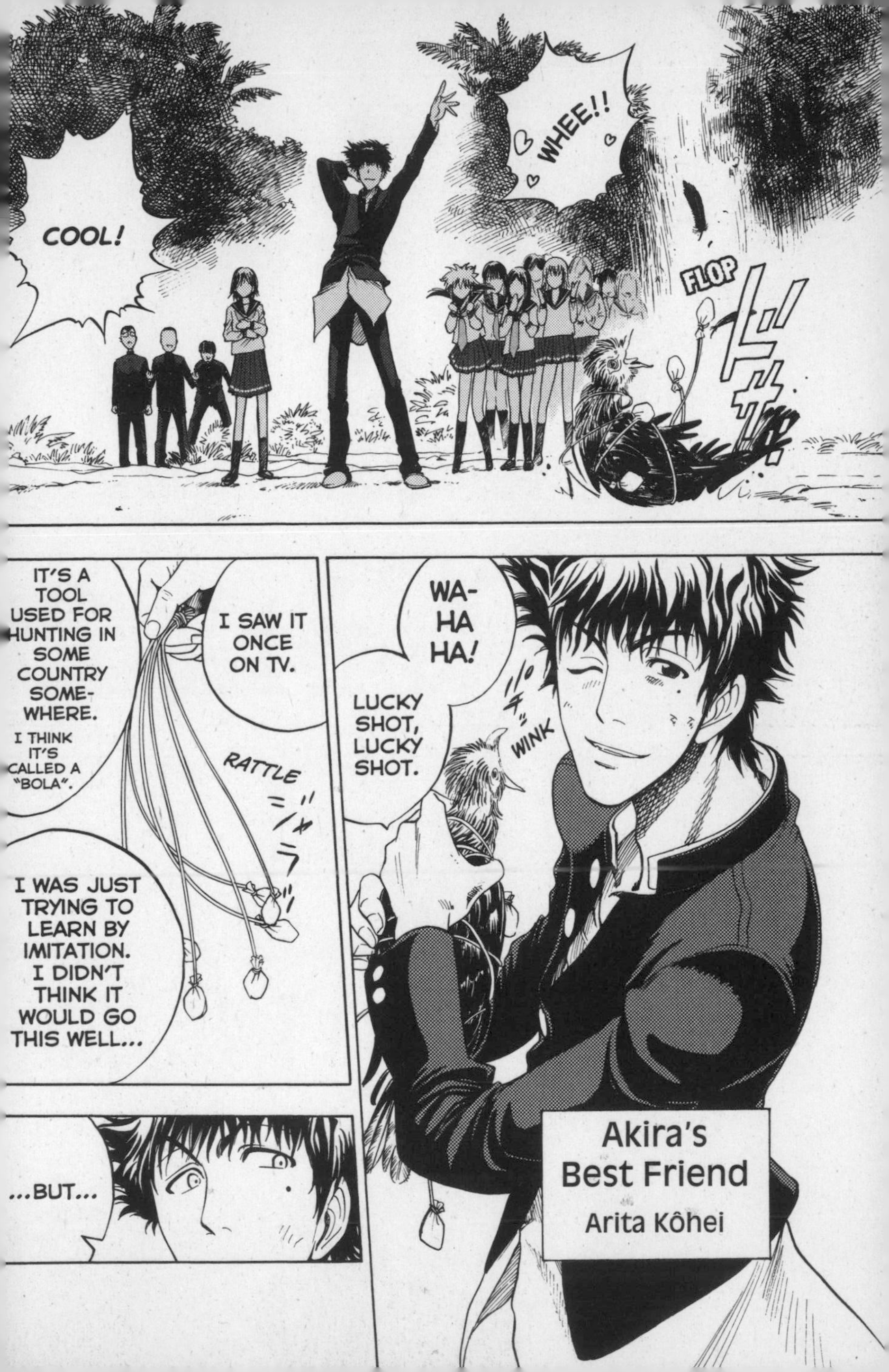
FLOP
WHEE!!
COOL!
WA-HA HA!
LUCKY SHOT, LUCKY SHOT.
WINK
Akira's Best Friend
Arita Kôhei
I SAW IT ONCE ON TV.
IT'S A TOOL USED FOR HUNTING IN SOME COUNTRY SOME-WHERE.
I THINK IT'S CALLED A "BOLA".
RATTLE
I WAS JUST TRYING TO LEARN BY IMITATION. I DIDN'T THINK IT WOULD GO THIS WELL...
...BUT...

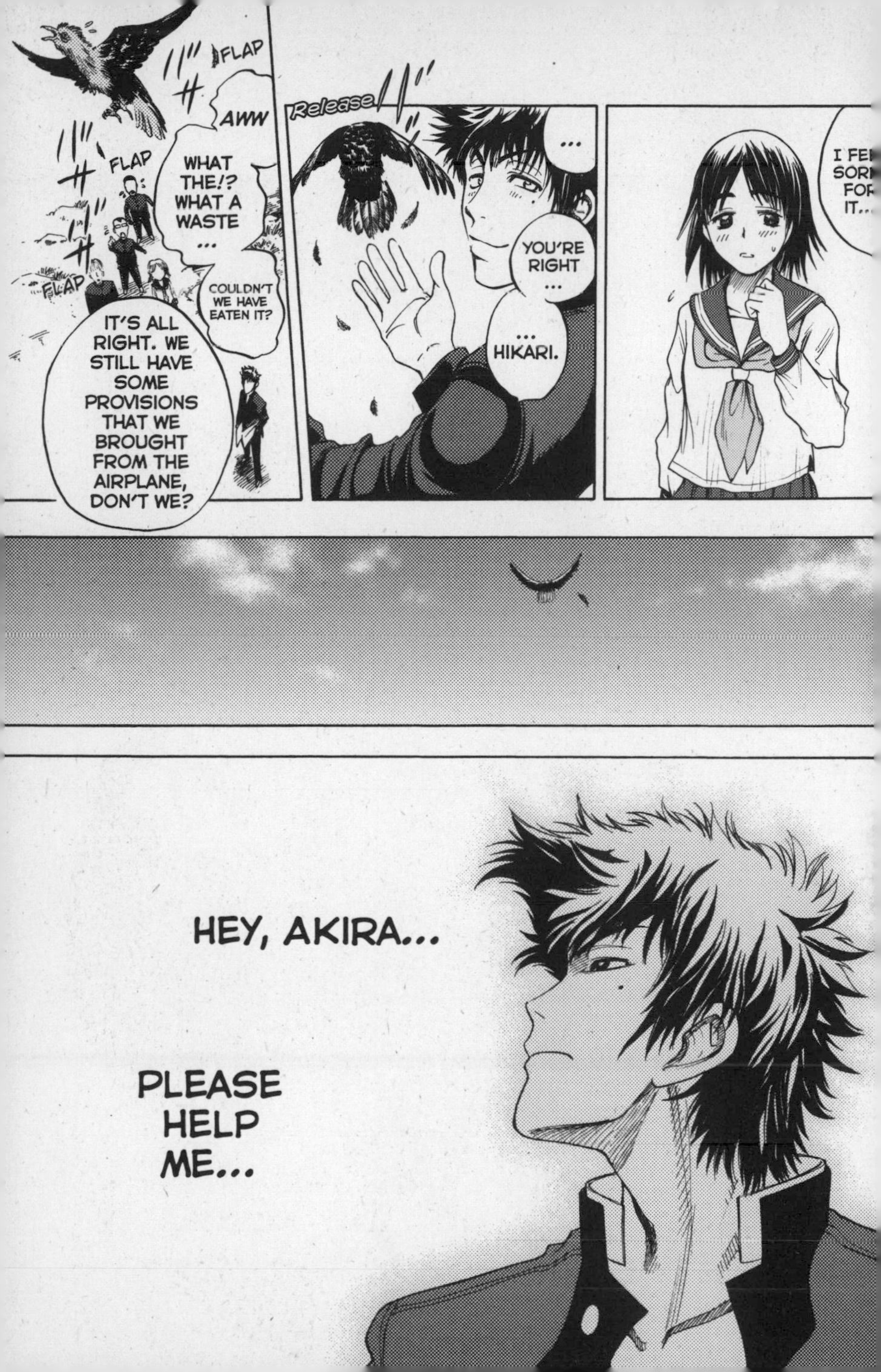
I FE SOR FO IT...
Release
...
YOU'RE RIGHT ...
... HIKARI.
FLAP
AWW
WHAT THE!? WHAT A WASTE ...
COULDN'T WE HAVE EATEN IT?
FLAP
FLAP
IT'S ALL RIGHT. WE STILL HAVE SOME PROVISIONS THAT WE BROUGHT FROM THE AIRPLANE, DON'T WE?
HEY, AKIRA...
PLEASE HELP ME...

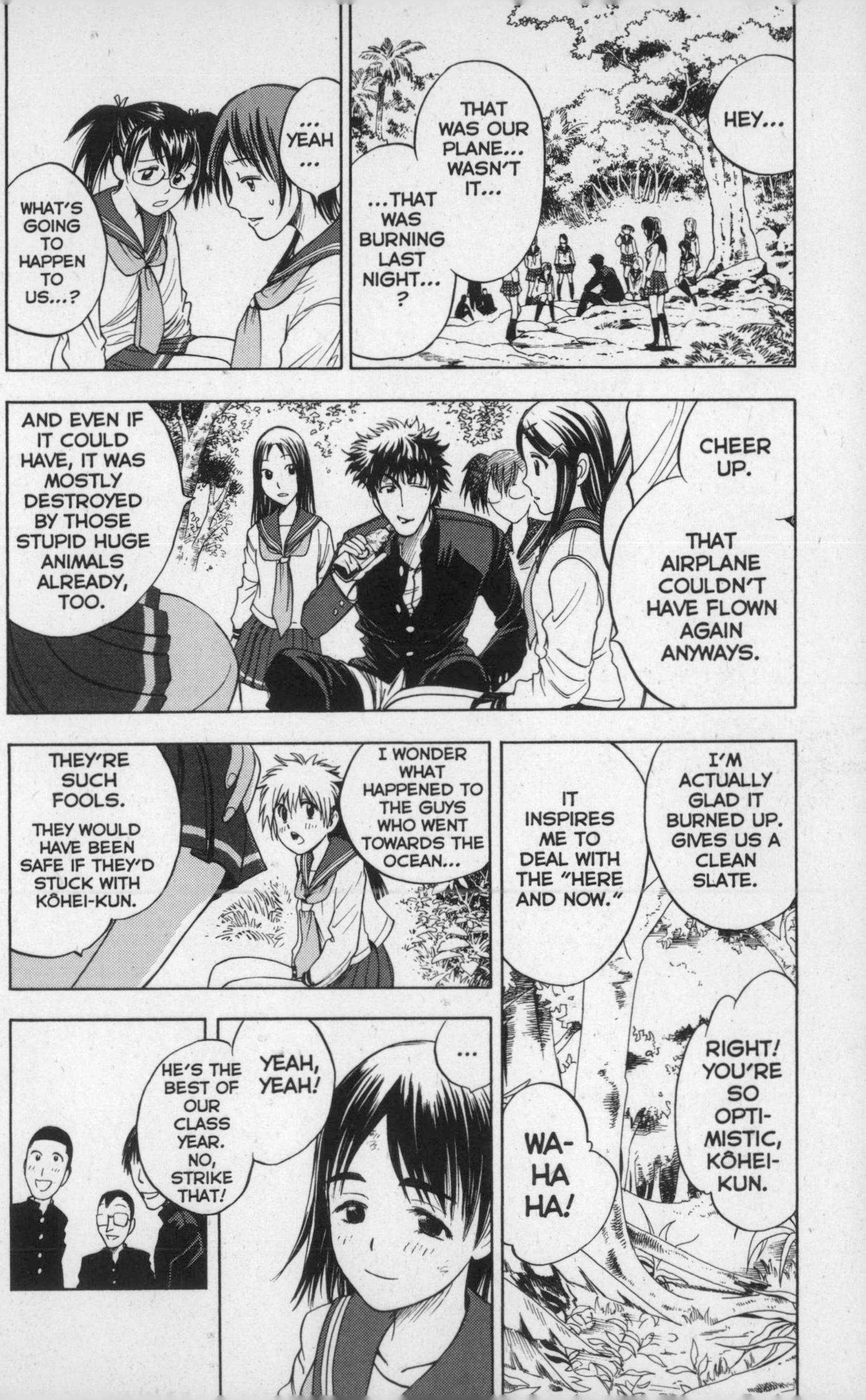
HEY...
THAT WAS OUR PLANE... WASN'T IT...
...THAT WAS BURNING LAST NIGHT...?
...YEAH...
WHAT'S GOING TO HAPPEN TO US...?
CHEER UP.
THAT AIRPLANE COULDN'T HAVE FLOWN AGAIN ANYWAYS.
AND EVEN IF IT COULD HAVE, IT WAS MOSTLY DESTROYED BY THOSE STUPID HUGE ANIMALS ALREADY, TOO.
I'M ACTUALLY GLAD IT BURNED UP. GIVES US A CLEAN SLATE.
IT INSPIRES ME TO DEAL WITH THE "HERE AND NOW."
RIGHT! YOU'RE SO OPTI-MISTIC, KÔHEI-KUN.
WA-HA HA!
I WONDER WHAT HAPPENED TO THE GUYS WHO WENT TOWARDS THE OCEAN...
THEY'RE SUCH FOOLS.
THEY WOULD HAVE BEEN SAFE IF THEY'D STUCK WITH KÔHEI-KUN.
...
YEAH, YEAH!
HE'S THE BEST OF OUR CLASS YEAR. NO, STRIKE THAT!

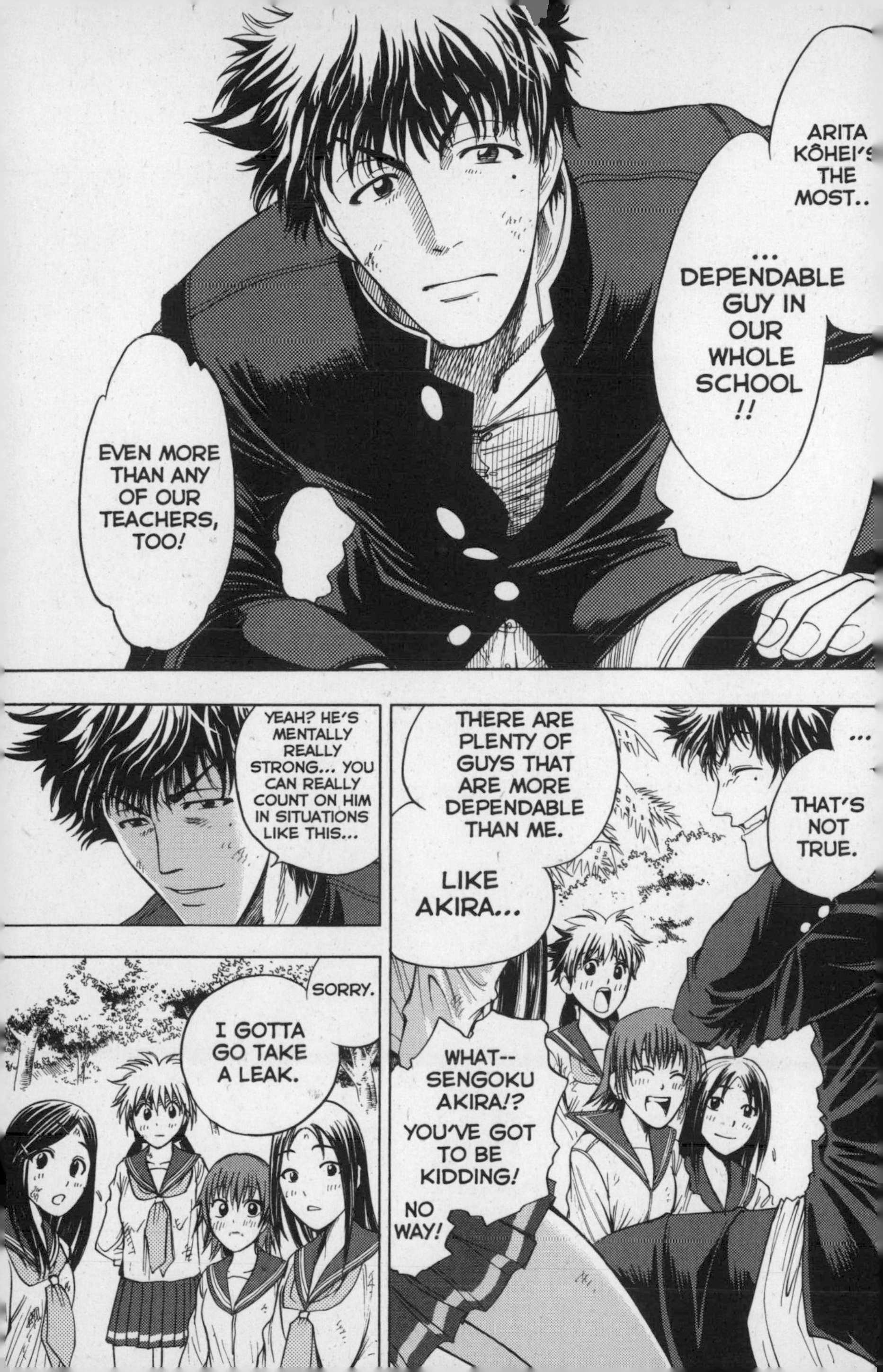
ARITA KÔHEI'S THE MOST..
... DEPENDABLE GUY IN OUR WHOLE SCHOOL !!
EVEN MORE THAN ANY OF OUR TEACHERS, TOO!
...
THAT'S NOT TRUE.
THERE ARE PLENTY OF GUYS THAT ARE MORE DEPENDABLE THAN ME.
LIKE AKIRA...
WHAT-- SENGOKU AKIRA!?
YOU'VE GOT TO BE KIDDING!
NO WAY!
YEAH? HE'S MENTALLY REALLY STRONG... YOU CAN REALLY COUNT ON HIM IN SITUATIONS LIKE THIS...
SORRY.
I GOTTA GO TAKE A LEAK.

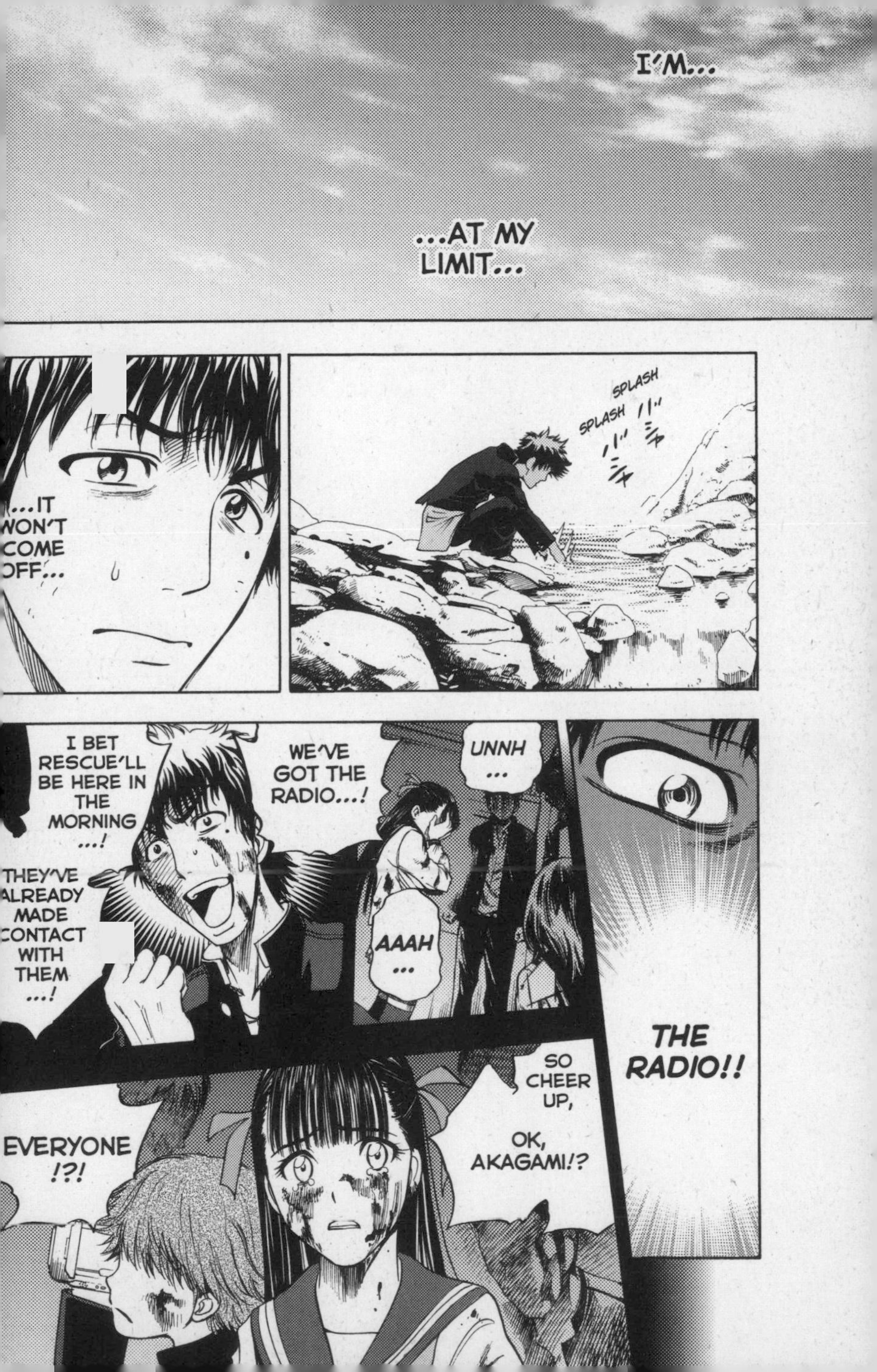
I'M...
...AT MY LIMIT...
SPLASH
SPLASH
...IT WON'T COME OFF...
THE RADIO!!
UNNH ...
WE'VE GOT THE RADIO...!
I BET RESCUE'LL BE HERE IN THE MORNING ...!
THEY'VE ALREADY MADE CONTACT WITH THEM ...!
AAAH ...
SO CHEER UP,
OK, AKAGAMI!?
EVERYONE !?!

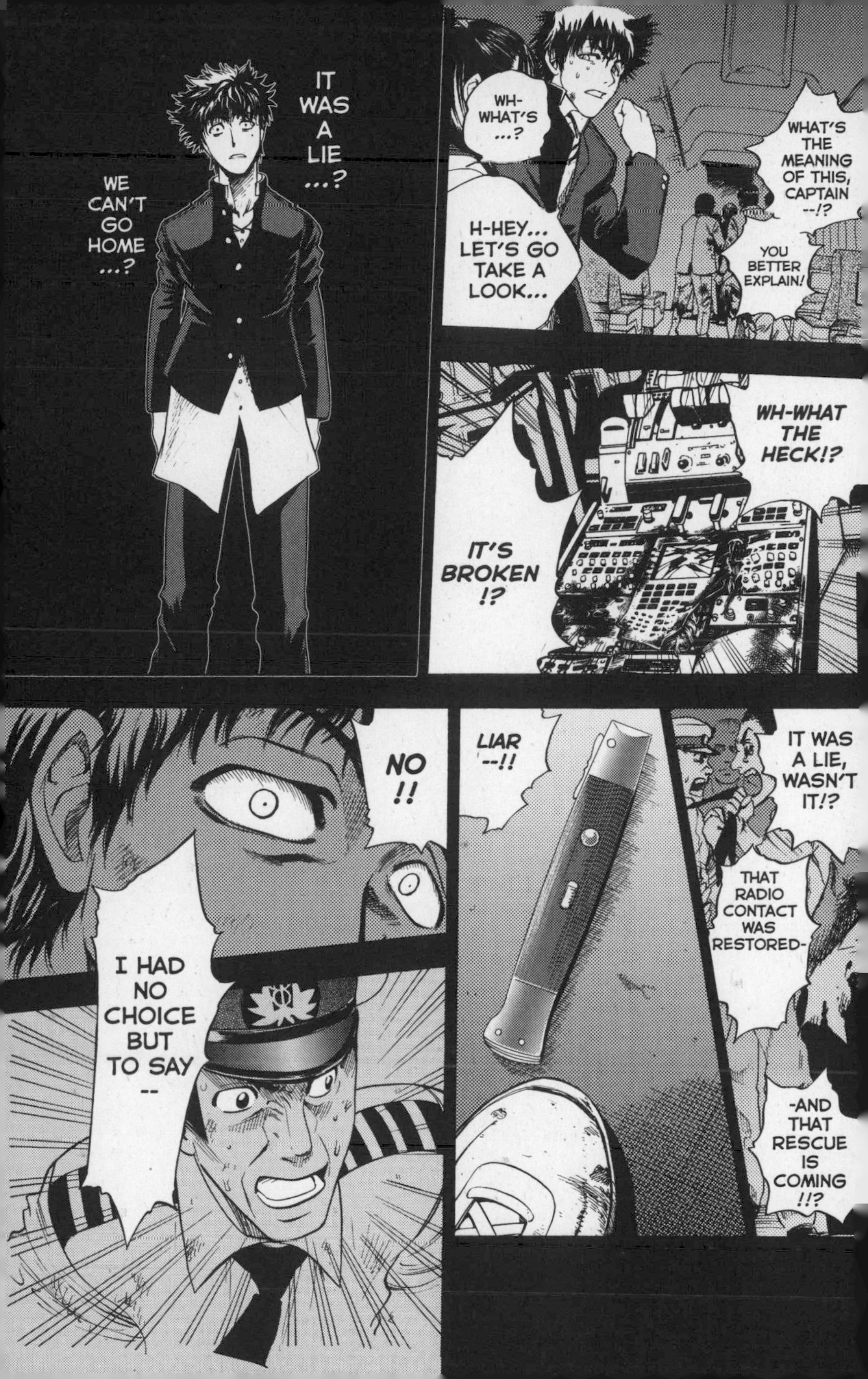
WHAT'S THE MEANING OF THIS, CAPTAIN --!?
YOU BETTER EXPLAIN!
WH- WHAT'S ...?
H-HEY... LET'S GO TAKE A LOOK...
WH-WHAT THE HECK!?
IT'S BROKEN !?
IT WAS A LIE ...?
WE CAN'T GO HOME ...?
IT WAS A LIE, WASN'T IT!?
THAT RADIO CONTACT WAS RESTORED-
-AND THAT RESCUE IS COMING !!?
LIAR --!!
NO !!
I HAD NO CHOICE BUT TO SAY --

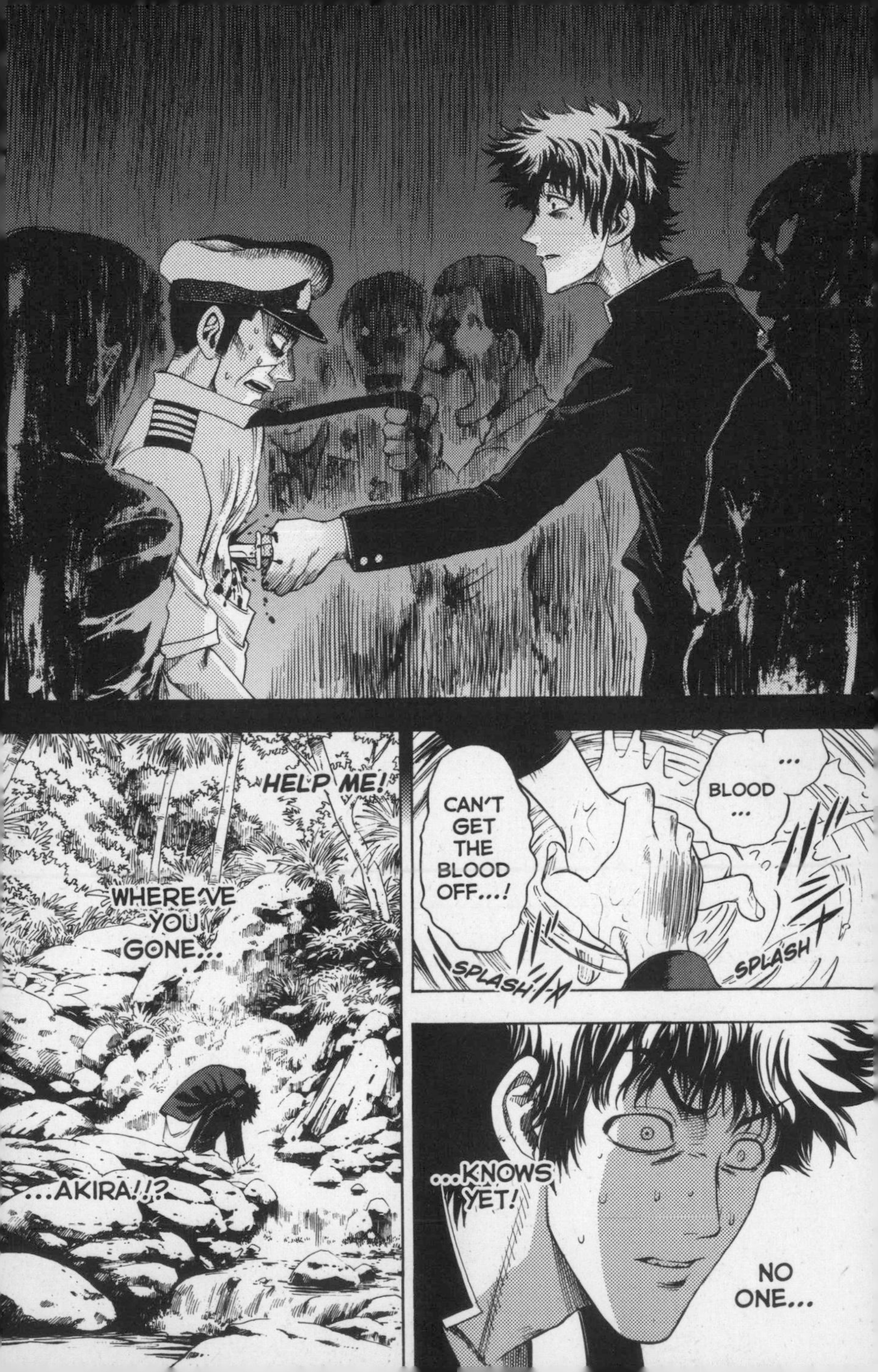
... BLOOD ...
CAN'T GET THE BLOOD OFF...!
SPLASH
SPLASH
NO ONE...
...KNOWS YET!
HELP ME!
WHERE'VE YOU GONE...
...AKIRA!!?

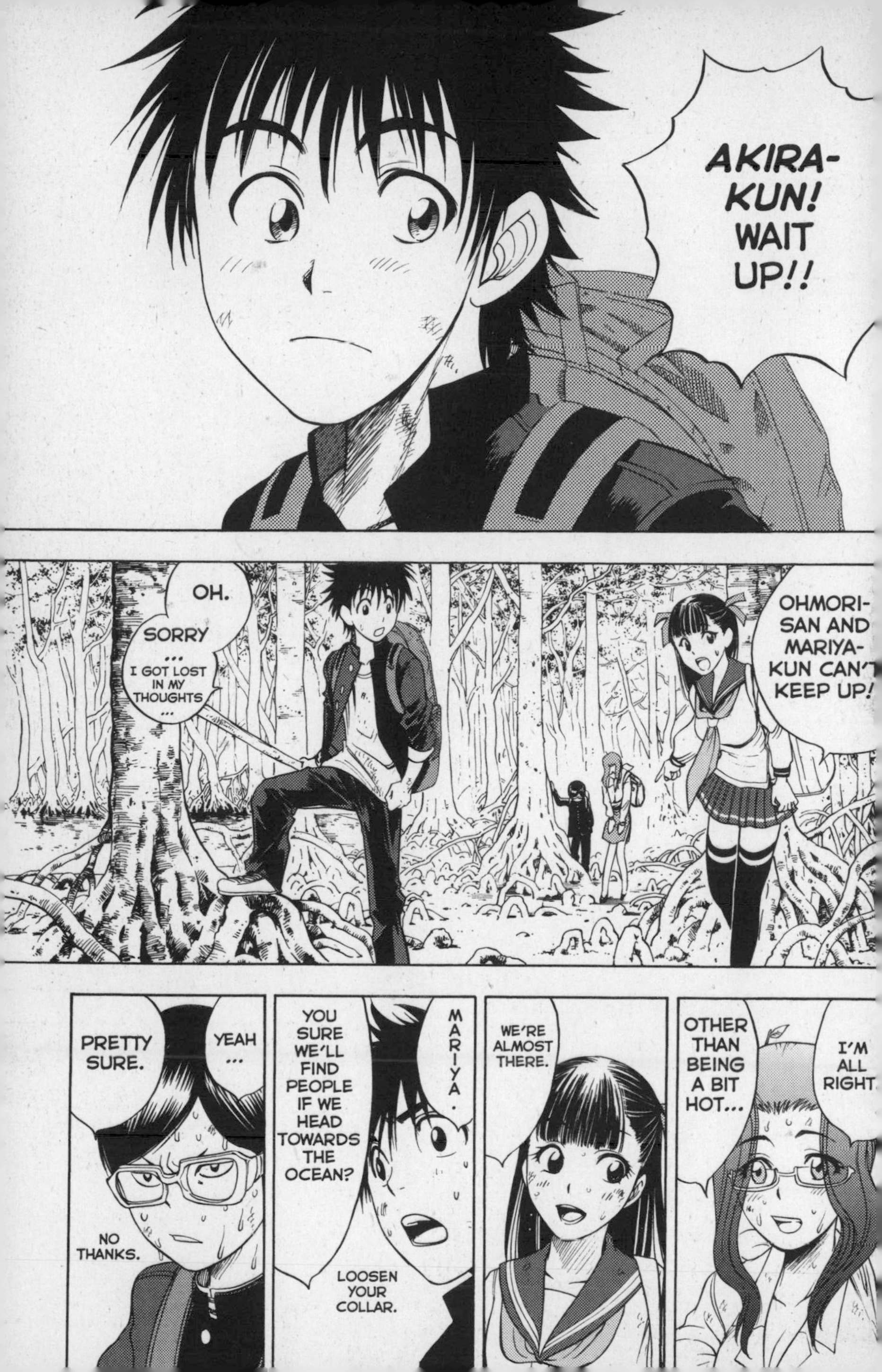
AKIRA-KUN! WAIT UP!!
OHMORI-SAN AND MARIYA-KUN CAN'T KEEP UP!
OH.
SORRY ... I GOT LOST IN MY THOUGHTS ...
I'M ALL RIGHT.
OTHER THAN BEING A BIT HOT...
WE'RE ALMOST THERE.
MARIYA.
YOU SURE WE'LL FIND PEOPLE IF WE HEAD TOWARDS THE OCEAN?
LOOSEN YOUR COLLAR.
YEAH ...
PRETTY SURE.
NO THANKS.

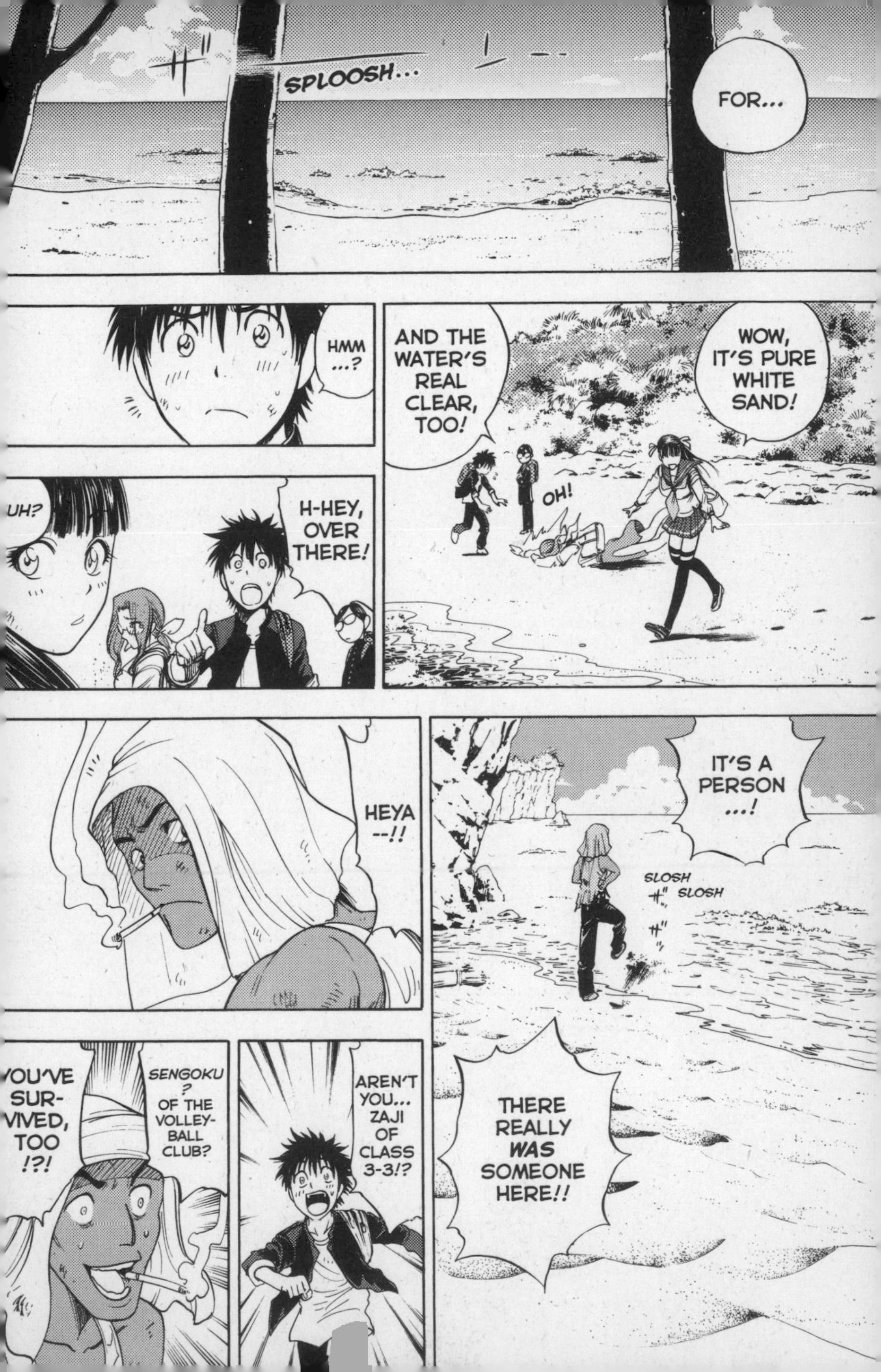
FOR...
SPLOOSH...
WOW, IT'S PURE WHITE SAND!
AND THE WATER'S REAL CLEAR, TOO!
OH!
HMM ...?
H-HEY, OVER THERE!
UH?
IT'S A PERSON ...!
SLOSH SLOSH
THERE REALLY WAS SOMEONE HERE!!
HEYA --!!
AREN'T YOU... ZAJI OF CLASS 3-3!?
SENGOKU? OF THE VOLLEY-BALL CLUB?
YOU'VE SUR-VIVED, TOO !?!

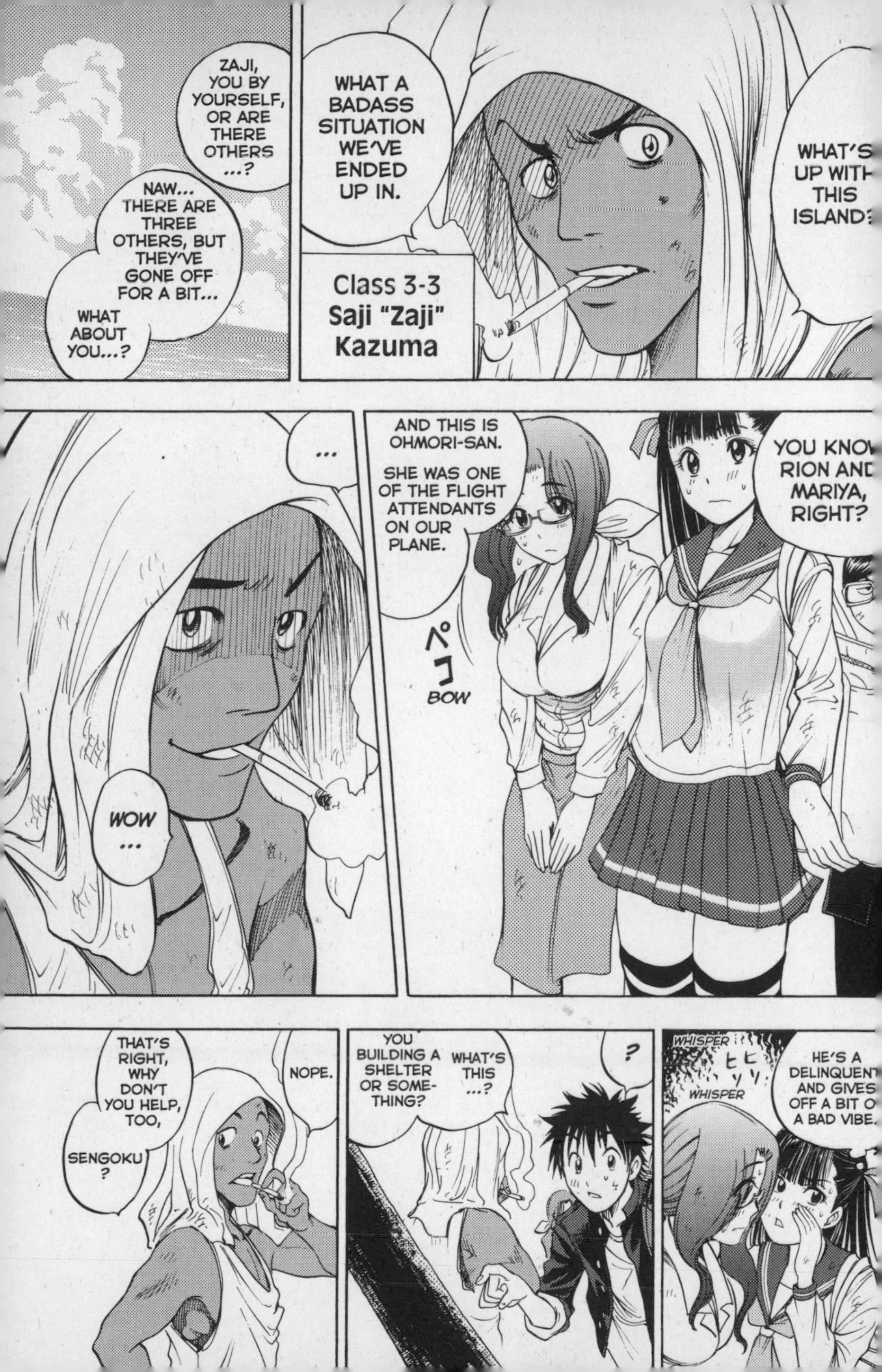
WHAT'S UP WITH THIS ISLAND?
WHAT A BADASS SITUATION WE'VE ENDED UP IN.
Class 3-3 Saji "Zaji" Kazuma
ZAJI, YOU BY YOURSELF, OR ARE THERE OTHERS ...?
NAW... THERE ARE THREE OTHERS, BUT THEY'VE GONE OFF FOR A BIT...
WHAT ABOUT YOU...?
YOU KNO RION AND MARIYA, RIGHT?
AND THIS IS OHMORI-SAN.
SHE WAS ONE OF THE FLIGHT ATTENDANTS ON OUR PLANE.
ペコ
BOW
...
WOW ...
WHISPER
ヒソ
WHISPER
HE'S A DELINQUENT AND GIVES OFF A BIT O A BAD VIBE.
?
WHAT'S THIS ...?
YOU BUILDING A SHELTER OR SOME-THING?
NOPE.
THAT'S RIGHT, WHY DON'T YOU HELP, TOO,
SENGOKU ?

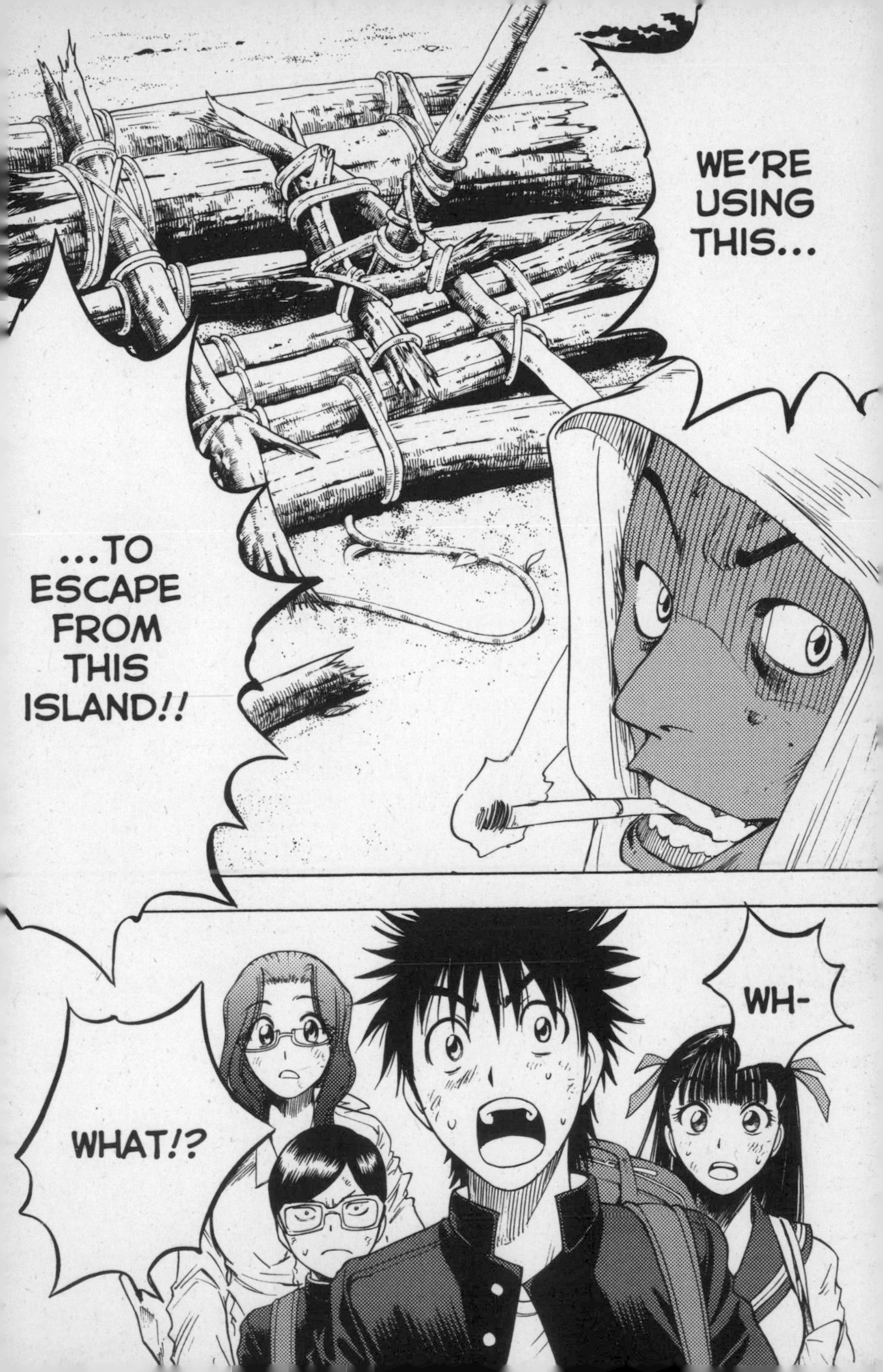
WE'RE USING THIS...
...TO ESCAPE FROM THIS ISLAND!!
WH-
WHAT!?

Episode 9 The King of Hell

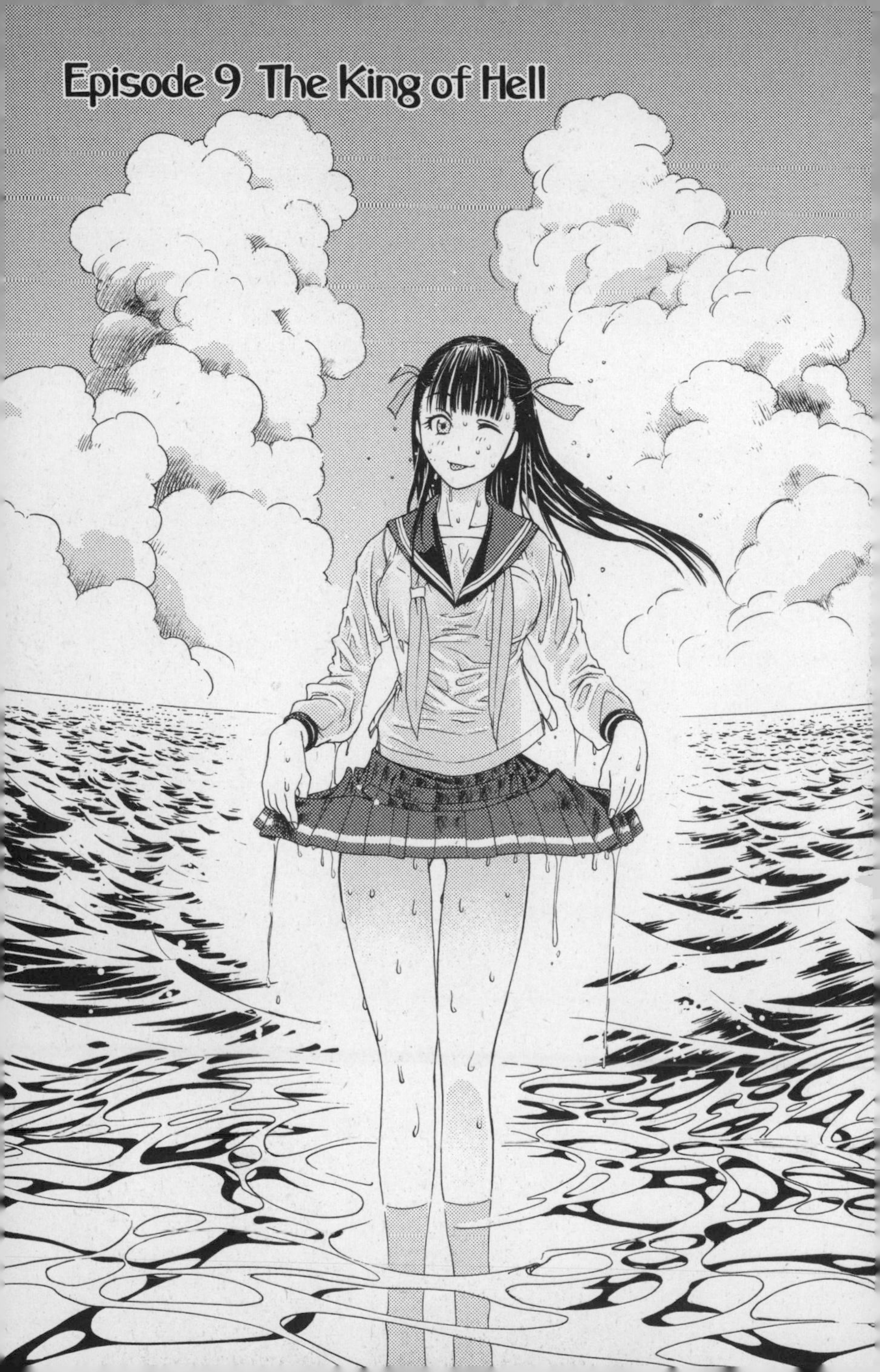

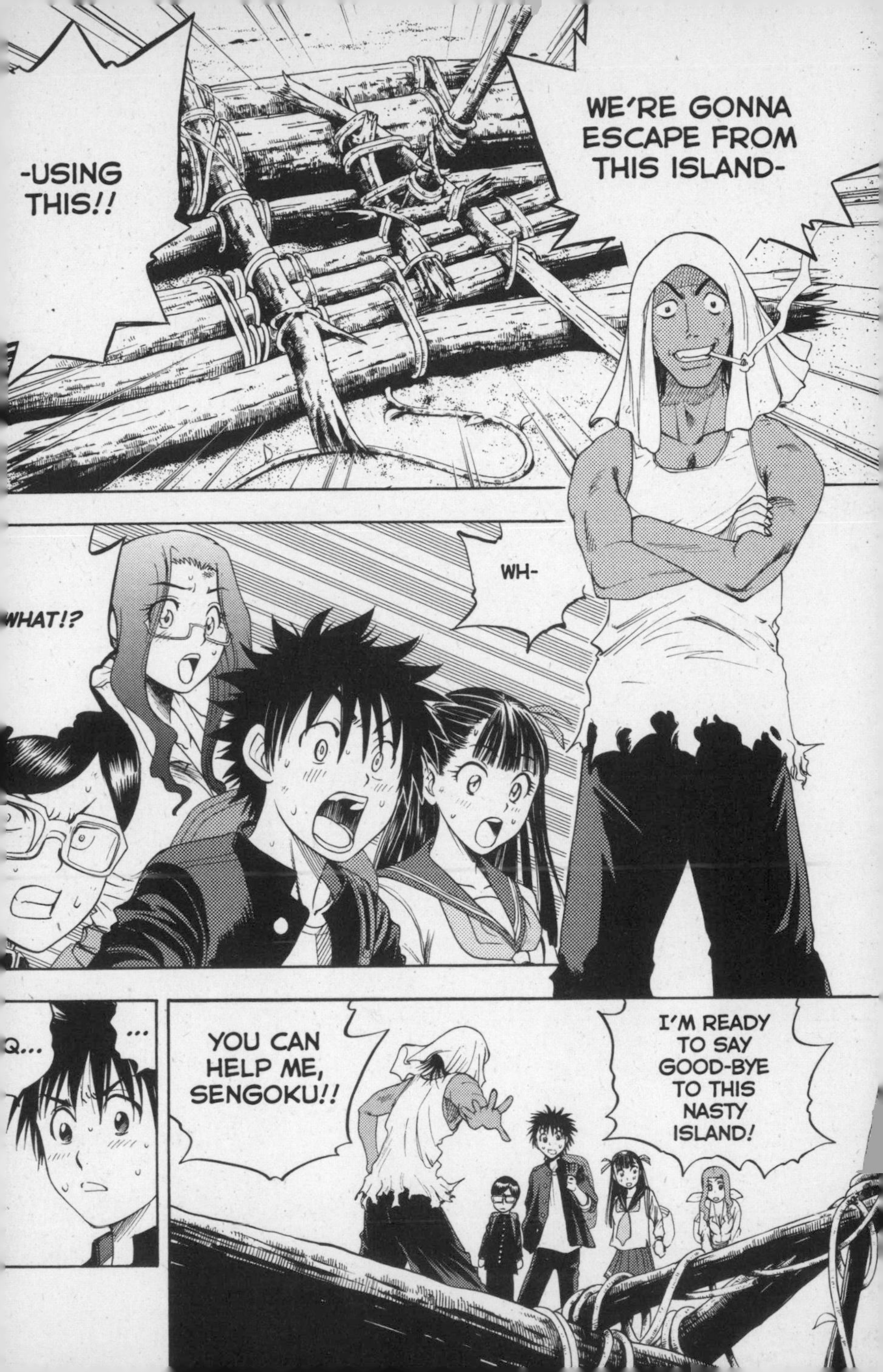
WE'RE GONNA ESCAPE FROM THIS ISLAND-
-USING THIS!!
WH-
WHAT!?
I'M READY TO SAY GOOD-BYE TO THIS NASTY ISLAND!
YOU CAN HELP ME, SENGOKU!!
...
Q...

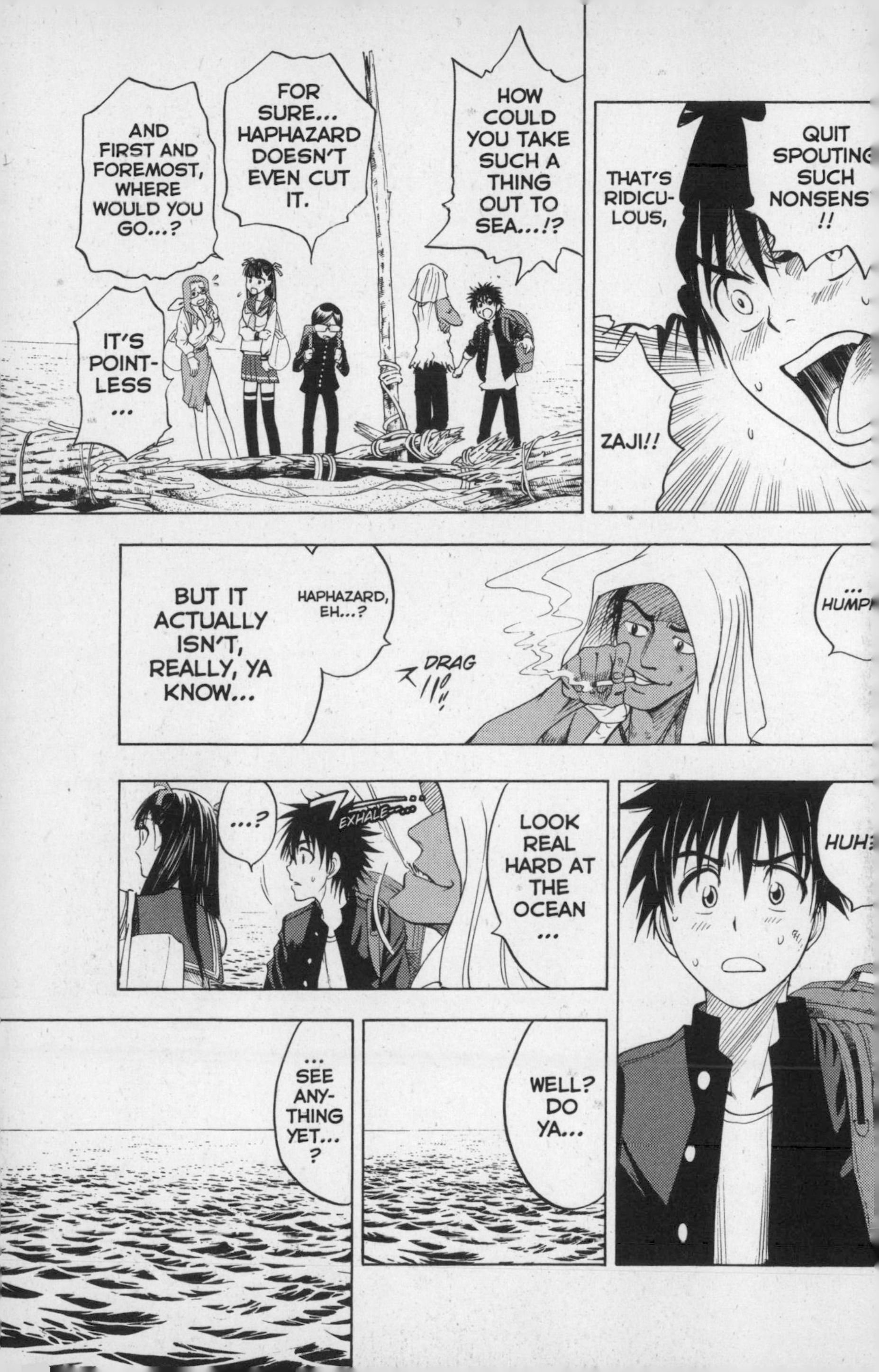
QUIT SPOUTING SUCH NONSENS!!
THAT'S RIDICULOUS,
ZAJI!!
HOW COULD YOU TAKE SUCH A THING OUT TO SEA...!?
FOR SURE... HAPHAZARD DOESN'T EVEN CUT IT.
AND FIRST AND FOREMOST, WHERE WOULD YOU GO...?
IT'S POINTLESS...
... HUMP
DRAG
HAPHAZARD, EH...?
BUT IT ACTUALLY ISN'T, REALLY, YA KNOW...
HUH
LOOK REAL HARD AT THE OCEAN...
EXHALE
...?
WELL? DO YA...
... SEE ANYTHING YET...?

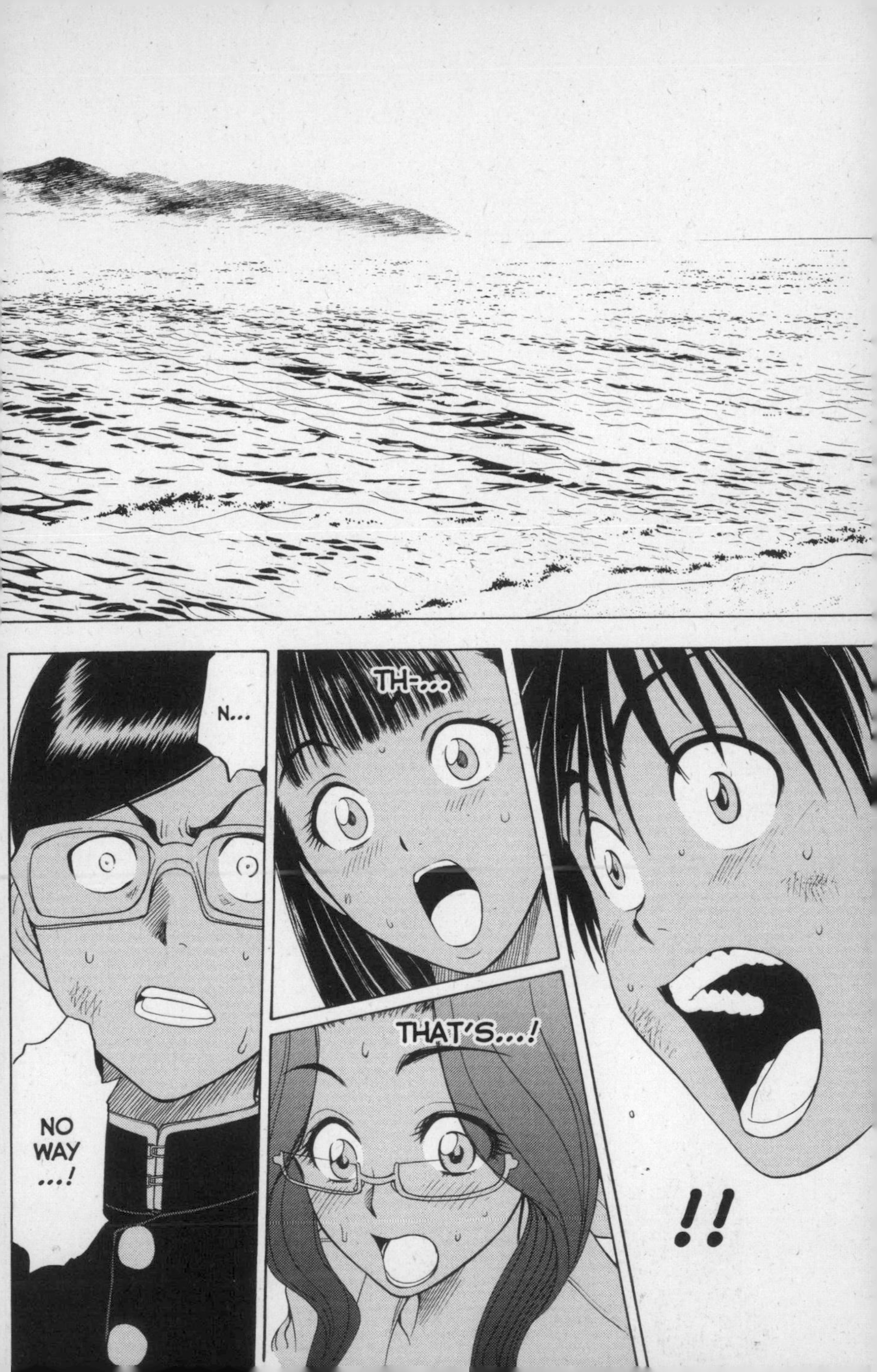
!!
TH-...
THAT'S...!
N...
NO WAY ...!

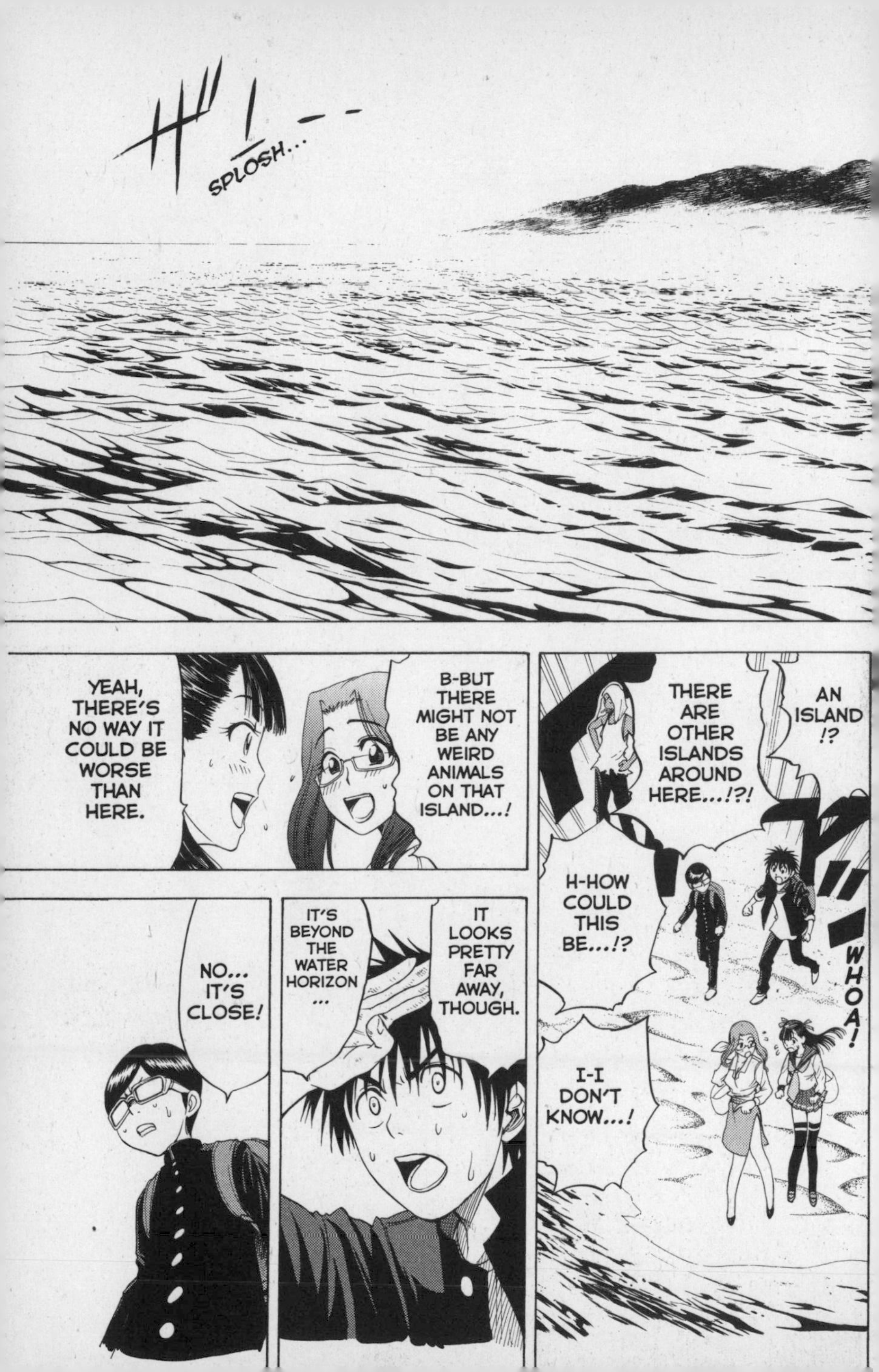
SPLOSH...
AN ISLAND!?
THERE ARE OTHER ISLANDS AROUND HERE...!?!
WHOA!
H-HOW COULD THIS BE...!?
I-I DON'T KNOW...!
B-BUT THERE MIGHT NOT BE ANY WEIRD ANIMALS ON THAT ISLAND...!
YEAH, THERE'S NO WAY IT COULD BE WORSE THAN HERE.
IT LOOKS PRETTY FAR AWAY, THOUGH.
IT'S BEYOND THE WATER HORIZON ...
NO... IT'S CLOSE!

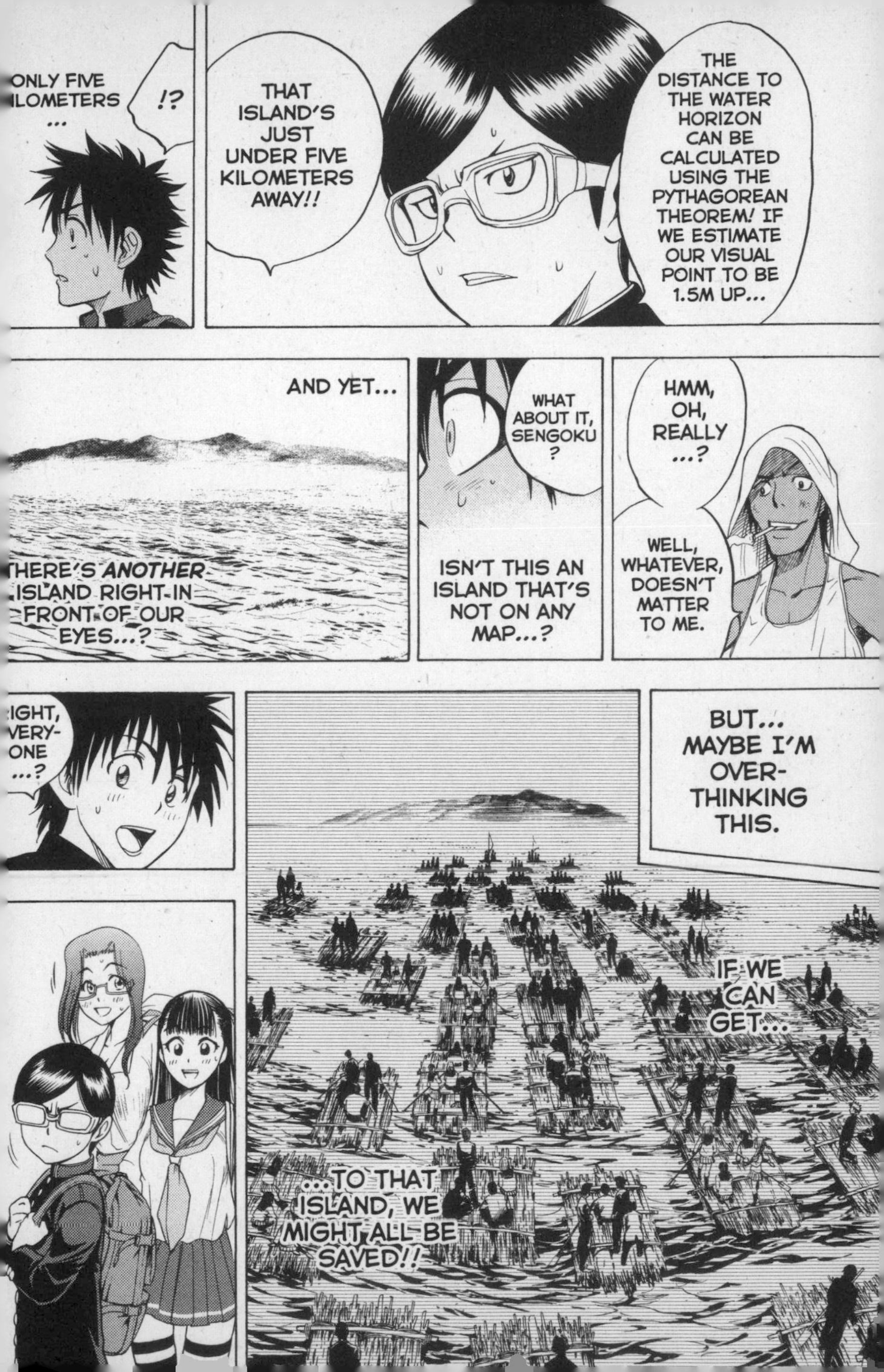
THE DISTANCE TO THE WATER HORIZON CAN BE CALCULATED USING THE PYTHAGOREAN THEOREM! IF WE ESTIMATE OUR VISUAL POINT TO BE 1.5M UP...
THAT ISLAND'S JUST UNDER FIVE KILOMETERS AWAY!!
!?
ONLY FIVE ILOMETERS ...
HMM, OH, REALLY ...?
WELL, WHATEVER, DOESN'T MATTER TO ME.
WHAT ABOUT IT, SENGOKU ?
ISN'T THIS AN ISLAND THAT'S NOT ON ANY MAP...?
AND YET...
THERE'S ANOTHER ISLAND RIGHT IN FRONT OF OUR EYES...?
BUT... MAYBE I'M OVER-THINKING THIS.
IF WE CAN GET...
...TO THAT ISLAND, WE MIGHT ALL BE SAVED!!
IGHT, VERY- ONE ...?

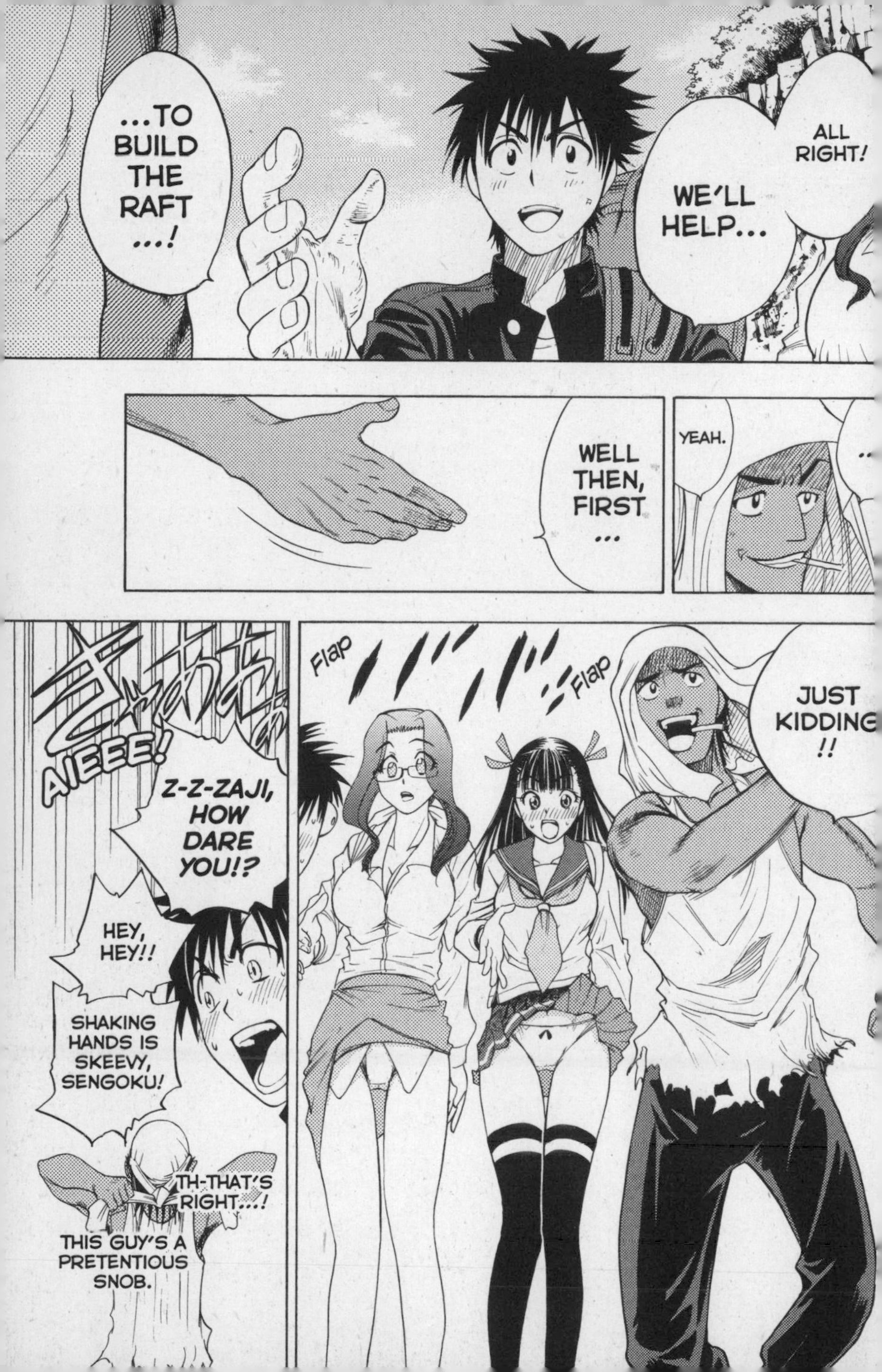
ALL RIGHT!
WE'LL HELP...
...TO BUILD THE RAFT...!
YEAH.
WELL THEN, FIRST...
JUST KIDDING!!
Flap
Flap
AIEEE!
Z-Z-ZAJI, HOW DARE YOU!?
HEY, HEY!!
SHAKING HANDS IS SKEEVY, SENGOKU!
TH-THAT'S RIGHT...!
THIS GUY'S A PRETENTIOUS SNOB.

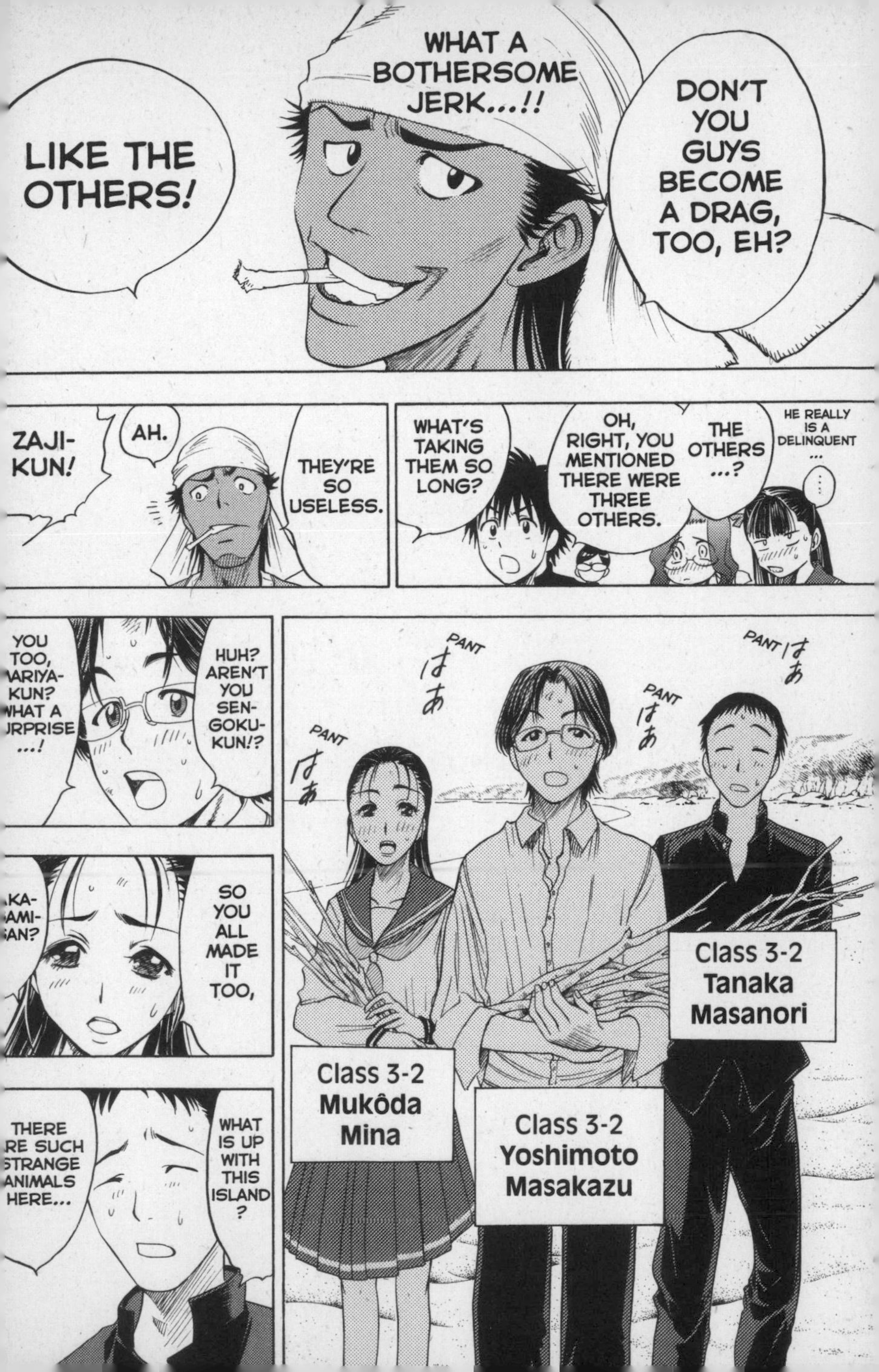

WHAT A BOTHERSOME JERK...!!
DON'T YOU GUYS BECOME A DRAG, TOO, EH?
LIKE THE OTHERS!
HE REALLY IS A DELINQUENT ...
...
THE OTHERS ...?
OH, RIGHT, YOU MENTIONED THERE WERE THREE OTHERS.
WHAT'S TAKING THEM SO LONG?
THEY'RE SO USELESS.
AH.
ZAJI-KUN!
PANT はあ
PANT はあ
PANT はあ
PANT はあ
Class 3-2 Tanaka Masanori
Class 3-2 Yoshimoto Masakazu
Class 3-2 Mukôda Mina
HUH? AREN'T YOU SEN-GOKU-KUN!?
YOU TOO, ARIYA-KUN? WHAT A URPRISE ...!
SO YOU ALL MADE IT TOO,
KA-AMI-AN?
WHAT IS UP WITH THIS ISLAND?
THERE RE SUCH STRANGE ANIMALS HERE...

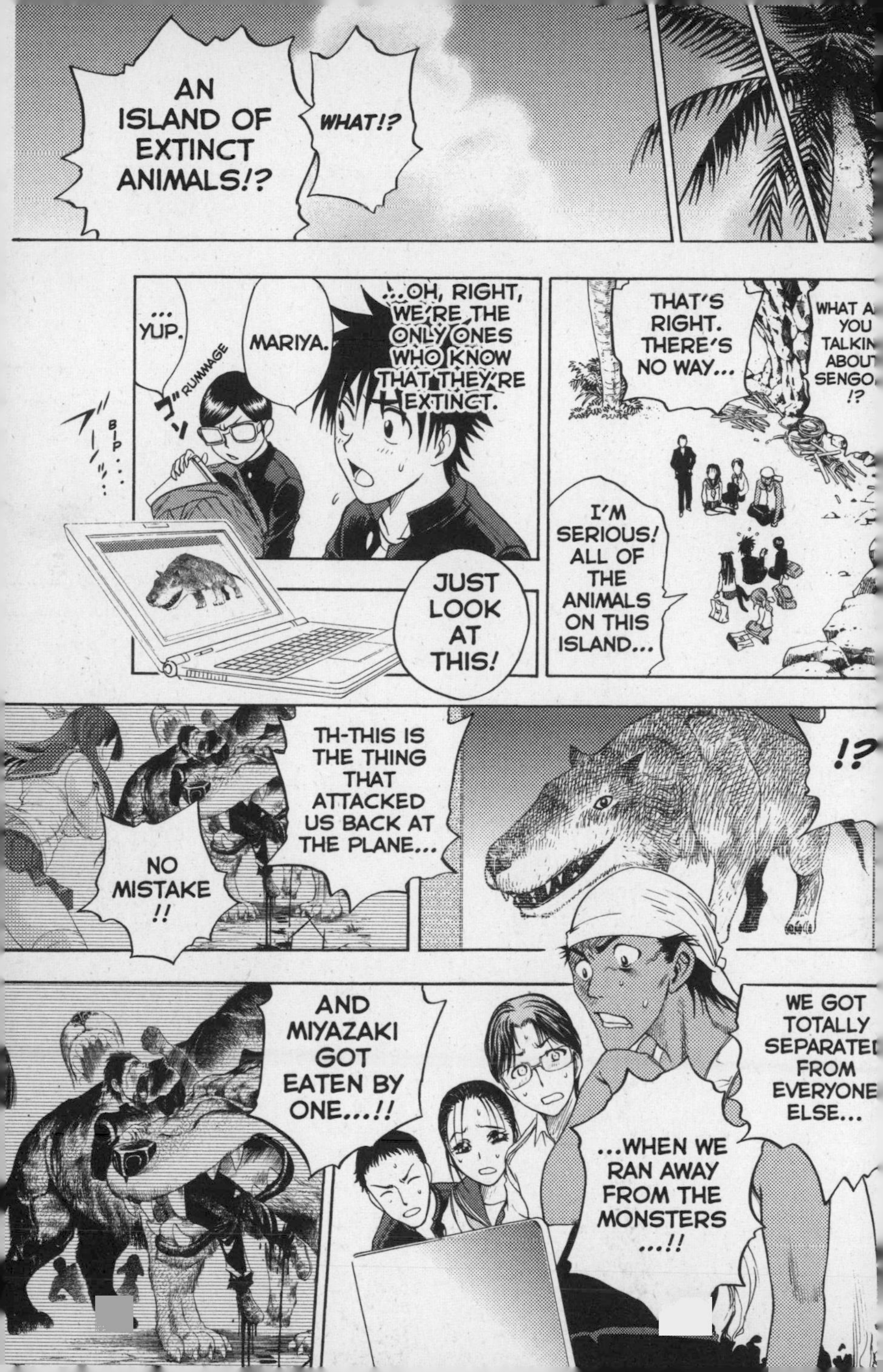
WHAT!?
AN ISLAND OF EXTINCT ANIMALS!?
WHAT A YOU TALKIN ABOUT SENGO !?
THAT'S RIGHT. THERE'S NO WAY...
I'M SERIOUS! ALL OF THE ANIMALS ON THIS ISLAND...
...OH, RIGHT, WE'RE THE ONLY ONES WHO KNOW THAT THEY'RE EXTINCT.
MARIYA.
...YUP.
RUMMAGE
BIP...
JUST LOOK AT THIS!
!?
TH-THIS IS THE THING THAT ATTACKED US BACK AT THE PLANE...
NO MISTAKE!!
WE GOT TOTALLY SEPARATE FROM EVERYONE ELSE...
...WHEN WE RAN AWAY FROM THE MONSTERS...!!
AND MIYAZAKI GOT EATEN BY ONE...!!

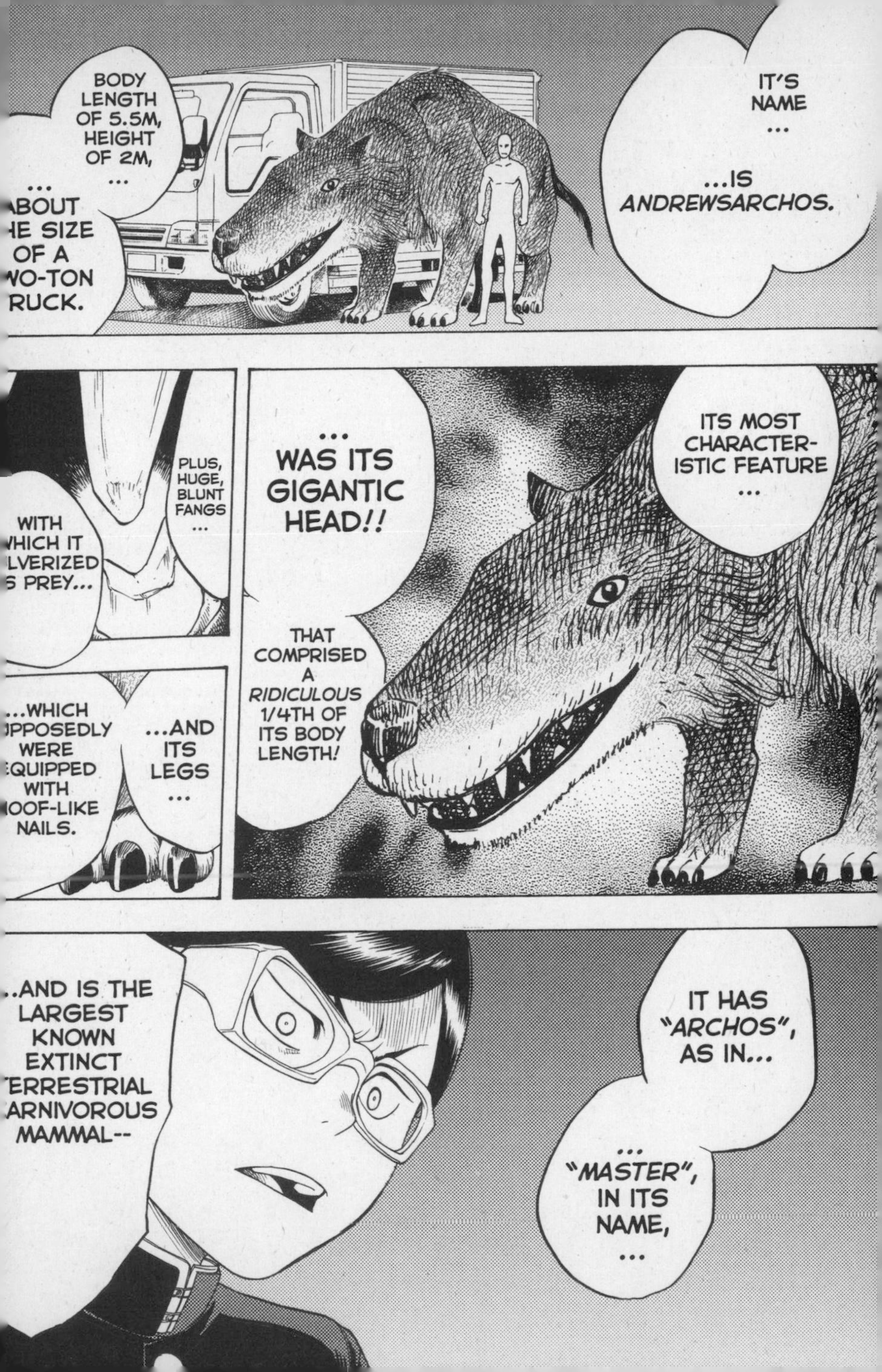
IT'S NAME ... ...IS *ANDREWSARCHOS.*
BODY LENGTH OF 5.5M, HEIGHT OF 2M, ...
... ABOUT HE SIZE OF A WO-TON RUCK.
ITS MOST CHARACTER-ISTIC FEATURE ...
... WAS ITS GIGANTIC HEAD!!
THAT COMPRISED A *RIDICULOUS* 1/4TH OF ITS BODY LENGTH!
PLUS, HUGE, BLUNT FANGS ...
WITH HICH IT LVERIZED S PREY...
...AND ITS LEGS ...
...WHICH UPPOSEDLY WERE QUIPPED WITH OOF-LIKE NAILS.
IT HAS "*ARCHOS*", AS IN...
... "*MASTER*", IN ITS NAME, ...
..AND IS THE LARGEST KNOWN EXTINCT ERRESTRIAL ARNIVOROUS MAMMAL--

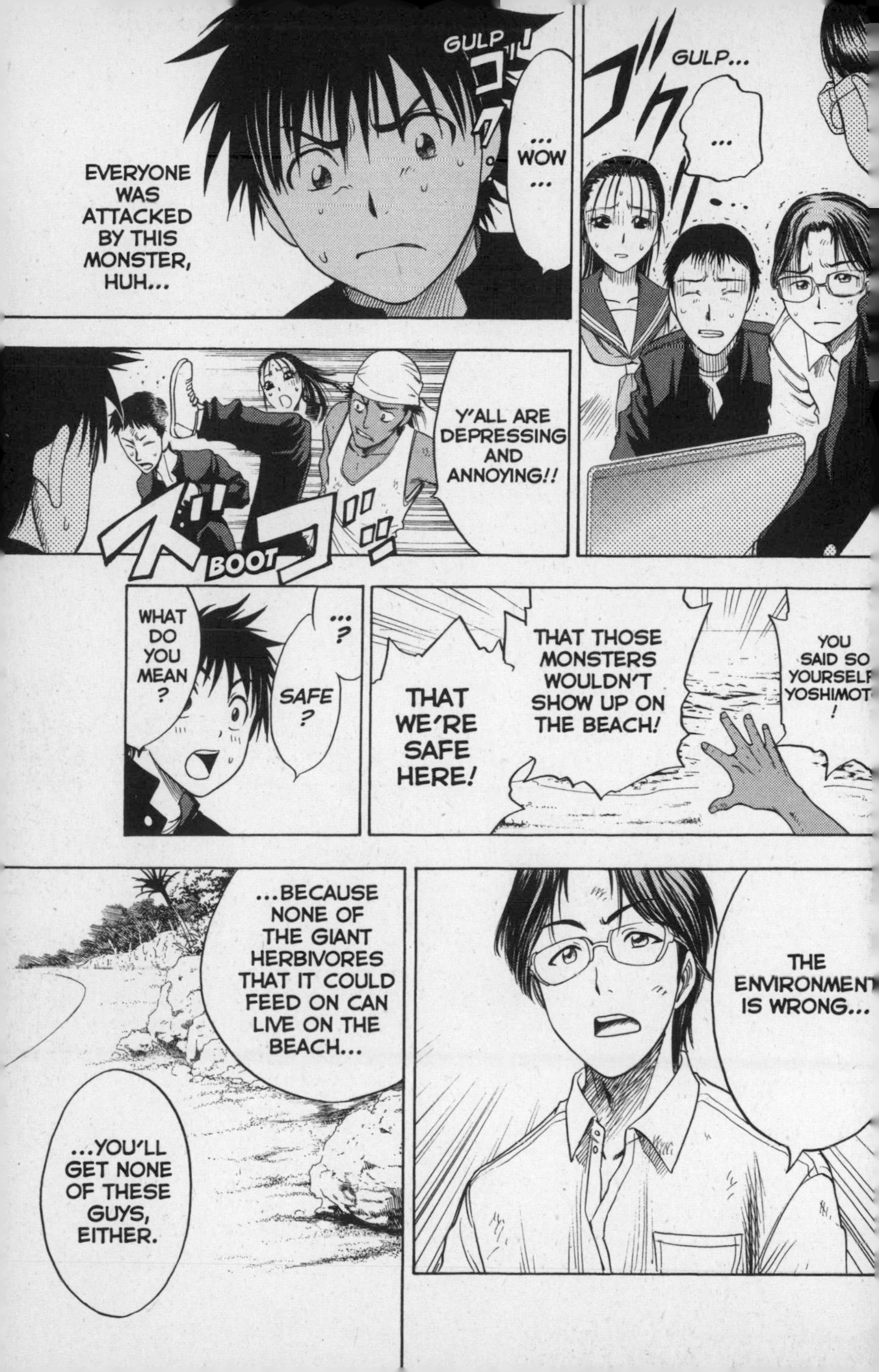
GULP...
...
GULP
...WOW...
EVERYONE WAS ATTACKED BY THIS MONSTER, HUH...
Y'ALL ARE DEPRESSING AND ANNOYING!!
BOOT
YOU SAID SO YOURSELF YOSHIMOT
!
THAT THOSE MONSTERS WOULDN'T SHOW UP ON THE BEACH!
THAT WE'RE SAFE HERE!
...? SAFE?
WHAT DO YOU MEAN?
THE ENVIRONMENT IS WRONG...
...BECAUSE NONE OF THE GIANT HERBIVORES THAT IT COULD FEED ON CAN LIVE ON THE BEACH...
...YOU'LL GET NONE OF THESE GUYS, EITHER.

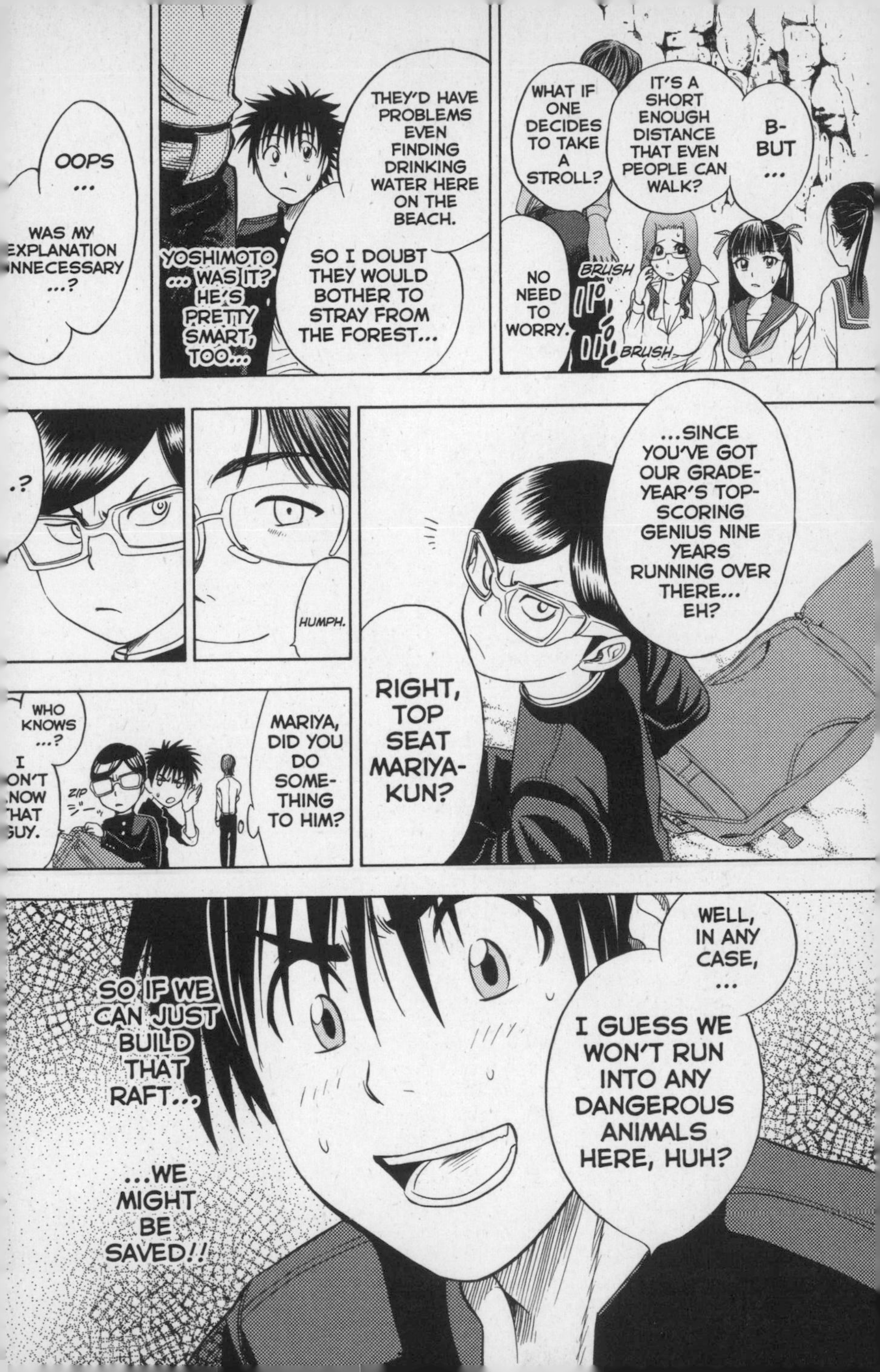
B-BUT ...
IT'S A SHORT ENOUGH DISTANCE THAT EVEN PEOPLE CAN WALK?
WHAT IF ONE DECIDES TO TAKE A STROLL?
NO NEED TO WORRY.
BRUSH
BRUSH
THEY'D HAVE PROBLEMS EVEN FINDING DRINKING WATER HERE ON THE BEACH.
SO I DOUBT THEY WOULD BOTHER TO STRAY FROM THE FOREST...
YOSHIMOTO ... WAS IT? HE'S PRETTY SMART, TOO...
OOPS ...
WAS MY EXPLANATION NNECESSARY ...?
...SINCE YOU'VE GOT OUR GRADE-YEAR'S TOP-SCORING GENIUS NINE YEARS RUNNING OVER THERE... EH?
HUMPH.
.?
RIGHT, TOP SEAT MARIYA-KUN?
MARIYA, DID YOU DO SOME-THING TO HIM?
WHO KNOWS ...?
I ON'T NOW THAT GUY.
ZIP
WELL, IN ANY CASE, ...
I GUESS WE WON'T RUN INTO ANY DANGEROUS ANIMALS HERE, HUH?
SO IF WE CAN JUST BUILD THAT RAFT...
...WE MIGHT BE SAVED!!

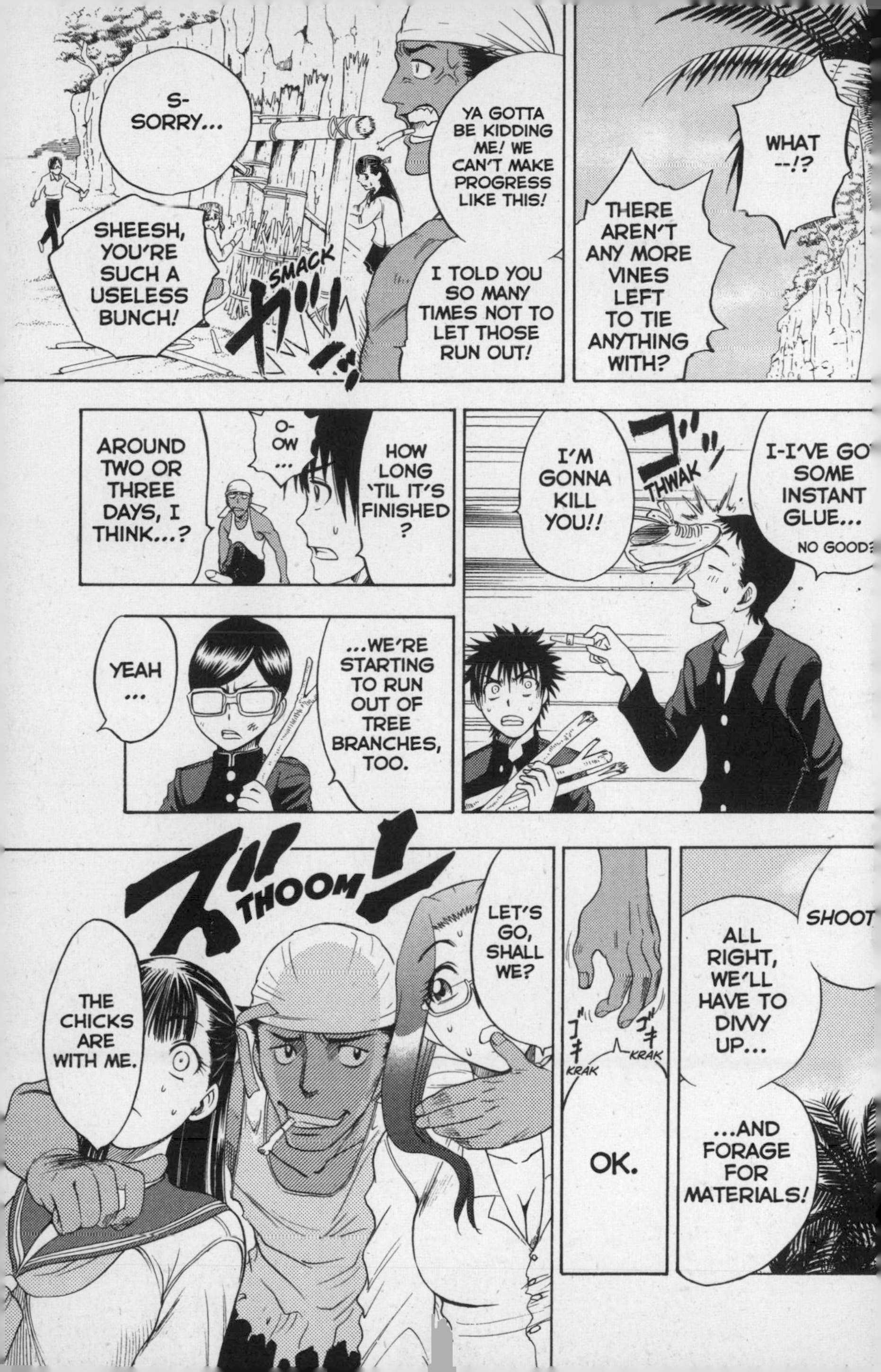
WHAT --!?
THERE AREN'T ANY MORE VINES LEFT TO TIE ANYTHING WITH?
YA GOTTA BE KIDDING ME! WE CAN'T MAKE PROGRESS LIKE THIS!
I TOLD YOU SO MANY TIMES NOT TO LET THOSE RUN OUT!
SMACK
S- SORRY...
SHEESH, YOU'RE SUCH A USELESS BUNCH!
I-I'VE GO SOME INSTANT GLUE...
NO GOOD?
THWAK
I'M GONNA KILL YOU!!
HOW LONG 'TIL IT'S FINISHED?
O-OW...
AROUND TWO OR THREE DAYS, I THINK...?
...WE'RE STARTING TO RUN OUT OF TREE BRANCHES, TOO.
YEAH...
SHOOT
ALL RIGHT, WE'LL HAVE TO DIVVY UP...
...AND FORAGE FOR MATERIALS!
KRAK
KRAK
OK.
LET'S GO, SHALL WE?
THOOM
THE CHICKS ARE WITH ME.

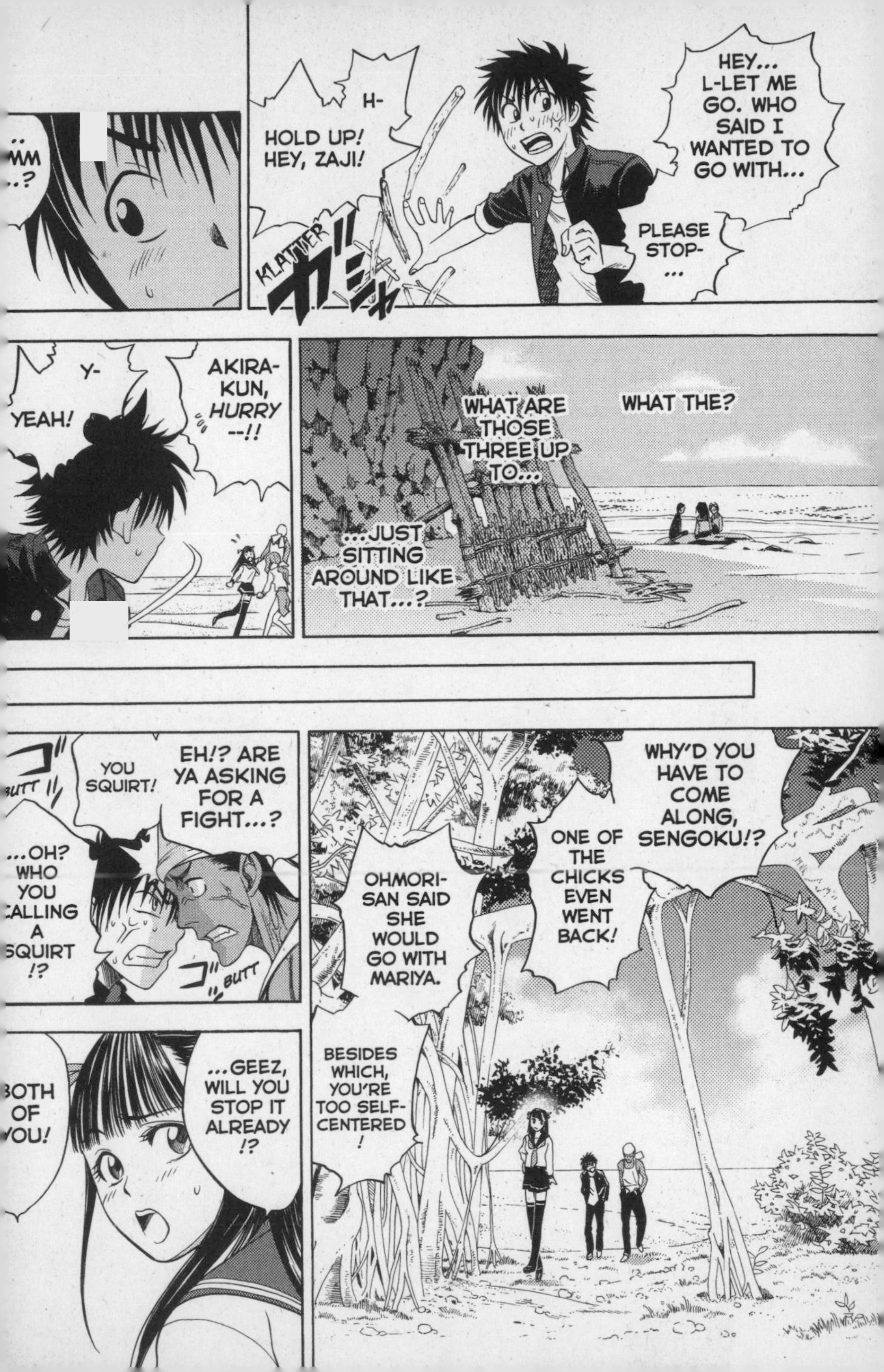
HEY... L-LET ME GO. WHO SAID I WANTED TO GO WITH...
PLEASE STOP- ...
H- HOLD UP! HEY, ZAJI!
KLATTER
.. MM ..?
WHAT THE?
WHAT ARE THOSE THREE UP TO...
...JUST SITTING AROUND LIKE THAT...?
AKIRA-KUN, HURRY--!!
Y- YEAH!
WHY'D YOU HAVE TO COME ALONG, SENGOKU!?
ONE OF THE CHICKS EVEN WENT BACK!
OHMORI-SAN SAID SHE WOULD GO WITH MARIYA.
BESIDES WHICH, YOU'RE TOO SELF-CENTERED!
EH!? ARE YA ASKING FOR A FIGHT...?
YOU SQUIRT!
BUTT
...OH? WHO YOU CALLING A SQUIRT!?
BUTT
...GEEZ, WILL YOU STOP IT ALREADY!?
OTH OF OU!

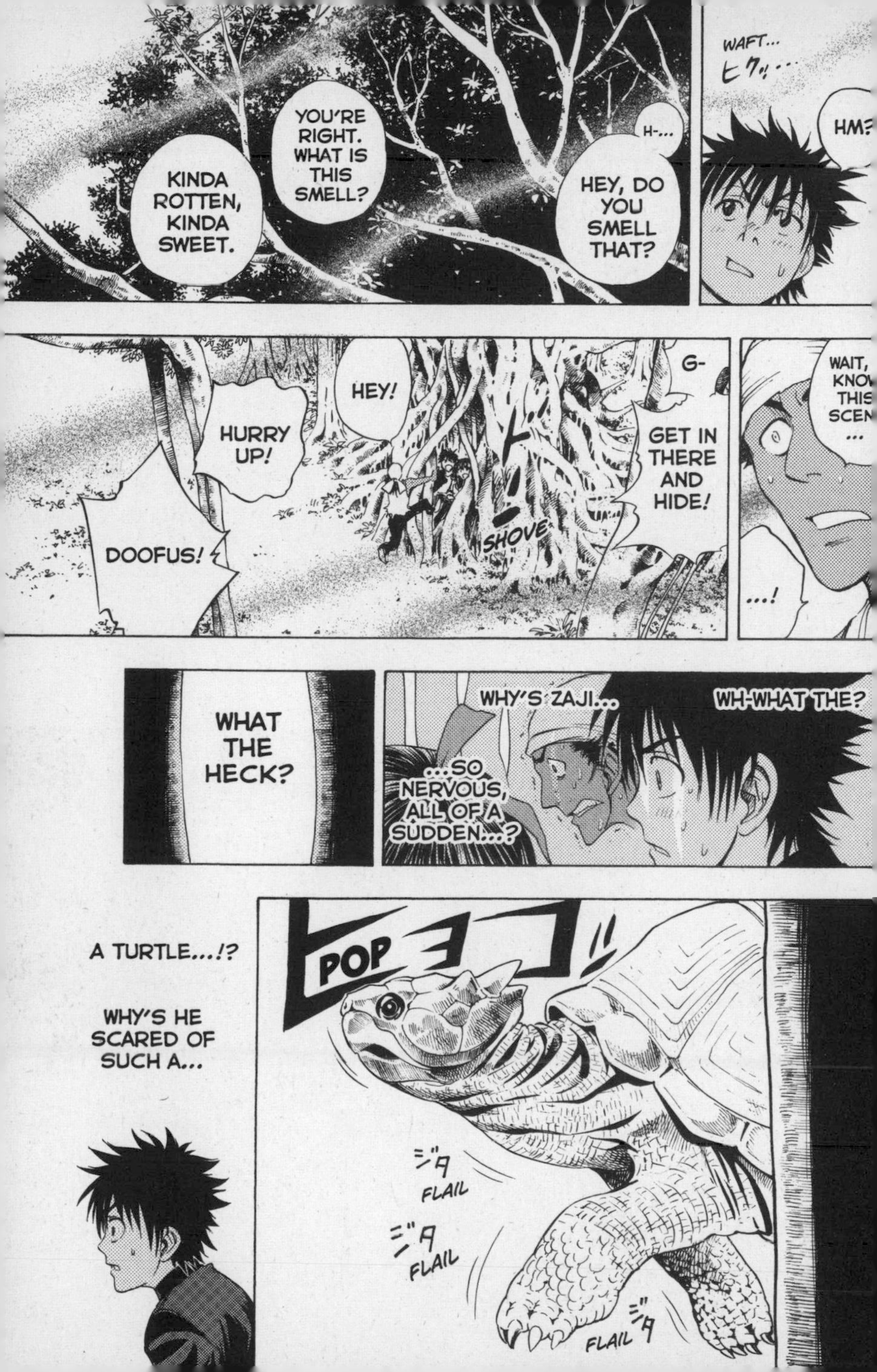
WAFT... ヒクッ...
HM?
H-...
HEY, DO YOU SMELL THAT?
YOU'RE RIGHT. WHAT IS THIS SMELL?
KINDA ROTTEN, KINDA SWEET.
WAIT, KNOW THIS SCEN ...
...!
G-
GET IN THERE AND HIDE!
SHOVE
HEY!
HURRY UP!
DOOFUS!
WH-WHAT THE?
WHY'S ZAJI...
...SO NERVOUS, ALL OF A SUDDEN...?
WHAT THE HECK?
POP
ジタ FLAIL
ジタ FLAIL
ジタ FLAIL
A TURTLE...!?
WHY'S HE SCARED OF SUCH A...

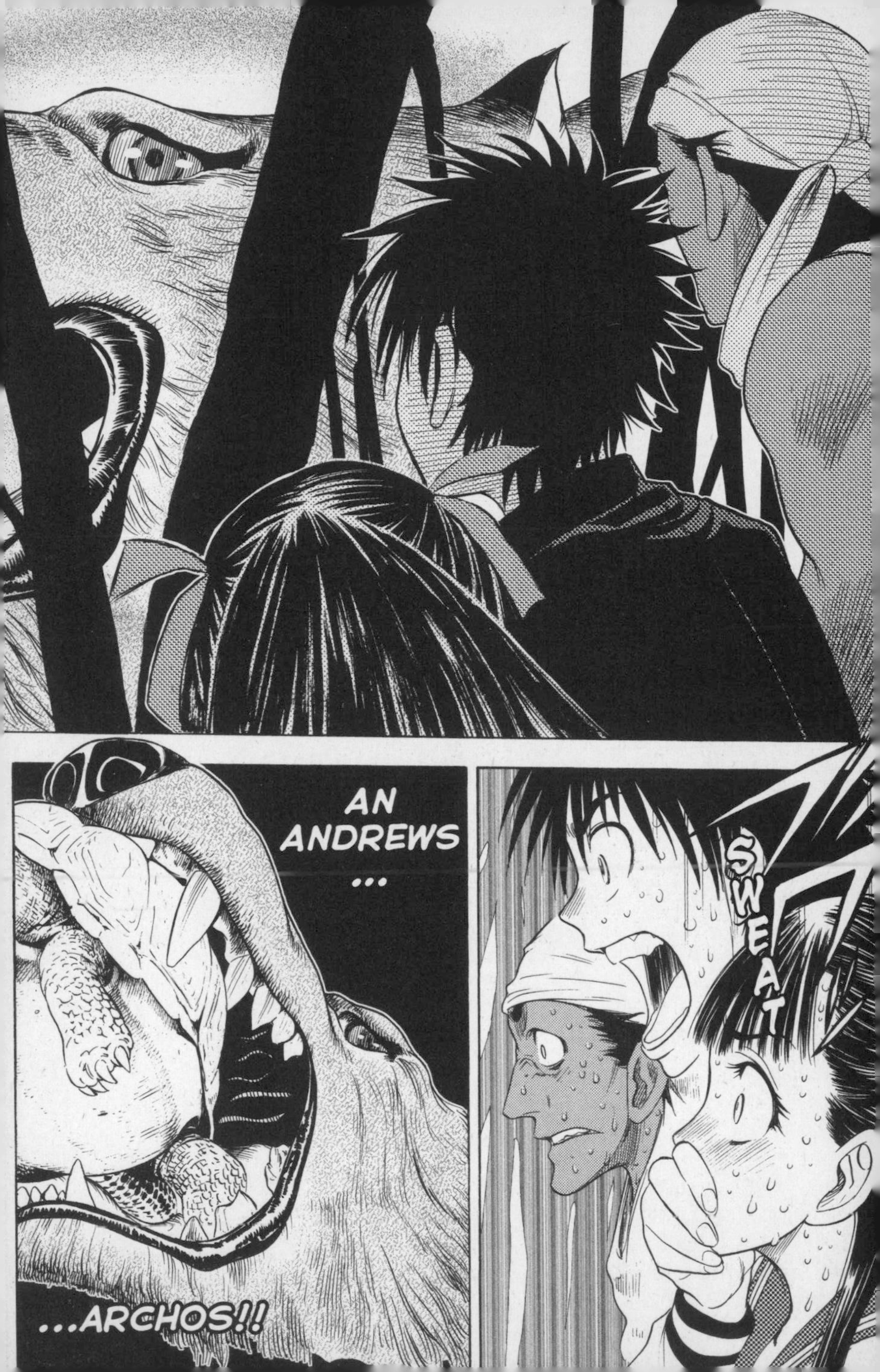
SWEAT
AN ANDREWS ...
...ARCHOS!!

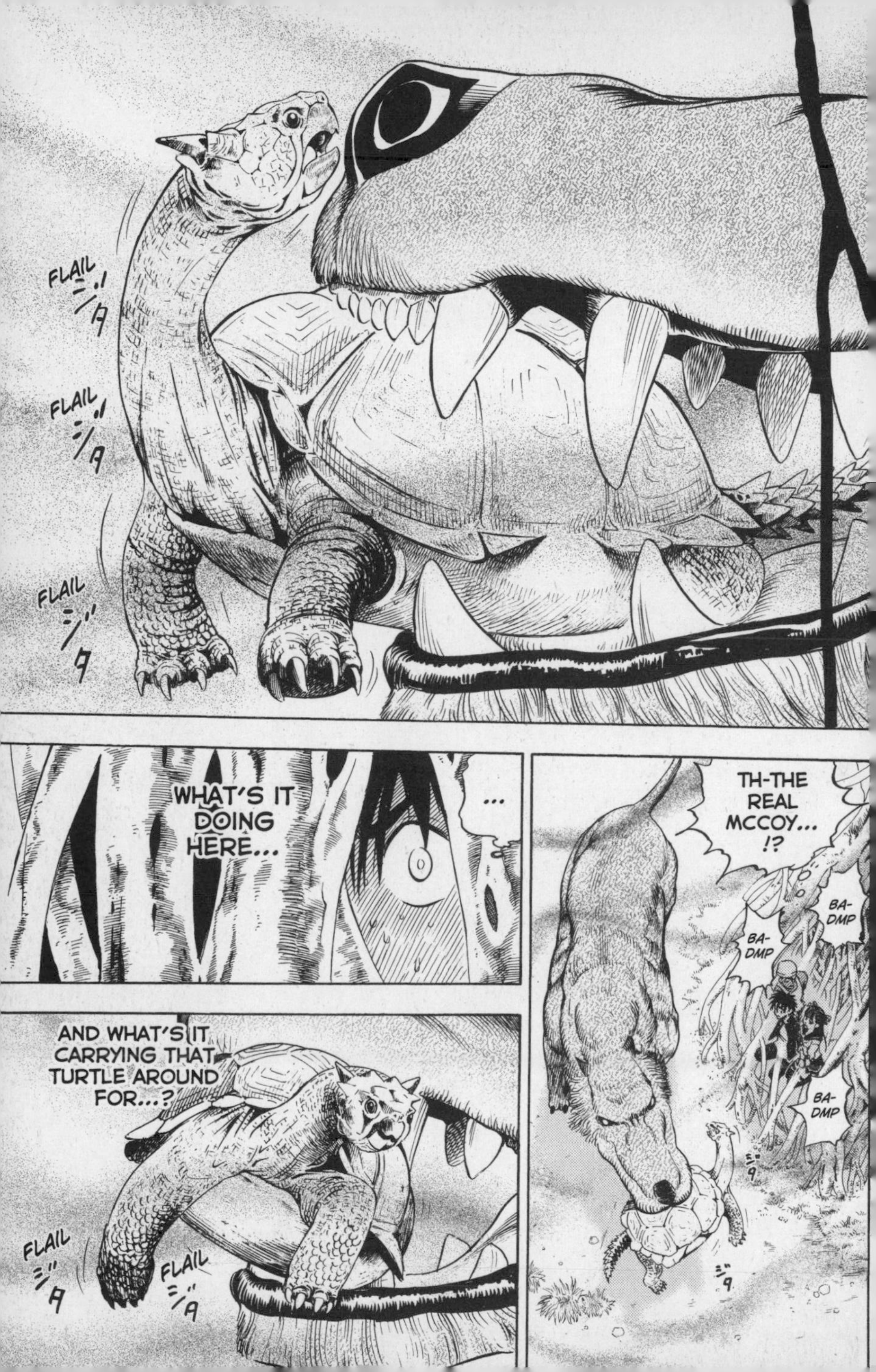
FLAIL
ジタ
FLAIL
ジタ
FLAIL
ジタ
TH-THE REAL MCCOY...!?
BA-DMP
BA-DMP
BA-DMP
ジタ
ジタ
...
WHAT'S IT DOING HERE...
AND WHAT'S IT CARRYING THAT TURTLE AROUND FOR...?
FLAIL
ジタ
FLAIL
ジタ

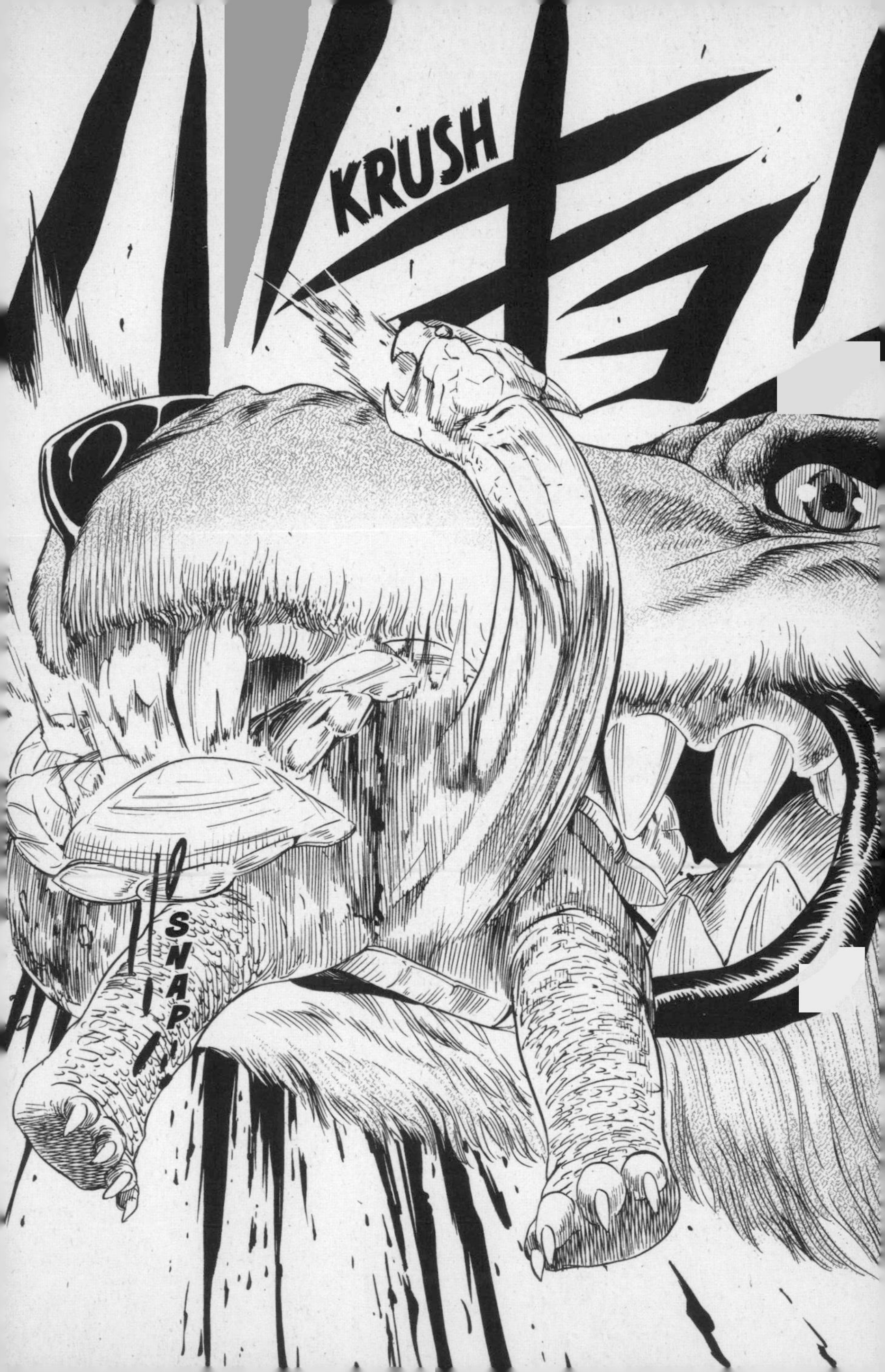
KRUSH
SNAP

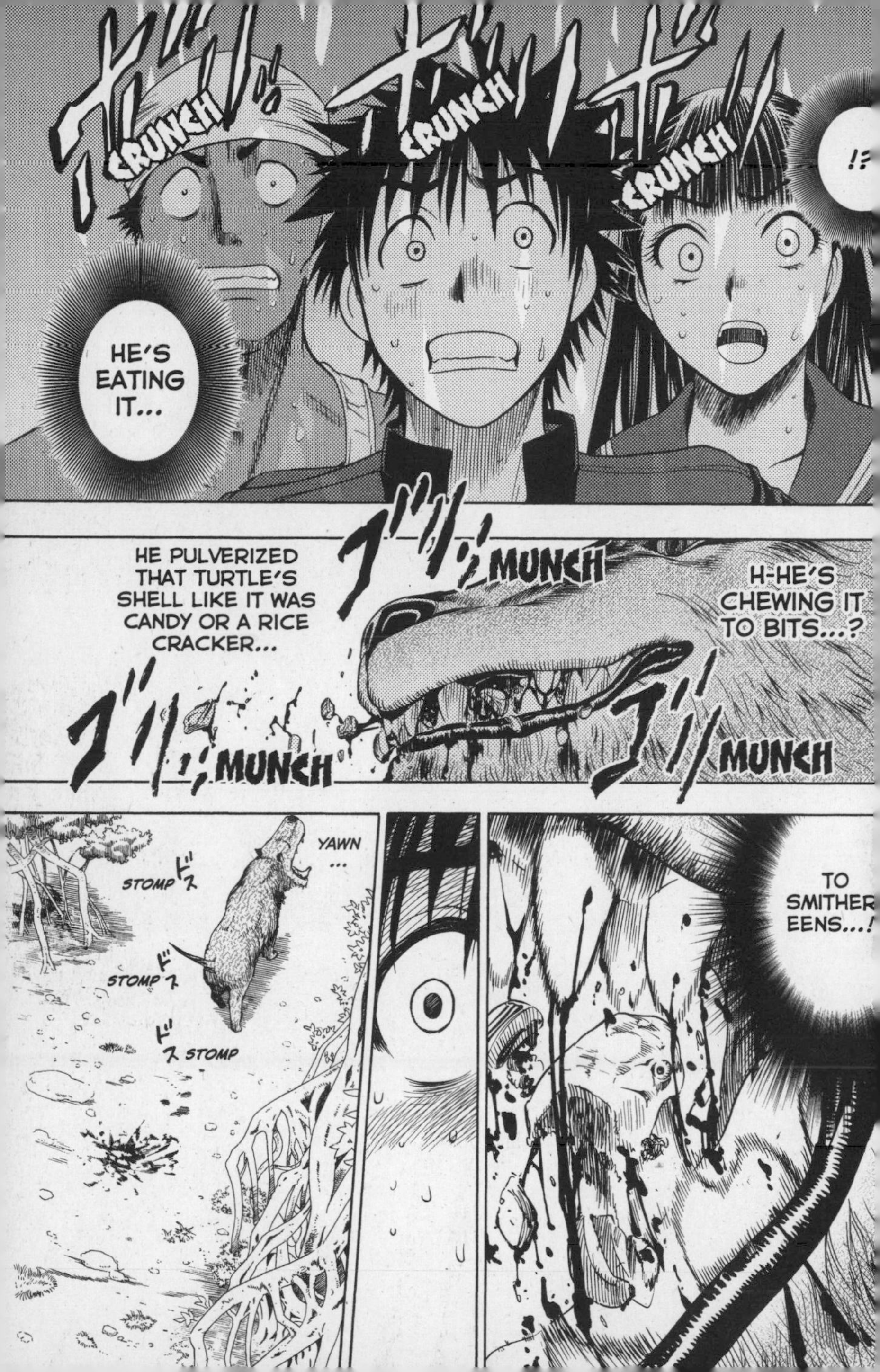
!?
CRUNCH
CRUNCH
CRUNCH
HE'S EATING IT...
H-HE'S CHEWING IT TO BITS...?
MUNCH
HE PULVERIZED THAT TURTLE'S SHELL LIKE IT WAS CANDY OR A RICE CRACKER...
MUNCH
MUNCH
TO SMITHER EENS...!
YAWN ...
STOMP ドス
STOMP ドス
ドス STOMP

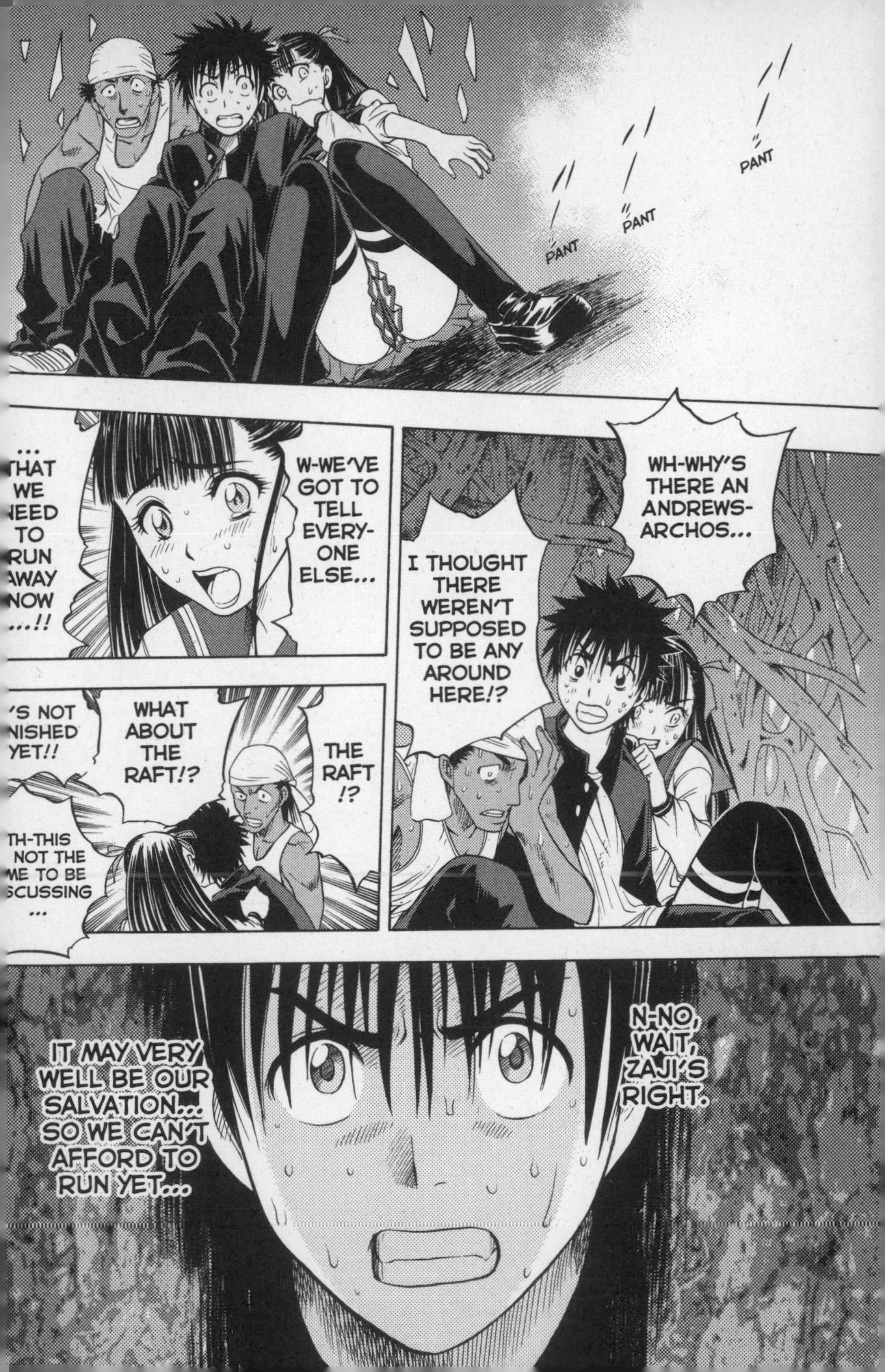
PANT
PANT
PANT
WH-WHY'S THERE AN ANDREWS-ARCHOS...
I THOUGHT THERE WEREN'T SUPPOSED TO BE ANY AROUND HERE!?
W-WE'VE GOT TO TELL EVERY-ONE ELSE...
...THAT WE NEED TO RUN AWAY NOW ...!!
THE RAFT!?
WHAT ABOUT THE RAFT!?
'S NOT NISHED YET!!
TH-THIS NOT THE ME TO BE SCUSSING ...
N-NO, WAIT, ZAJI'S RIGHT.
IT MAY VERY WELL BE OUR SALVATION... SO WE CAN'T AFFORD TO RUN YET...

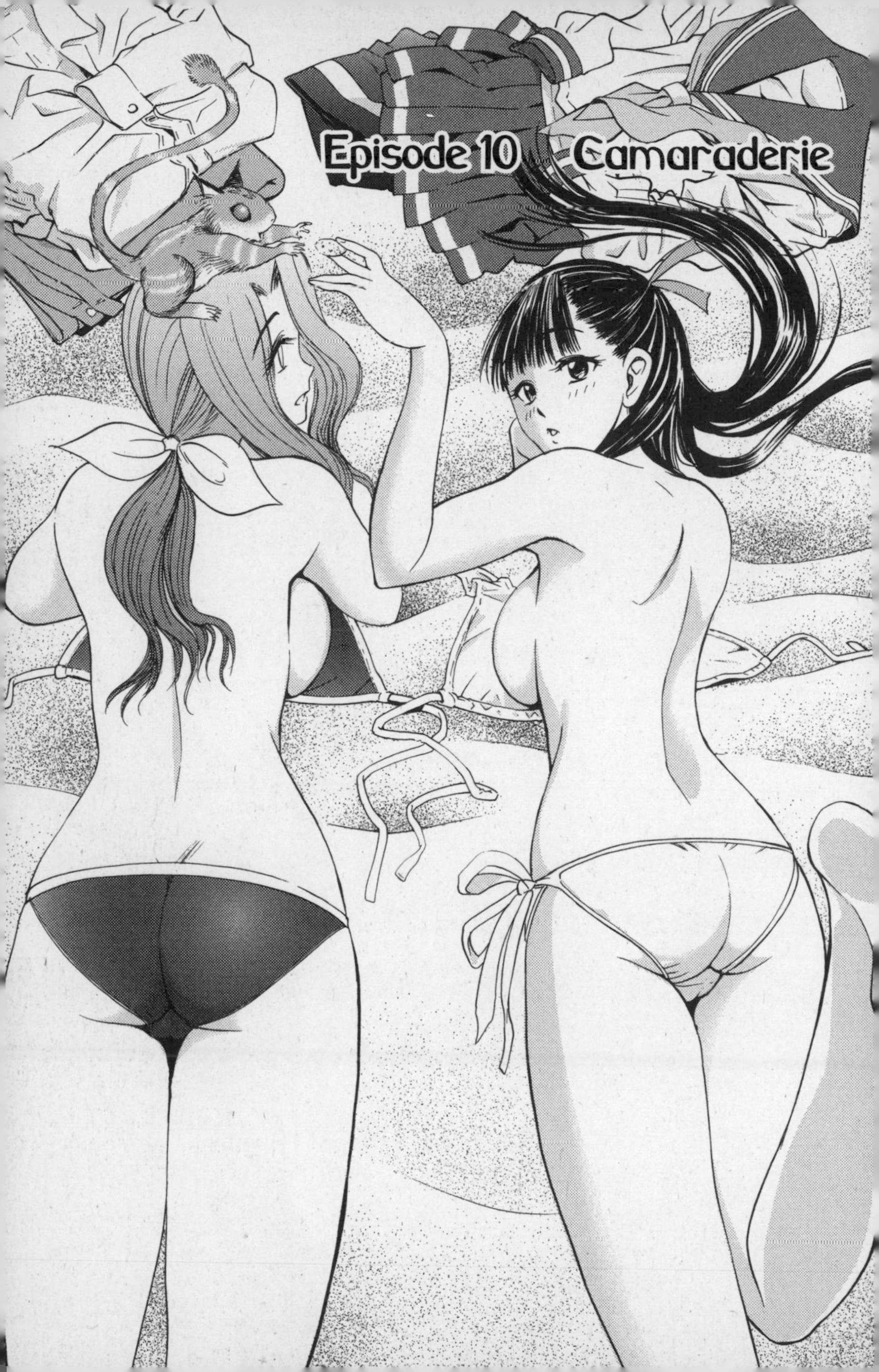
Episode 10 Camaraderie

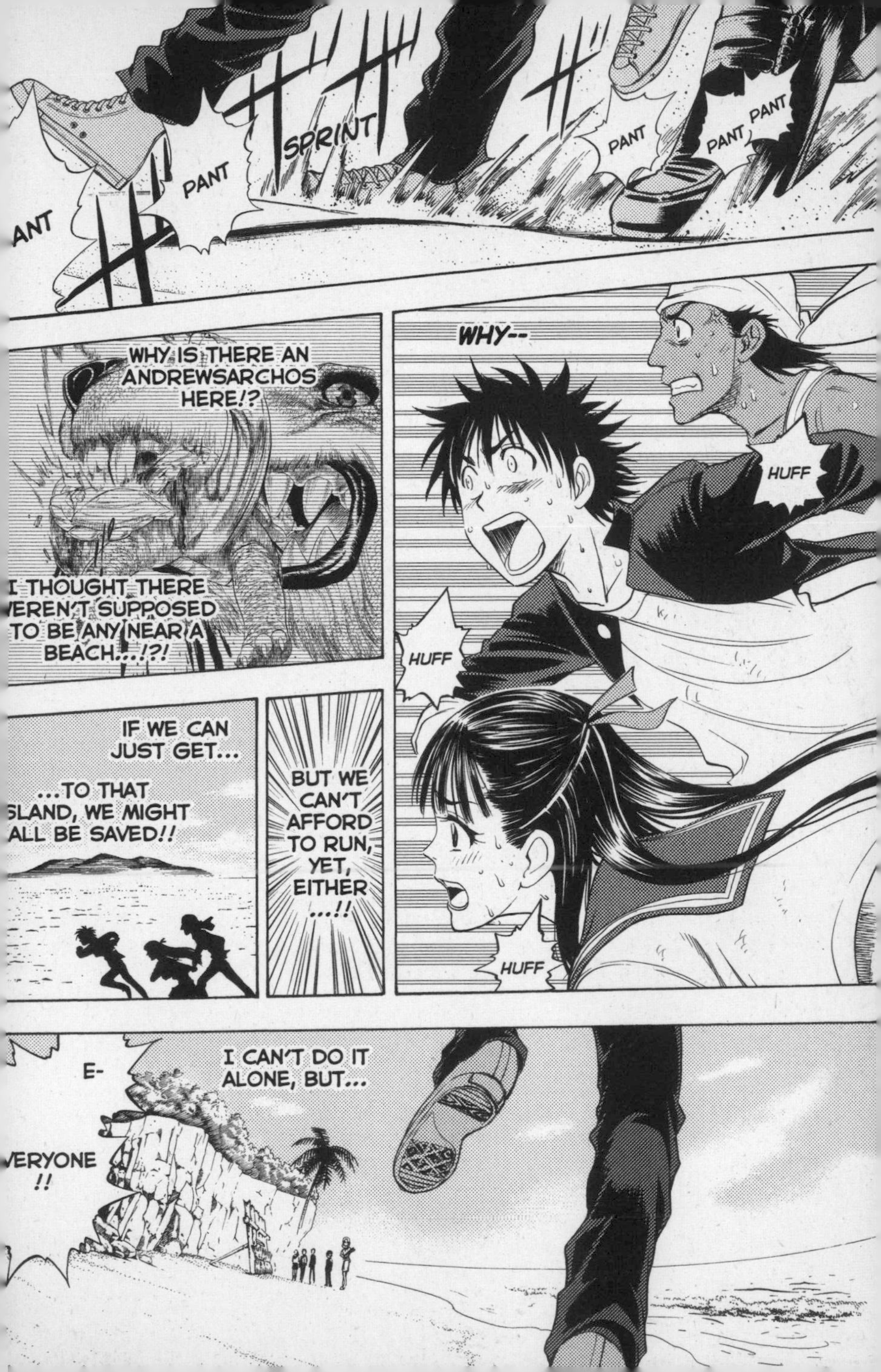
PANT PANT
PANT
PANT
SPRINT
PANT
ANT
WHY--
HUFF
HUFF
HUFF
WHY IS THERE AN ANDREWSARCHOS HERE!?
I THOUGHT THERE VEREN'T SUPPOSED TO BE ANY NEAR A BEACH...!?!
BUT WE CAN'T AFFORD TO RUN, YET, EITHER ...!!
IF WE CAN JUST GET...
...TO THAT SLAND, WE MIGHT ALL BE SAVED!!
I CAN'T DO IT ALONE, BUT...
E-
VERYONE !!

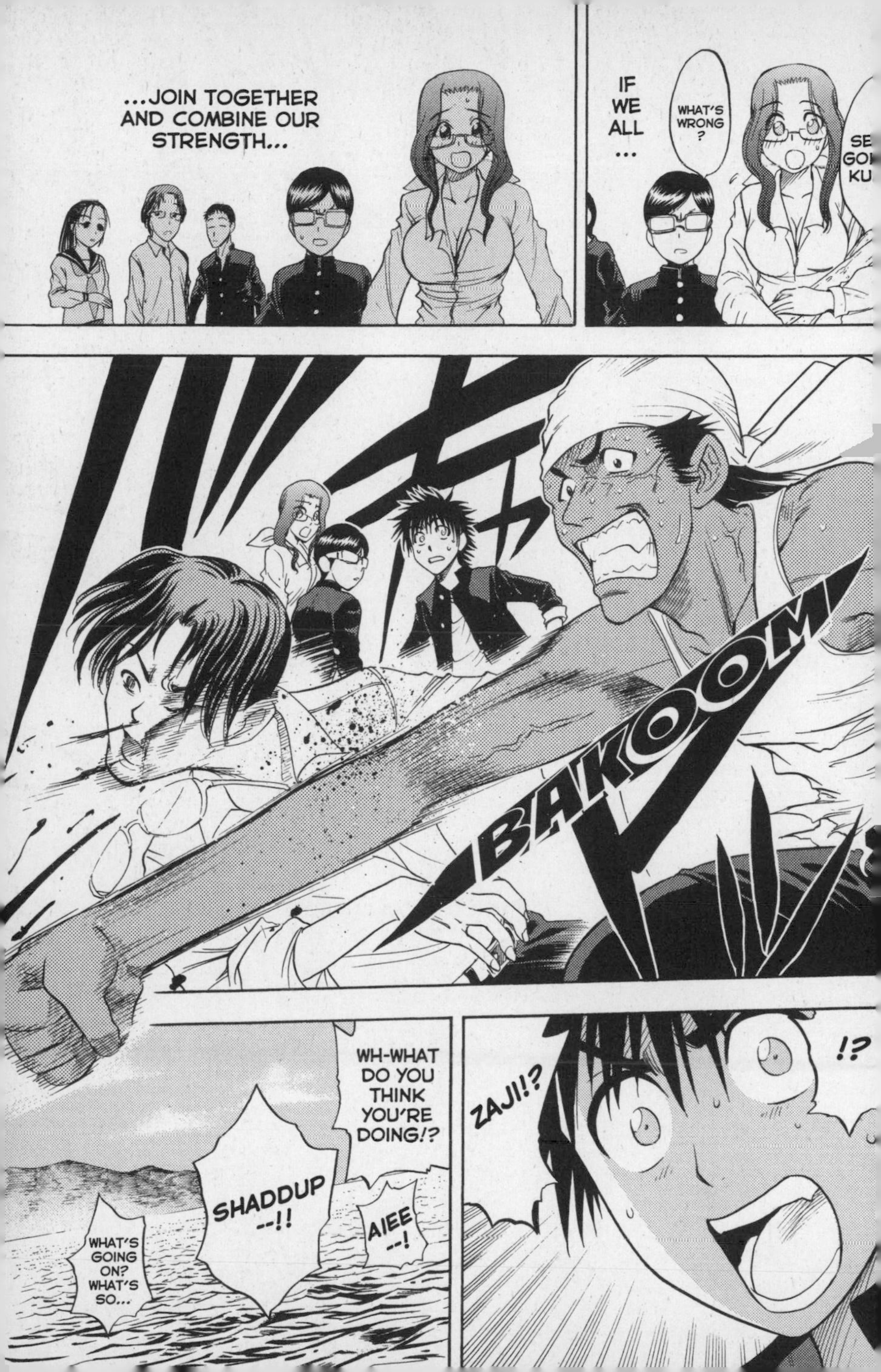
SE GO KU
WHAT'S WRONG ?
IF WE ALL ...
...JOIN TOGETHER AND COMBINE OUR STRENGTH...
BAKOOM
!?
ZAJI!?
WH-WHAT DO YOU THINK YOU'RE DOING!?
AIEE --!
SHADDUP --!!
WHAT'S GOING ON? WHAT'S SO...

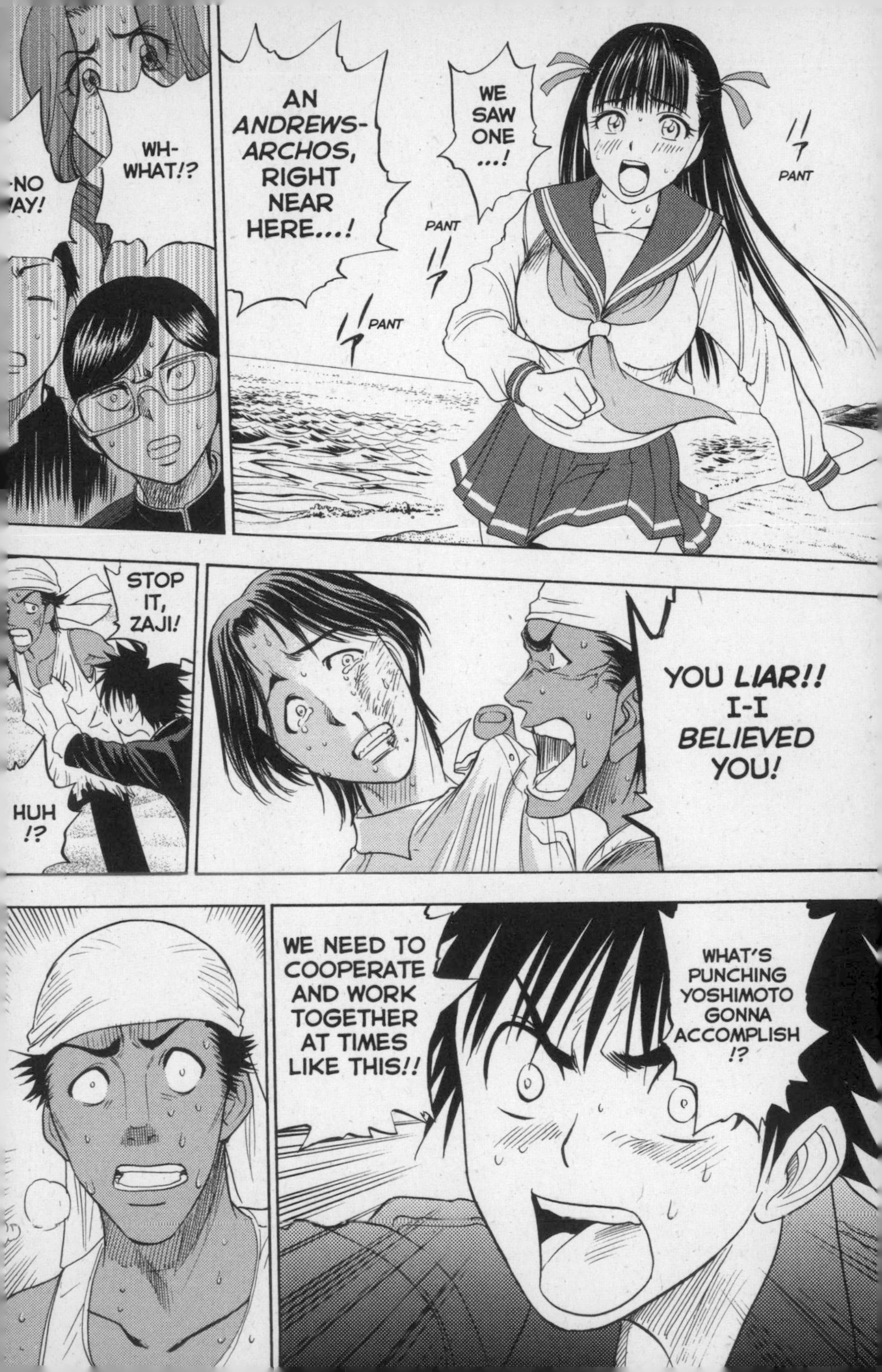
PANT
WE SAW ONE ...!
AN ANDREWS-ARCHOS, RIGHT NEAR HERE...!
PANT
PANT
WH-WHAT!?
-NO AY!
YOU LIAR!! I-I BELIEVED YOU!
STOP IT, ZAJI!
HUH !?
WHAT'S PUNCHING YOSHIMOTO GONNA ACCOMPLISH !?
WE NEED TO COOPERATE AND WORK TOGETHER AT TIMES LIKE THIS!!

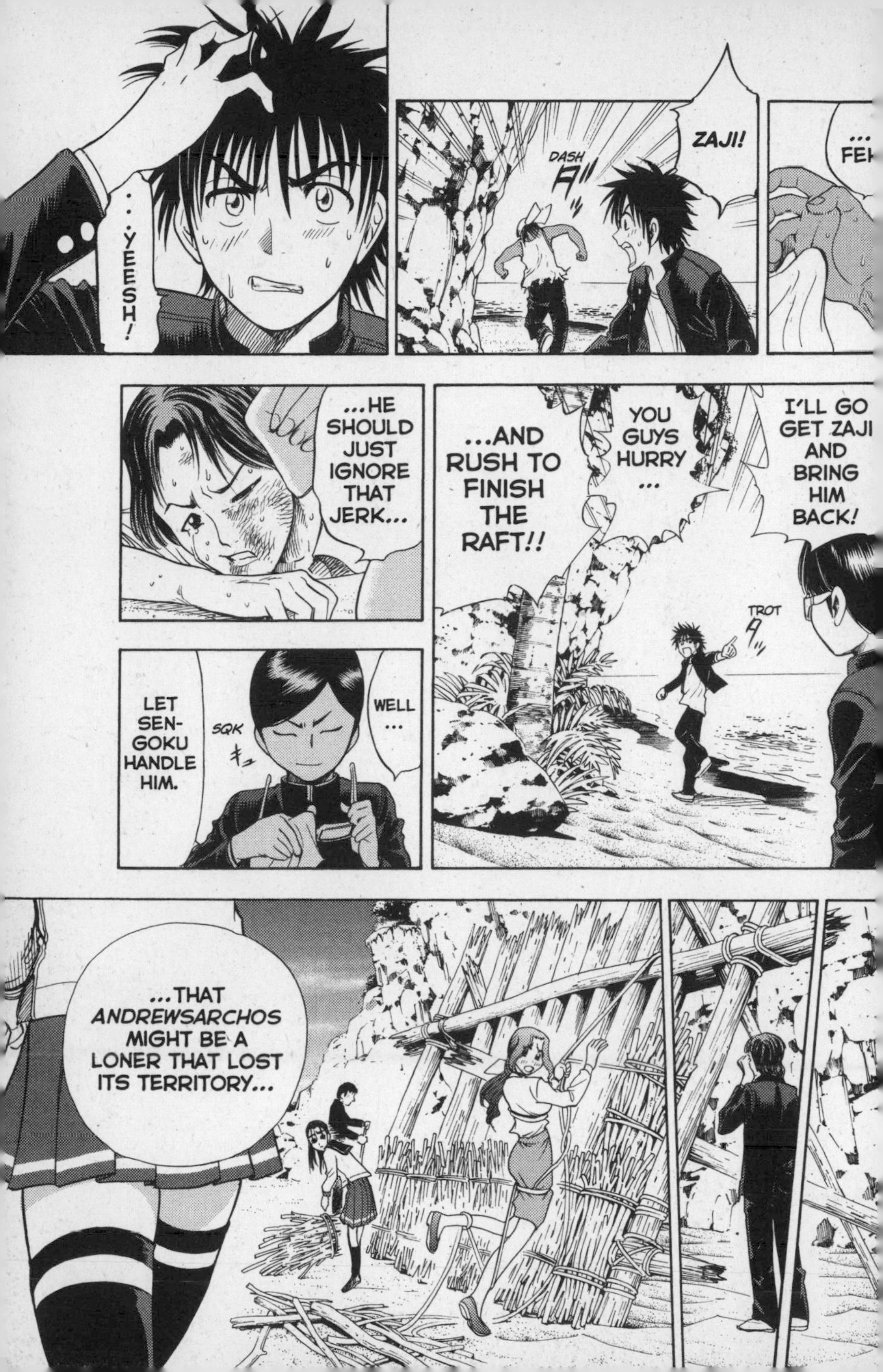
... FEH
ZAJI!
DASH
...YEESH!
I'LL GO GET ZAJI AND BRING HIM BACK!
YOU GUYS HURRY ...
...AND RUSH TO FINISH THE RAFT!!
TROT
...HE SHOULD JUST IGNORE THAT JERK...
WELL ...
LET SEN-GOKU HANDLE HIM.
SQK
...THAT *ANDREWSARCHOS* MIGHT BE A LONER THAT LOST ITS TERRITORY...

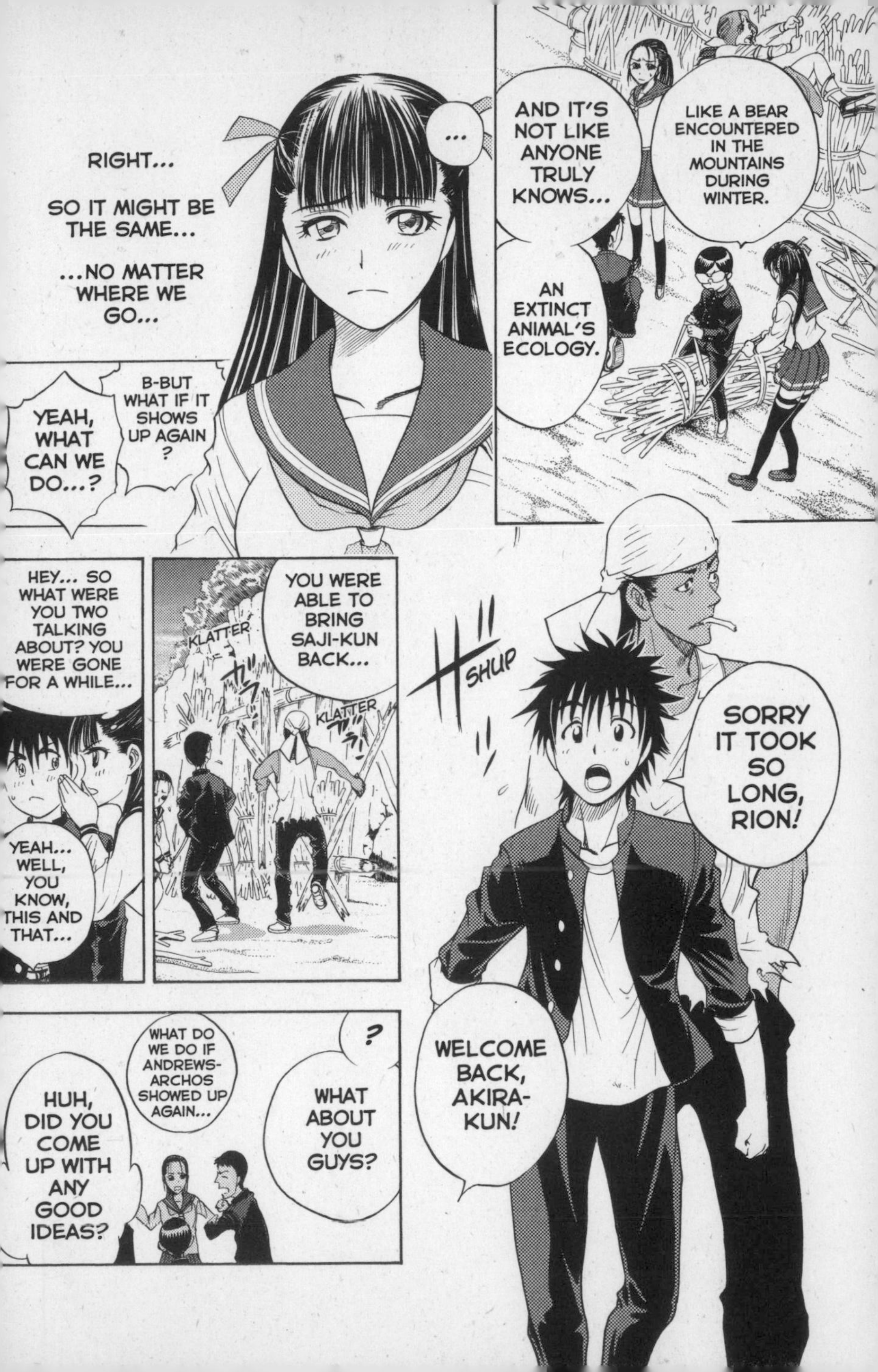
LIKE A BEAR ENCOUNTERED IN THE MOUNTAINS DURING WINTER.
AND IT'S NOT LIKE ANYONE TRULY KNOWS...
AN EXTINCT ANIMAL'S ECOLOGY.
...
RIGHT...
SO IT MIGHT BE THE SAME...
...NO MATTER WHERE WE GO...
B-BUT WHAT IF IT SHOWS UP AGAIN?
YEAH, WHAT CAN WE DO...?
SORRY IT TOOK SO LONG, RION!
SHUP
WELCOME BACK, AKIRA-KUN!
YOU WERE ABLE TO BRING SAJI-KUN BACK...
KLATTER
KLATTER
HEY... SO WHAT WERE YOU TWO TALKING ABOUT? YOU WERE GONE FOR A WHILE...
YEAH... WELL, YOU KNOW, THIS AND THAT...
?
WHAT ABOUT YOU GUYS?
WHAT DO WE DO IF ANDREWS-ARCHOS SHOWED UP AGAIN...
HUH, DID YOU COME UP WITH ANY GOOD IDEAS?

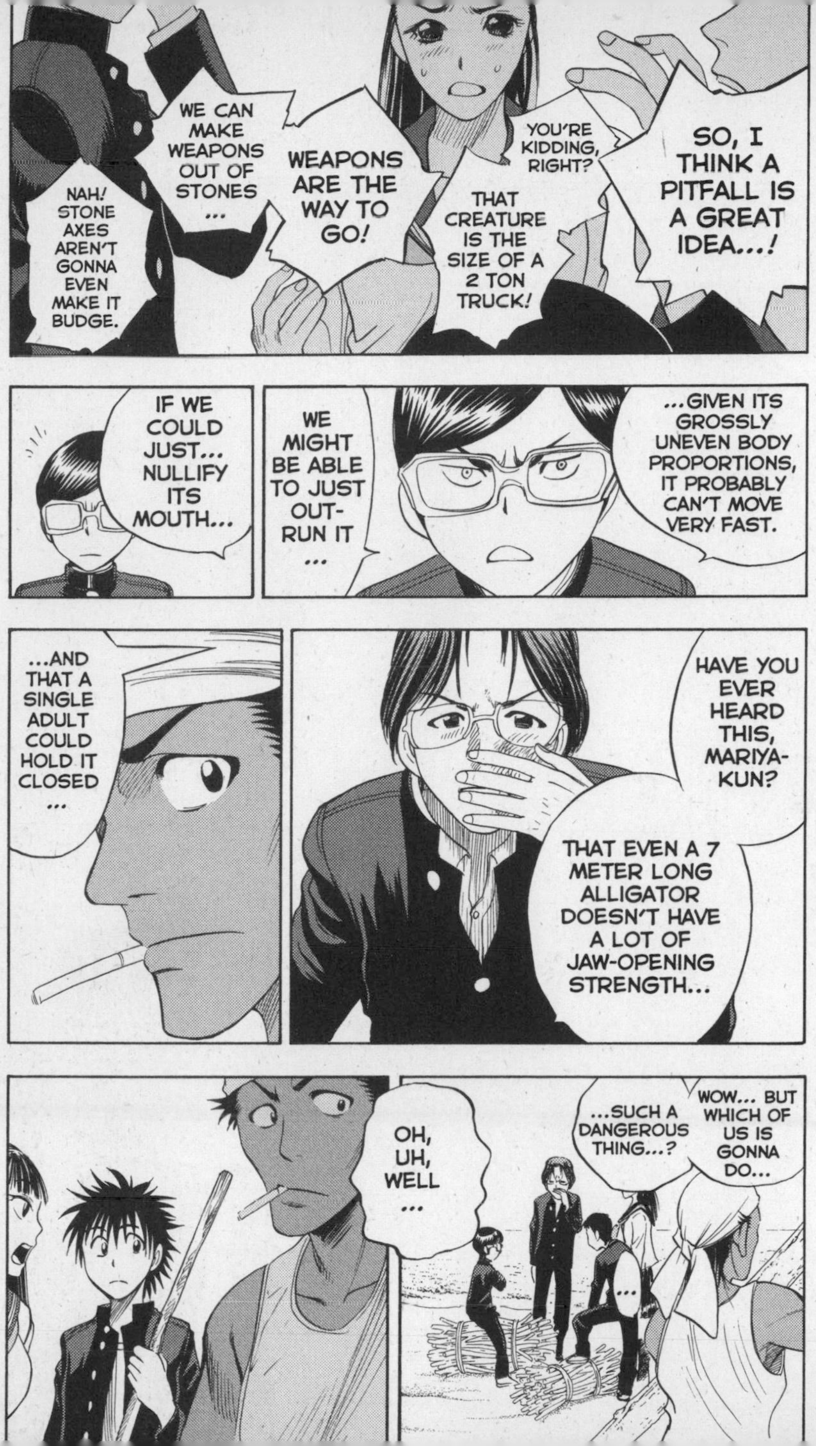
SO, I THINK A PITFALL IS A GREAT IDEA...!
YOU'RE KIDDING, RIGHT?
THAT CREATURE IS THE SIZE OF A 2 TON TRUCK!
WEAPONS ARE THE WAY TO GO!
WE CAN MAKE WEAPONS OUT OF STONES ...
NAH! STONE AXES AREN'T GONNA EVEN MAKE IT BUDGE.
...GIVEN ITS GROSSLY UNEVEN BODY PROPORTIONS, IT PROBABLY CAN'T MOVE VERY FAST.
WE MIGHT BE ABLE TO JUST OUT-RUN IT ...
IF WE COULD JUST... NULLIFY ITS MOUTH...
HAVE YOU EVER HEARD THIS, MARIYA-KUN?
THAT EVEN A 7 METER LONG ALLIGATOR DOESN'T HAVE A LOT OF JAW-OPENING STRENGTH...
...AND THAT A SINGLE ADULT COULD HOLD IT CLOSED ...
WOW... BUT WHICH OF US IS GONNA DO...
...SUCH A DANGEROUS THING...?
...
OH, UH, WELL ...

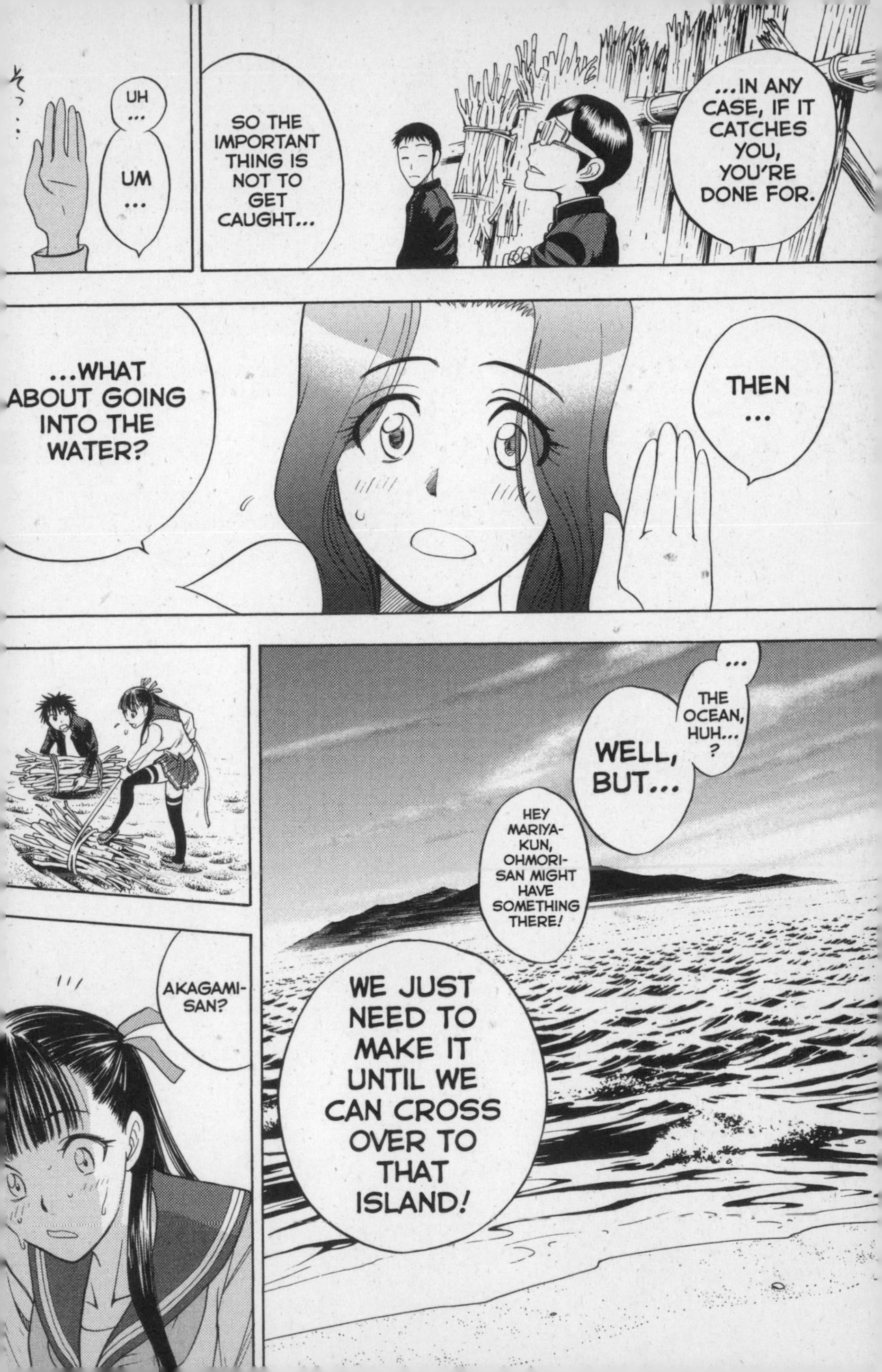
...IN ANY CASE, IF IT CATCHES YOU, YOU'RE DONE FOR.
SO THE IMPORTANT THING IS NOT TO GET CAUGHT...
そっ...
UH ... UM ...
THEN ...
...WHAT ABOUT GOING INTO THE WATER?
... THE OCEAN, HUH...?
WELL, BUT...
HEY MARIYA-KUN, OHMORI-SAN MIGHT HAVE SOMETHING THERE!
WE JUST NEED TO MAKE IT UNTIL WE CAN CROSS OVER TO THAT ISLAND!
AKAGAMI-SAN?

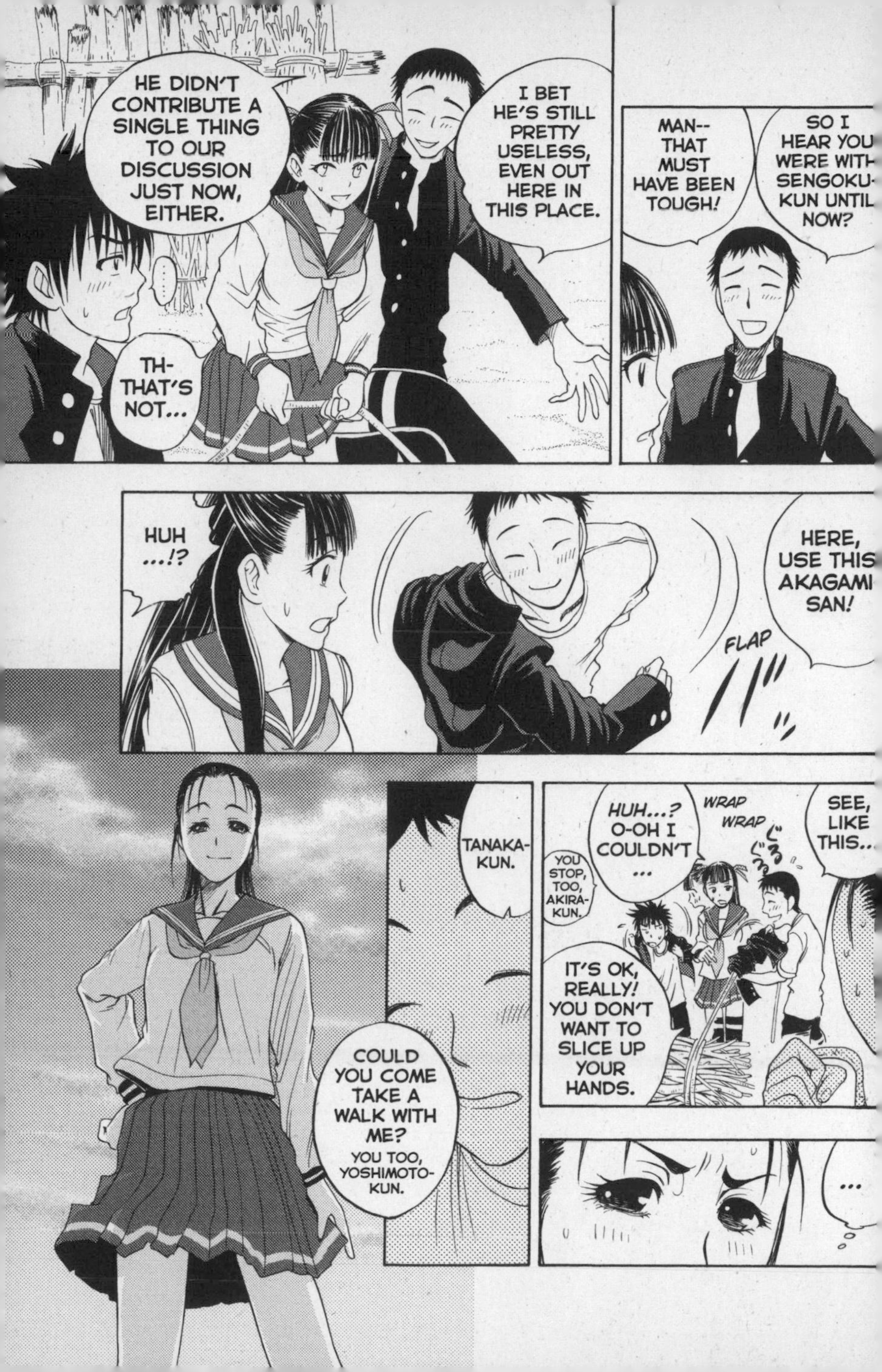
SO I HEAR YOU WERE WITH SENGOKU-KUN UNTIL NOW?
MAN-- THAT MUST HAVE BEEN TOUGH!
I BET HE'S STILL PRETTY USELESS, EVEN OUT HERE IN THIS PLACE.
HE DIDN'T CONTRIBUTE A SINGLE THING TO OUR DISCUSSION JUST NOW, EITHER.
...
TH- THAT'S NOT...
HERE, USE THIS AKAGAMI-SAN!
FLAP
HUH ...!?
SEE, LIKE THIS...
WRAP WRAP
HUH...? O-OH I COULDN'T ...
YOU STOP, TOO, AKIRA-KUN.
IT'S OK, REALLY! YOU DON'T WANT TO SLICE UP YOUR HANDS.
...
TANAKA-KUN.
COULD YOU COME TAKE A WALK WITH ME?
YOU TOO, YOSHIMOTO-KUN.

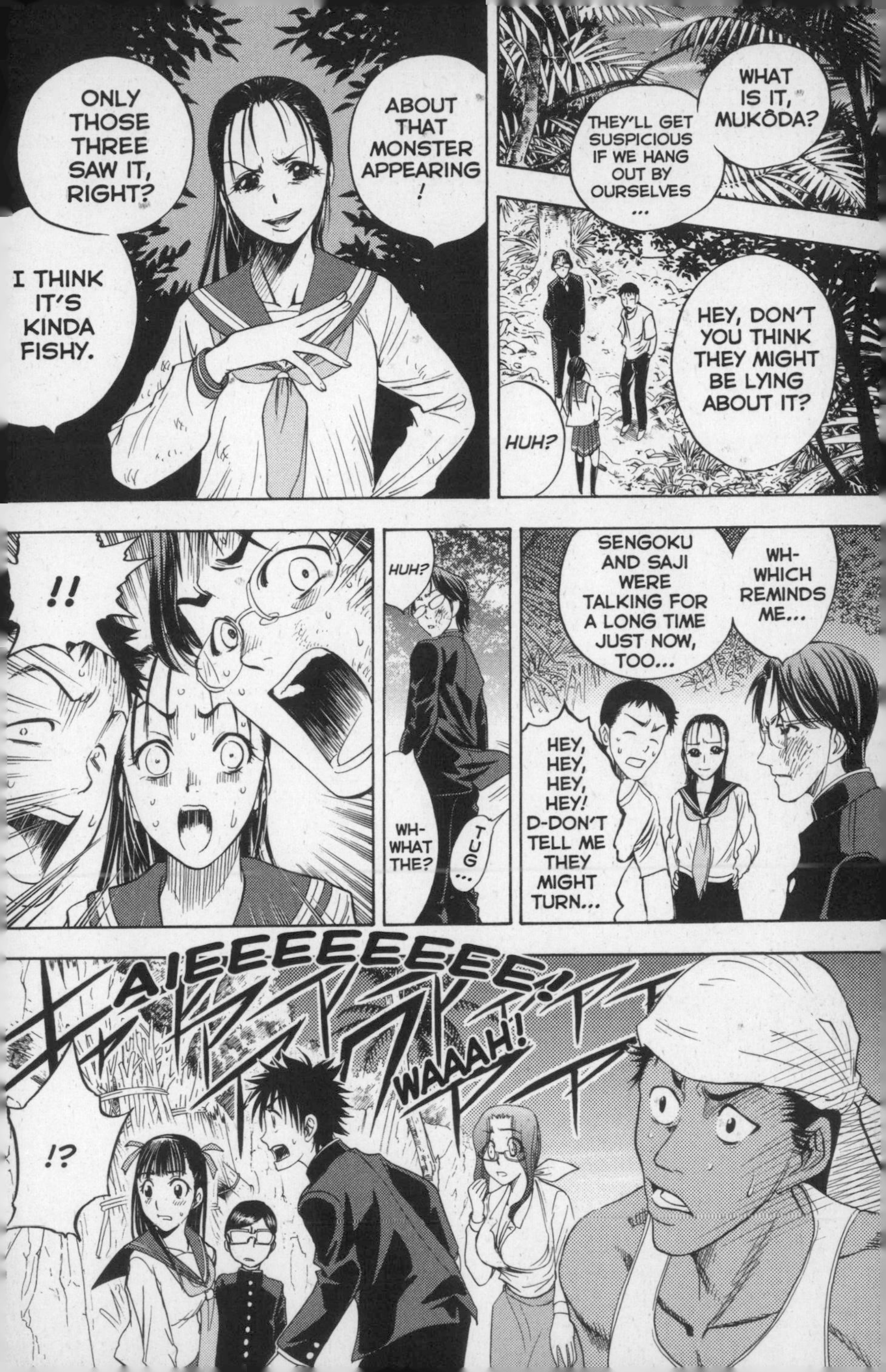
WHAT IS IT, MUKÔDA?
THEY'LL GET SUSPICIOUS IF WE HANG OUT BY OURSELVES ...
HEY, DON'T YOU THINK THEY MIGHT BE LYING ABOUT IT?
HUH?
ABOUT THAT MONSTER APPEARING!
ONLY THOSE THREE SAW IT, RIGHT?
I THINK IT'S KINDA FISHY.
WH- WHICH REMINDS ME...
SENGOKU AND SAJI WERE TALKING FOR A LONG TIME JUST NOW, TOO...
HEY, HEY, HEY, HEY! D-DON'T TELL ME THEY MIGHT TURN...
HUH?
TUG...
WH- WHAT THE?
!!
AIEEEEEEEEEE!
WAAAH!
!?

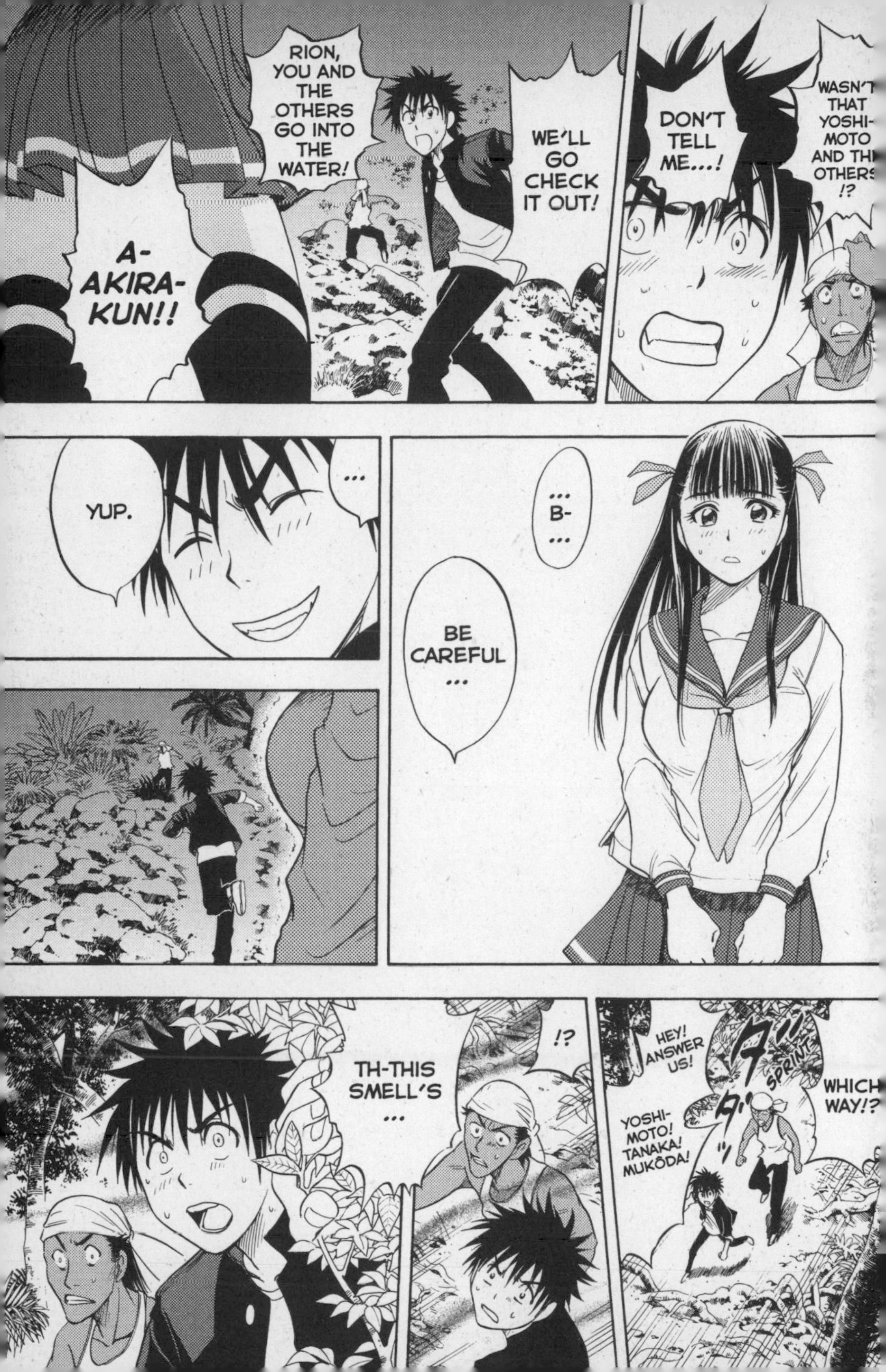
WASN'T THAT YOSHI-MOTO AND THE OTHERS !?
DON'T TELL ME...!
RION, YOU AND THE OTHERS GO INTO THE WATER!
WE'LL GO CHECK IT OUT!
A- AKIRA-KUN!!
... B- ...
BE CAREFUL ...
...
YUP.
HEY! ANSWER US!
SPRINT
WHICH WAY!?
YOSHI-MOTO! TANAKA! MUKŌDA!
!?
TH-THIS SMELL'S ...

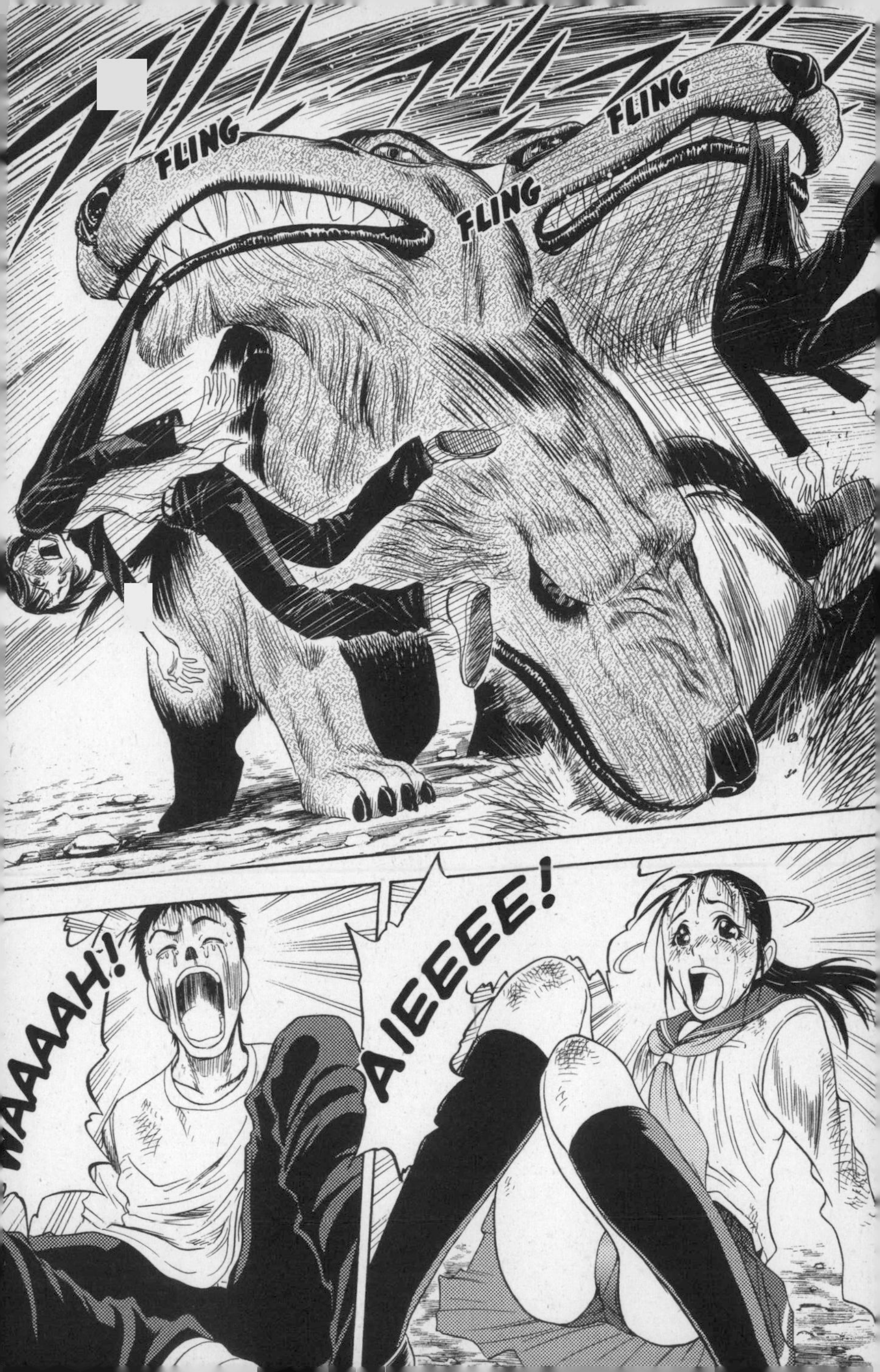
FLING
FLING
FLING
AIEEEE!
WAAAAH!

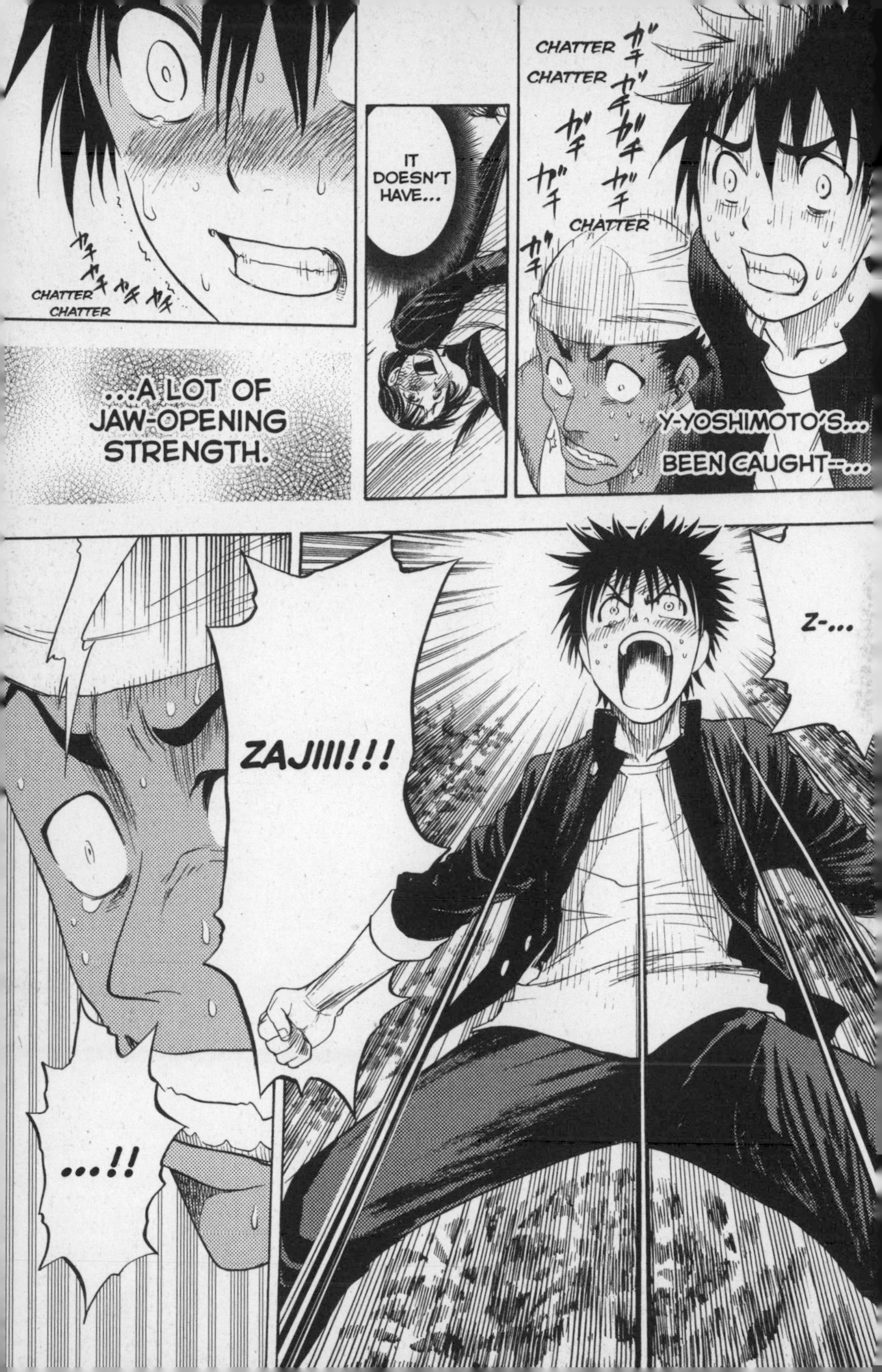
CHATTER
CHATTER
CHATTER
Y-YOSHIMOTO'S... BEEN CAUGHT--...
IT DOESN'T HAVE...
CHATTER
CHATTER
...A LOT OF JAW-OPENING STRENGTH.
Z-...
ZAJIIII!!!
...!!

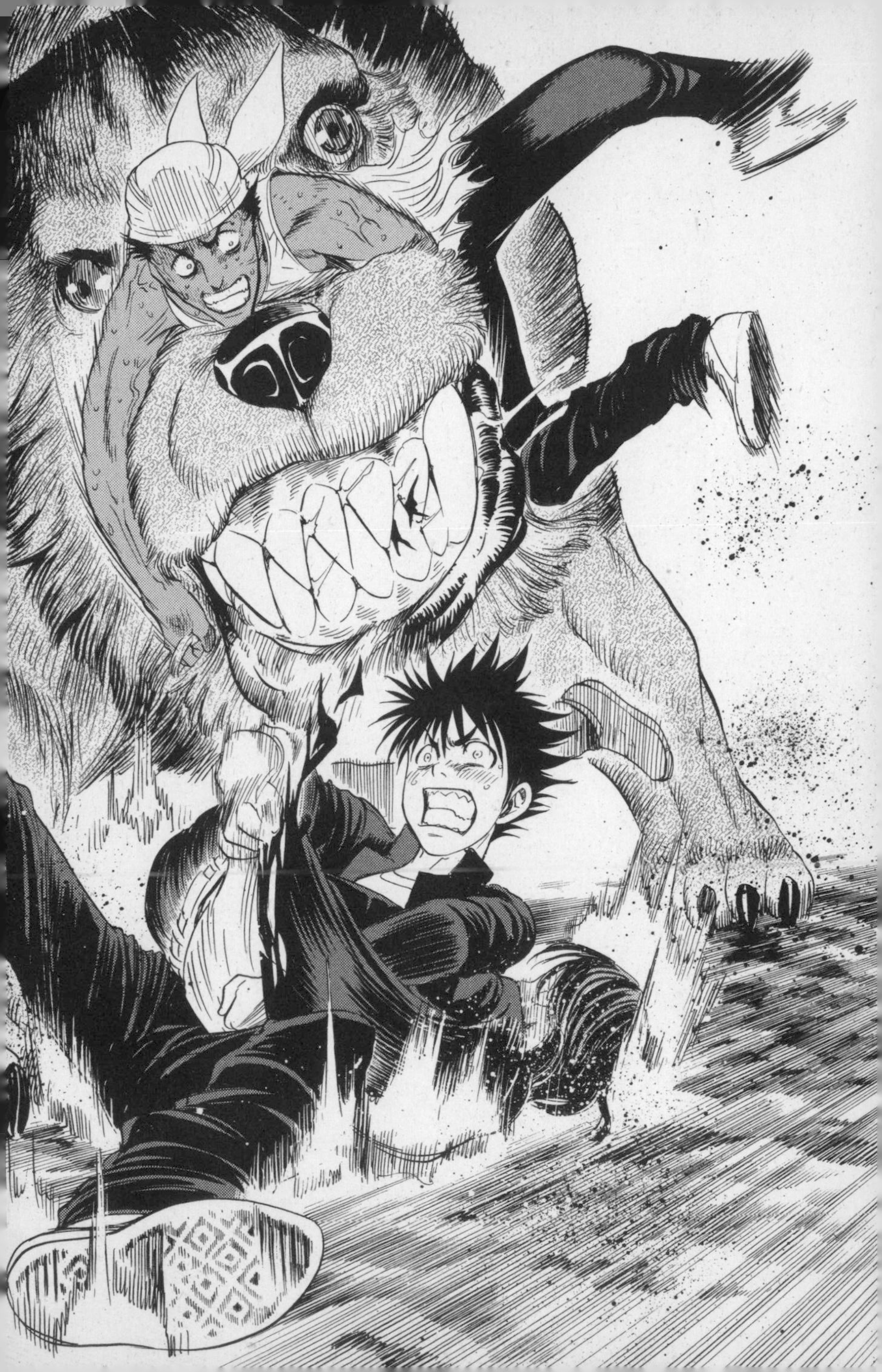

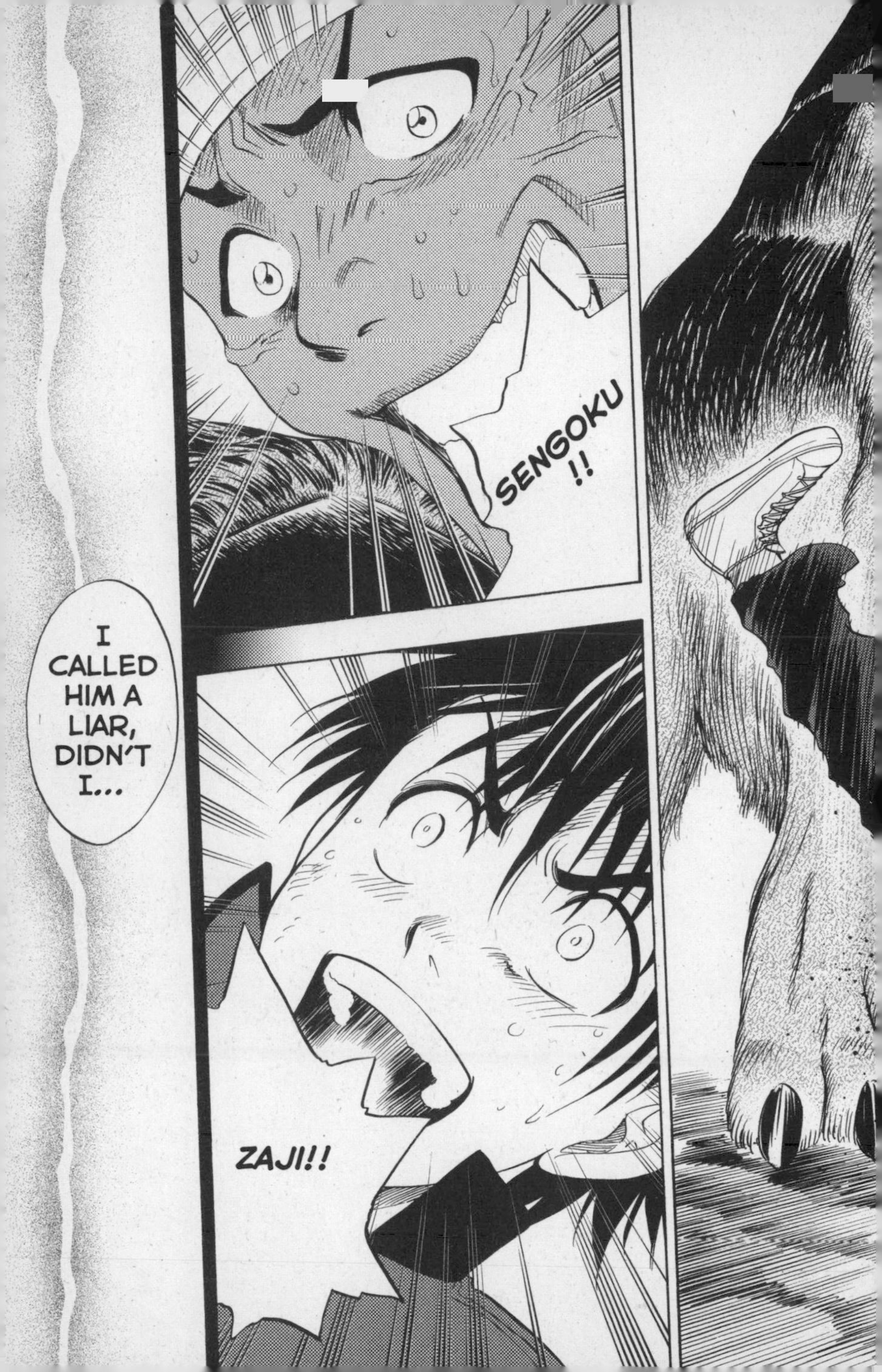
SENGOKU !!
ZAJI!!
I CALLED HIM A LIAR, DIDN'T I...

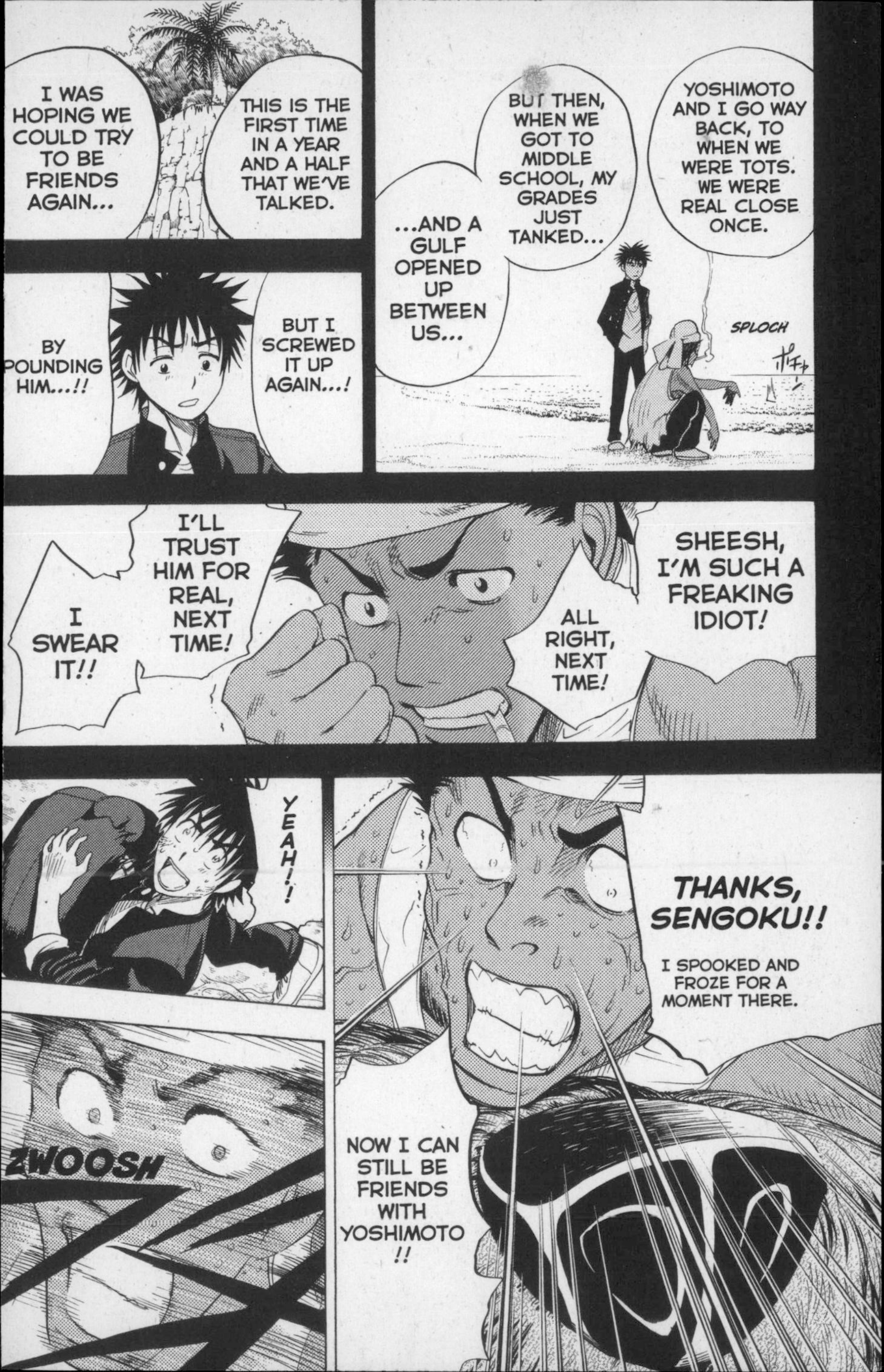
YOSHIMOTO AND I GO WAY BACK, TO WHEN WE WERE TOTS. WE WERE REAL CLOSE ONCE.
BUT THEN, WHEN WE GOT TO MIDDLE SCHOOL, MY GRADES JUST TANKED...
...AND A GULF OPENED UP BETWEEN US...
SPLOCH
THIS IS THE FIRST TIME IN A YEAR AND A HALF THAT WE'VE TALKED.
I WAS HOPING WE COULD TRY TO BE FRIENDS AGAIN...
BUT I SCREWED IT UP AGAIN...!
BY POUNDING HIM...!!
SHEESH, I'M SUCH A FREAKING IDIOT!
ALL RIGHT, NEXT TIME!
I'LL TRUST HIM FOR REAL, NEXT TIME!
I SWEAR IT!!
THANKS, SENGOKU!!
I SPOOKED AND FROZE FOR A MOMENT THERE.
NOW I CAN STILL BE FRIENDS WITH YOSHIMOTO!!
YEAH!!
ZWOOSH

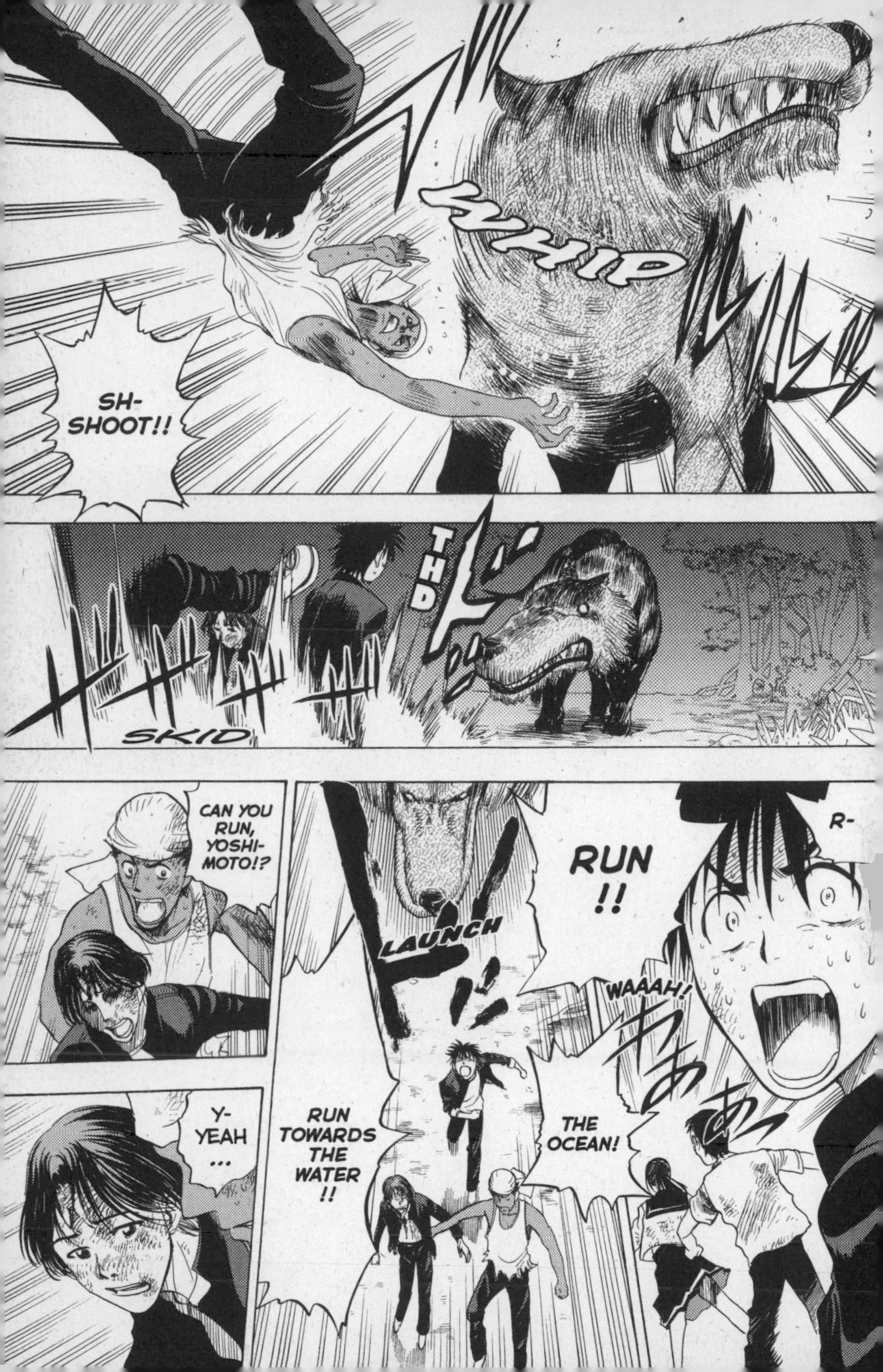
WHIP
SH-SHOOT!!
THD
SKID
R-
RUN!!
WAAAH!
LAUNCH
THE OCEAN!
RUN TOWARDS THE WATER!!
CAN YOU RUN, YOSHIMOTO!?
Y-YEAH ...

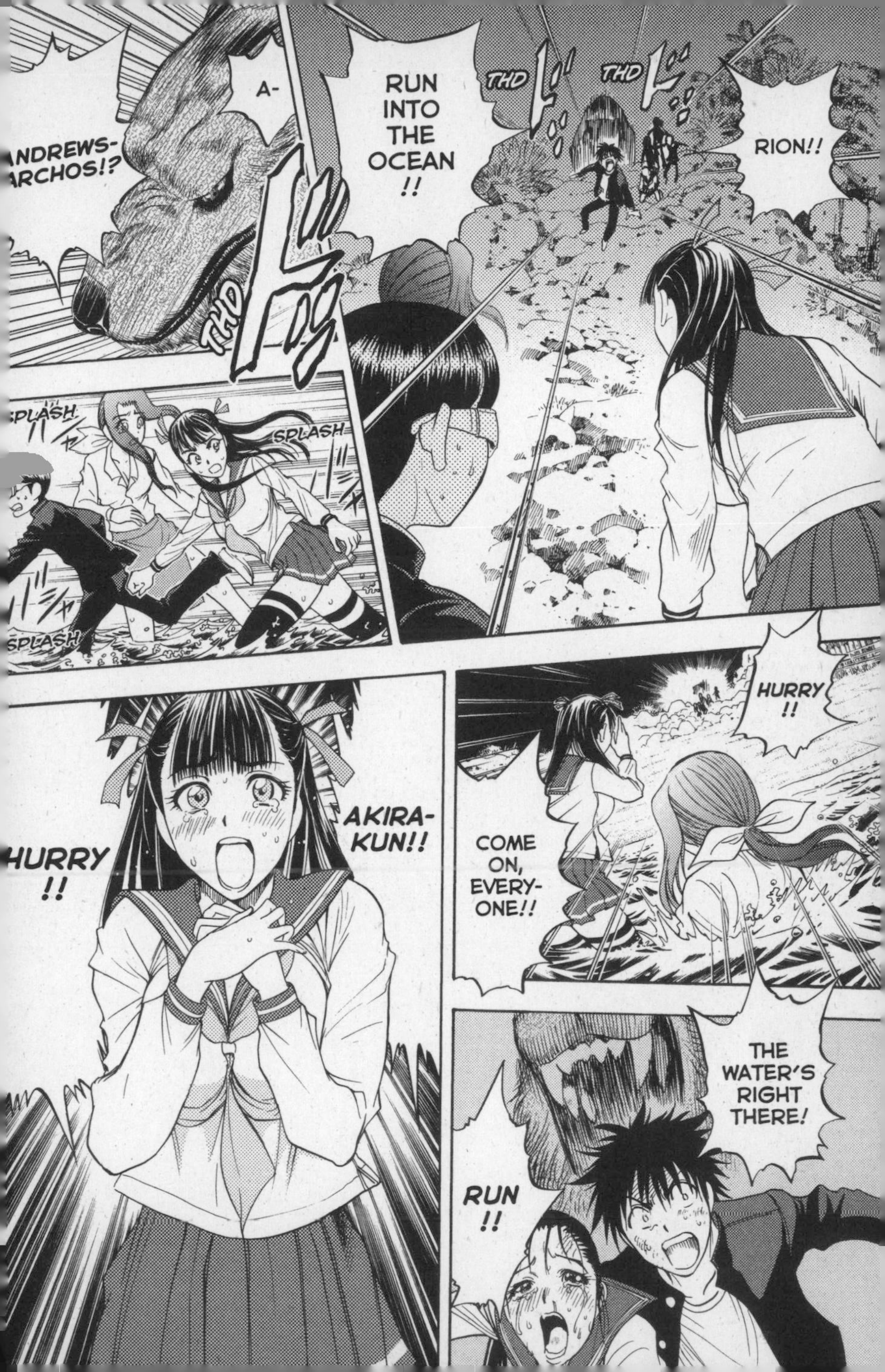
THD THD
RION!!
RUN INTO THE OCEAN!!
A-
ANDREWS-ARCHOS!?
THD
SPLASH
SPLASH
SPLASH
HURRY!!
COME ON, EVERY-ONE!!
THE WATER'S RIGHT THERE!
RUN!!
AKIRA-KUN!!
HURRY!!

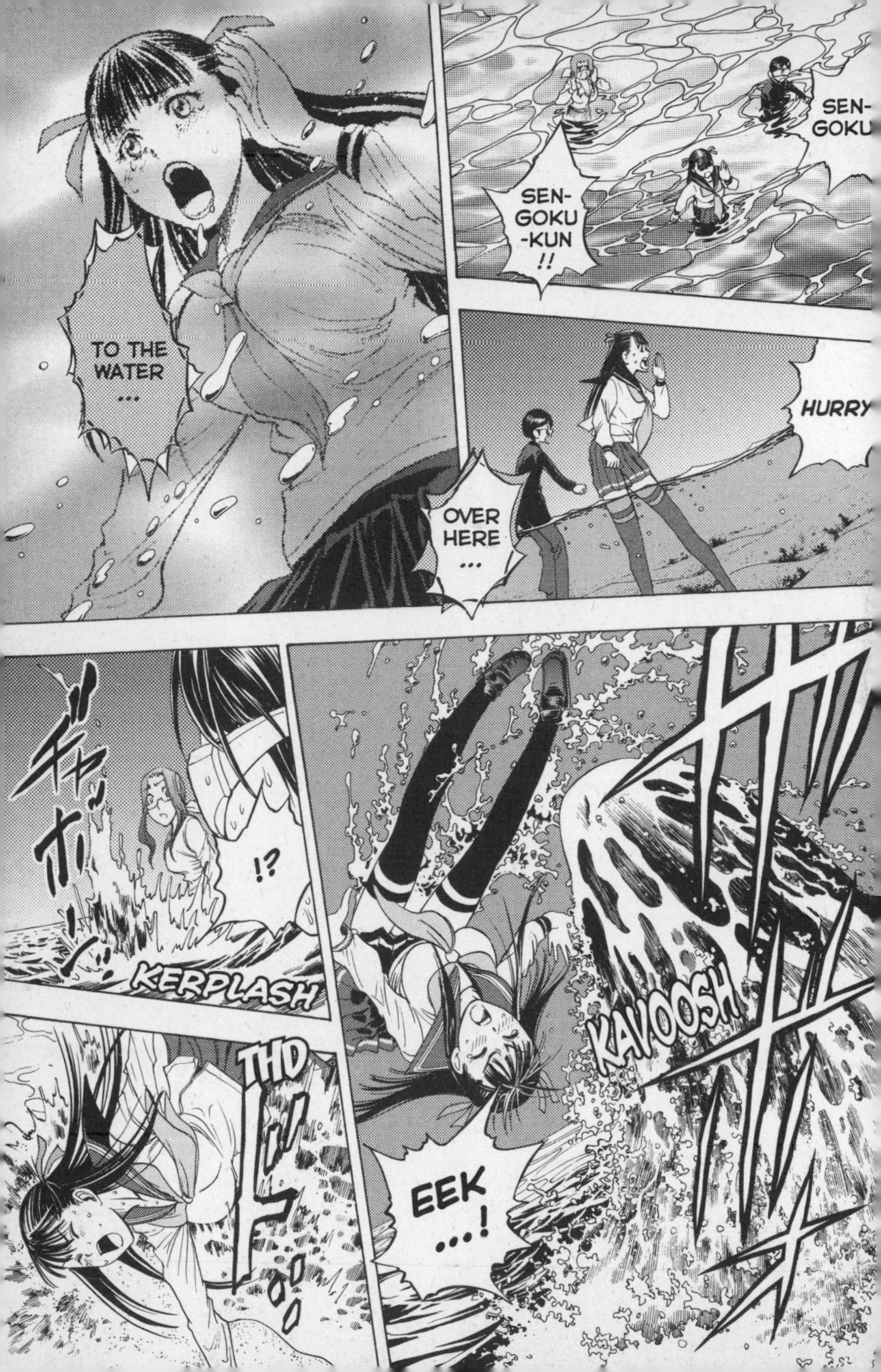
SEN-GOKU
SEN-GOKU-KUN!!
HURRY
OVER HERE...
TO THE WATER...
KAVOOSH
EEK...!
!?
KERPLASH
THD

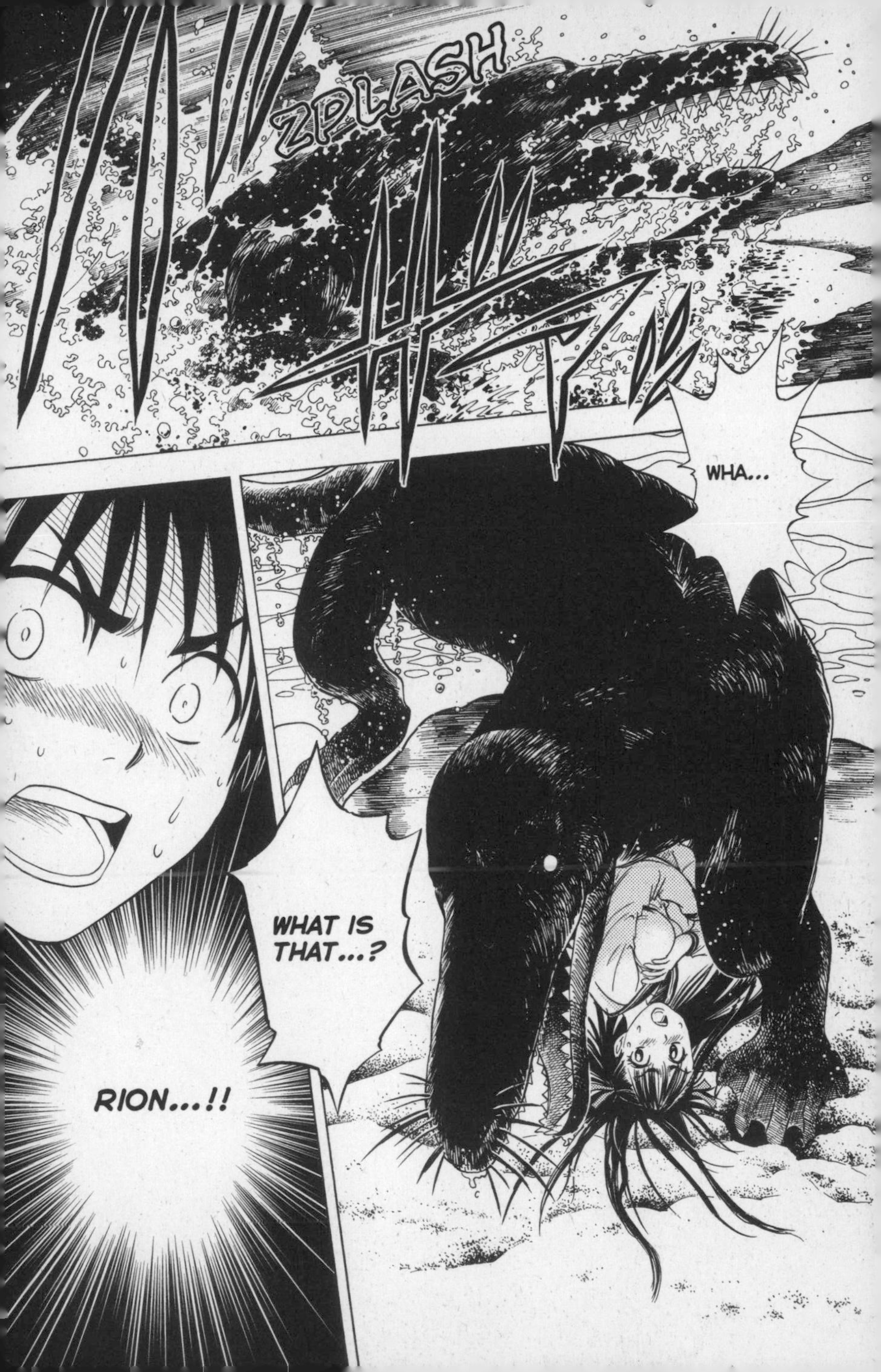
ZPLASH
WHA...
WHAT IS THAT...?
RION...!!

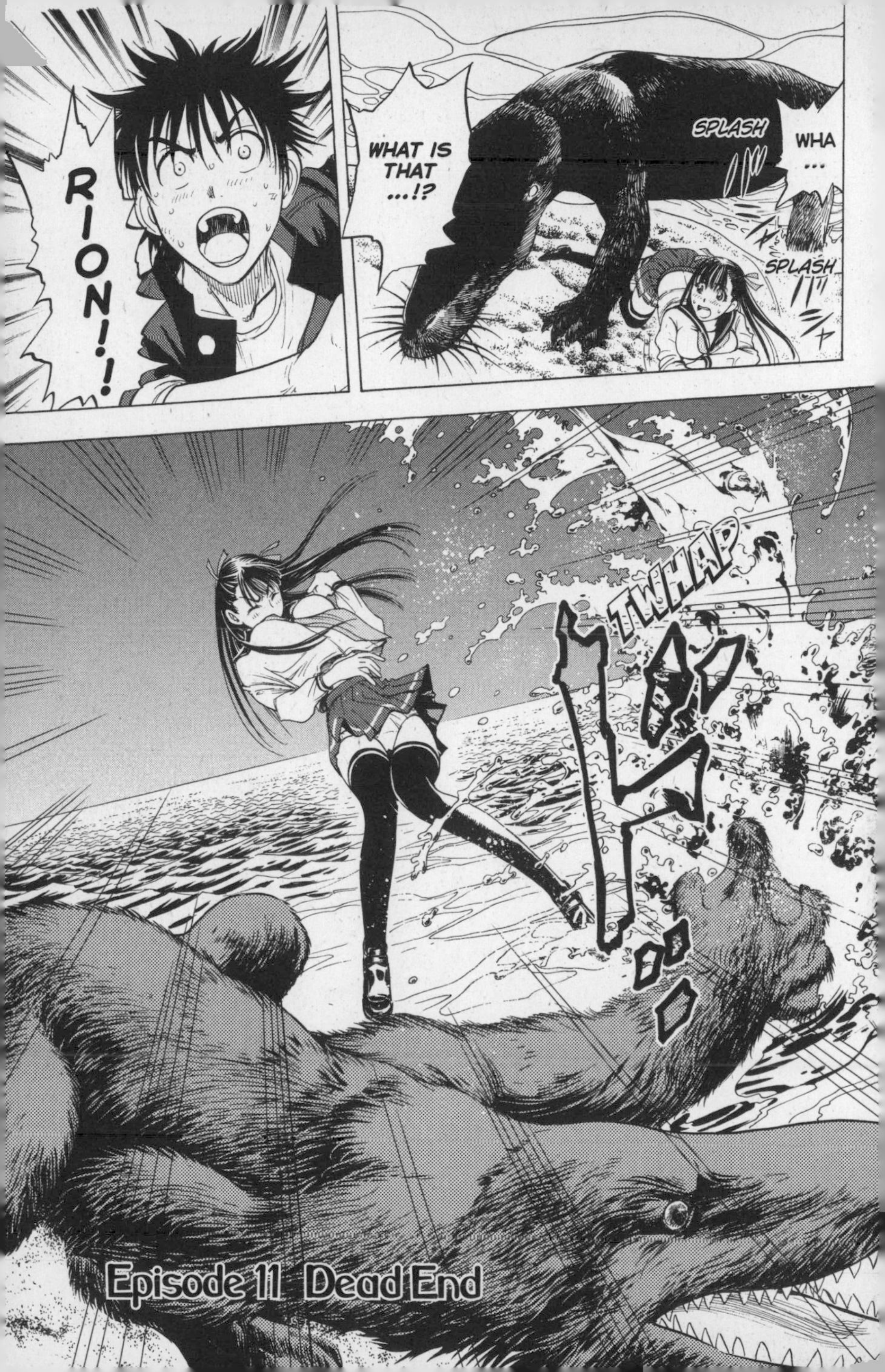
WHA ...
SPLASH
SPLASH
WHAT IS THAT ...!?
RION!!
TWHAP
Episode 11 Dead End

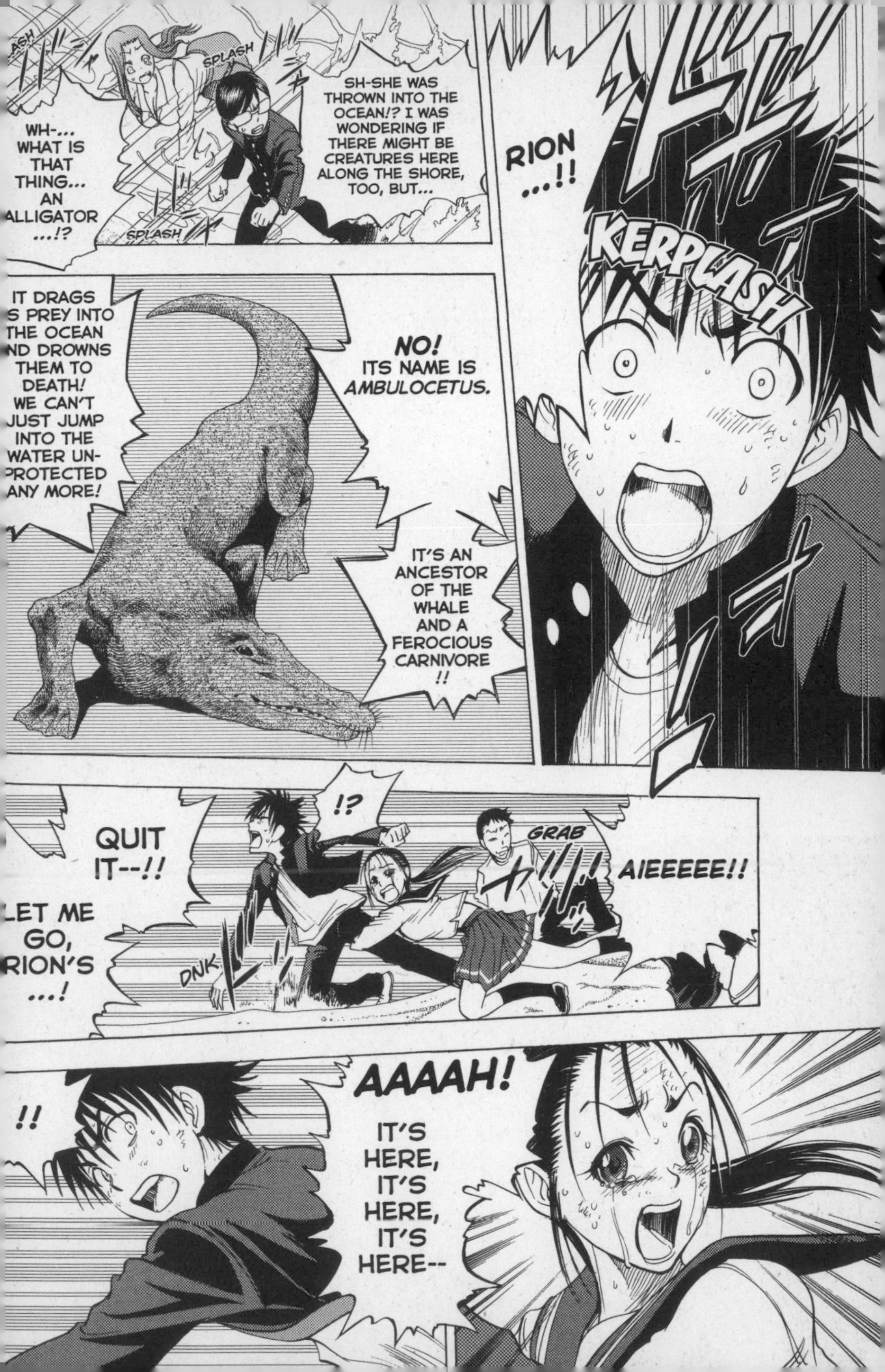
RION ...!!
KERPLASH
SPLASH
SH-SHE WAS THROWN INTO THE OCEAN!? I WAS WONDERING IF THERE MIGHT BE CREATURES HERE ALONG THE SHORE, TOO, BUT...
WH-... WHAT IS THAT THING... AN ALLIGATOR ...!?
SPLASH
NO! ITS NAME IS AMBULOCETUS.
IT'S AN ANCESTOR OF THE WHALE AND A FEROCIOUS CARNIVORE !!
IT DRAGS S PREY INTO THE OCEAN ND DROWNS THEM TO DEATH! WE CAN'T JUST JUMP INTO THE WATER UN-PROTECTED ANY MORE!
AIEEEEE!!
GRAB
!?
QUIT IT--!!
LET ME GO, RION'S ...!
DNK
AAAAH!
IT'S HERE, IT'S HERE, IT'S HERE--
!!

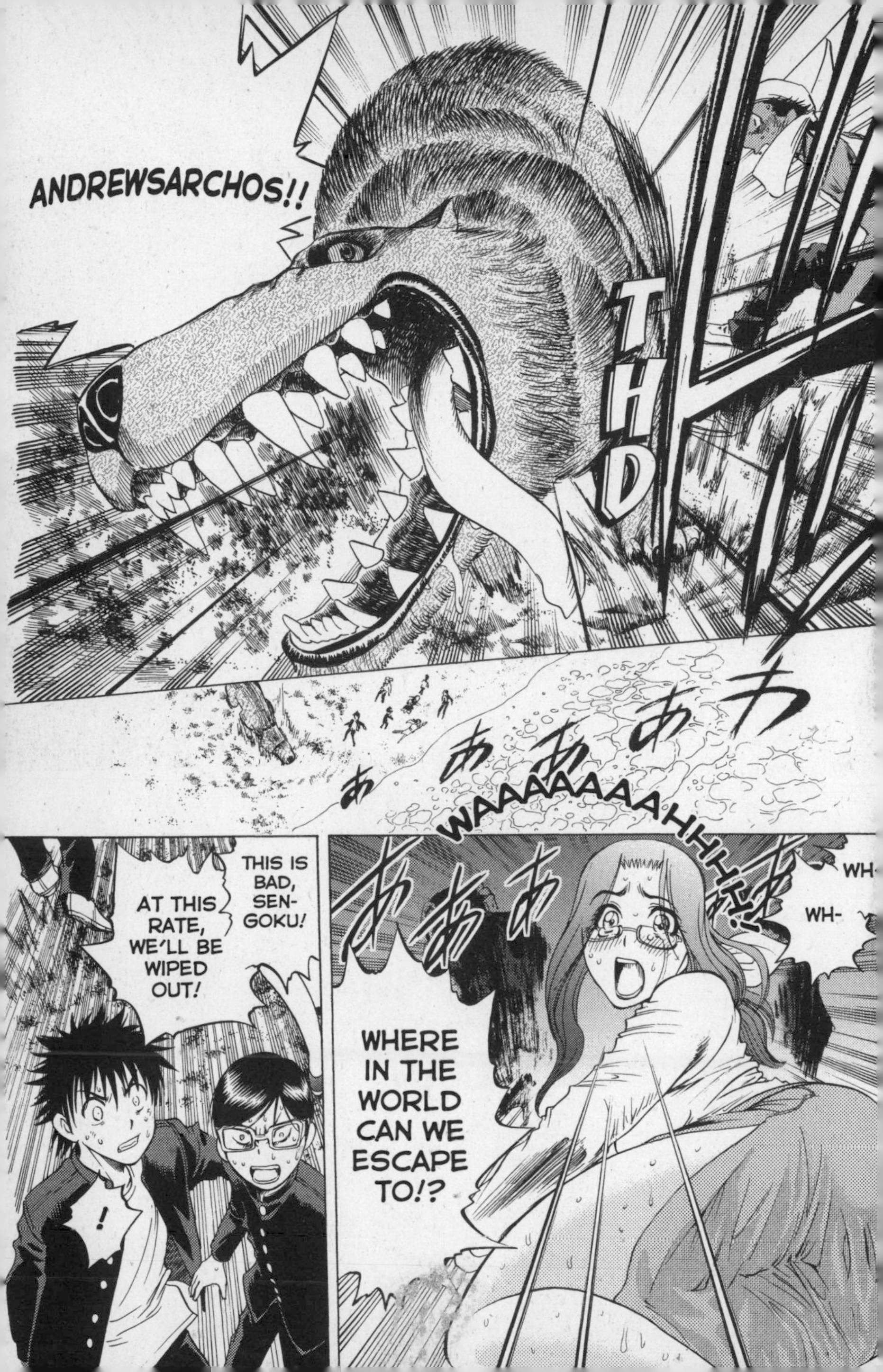
ANDREWSARCHOS!!
THD
あああああ
WAAAAAAAHHHH!!
あああ
WH-
WH-
WHERE IN THE WORLD CAN WE ESCAPE TO!?
THIS IS BAD, SENGOKU!
AT THIS RATE, WE'LL BE WIPED OUT!
!

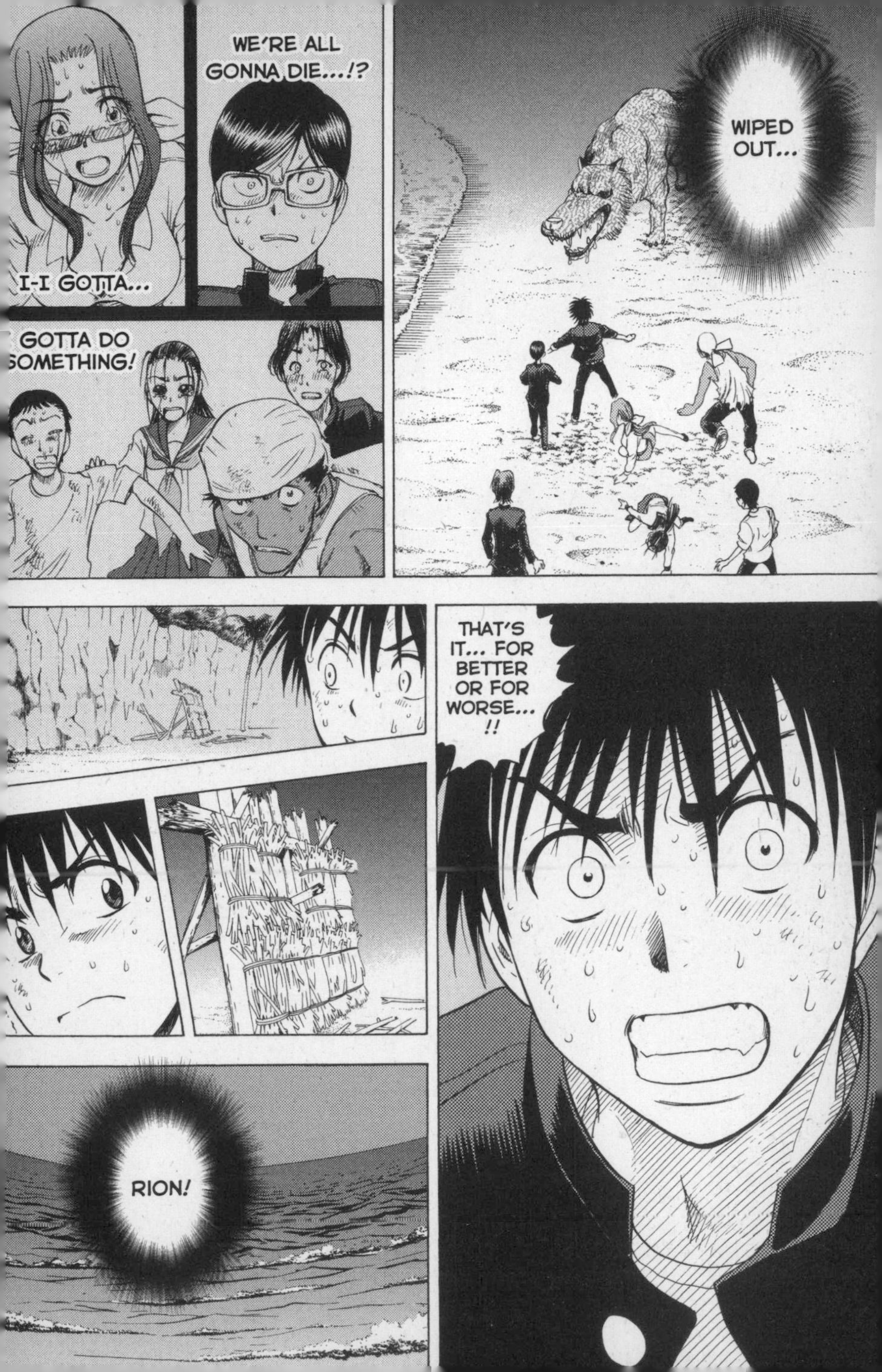
WIPED OUT...
WE'RE ALL GONNA DIE...!?
I-I GOTTA...
GOTTA DO SOMETHING!
THAT'S IT... FOR BETTER OR FOR WORSE... !!
RION!

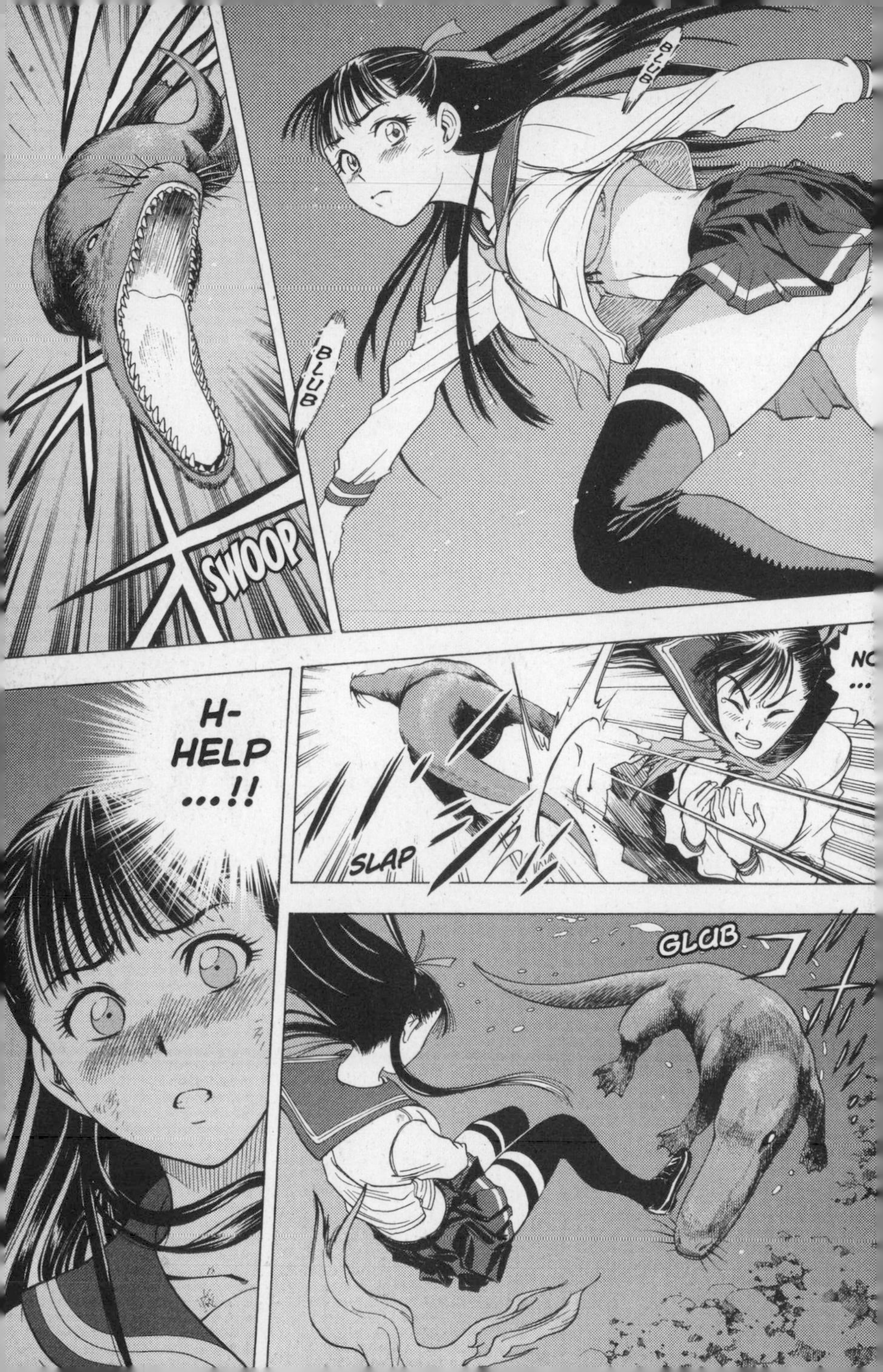
BLUB
BLUB
SWOOP
NO ...
SLAP
GLUB
H-HELP ...!!

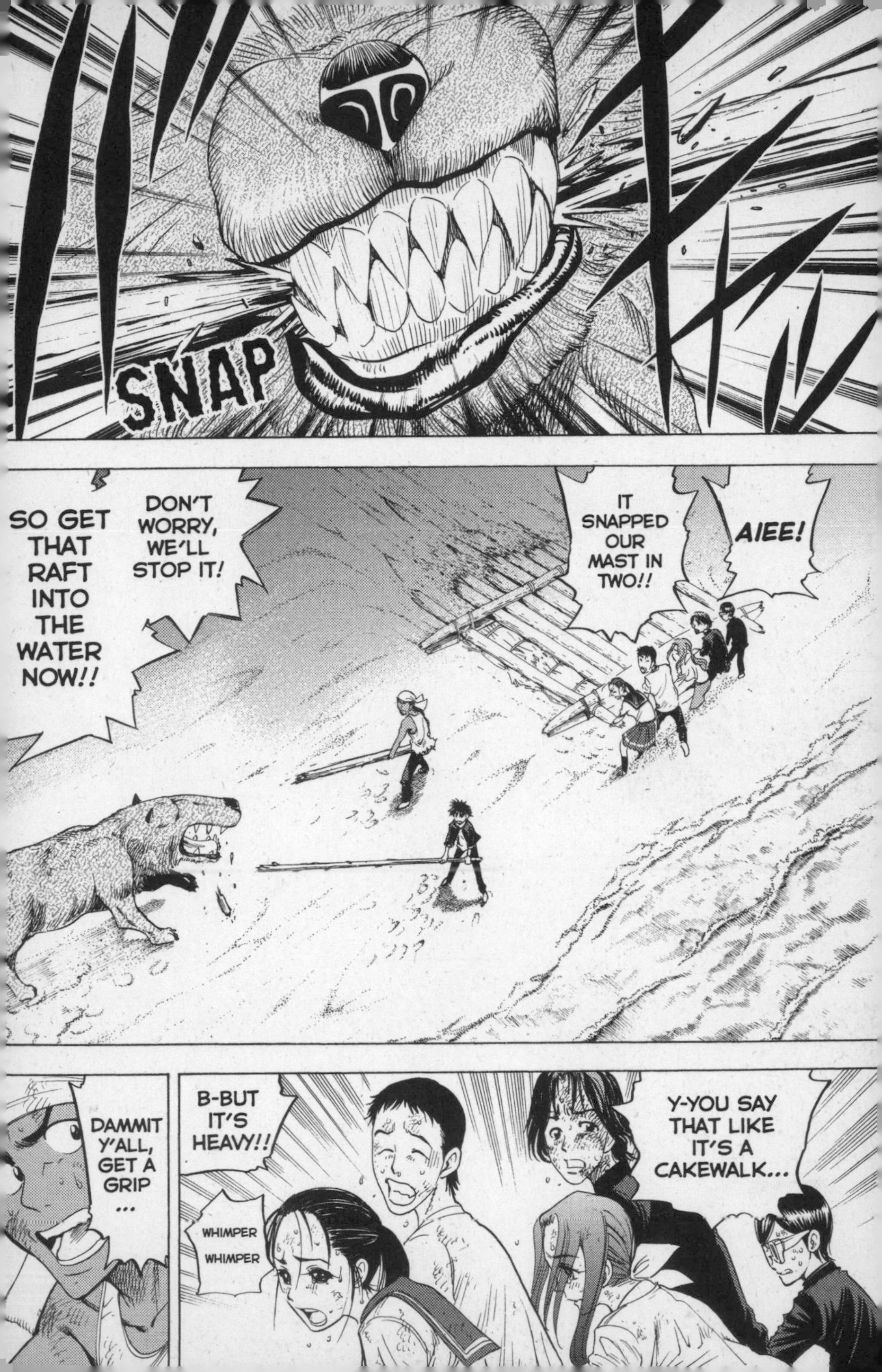
SNAP
AIEE!
IT SNAPPED OUR MAST IN TWO!!
DON'T WORRY, WE'LL STOP IT!
SO GET THAT RAFT INTO THE WATER NOW!!
Y-YOU SAY THAT LIKE IT'S A CAKEWALK...
B-BUT IT'S HEAVY!!
WHIMPER WHIMPER
DAMMIT Y'ALL, GET A GRIP ...

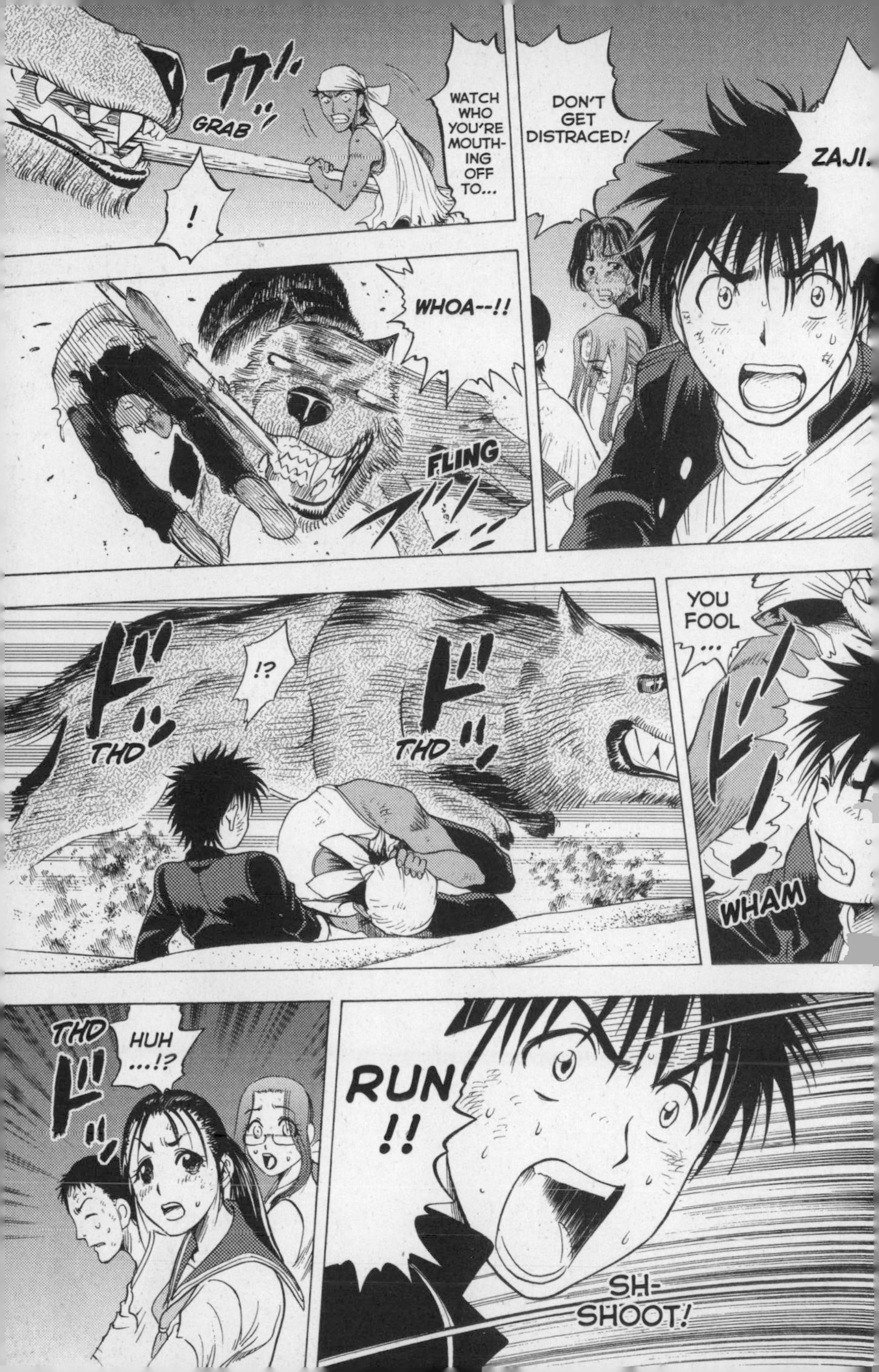
ZAJI.
DON'T GET DISTRACTED!
GRAB
WATCH WHO YOU'RE MOUTHING OFF TO...
!
WHOA--!!
FLING
YOU FOOL ...
WHAM
THD
!?
THD
RUN !!
SH-SHOOT!
HUH ...!?
THD

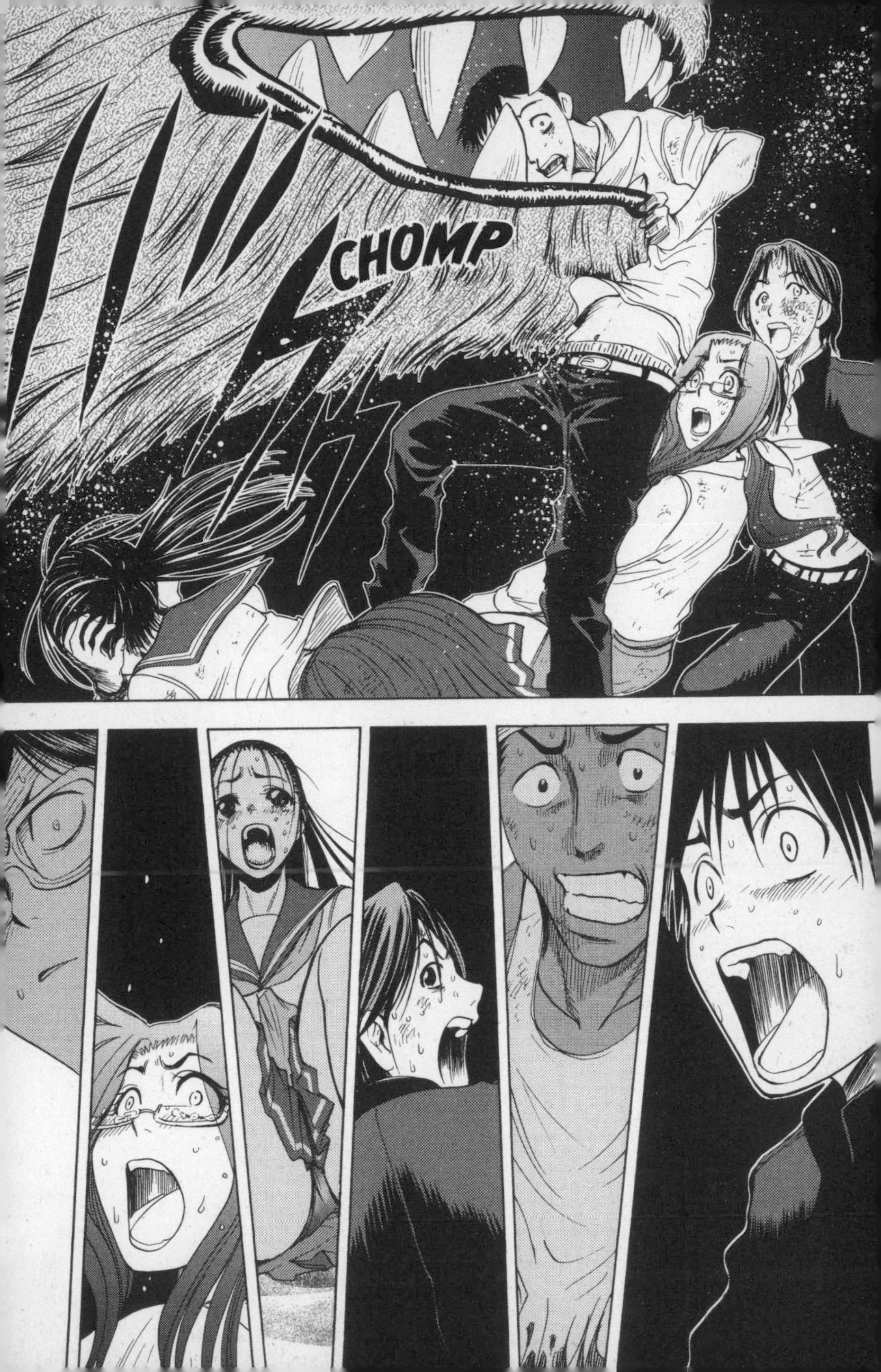
CHOMP

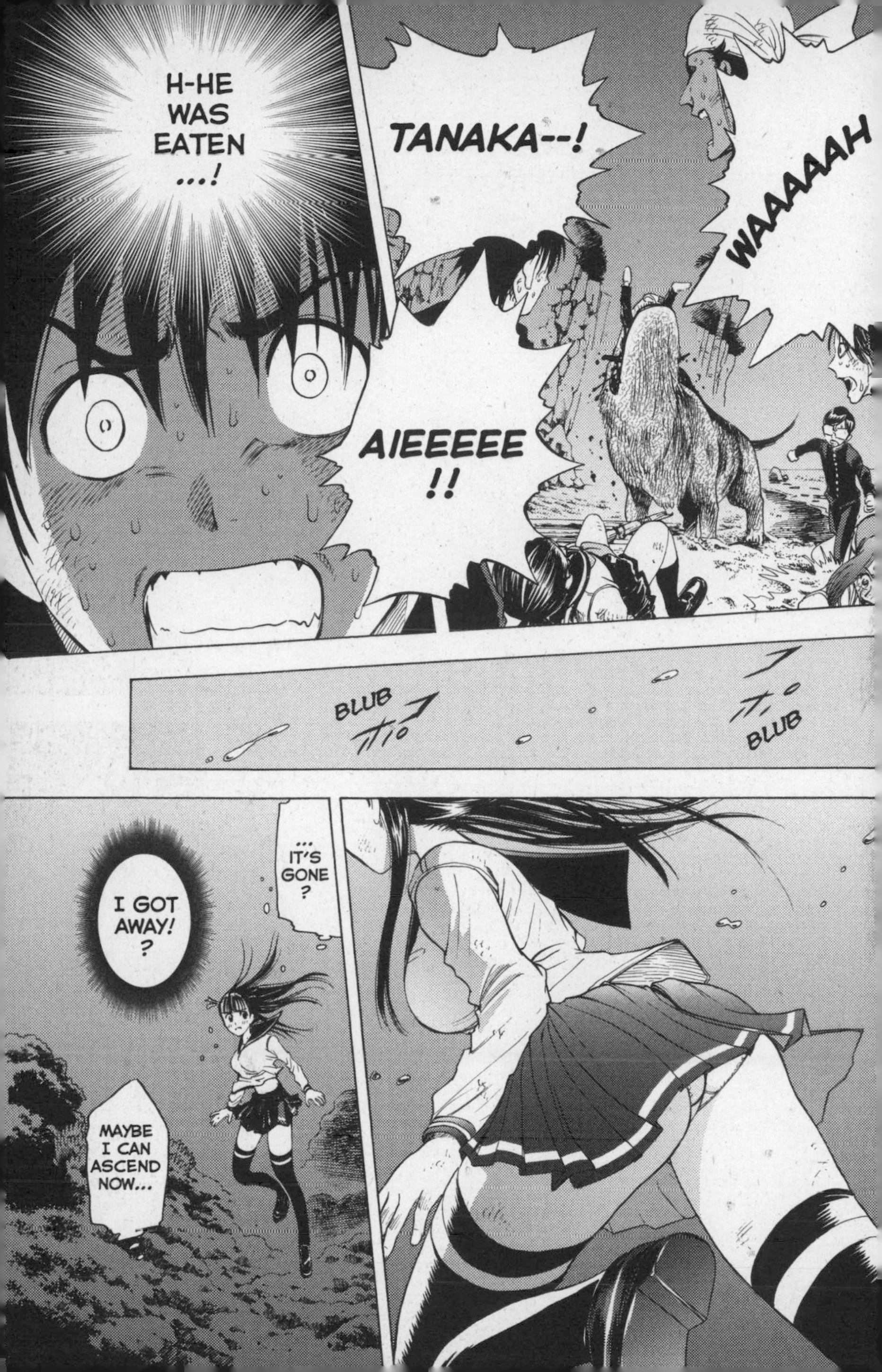

TANAKA--!
WAAAAAH
AIEEEEE !!
H-HE WAS EATEN ...!
BLUB
BLUB
... IT'S GONE ?
I GOT AWAY! ?
MAYBE I CAN ASCEND NOW...

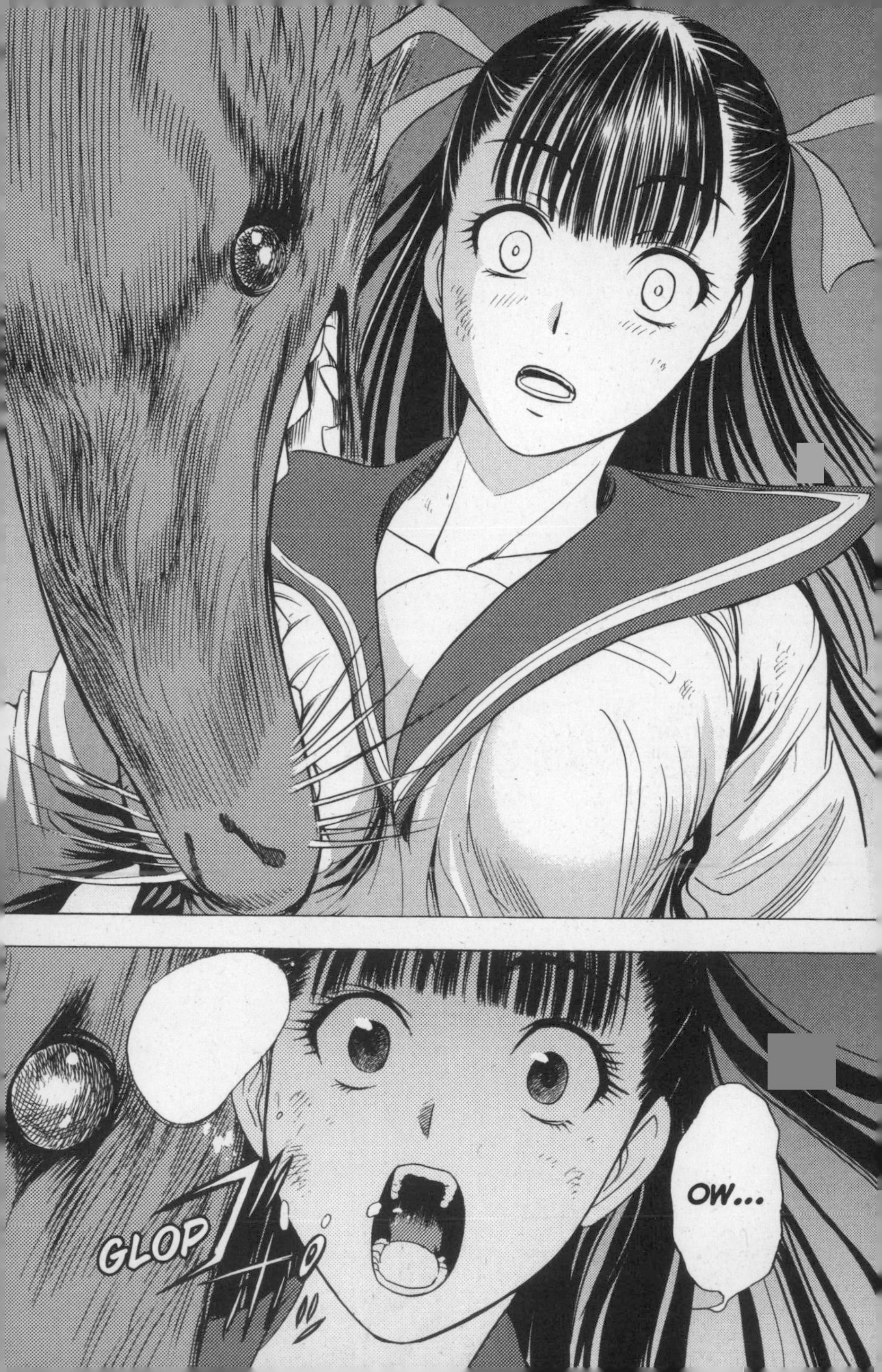
OW...
GLOP

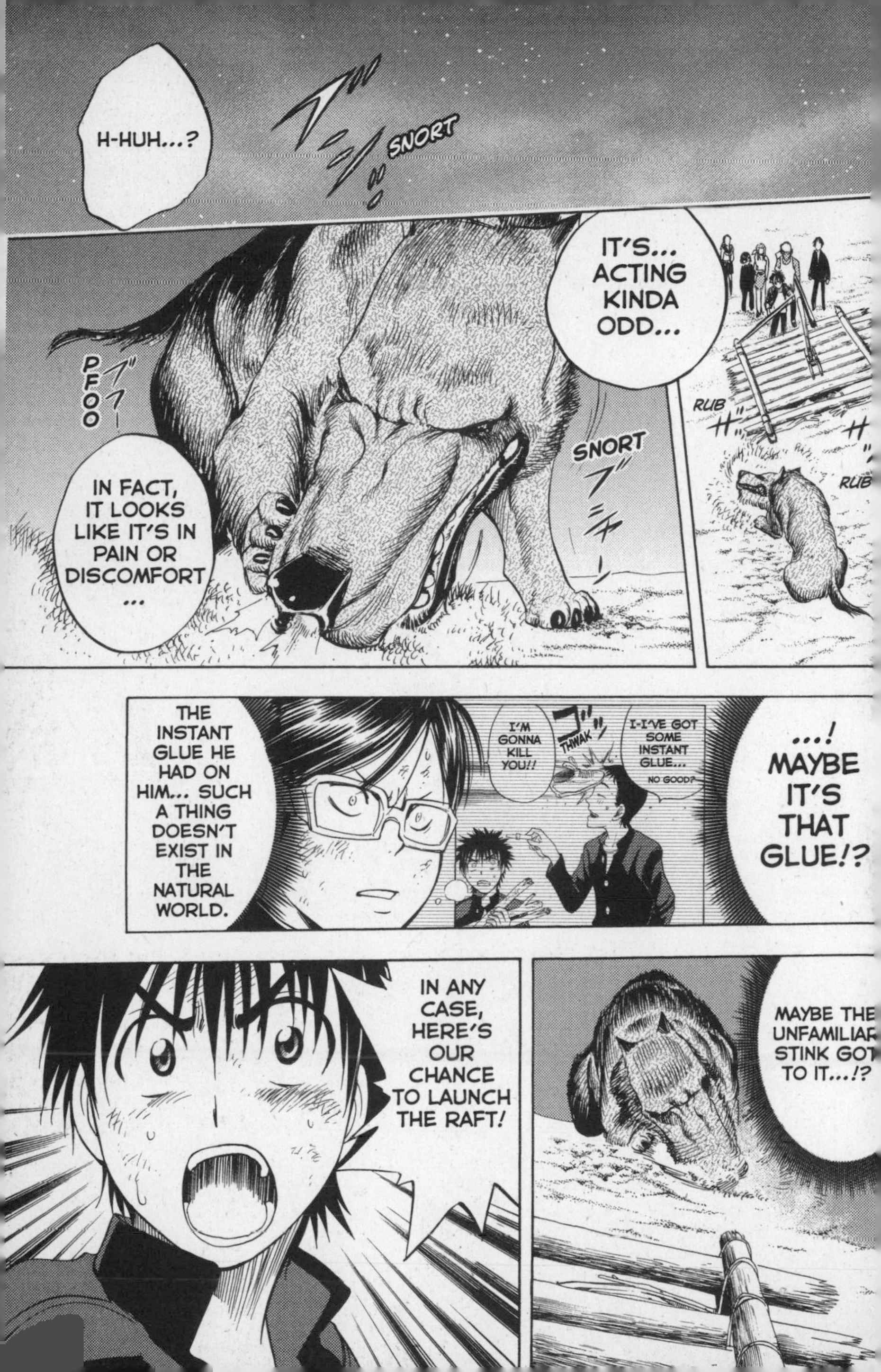
H-HUH...?
SNORT
RUB
RUB
IT'S... ACTING KINDA ODD...
SNORT
PFOO
IN FACT, IT LOOKS LIKE IT'S IN PAIN OR DISCOMFORT ...
...! MAYBE IT'S THAT GLUE!?
I-I'VE GOT SOME INSTANT GLUE...
NO GOOD?
THWAK
I'M GONNA KILL YOU!!
THE INSTANT GLUE HE HAD ON HIM... SUCH A THING DOESN'T EXIST IN THE NATURAL WORLD.
MAYBE THE UNFAMILIAR STINK GOT TO IT...!?
IN ANY CASE, HERE'S OUR CHANCE TO LAUNCH THE RAFT!

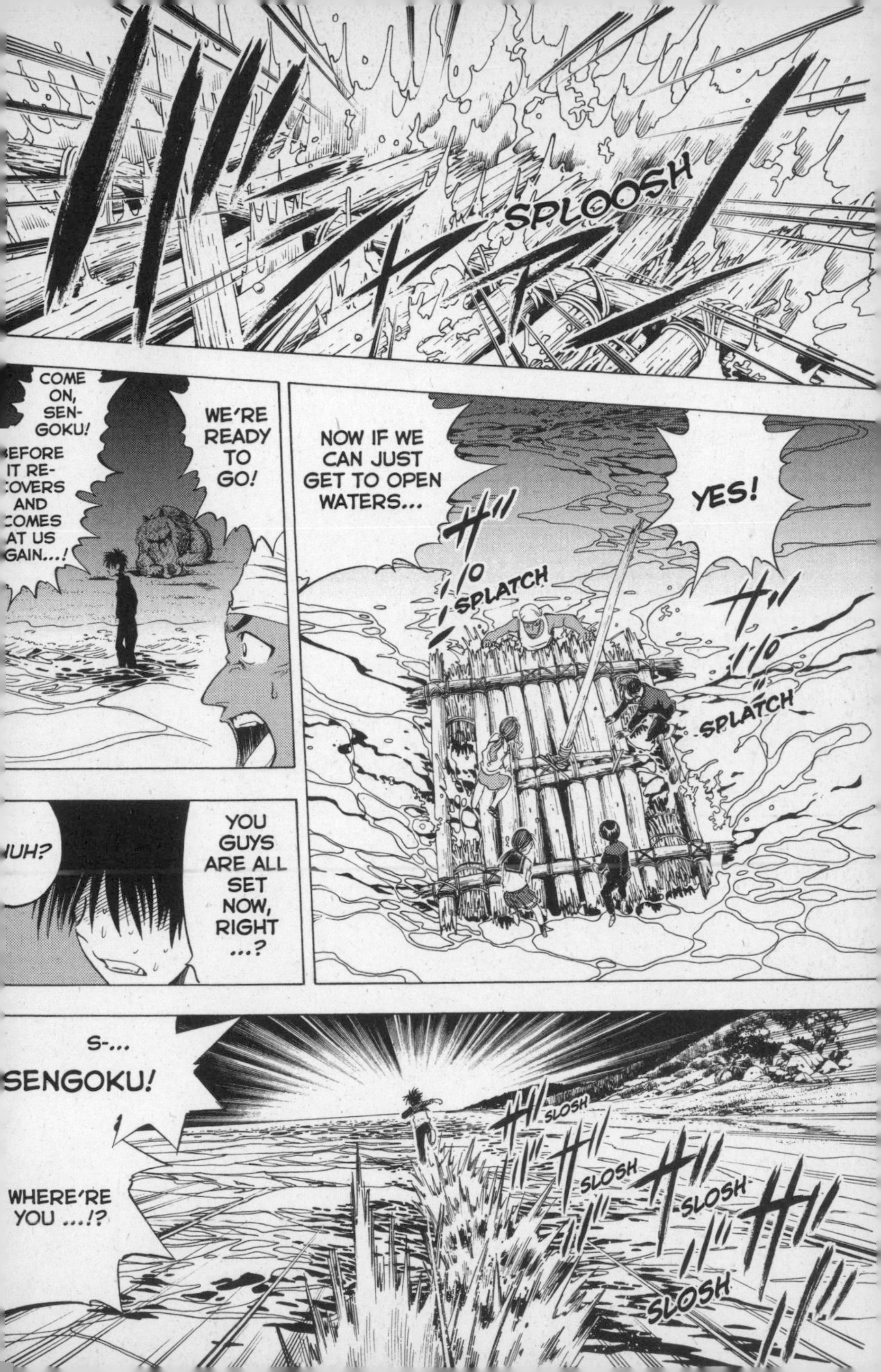
SPLOOSH
NOW IF WE CAN JUST GET TO OPEN WATERS...
YES!
SPLATCH
SPLATCH
WE'RE READY TO GO!
COME ON, SEN-GOKU!
EFORE IT RE-COVERS AND COMES AT US GAIN...!
YOU GUYS ARE ALL SET NOW, RIGHT ...?
UH?
S-...
SENGOKU!
WHERE'RE YOU ...!?
SLOSH
SLOSH
SLOSH
SLOSH

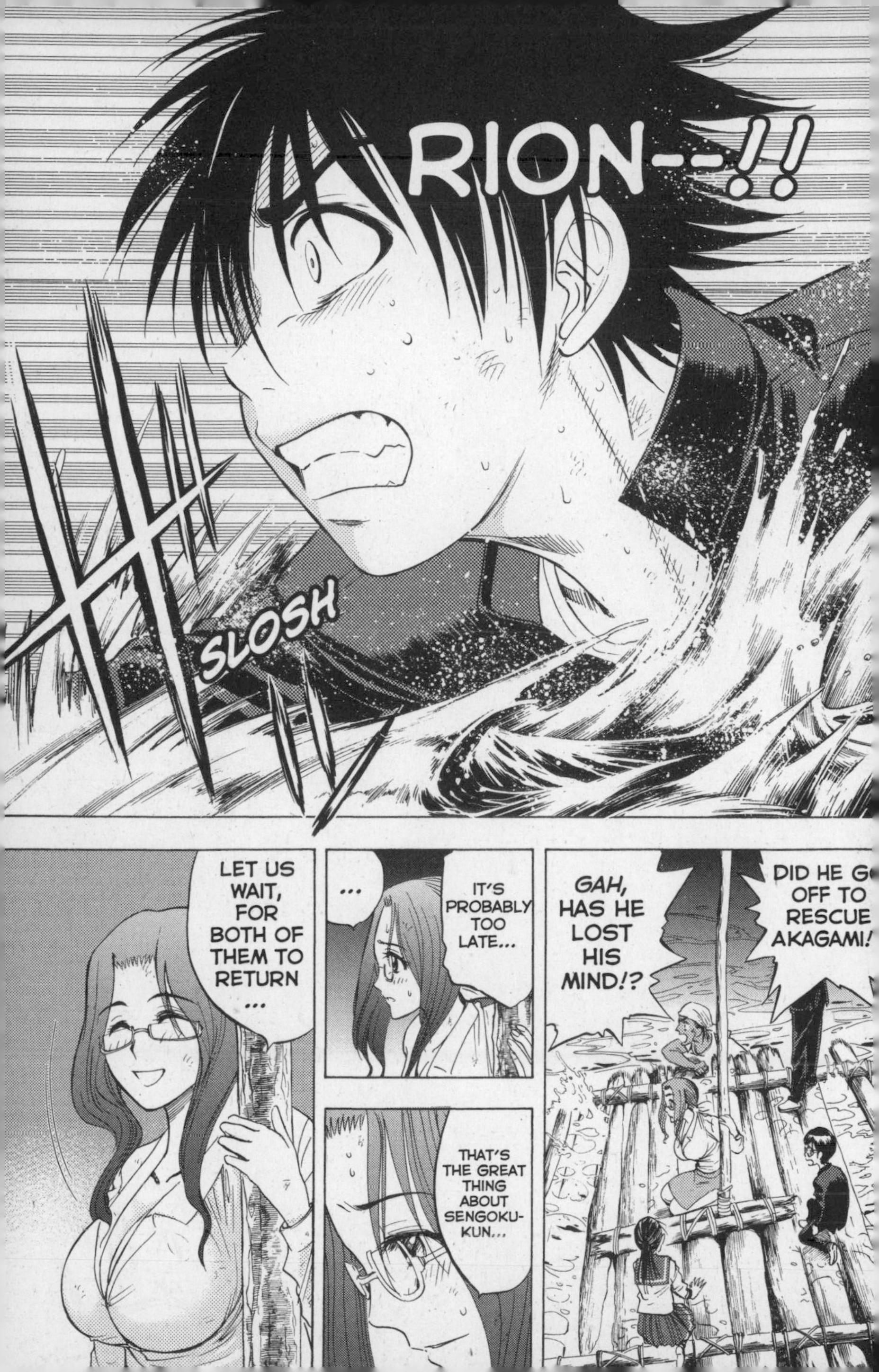
RION--!!
SLOSH
DID HE GO OFF TO RESCUE AKAGAMI!
GAH, HAS HE LOST HIS MIND!?
IT'S PROBABLY TOO LATE...
...
THAT'S THE GREAT THING ABOUT SENGOKU-KUN...
LET US WAIT, FOR BOTH OF THEM TO RETURN ...

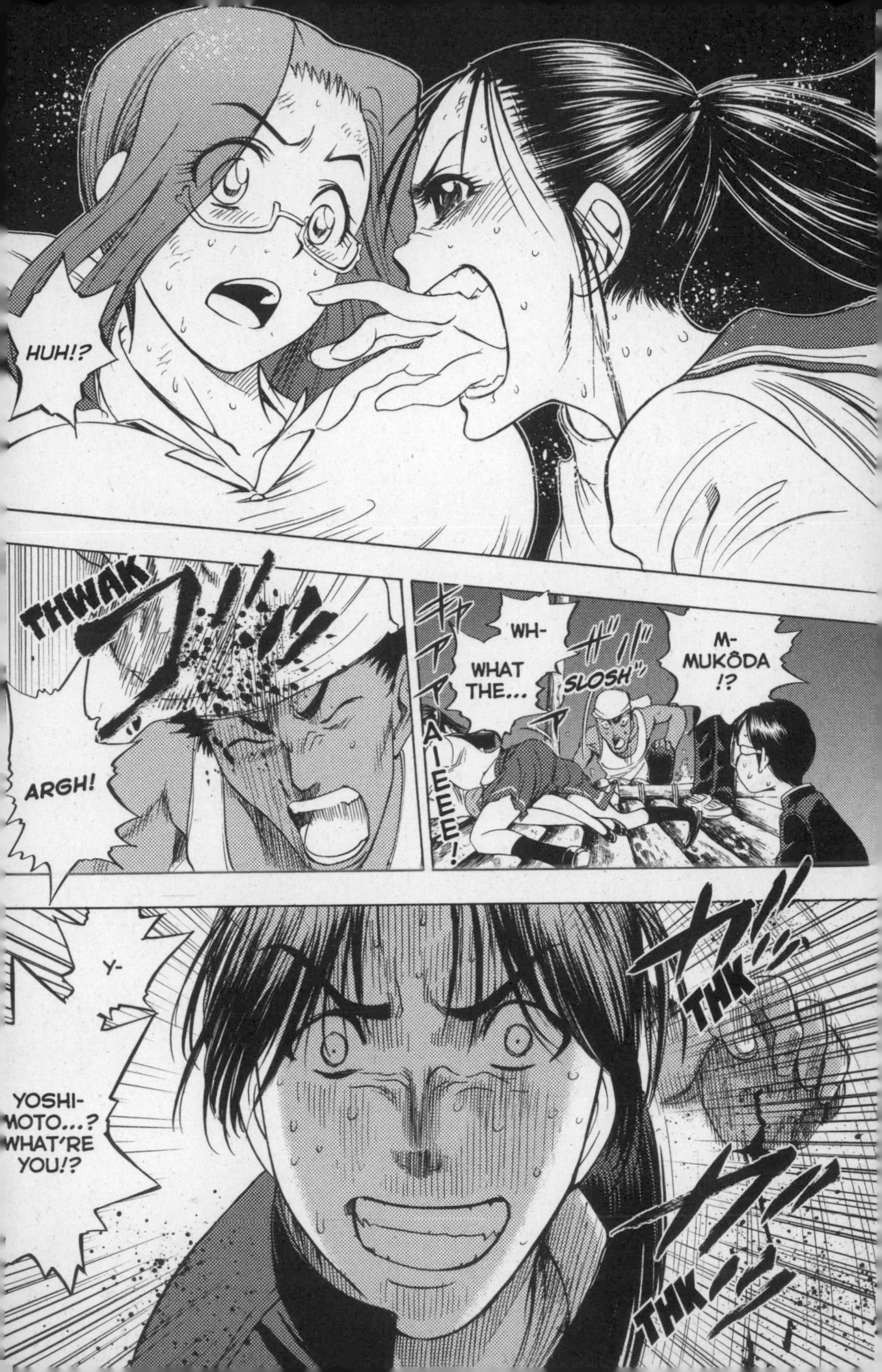
HUH!?
M-MUKÔDA!?
SLOSH
WH-WHAT THE...
AIEEE!
THWAK
ARGH!
THK
Y-
YOSHIMOTO...? WHAT'RE YOU!?
THK

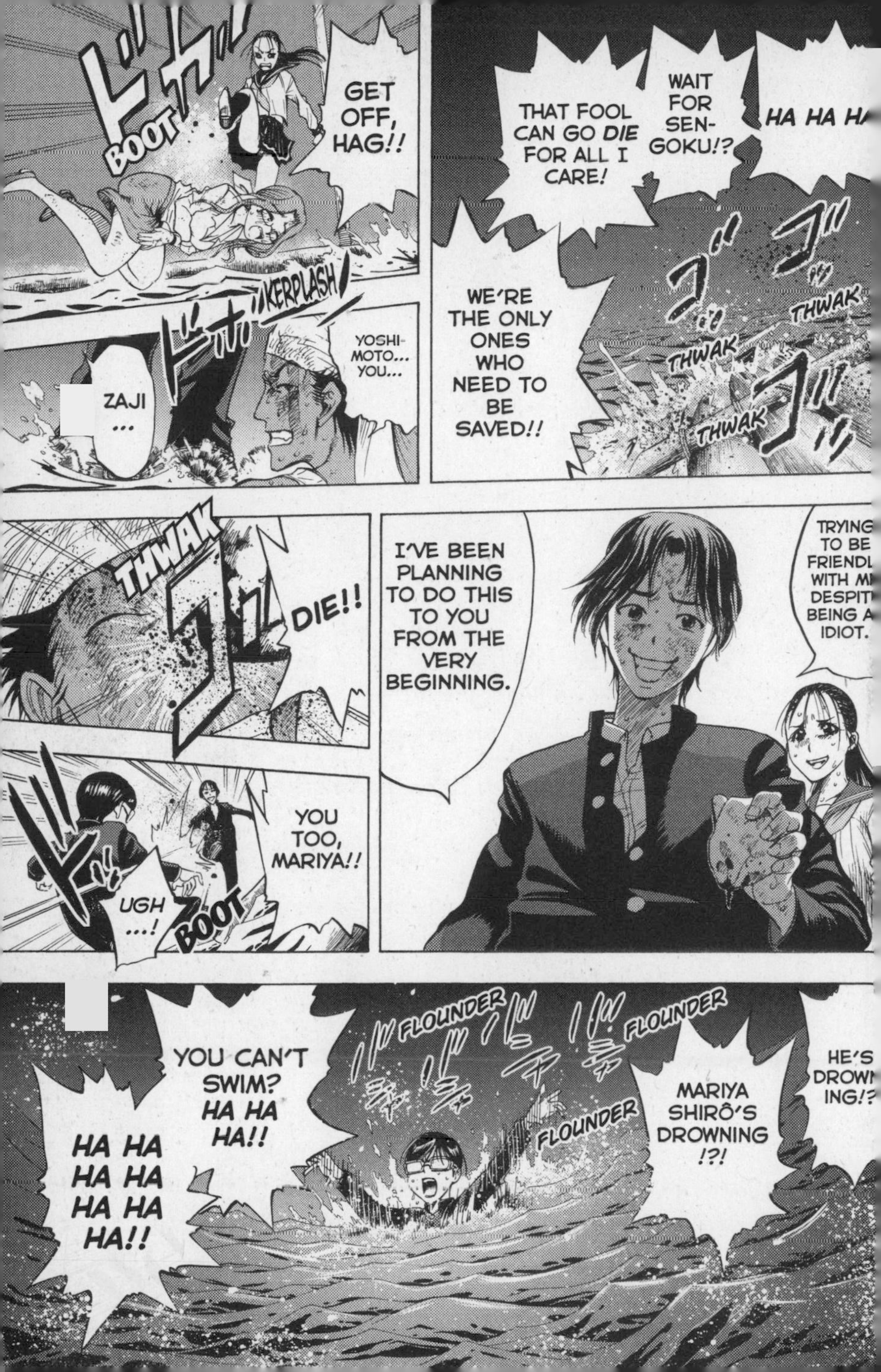
HA HA HA
WAIT FOR SEN-GOKU!?
THAT FOOL CAN GO DIE FOR ALL I CARE!
WE'RE THE ONLY ONES WHO NEED TO BE SAVED!!
THWAK
THWAK
THWAK
GET OFF, HAG!!
BOOT
KERPLASH
YOSHI-MOTO... YOU...
ZAJI ...
TRYING TO BE FRIENDL WITH M DESPIT BEING A IDIOT.
I'VE BEEN PLANNING TO DO THIS TO YOU FROM THE VERY BEGINNING.
THWAK
DIE!!
YOU TOO, MARIYA!!
UGH ...!
BOOT
HE'S DROWN ING!?
MARIYA SHIRÔ'S DROWNING !?!
FLOUNDER
FLOUNDER
FLOUNDER
YOU CAN'T SWIM? HA HA HA!!
HA HA HA HA HA HA HA!!

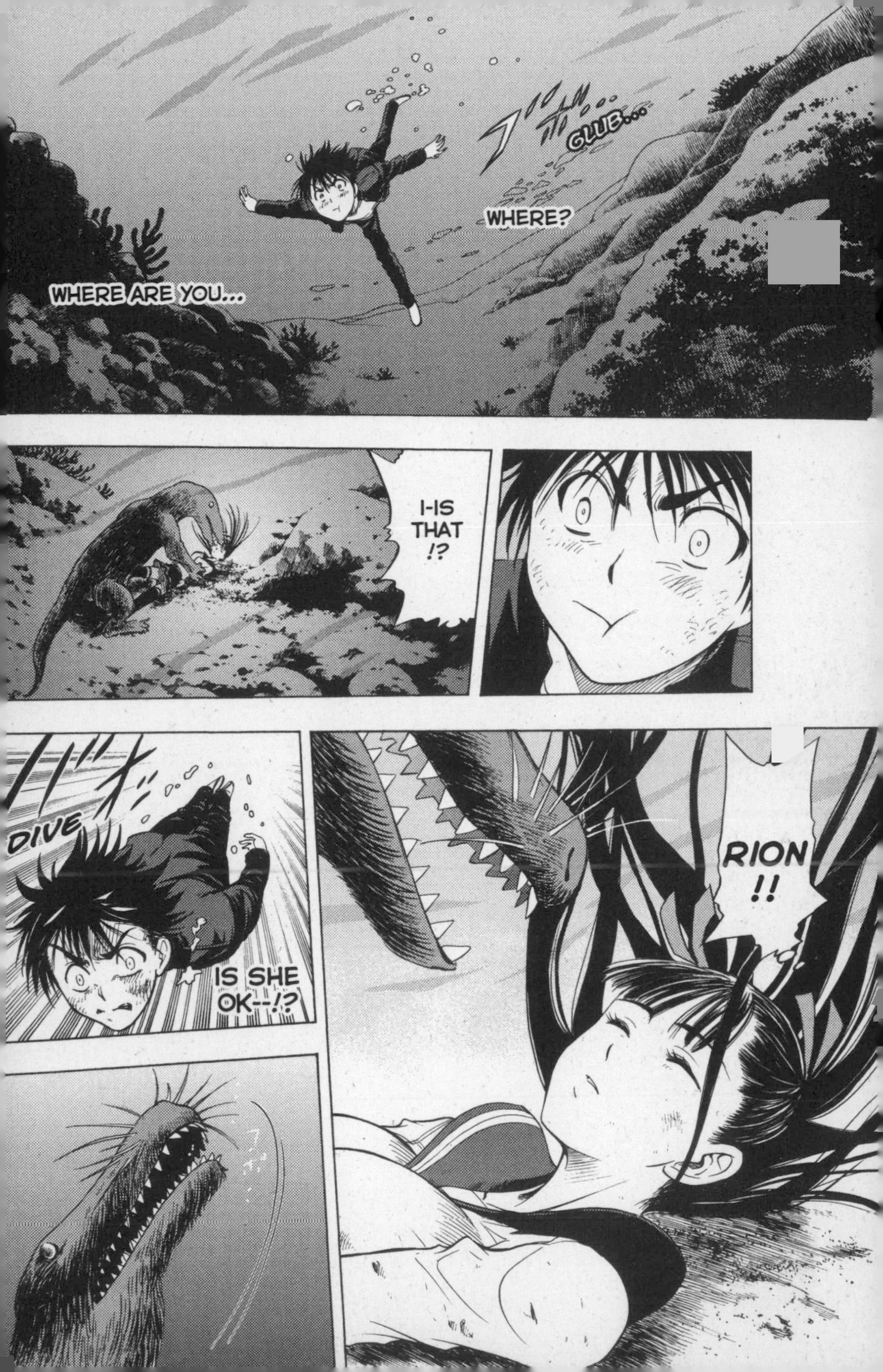
GLUB...
WHERE?
WHERE ARE YOU...
I-IS THAT !?
RION !!
DIVE
IS SHE OK--!?

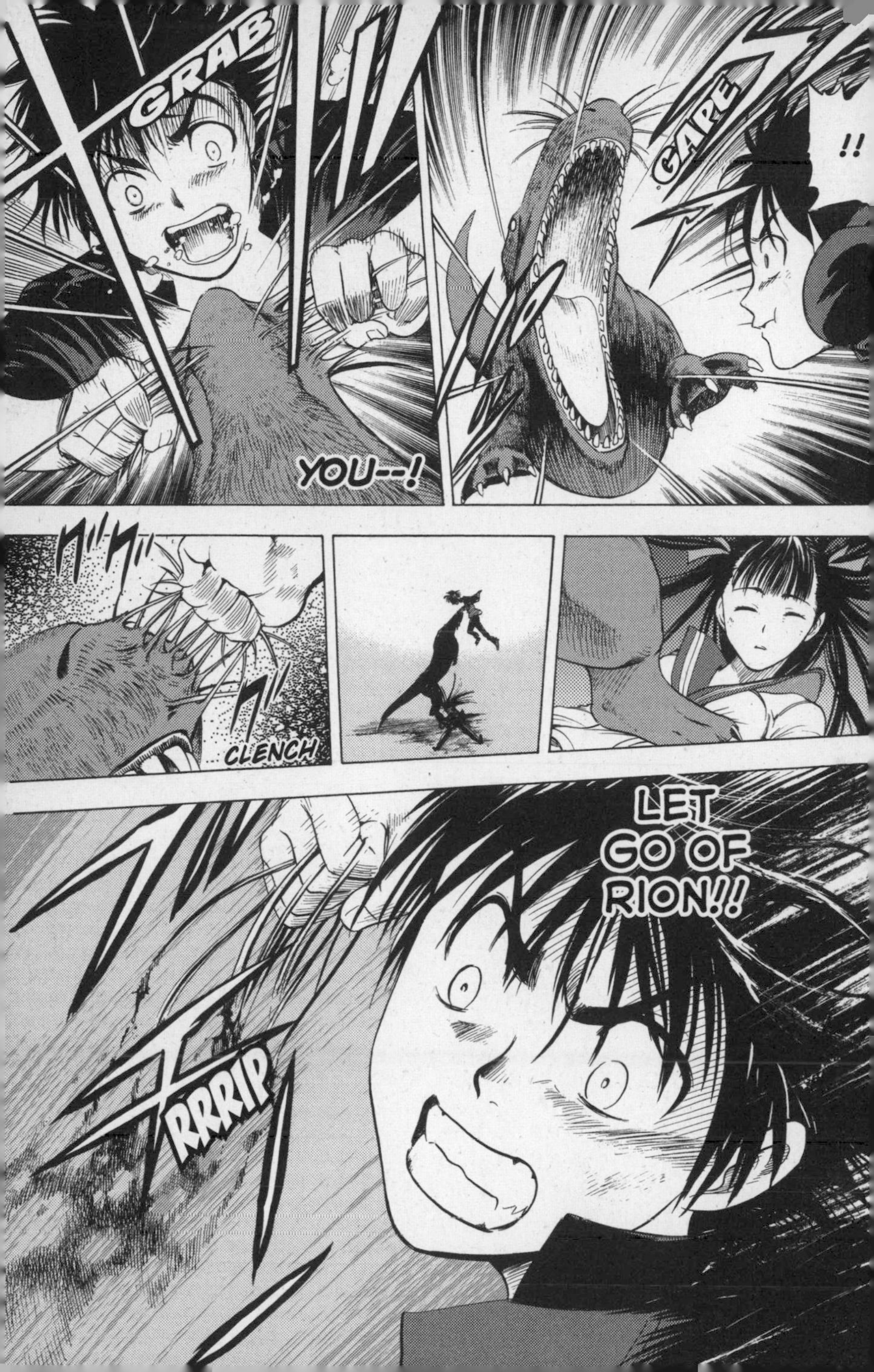
GAPE
!!
GRAB
YOU--!
CLENCH
LET GO OF RION!!
RRRIP

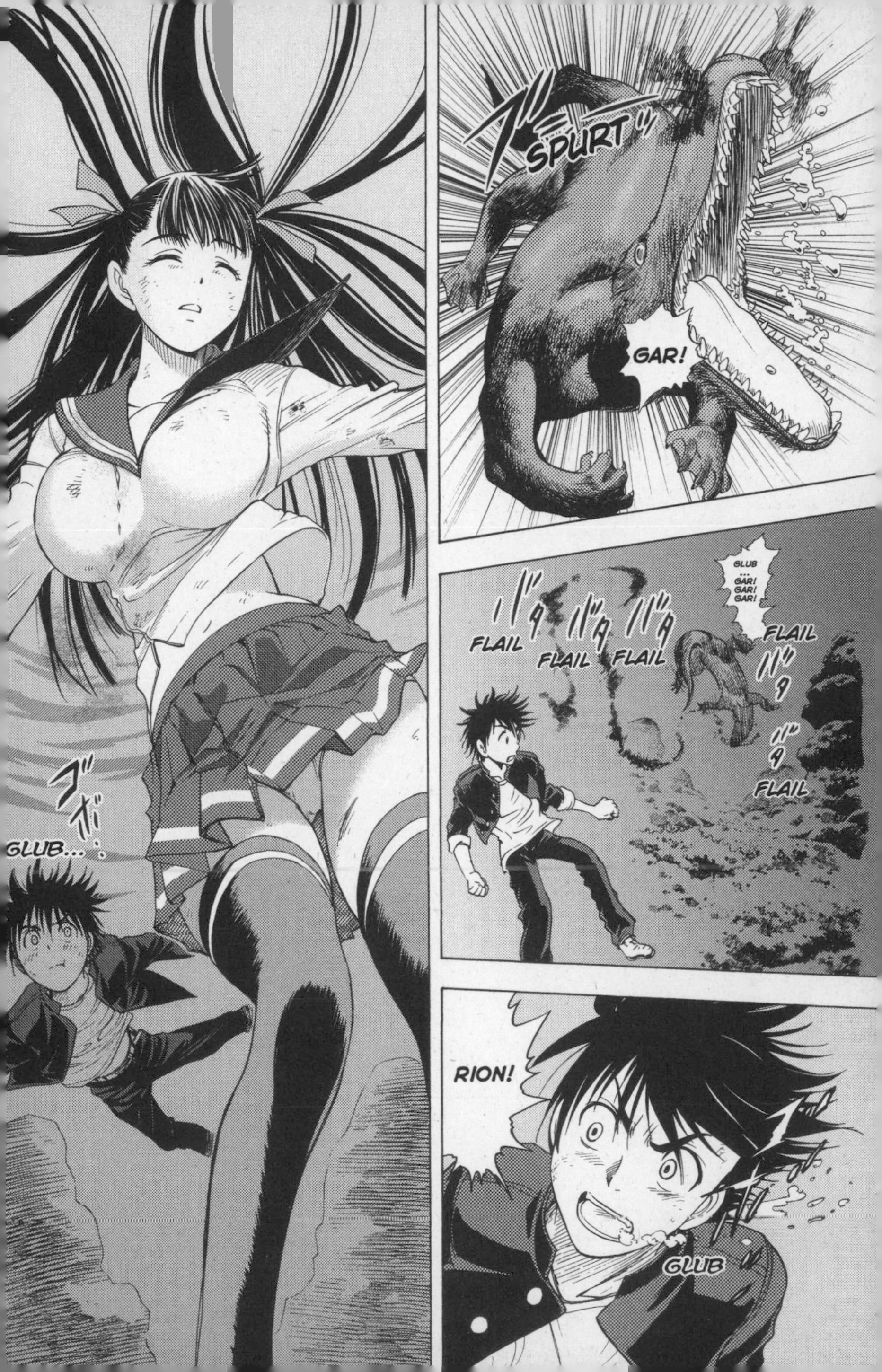
SPURT
GAR!
GLUB ... GAR! GAR! GAR!
FLAIL
FLAIL
FLAIL
FLAIL
FLAIL
RION!
GLUB
GLUB...

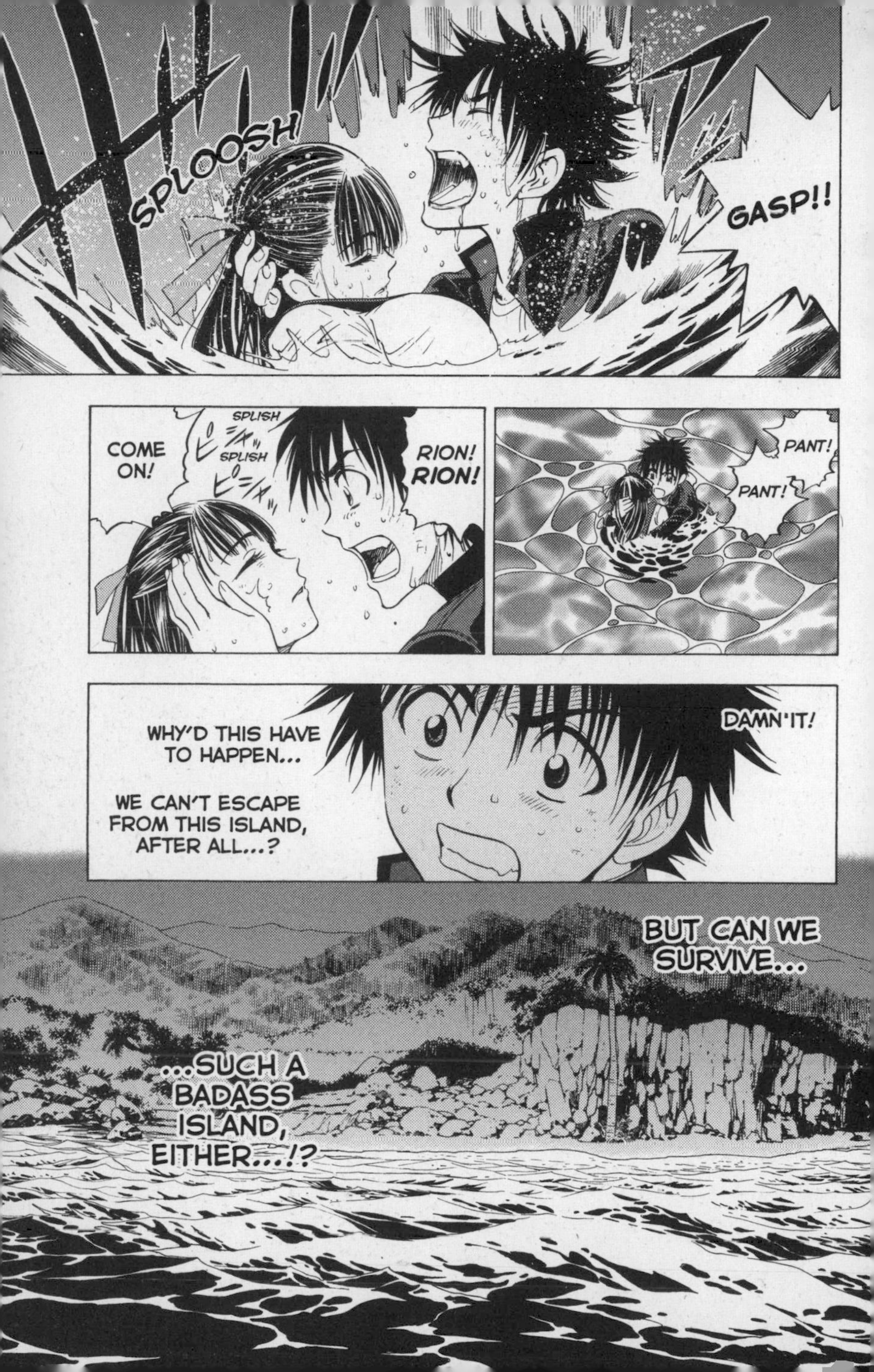
GASP!!
SPLOOSH
PANT!
PANT!
RION! RION!
SPLISH
SPLISH
COME ON!
DAMN'IT!
WHY'D THIS HAVE TO HAPPEN...
WE CAN'T ESCAPE FROM THIS ISLAND, AFTER ALL...?
BUT CAN WE SURVIVE...
...SUCH A BADASS ISLAND, EITHER...!?

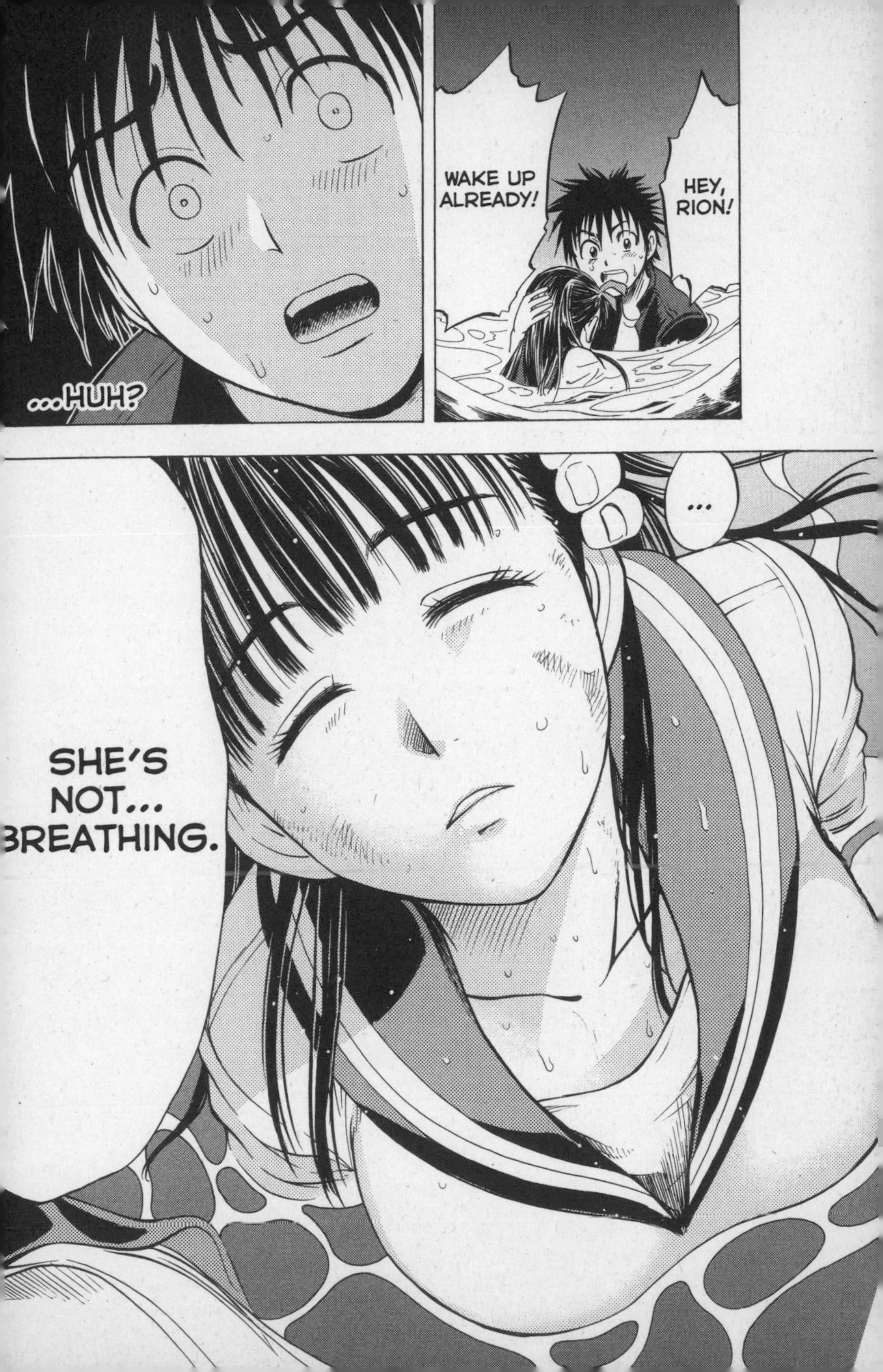
HEY, RION!
WAKE UP ALREADY!
...HUH?
...
SHE'S NOT... BREATHING.

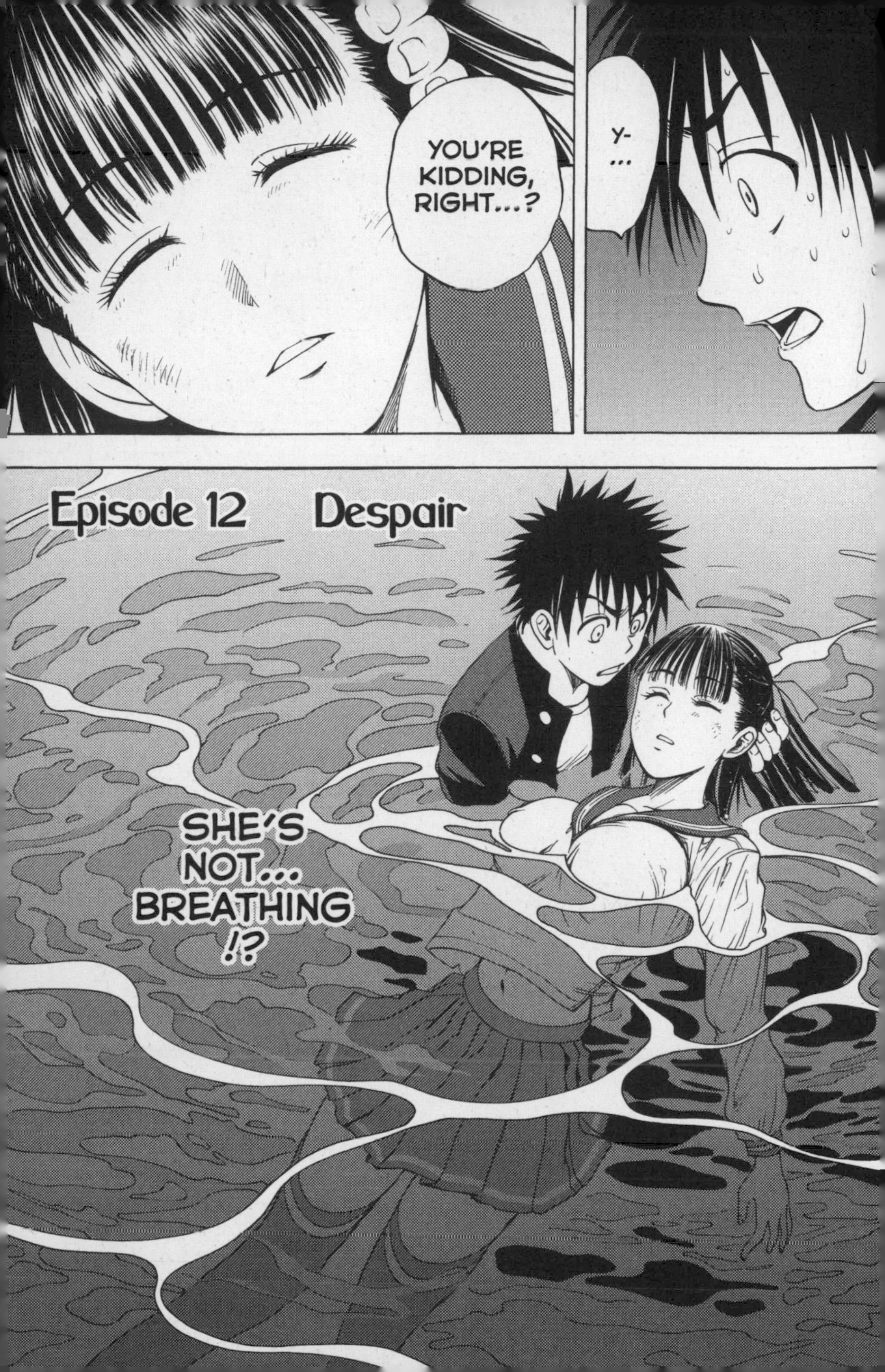
Y-
...
YOU'RE KIDDING, RIGHT...?
Episode 12 Despair
SHE'S NOT... BREATHING !?

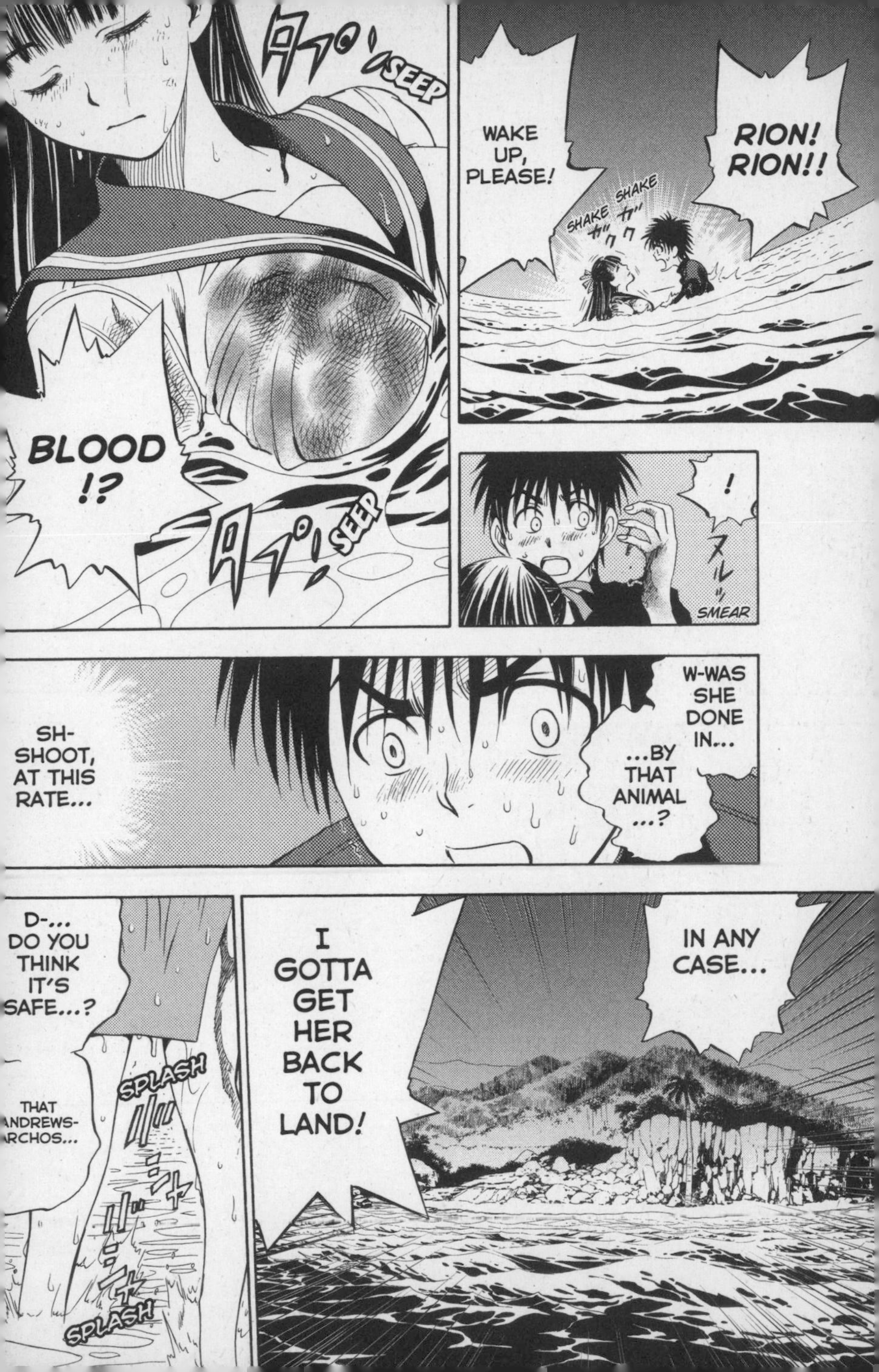
RION! RION!!
WAKE UP, PLEASE!
SHAKE SHAKE
!
SMEAR
SEEP
BLOOD !?
SEEP
W-WAS SHE DONE IN...
...BY THAT ANIMAL ...?
SH- SHOOT, AT THIS RATE...
IN ANY CASE...
I GOTTA GET HER BACK TO LAND!
D-... DO YOU THINK IT'S SAFE...?
THAT ANDREWS- ARCHOS...
SPLASH
SPLASH

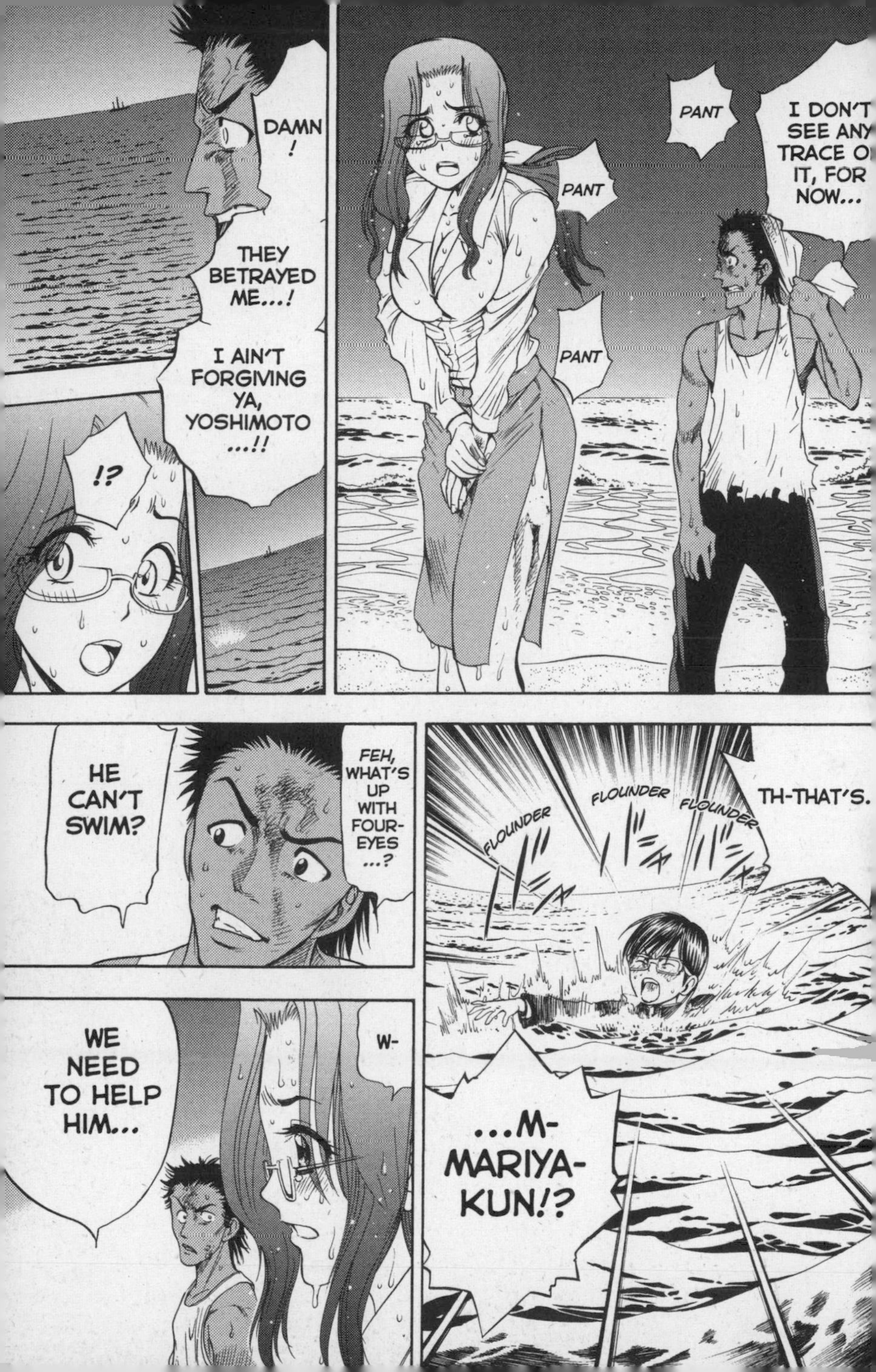
I DON'T SEE ANY TRACE O IT, FOR NOW...
PANT
PANT
PANT
DAMN!
THEY BETRAYED ME...!
I AIN'T FORGIVING YA, YOSHIMOTO...!!
!?
TH-THAT'S.
FLOUNDER
FLOUNDER
FLOUNDER
...M-MARIYA-KUN!?
FEH, WHAT'S UP WITH FOUR-EYES...?
HE CAN'T SWIM?
W-
WE NEED TO HELP HIM...

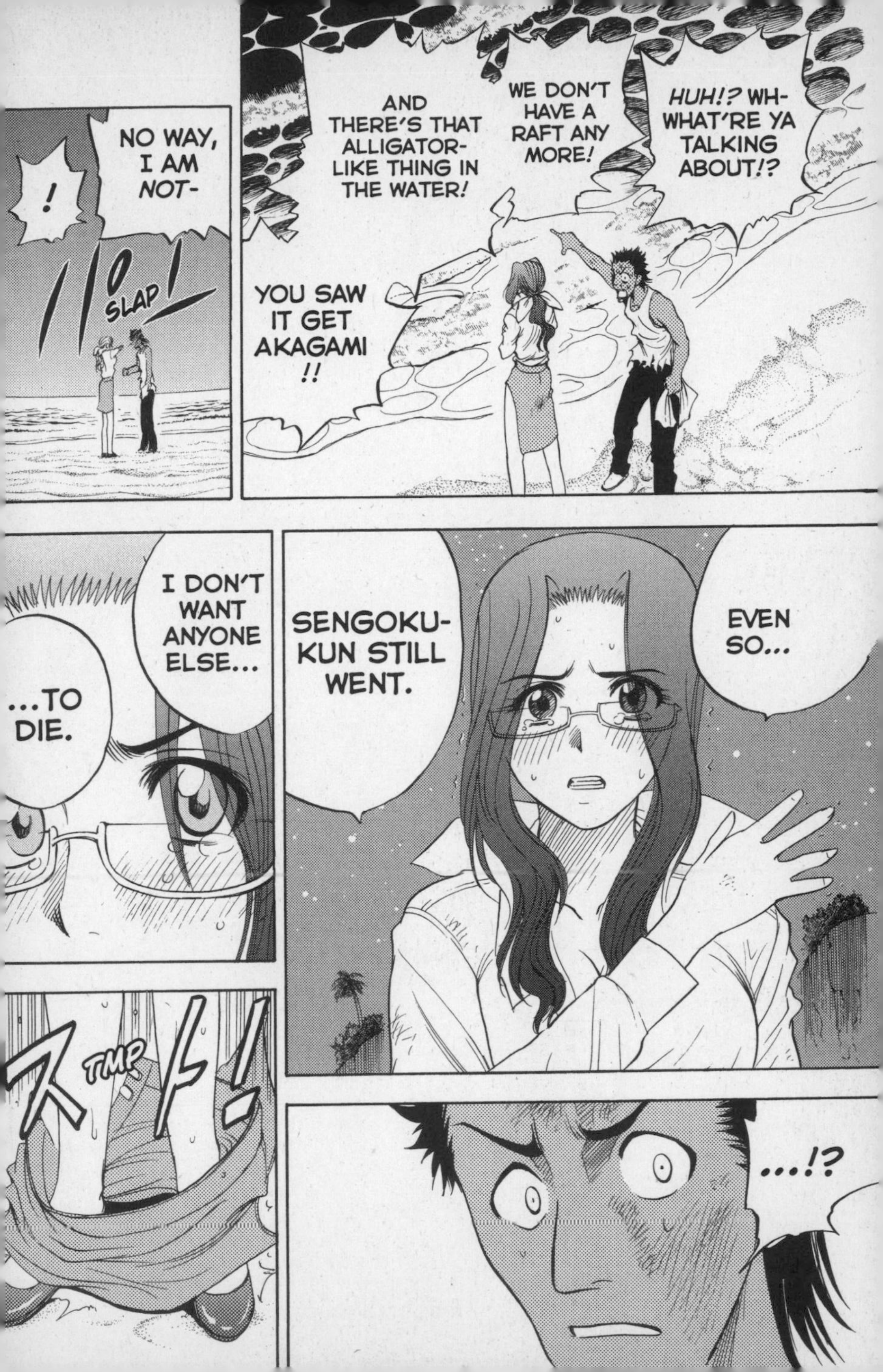
HUH!? WH-WHAT'RE YA TALKING ABOUT!?
WE DON'T HAVE A RAFT ANY MORE!
AND THERE'S THAT ALLIGATOR-LIKE THING IN THE WATER!
YOU SAW IT GET AKAGAMI!!
NO WAY, I AM NOT-
!
SLAP
EVEN SO...
SENGOKU-KUN STILL WENT.
I DON'T WANT ANYONE ELSE...
...TO DIE.
...!?
TMP

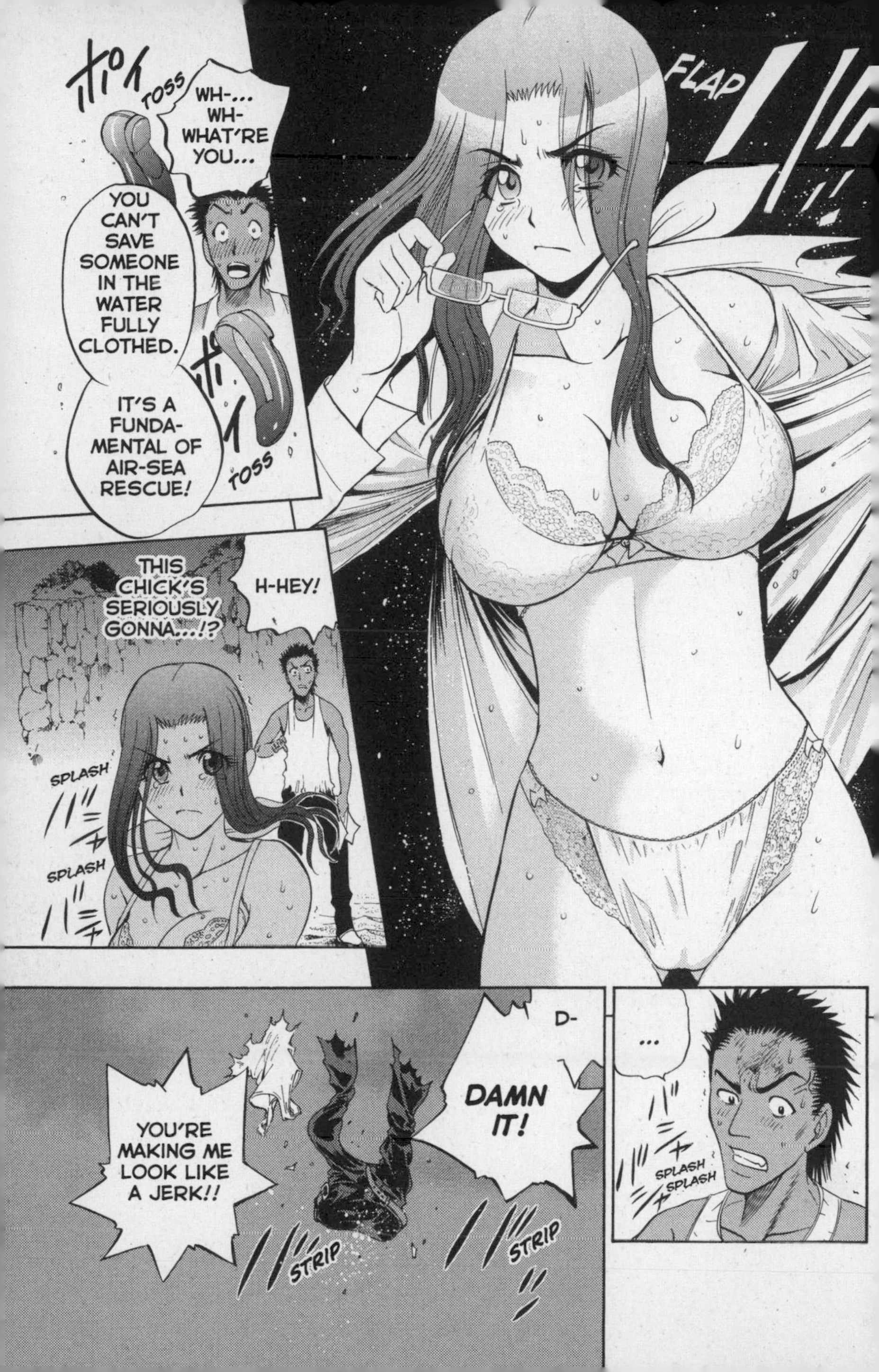
FLAP
TOSS
WH-... WH- WHAT'RE YOU...
YOU CAN'T SAVE SOMEONE IN THE WATER FULLY CLOTHED.
IT'S A FUNDA-MENTAL OF AIR-SEA RESCUE!
TOSS
H-HEY!
THIS CHICK'S SERIOUSLY GONNA...!?
SPLASH
SPLASH
...
SPLASH SPLASH
D-
DAMN IT!
YOU'RE MAKING ME LOOK LIKE A JERK!!
STRIP
STRIP

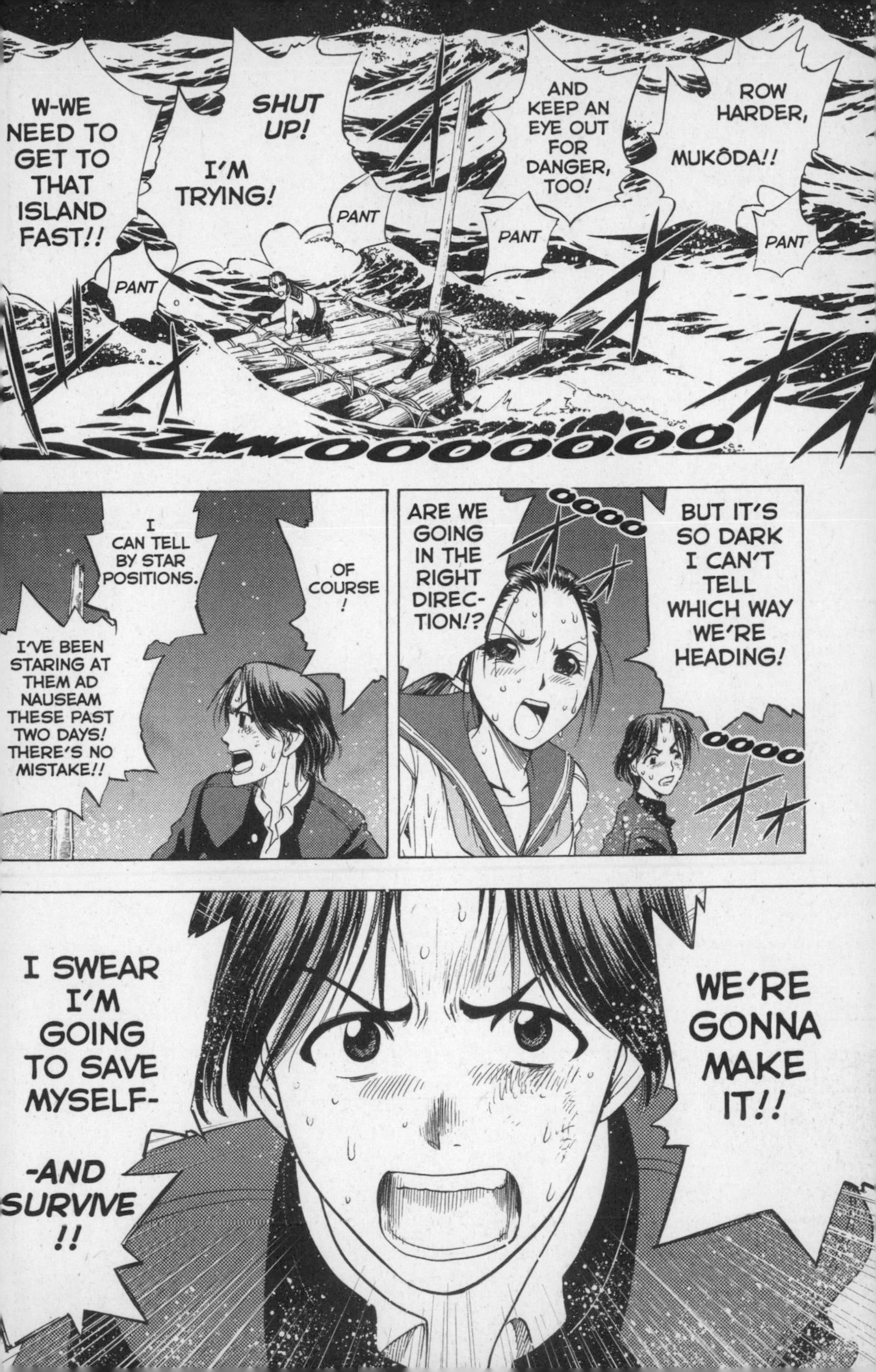
ROW HARDER, MUKÔDA!!
PANT
AND KEEP AN EYE OUT FOR DANGER, TOO!
PANT
PANT
SHUT UP!
I'M TRYING!
W-WE NEED TO GET TO THAT ISLAND FAST!!
PANT
ZWOOOOOOOOO
BUT IT'S SO DARK I CAN'T TELL WHICH WAY WE'RE HEADING!
OOOO
ARE WE GOING IN THE RIGHT DIRECTION!?
OOOO
OF COURSE!
I CAN TELL BY STAR POSITIONS.
I'VE BEEN STARING AT THEM AD NAUSEAM THESE PAST TWO DAYS! THERE'S NO MISTAKE!!
WE'RE GONNA MAKE IT!!
I SWEAR I'M GOING TO SAVE MYSELF-
-AND SURVIVE!!

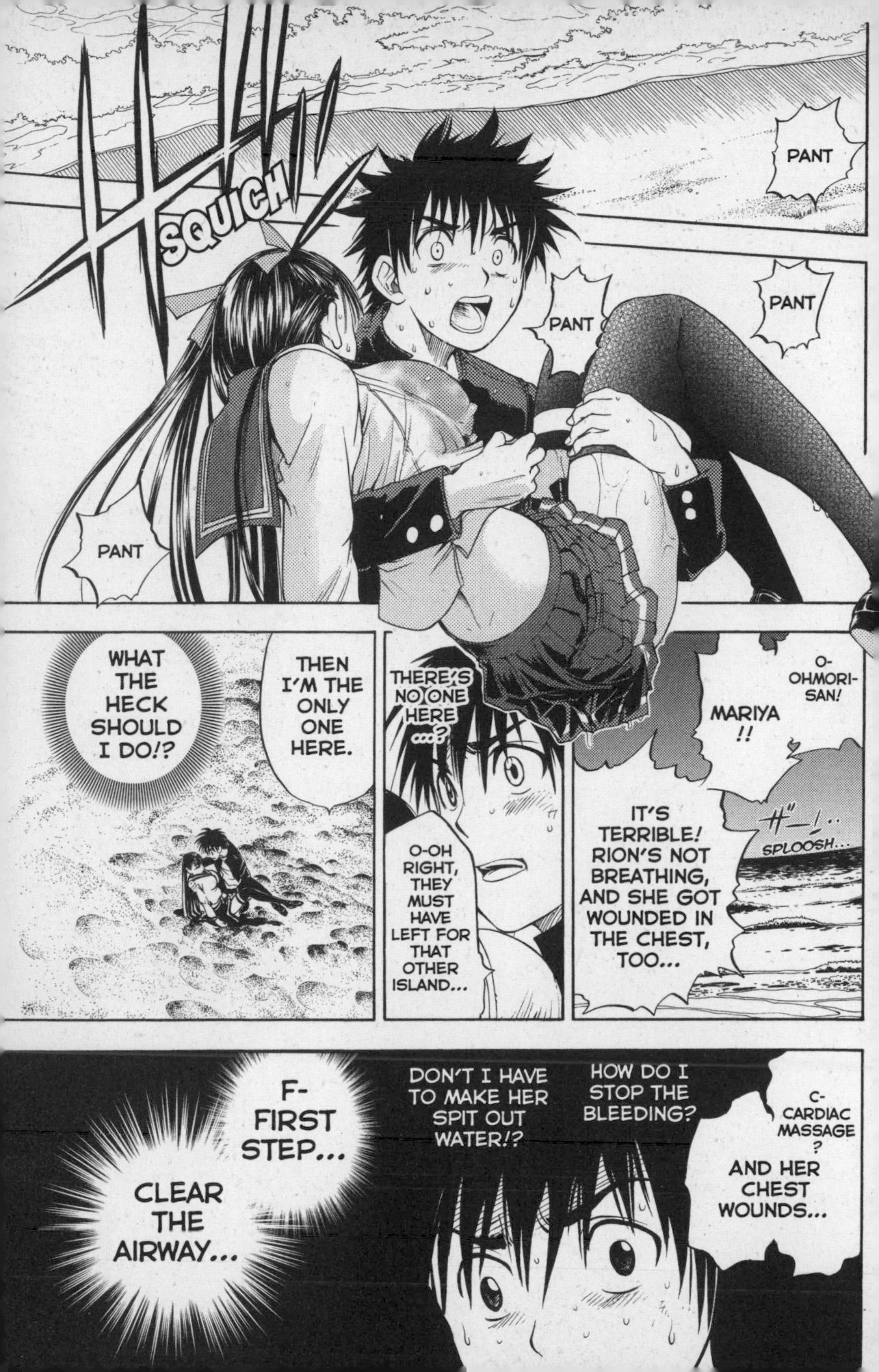
PANT
PANT
PANT
SQUICH
PANT
O- OHMORI-SAN!
MARIYA !!
IT'S TERRIBLE! RION'S NOT BREATHING, AND SHE GOT WOUNDED IN THE CHEST, TOO...
SPLOOSH...
THERE'S NO ONE HERE ...?
O-OH RIGHT, THEY MUST HAVE LEFT FOR THAT OTHER ISLAND...
THEN I'M THE ONLY ONE HERE.
WHAT THE HECK SHOULD I DO!?
C- CARDIAC MASSAGE ?
AND HER CHEST WOUNDS...
HOW DO I STOP THE BLEEDING?
DON'T I HAVE TO MAKE HER SPIT OUT WATER!?
F- FIRST STEP...
CLEAR THE AIRWAY...

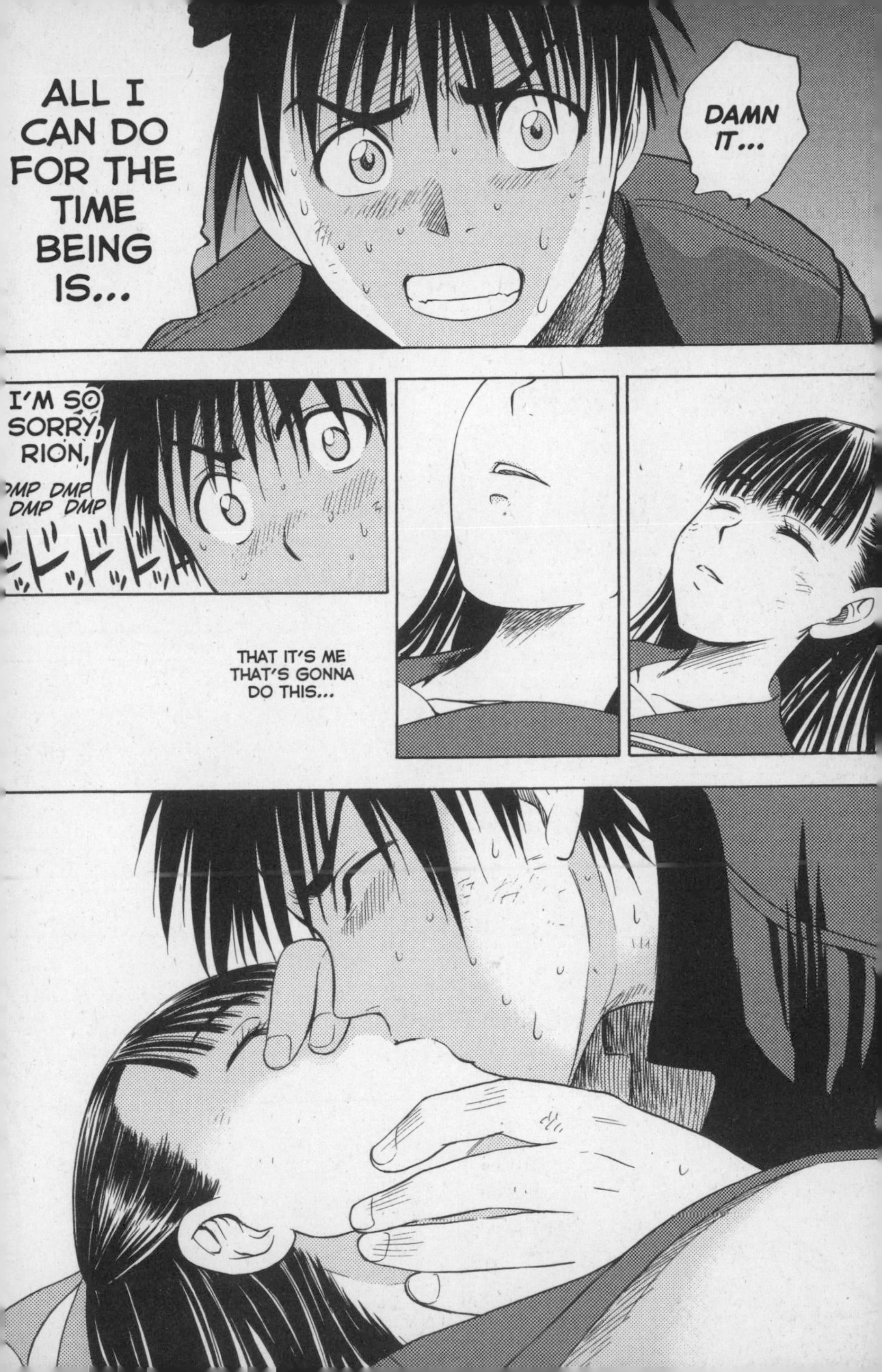
DAMN IT...
ALL I CAN DO FOR THE TIME BEING IS...
I'M SO SORRY, RION,
MP DMP
DMP DMP
ドッドッドッ
THAT IT'S ME THAT'S GONNA DO THIS...

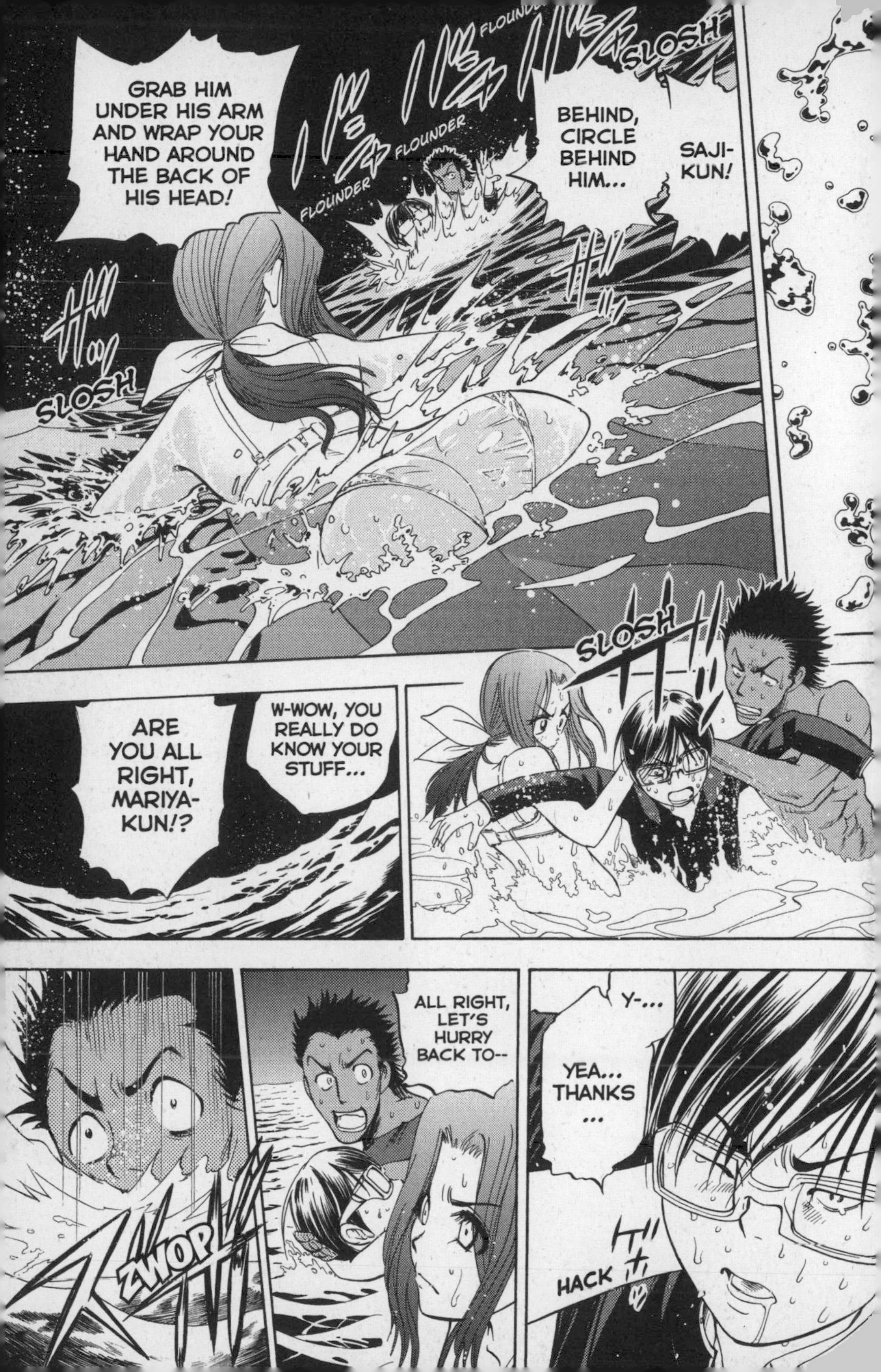
SLOSH
SAJI-KUN!
BEHIND, CIRCLE BEHIND HIM...
FLOUNDER
FLOUNDER
FLOUNDER
GRAB HIM UNDER HIS ARM AND WRAP YOUR HAND AROUND THE BACK OF HIS HEAD!
SLOSH
SLOSH
W-WOW, YOU REALLY DO KNOW YOUR STUFF...
ARE YOU ALL RIGHT, MARIYA-KUN!?
Y-...
YEA... THANKS ...
HACK
ALL RIGHT, LET'S HURRY BACK TO--
ZWOP

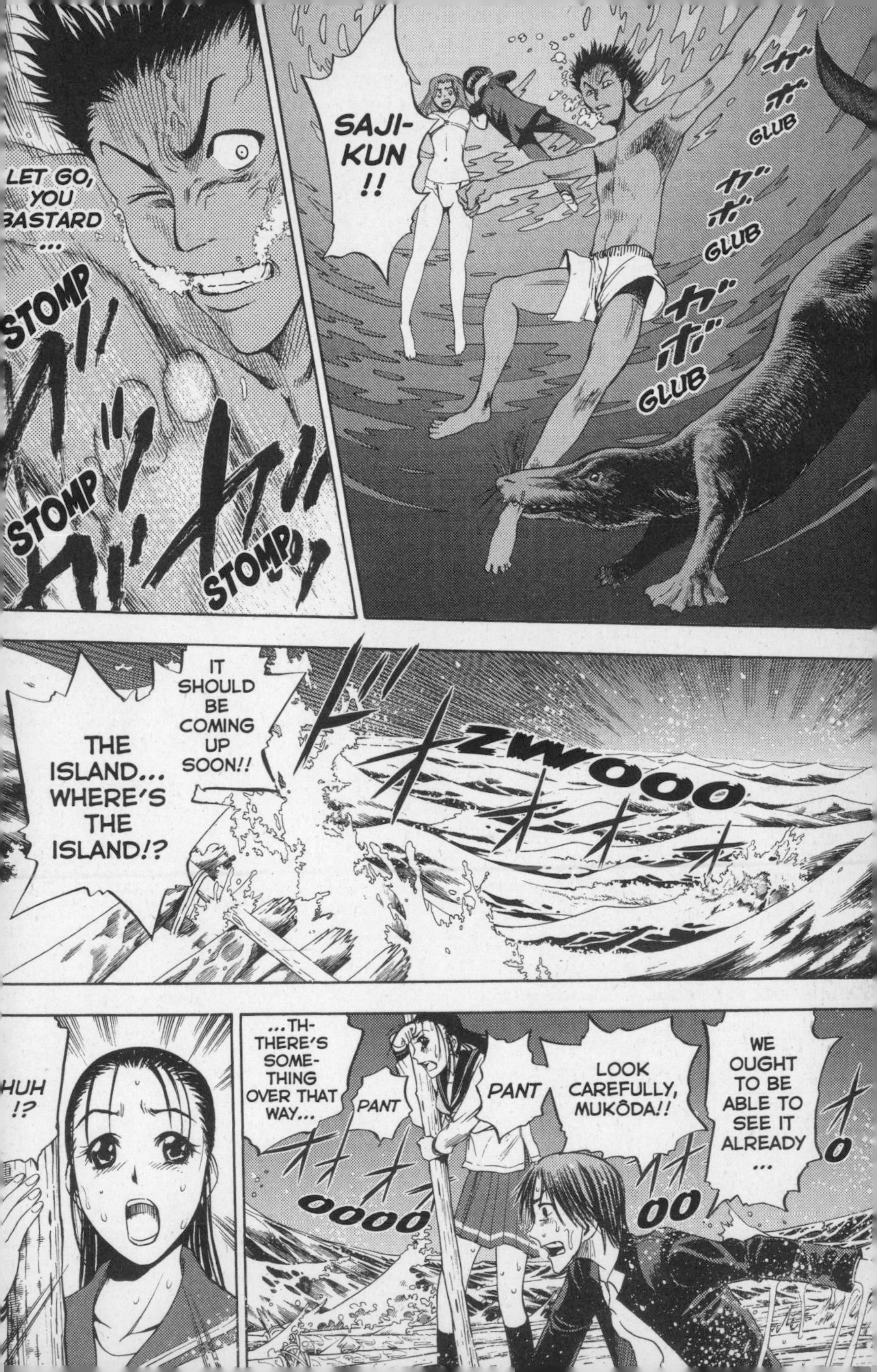
SAJI-KUN !!
GLUB
GLUB
GLUB
LET GO, YOU BASTARD ...
STOMP
STOMP
STOMP
ZWOOO
IT SHOULD BE COMING UP SOON!!
THE ISLAND... WHERE'S THE ISLAND!?
WE OUGHT TO BE ABLE TO SEE IT ALREADY ...
OO
LOOK CAREFULLY, MUKÔDA!!
PANT
PANT
...TH-THERE'S SOME-THING OVER THAT WAY...
OOOO
HUH !?

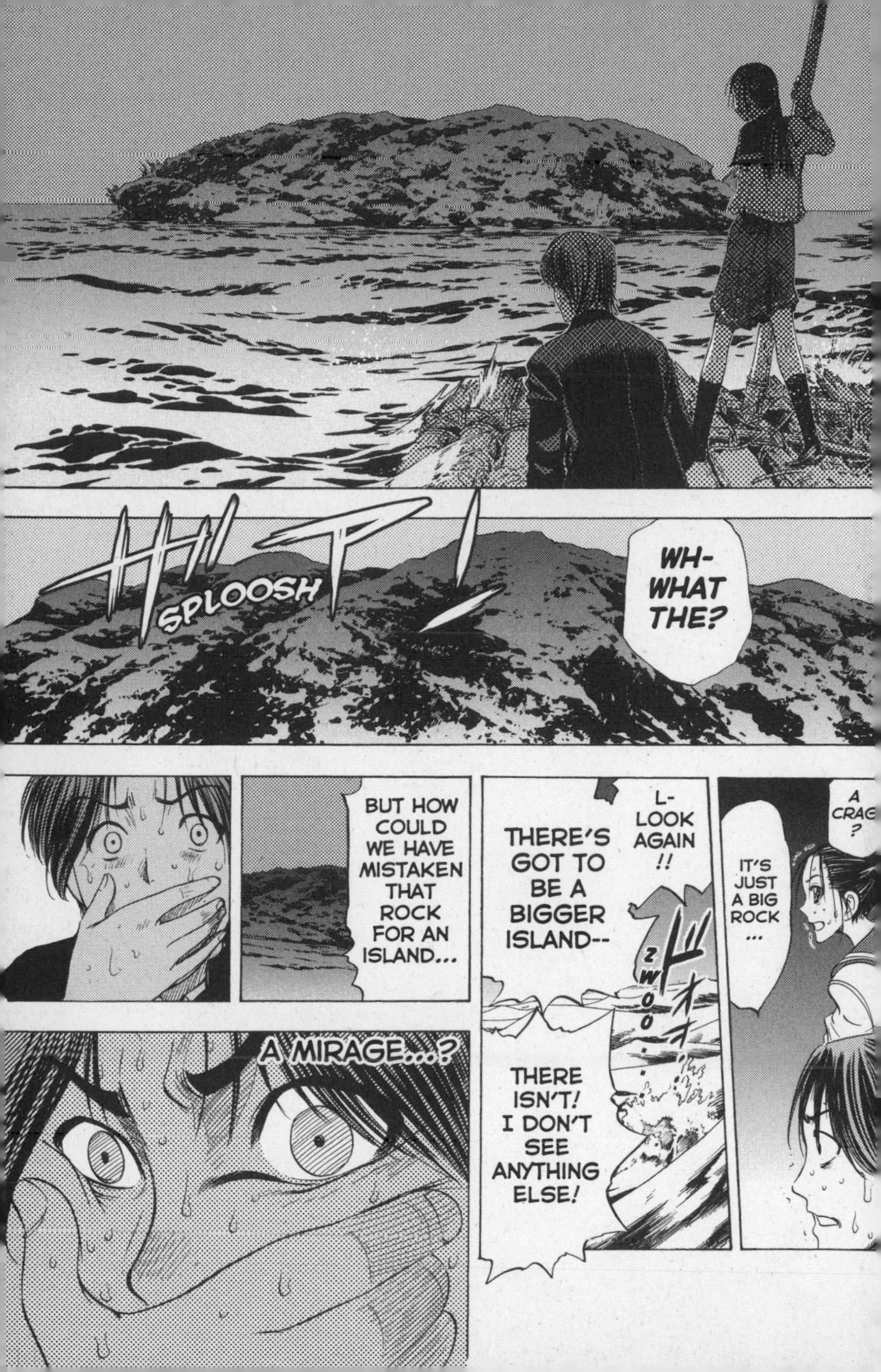
WH-WHAT THE?
SPLOOSH
A CRAG?
IT'S JUST A BIG ROCK...
L-LOOK AGAIN!!
THERE'S GOT TO BE A BIGGER ISLAND--
ZWOOO...
THERE ISN'T! I DON'T SEE ANYTHING ELSE!
BUT HOW COULD WE HAVE MISTAKEN THAT ROCK FOR AN ISLAND...
A MIRAGE...?

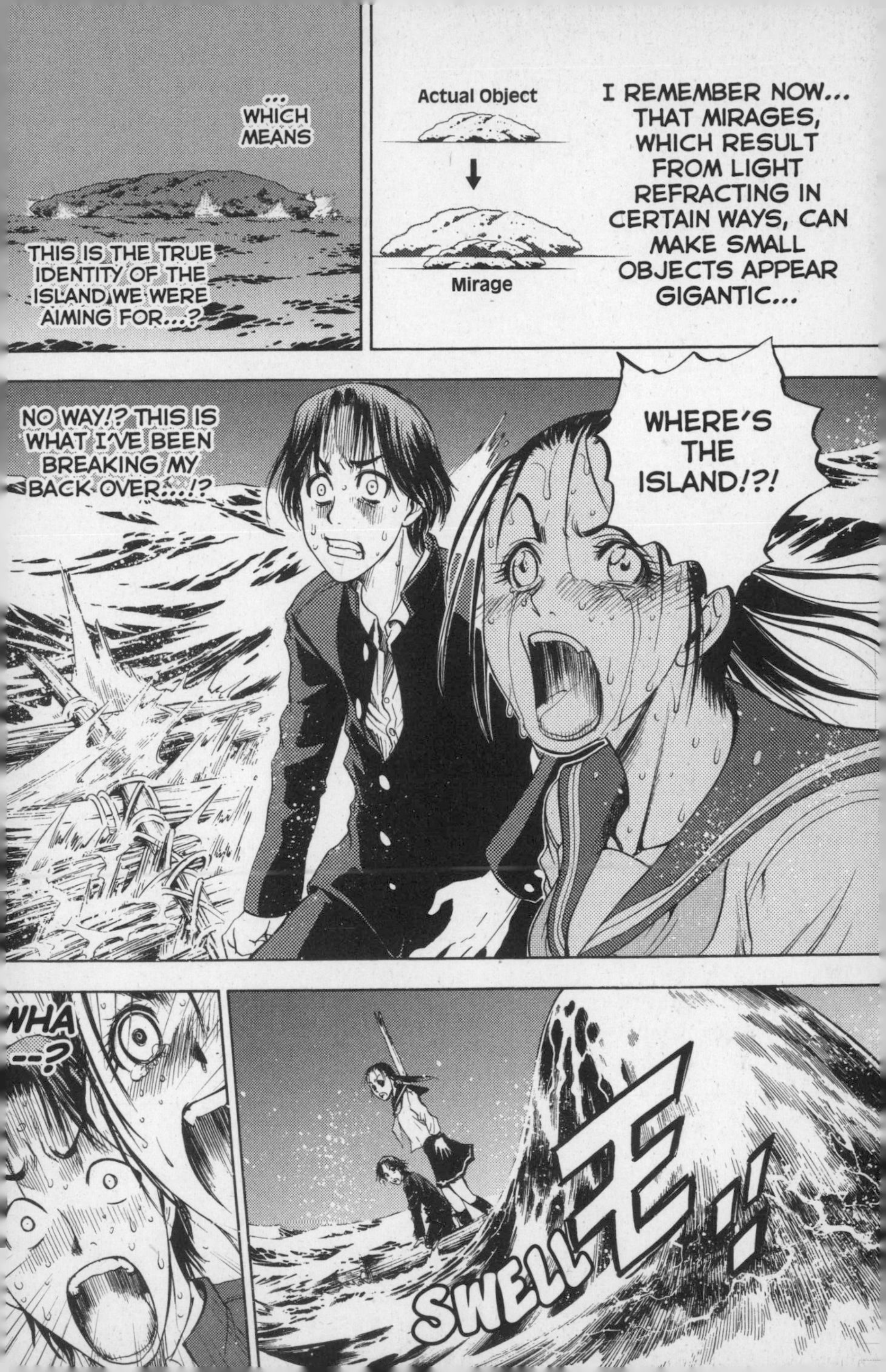
Actual Object
Mirage
I REMEMBER NOW... THAT MIRAGES, WHICH RESULT FROM LIGHT REFRACTING IN CERTAIN WAYS, CAN MAKE SMALL OBJECTS APPEAR GIGANTIC...
...WHICH MEANS
THIS IS THE TRUE IDENTITY OF THE ISLAND WE WERE AIMING FOR...?
WHERE'S THE ISLAND!?!
NO WAY!? THIS IS WHAT I'VE BEEN BREAKING MY BACK OVER...!?
SWELL
WHA--?

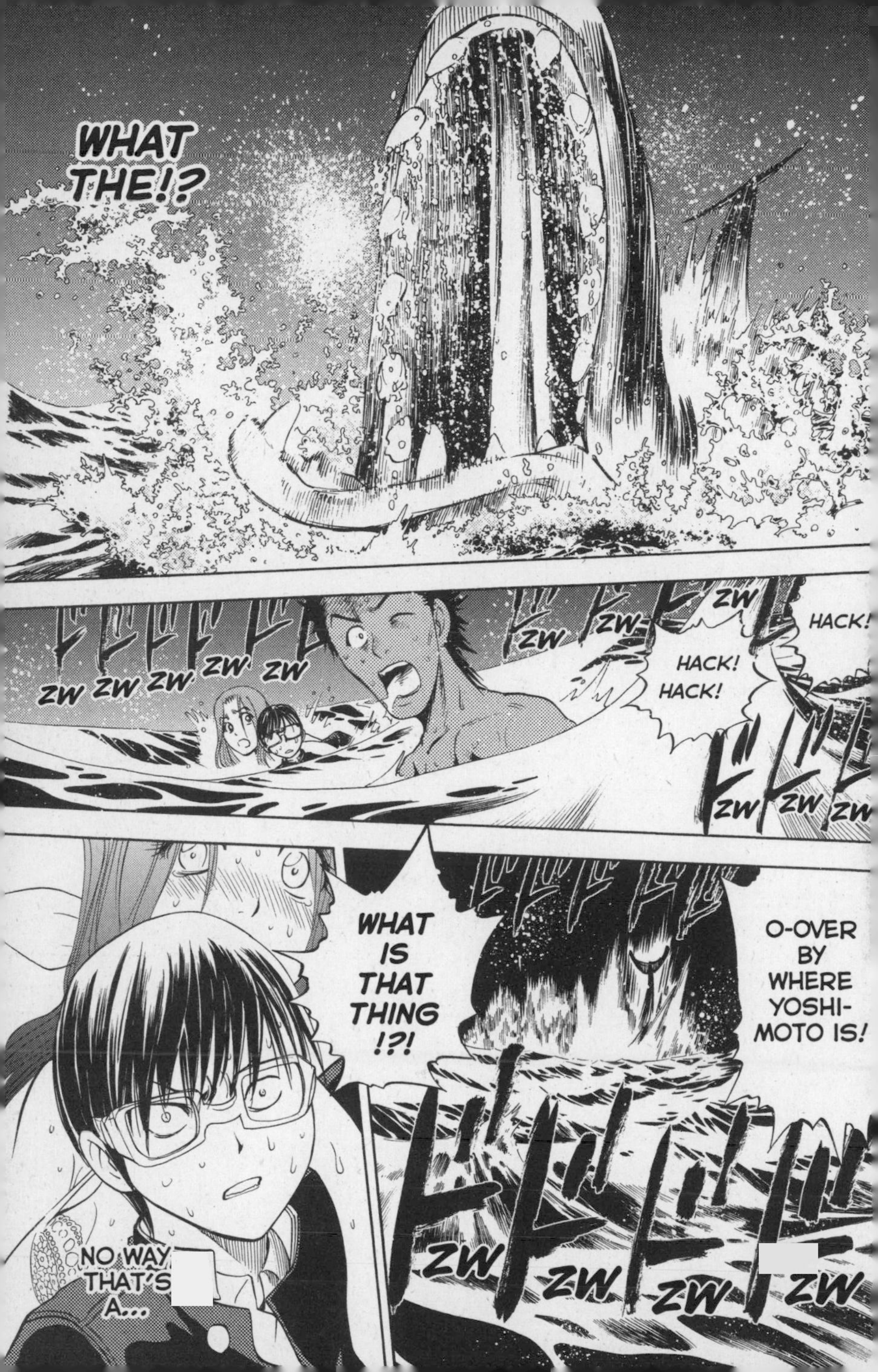
WHAT THE!?
ZW ZW
ZW ZW
HACK!
HACK! HACK!
ZW ZW ZW
ZW ZW ZW ZW ZW
O-OVER BY WHERE YOSHI-MOTO IS!
WHAT IS THAT THING !?!
ZW ZW ZW ZW
NO WAY THAT'S A...

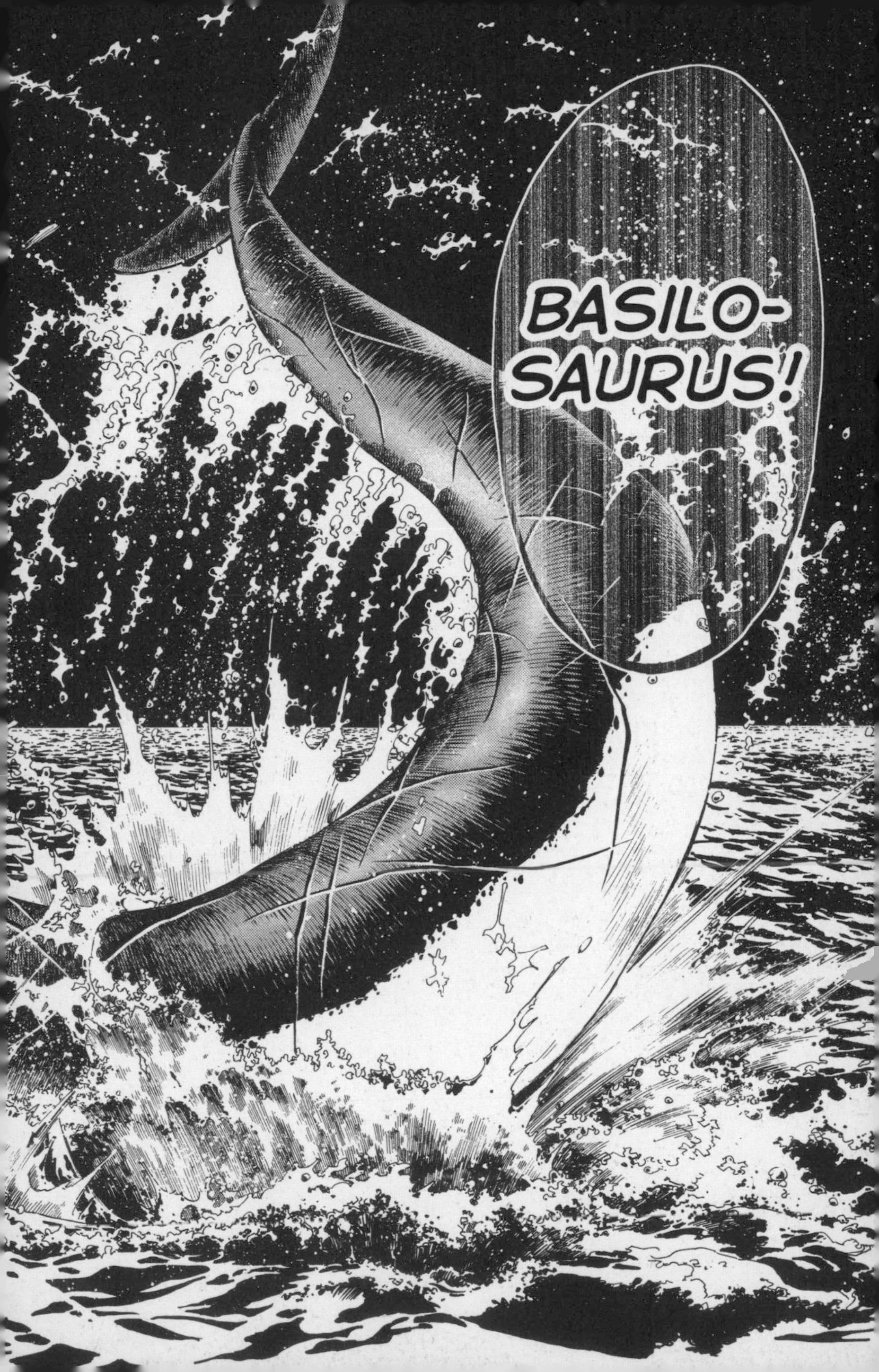
BASILO-
SAURUS!

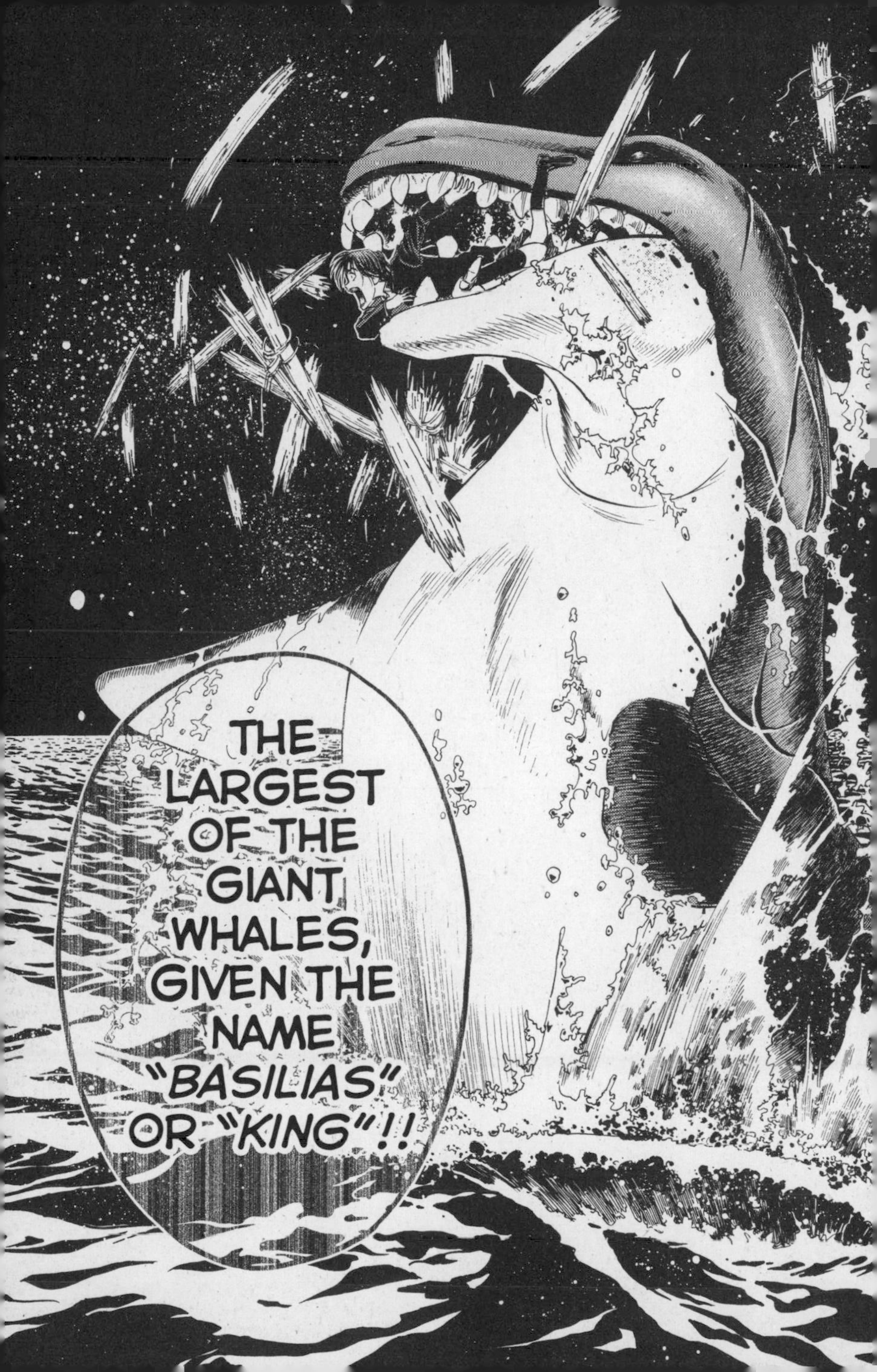
THE LARGEST OF THE GIANT WHALES, GIVEN THE NAME "BASILIAS" OR "KING"!!

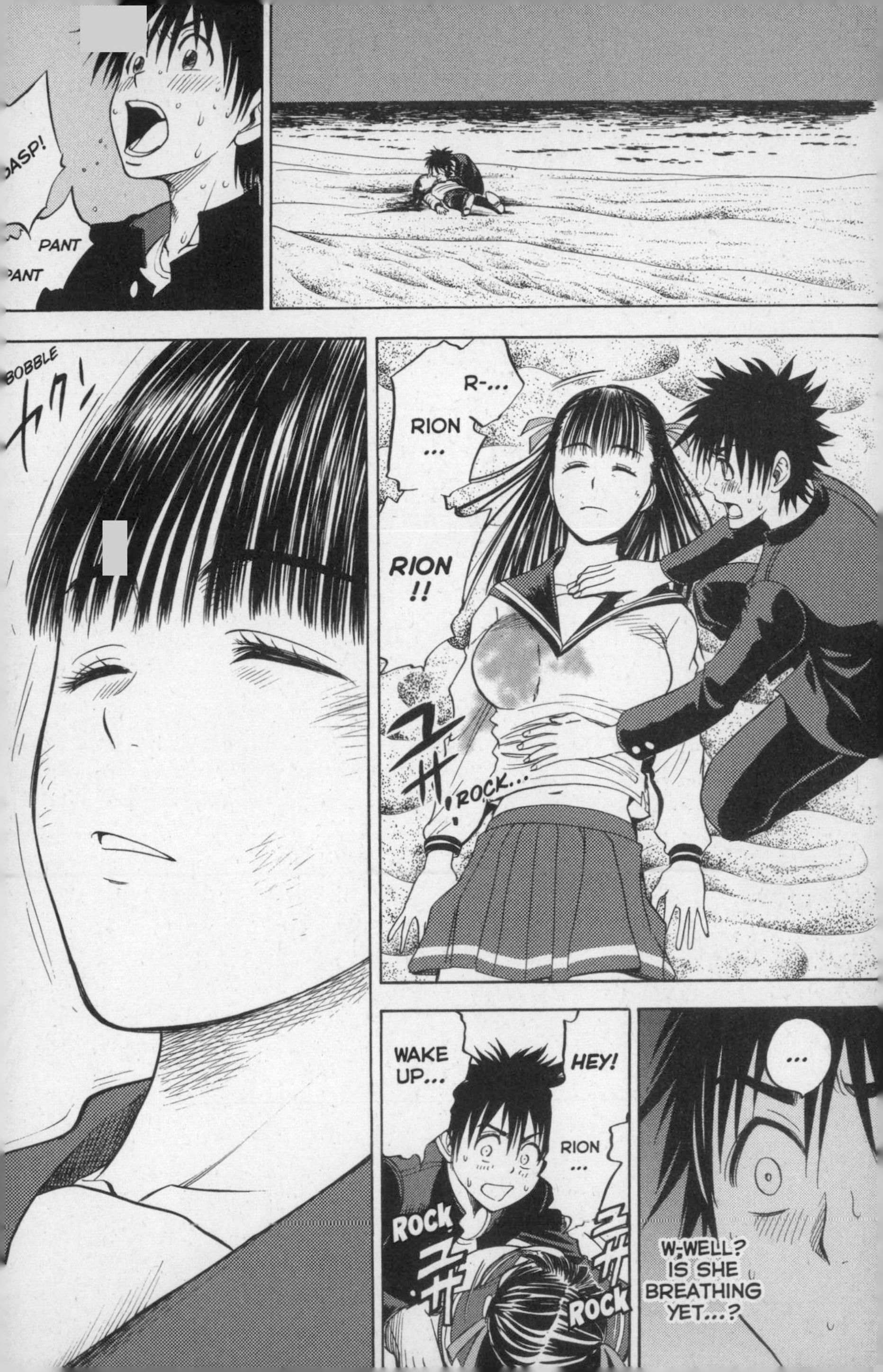
ASP!
PANT
PANT
R-...
RION ...
RION !!
ROCK...
...
W-WELL? IS SHE BREATHING YET...?
HEY!
WAKE UP...
RION ...
ROCK
ROCK
BOBBLE

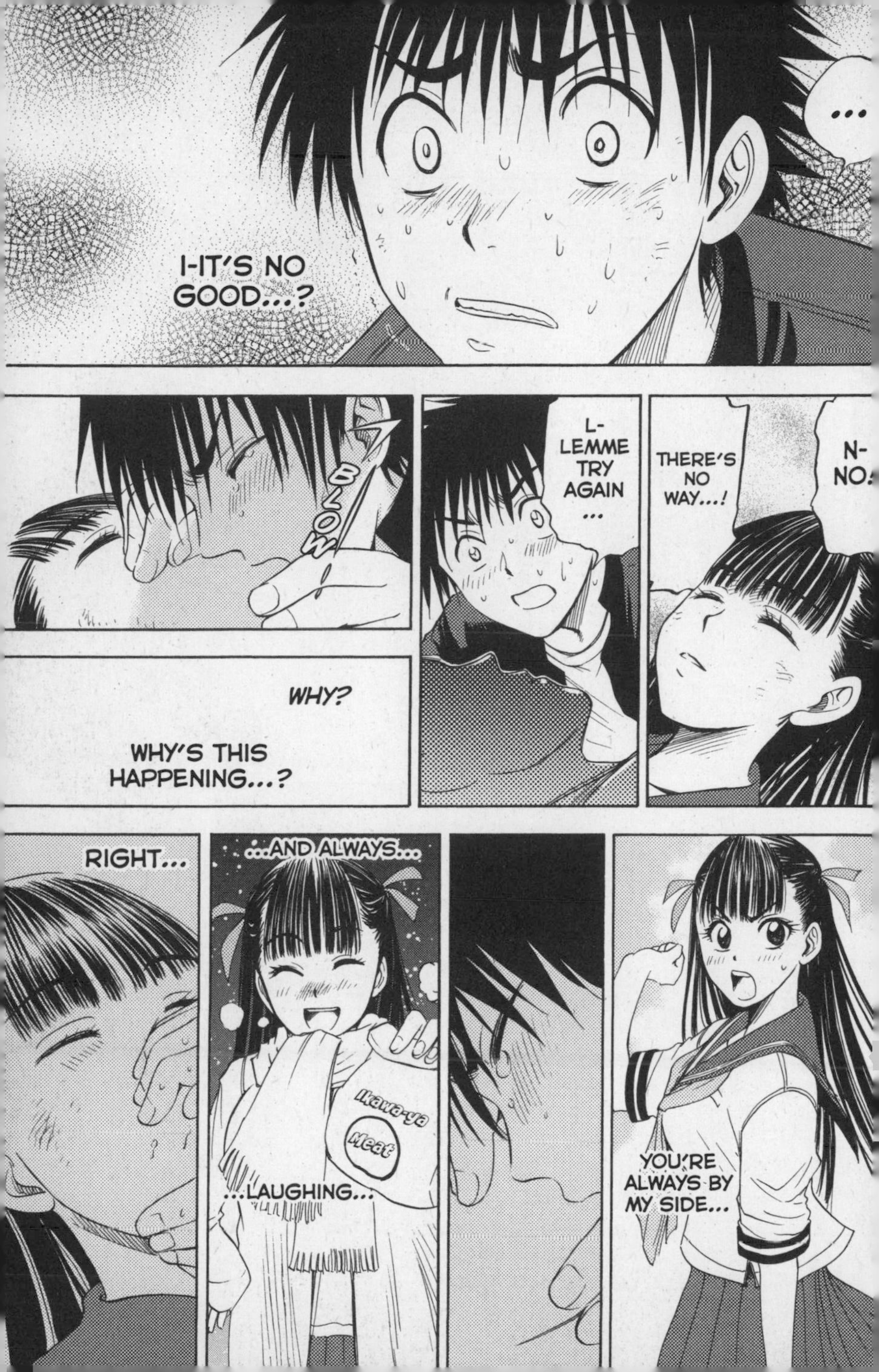
...
I-IT'S NO GOOD...?
N-NO!
THERE'S NO WAY...!
L-LEMME TRY AGAIN ...
BLOW
WHY?
WHY'S THIS HAPPENING...?
YOU'RE ALWAYS BY MY SIDE...
...AND ALWAYS...
Ikawa-ya
Meat
...LAUGHING...
RIGHT...

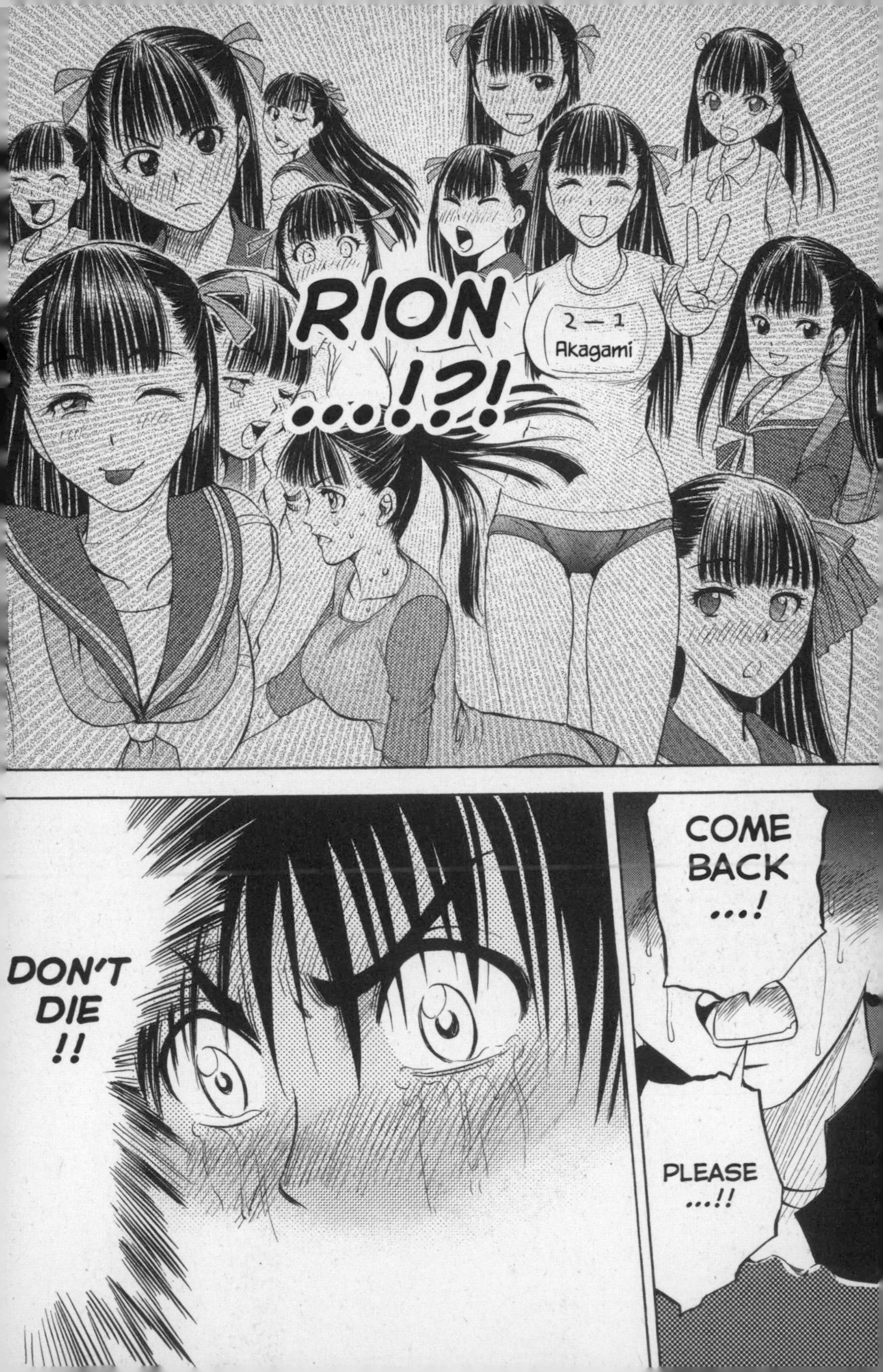
RION ...!?!
2—1
Akagami
COME BACK ...!
PLEASE ...!!
DON'T DIE !!

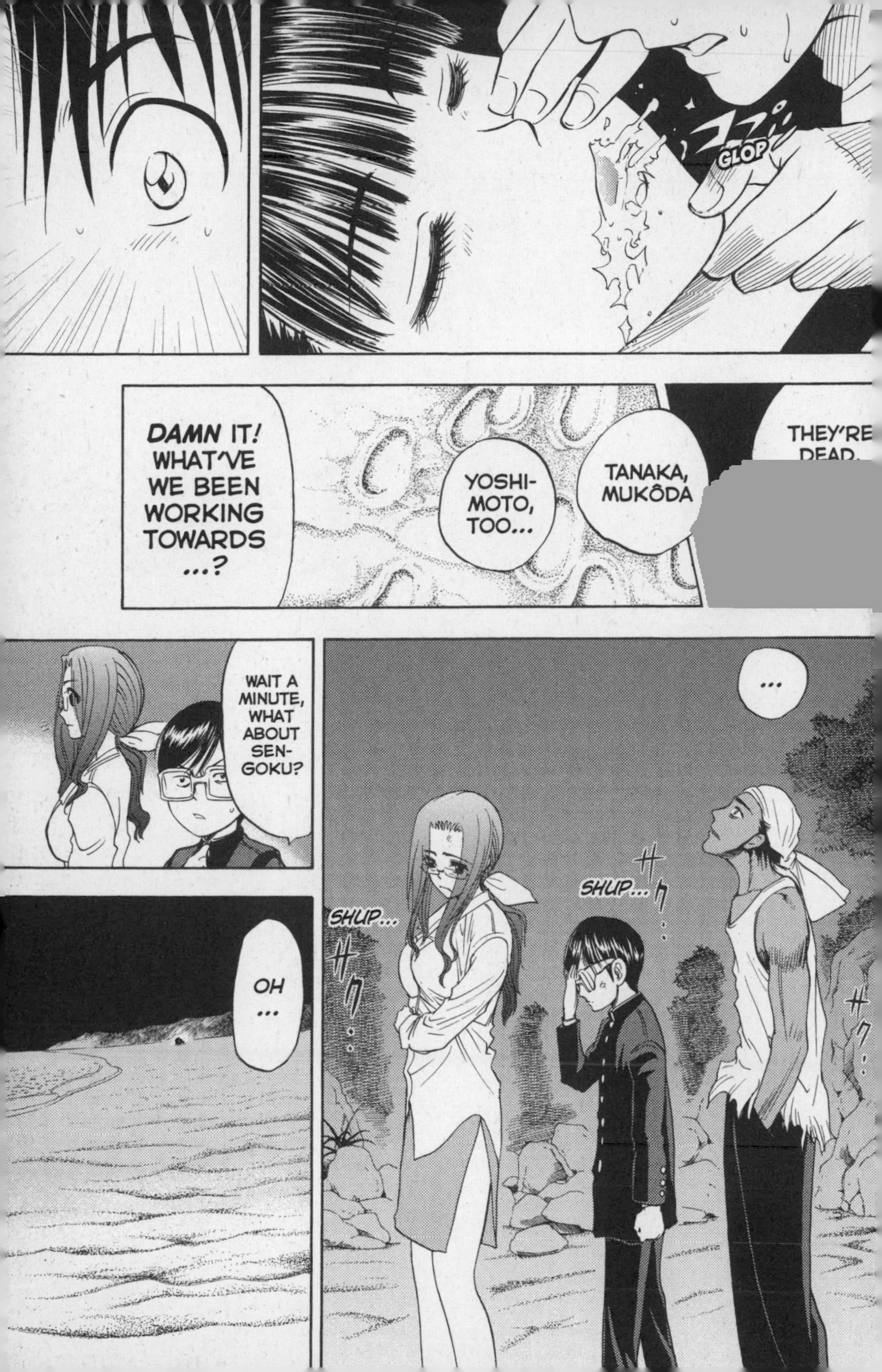
GLOP
THEY'RE DEAD.
TANAKA, MUKÔDA
YOSHI-MOTO, TOO...
DAMN IT! WHAT'VE WE BEEN WORKING TOWARDS ...?
...
SHUP...
SHUP...
WAIT A MINUTE, WHAT ABOUT SEN-GOKU?
OH ...

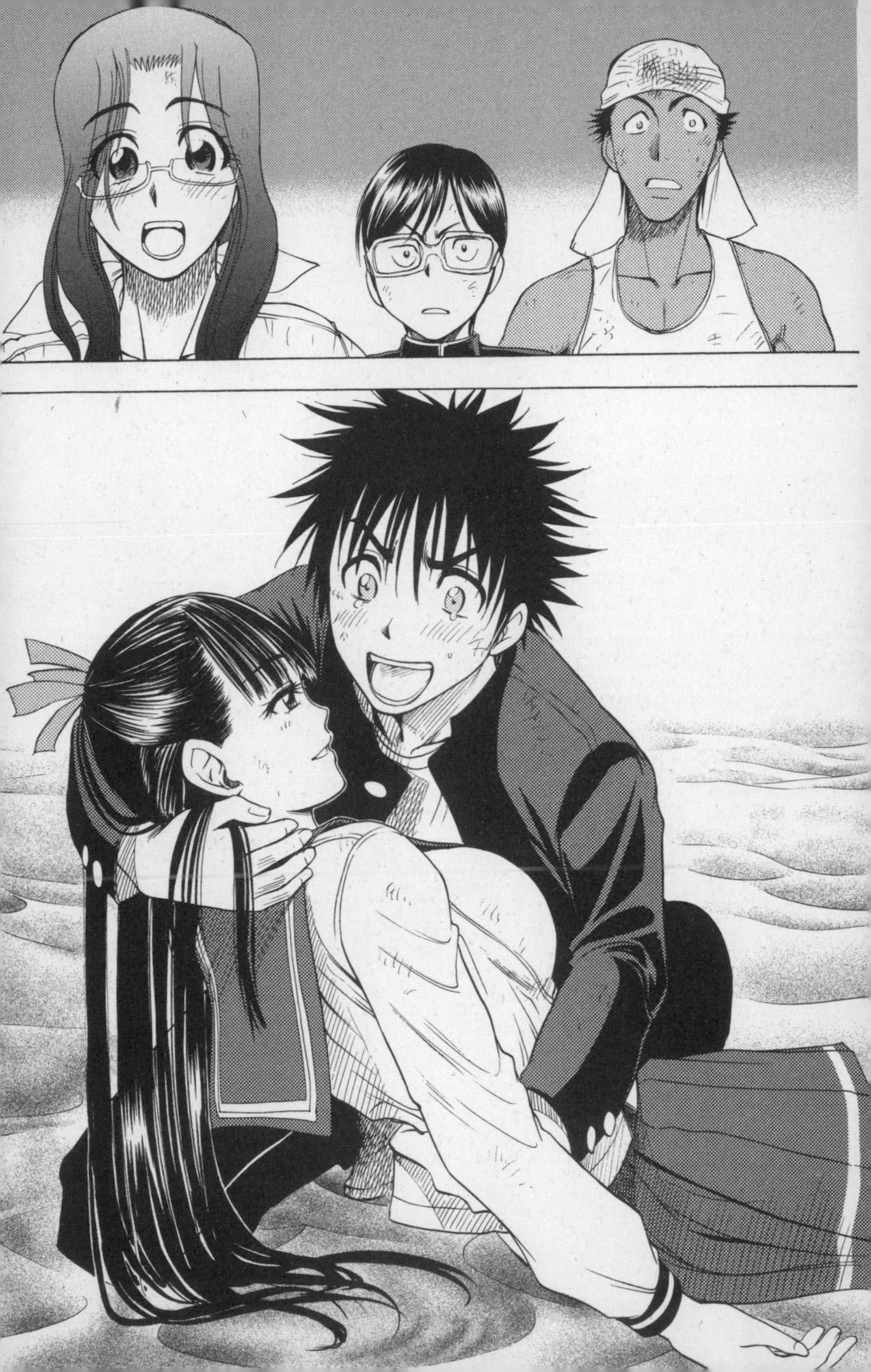

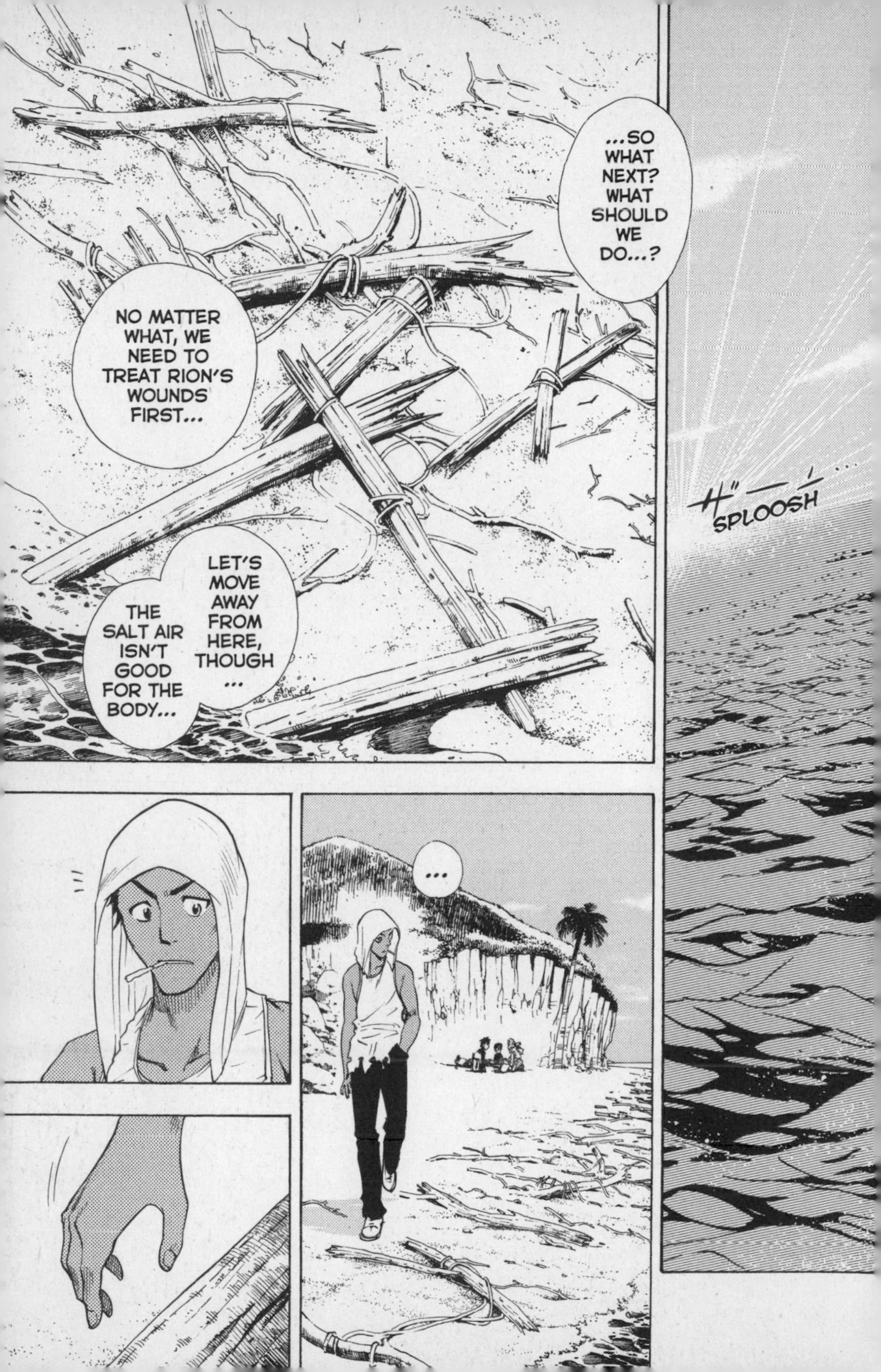
SPLOOSH
...SO WHAT NEXT? WHAT SHOULD WE DO...?
NO MATTER WHAT, WE NEED TO TREAT RION'S WOUNDS FIRST...
LET'S MOVE AWAY FROM HERE, THOUGH ...
THE SALT AIR ISN'T GOOD FOR THE BODY...
...

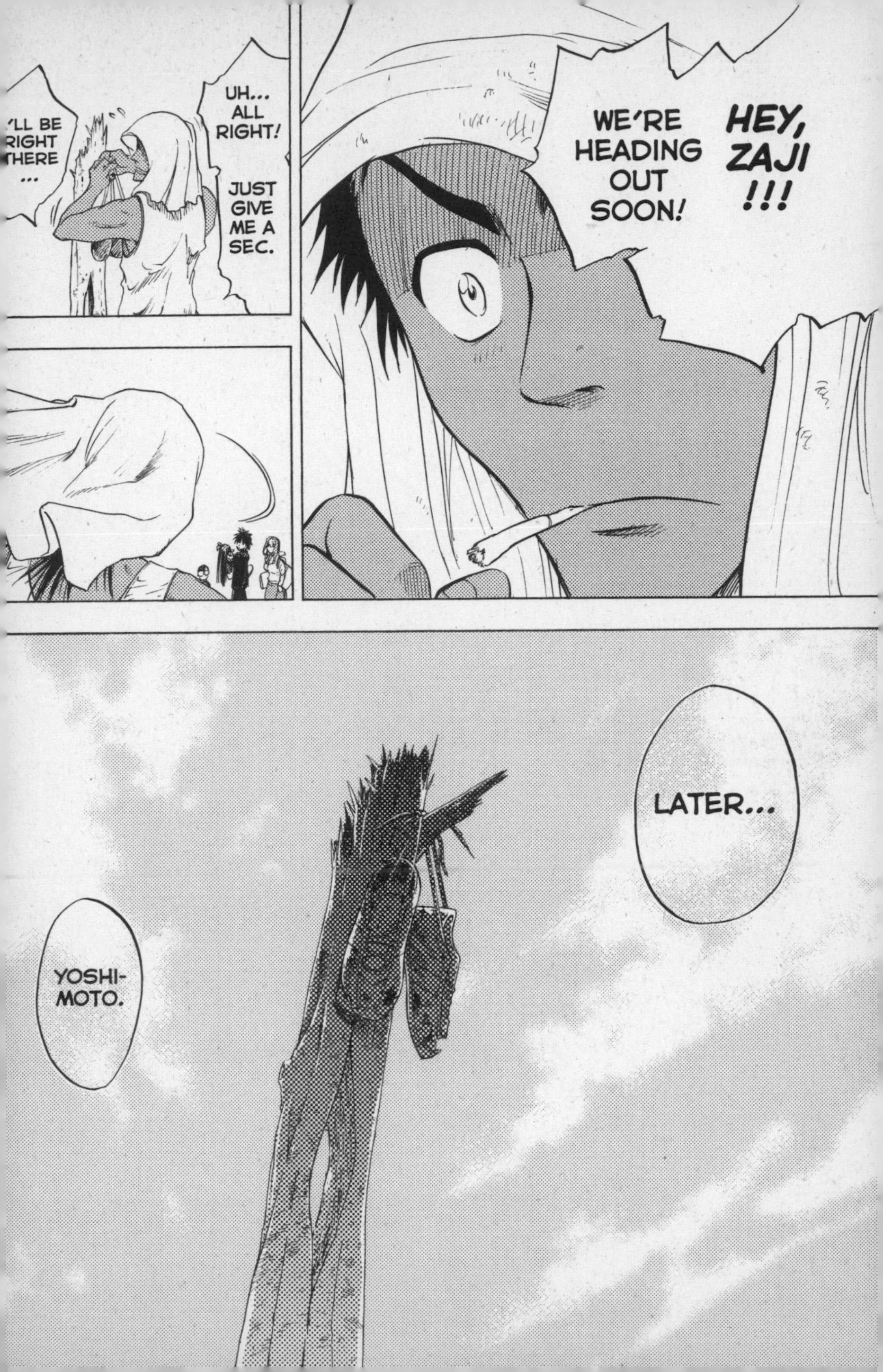
HEY, ZAJI!!!
WE'RE HEADING OUT SOON!
UH... ALL RIGHT!
JUST GIVE ME A SEC.
'LL BE RIGHT THERE ...
LATER...
YOSHI-MOTO.

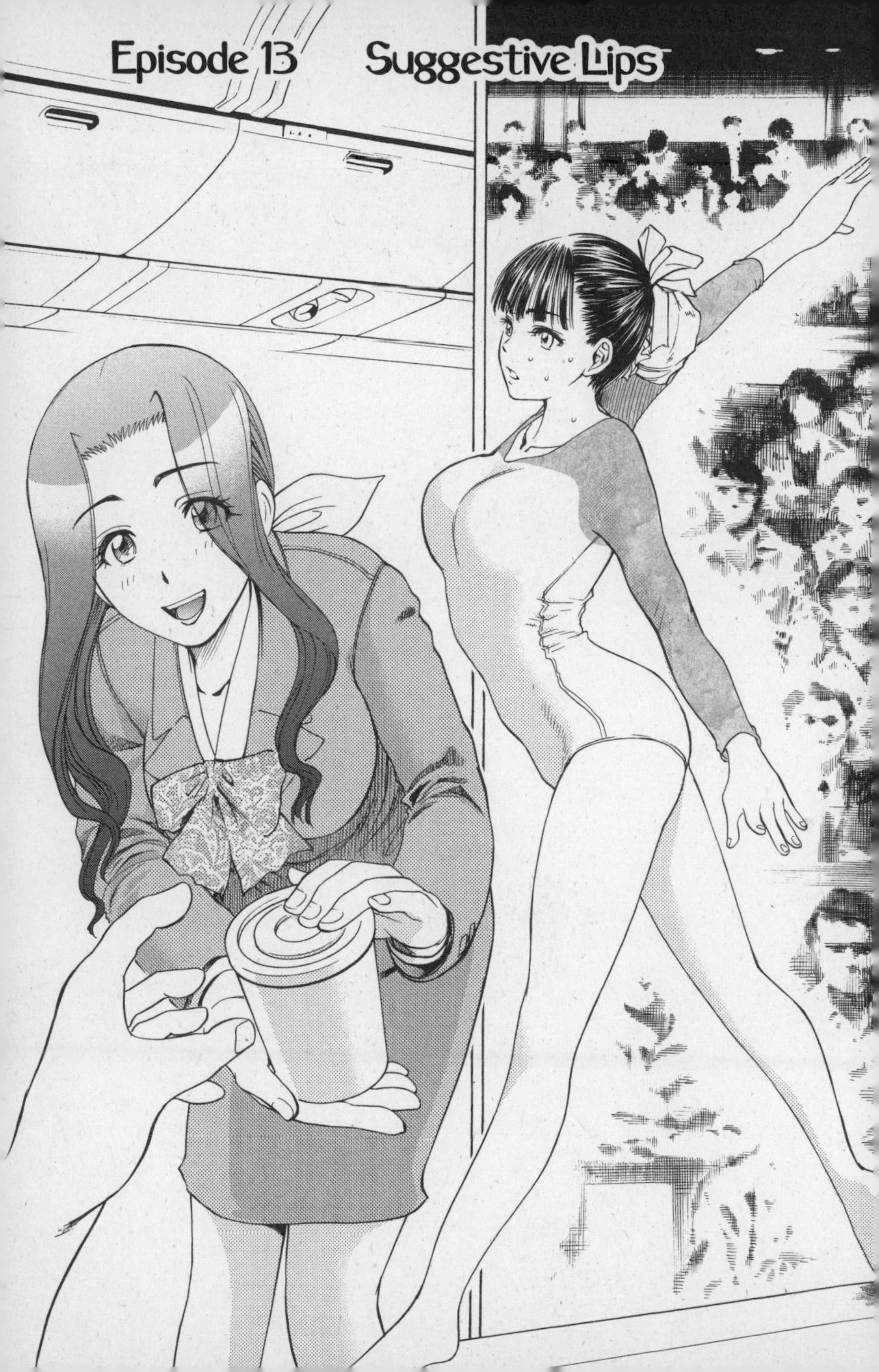
Episode 13
Suggestive Lips

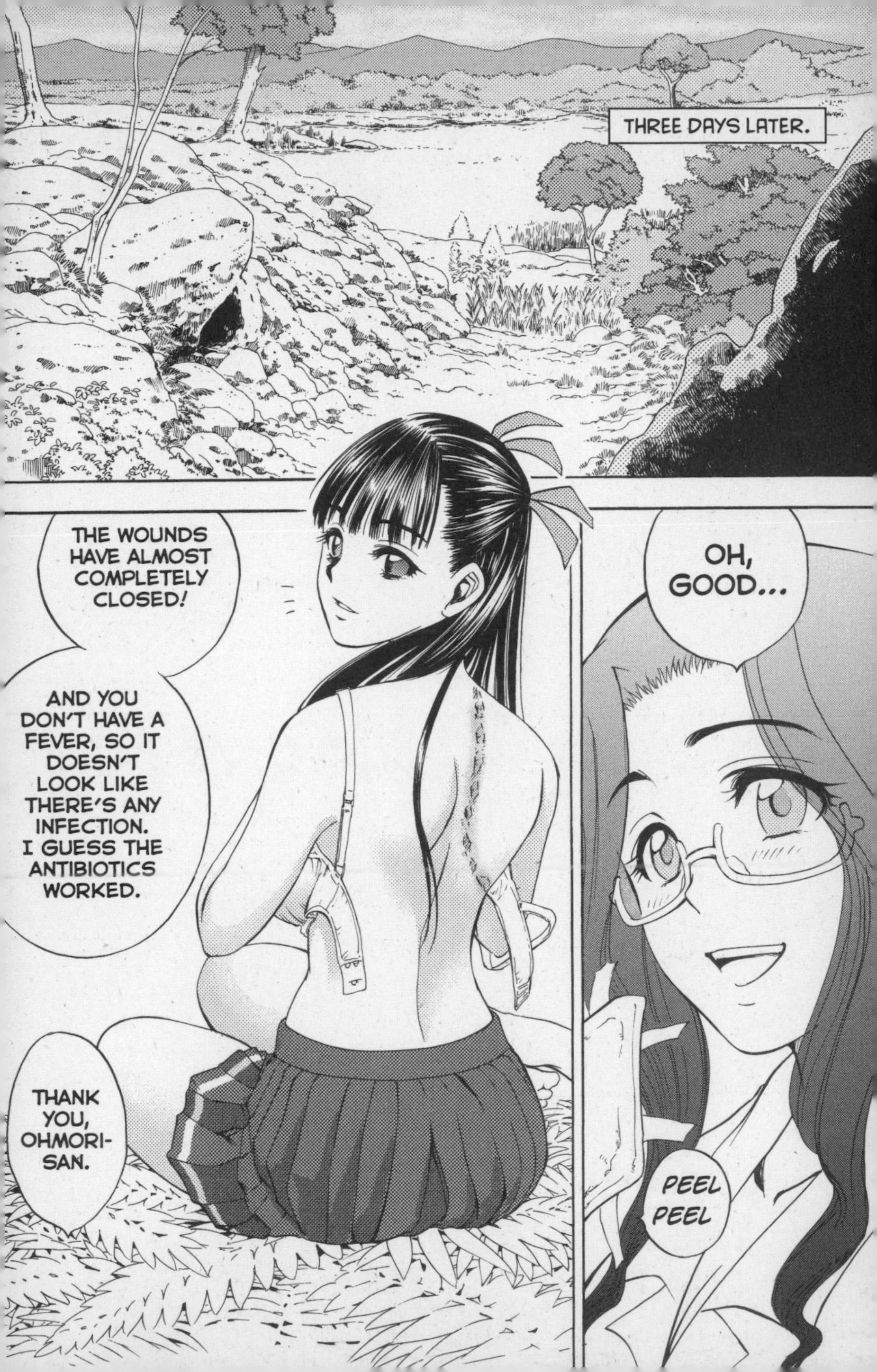
THREE DAYS LATER.
OH, GOOD...
PEEL PEEL
THE WOUNDS HAVE ALMOST COMPLETELY CLOSED!
AND YOU DON'T HAVE A FEVER, SO IT DOESN'T LOOK LIKE THERE'S ANY INFECTION. I GUESS THE ANTIBIOTICS WORKED.
THANK YOU, OHMORI-SAN.

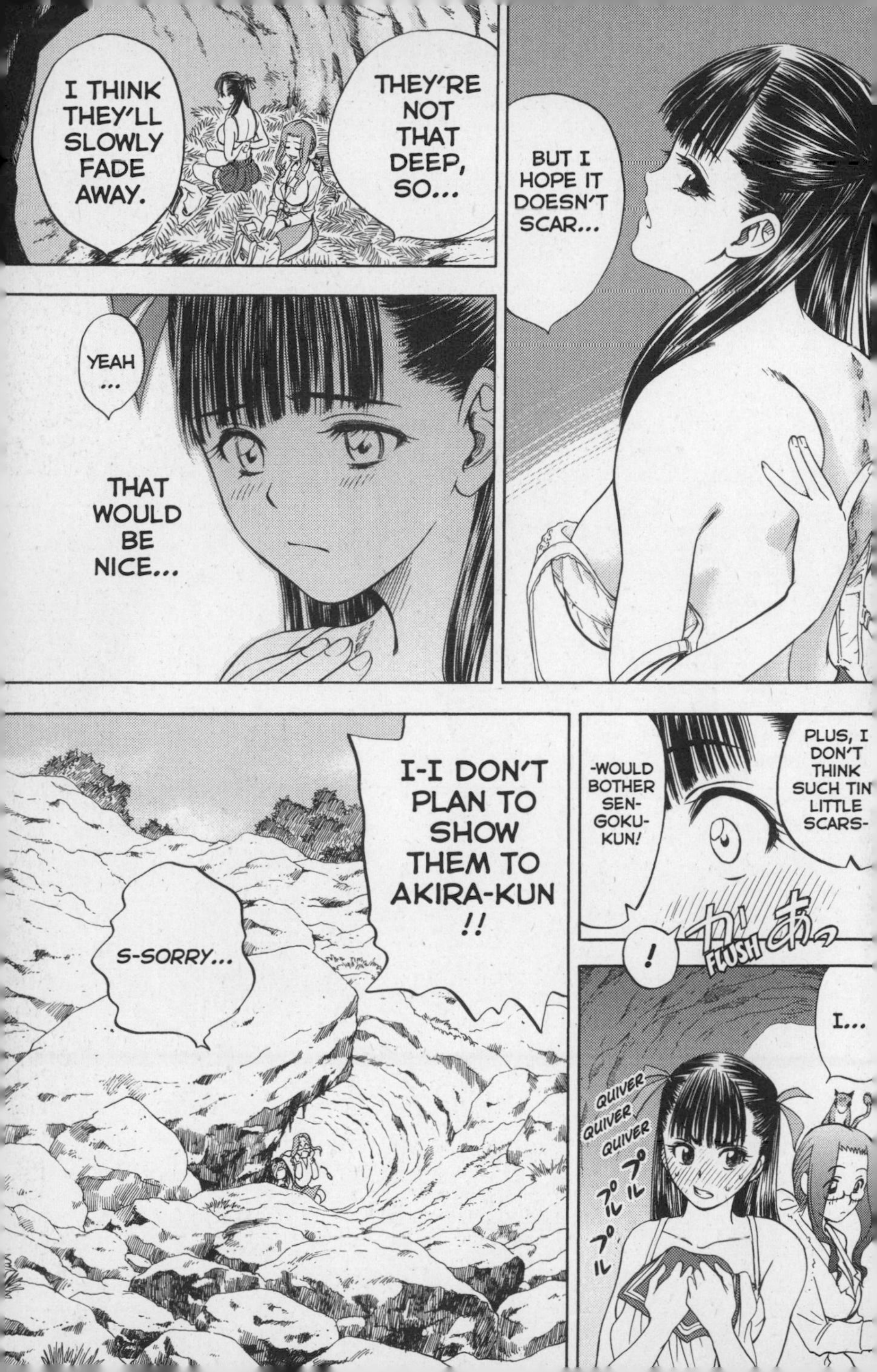
BUT I HOPE IT DOESN'T SCAR...
THEY'RE NOT THAT DEEP, SO...
I THINK THEY'LL SLOWLY FADE AWAY.
YEAH...
THAT WOULD BE NICE...
PLUS, I DON'T THINK SUCH TIN LITTLE SCARS-
-WOULD BOTHER SEN-GOKU-KUN!
かあっ
FLUSH
!
I...
QUIVER QUIVER QUIVER
プルプル
プルプル
I-I DON'T PLAN TO SHOW THEM TO AKIRA-KUN!!
S-SORRY...

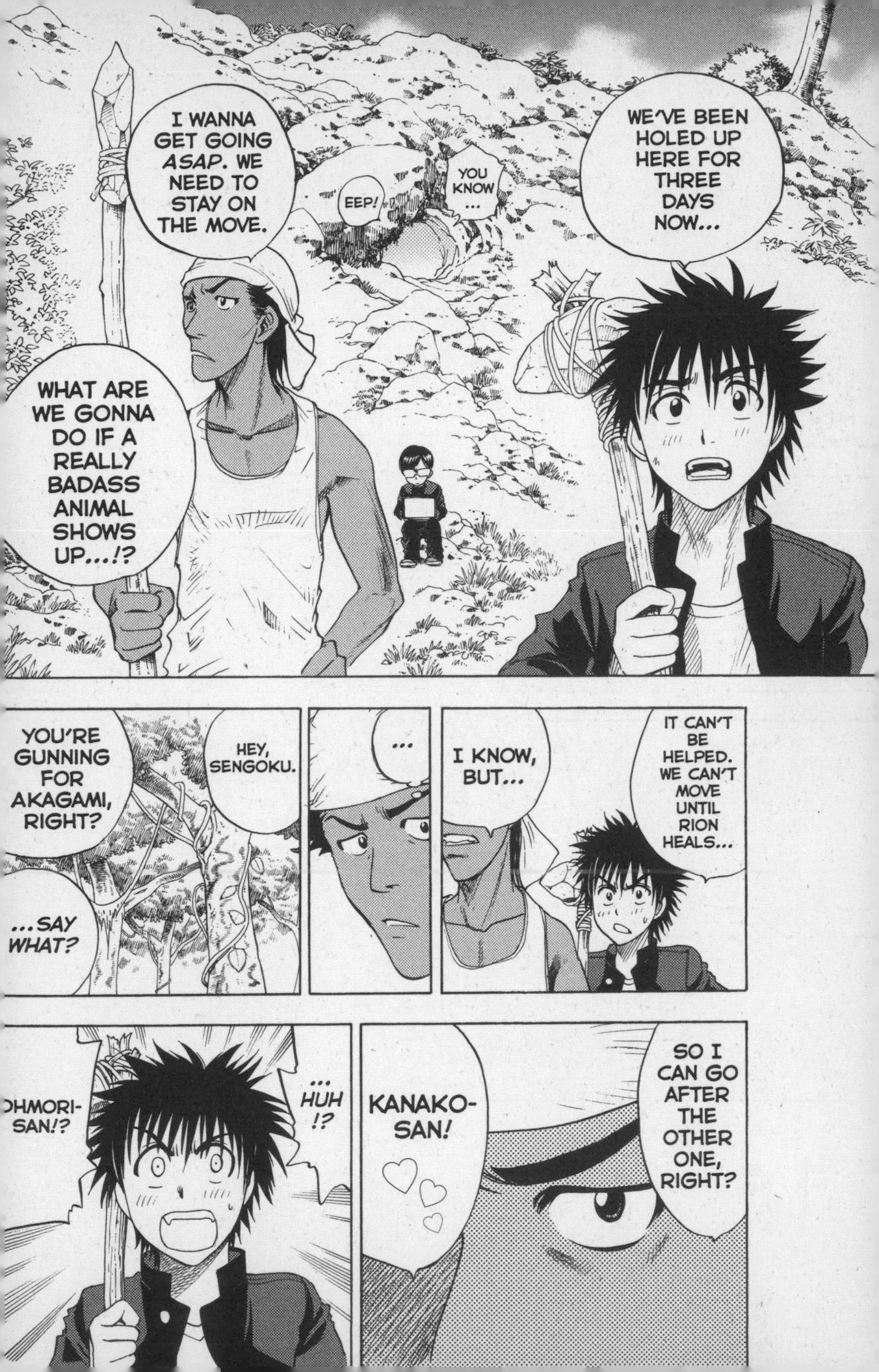
WE'VE BEEN HOLED UP HERE FOR THREE DAYS NOW...
YOU KNOW ...
EEP!
I WANNA GET GOING *ASAP*. WE NEED TO STAY ON THE MOVE.
WHAT ARE WE GONNA DO IF A REALLY BADASS ANIMAL SHOWS UP...!?
IT CAN'T BE HELPED. WE CAN'T MOVE UNTIL RION HEALS...
I KNOW, BUT...
...
HEY, SENGOKU.
YOU'RE GUNNING FOR AKAGAMI, RIGHT?
...SAY WHAT?
SO I CAN GO AFTER THE OTHER ONE, RIGHT?
KANAKO-SAN!
...HUH!?
OHMORI-SAN!?

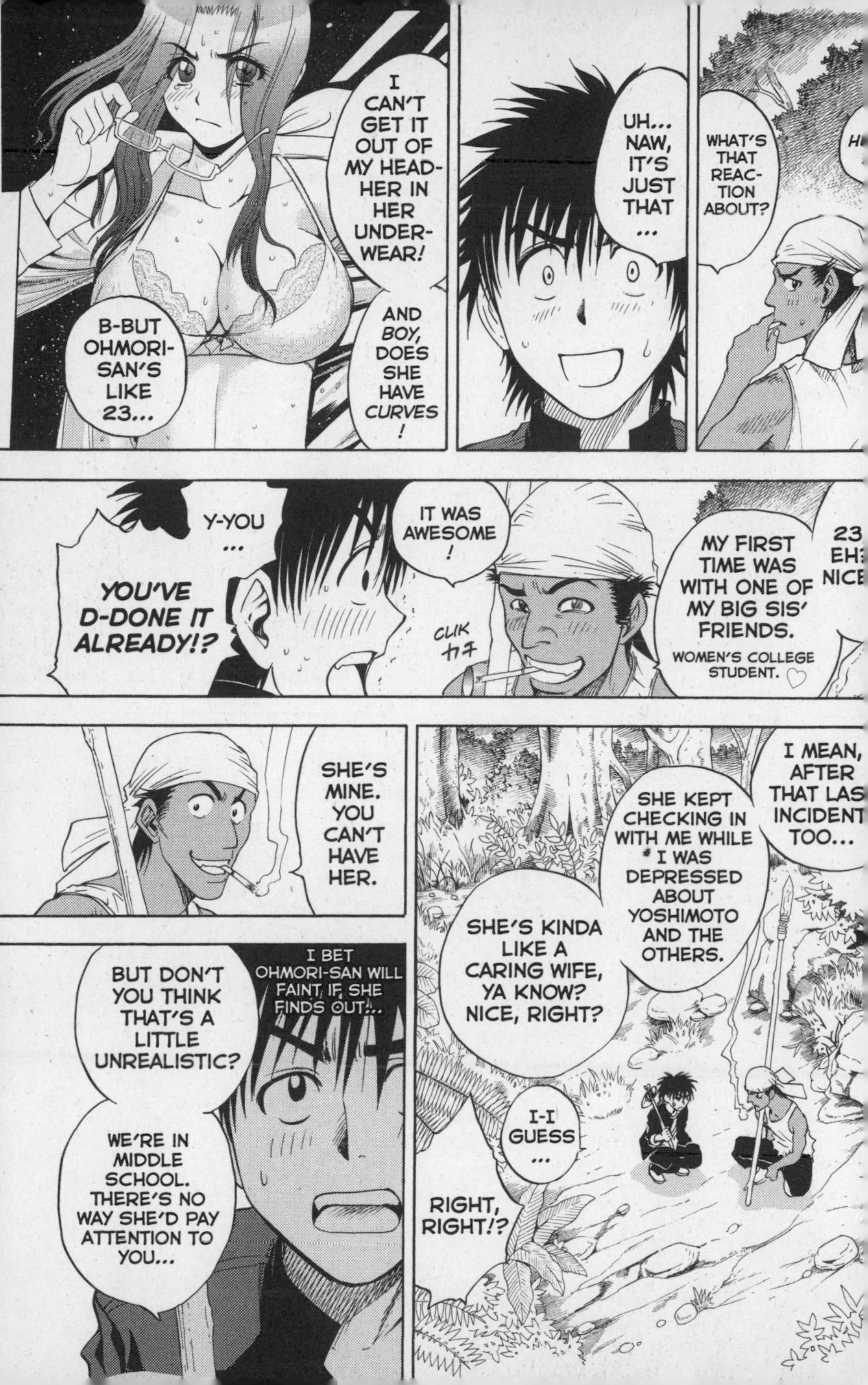
WHAT'S THAT REACTION ABOUT?
UH... NAW, IT'S JUST THAT ...
I CAN'T GET IT OUT OF MY HEAD- HER IN HER UNDERWEAR!
AND *BOY*, DOES SHE HAVE *CURVES*!
B-BUT OHMORI-SAN'S LIKE 23...
23 EH NICE
MY FIRST TIME WAS WITH ONE OF MY BIG SIS' FRIENDS.
WOMEN'S COLLEGE STUDENT. ♡
CLIK カチ
IT WAS AWESOME!
Y-YOU ...
YOU'VE D-DONE IT ALREADY!?
I MEAN, AFTER THAT LAS INCIDENT TOO...
SHE KEPT CHECKING IN WITH ME WHILE I WAS DEPRESSED ABOUT YOSHIMOTO AND THE OTHERS.
SHE'S KINDA LIKE A CARING WIFE, YA KNOW? NICE, RIGHT?
I-I GUESS ...
RIGHT, RIGHT!?
SHE'S MINE. YOU CAN'T HAVE HER.
I BET OHMORI-SAN WILL FAINT IF SHE FINDS OUT...
BUT DON'T YOU THINK THAT'S A LITTLE UNREALISTIC?
WE'RE IN MIDDLE SCHOOL. THERE'S NO WAY SHE'D PAY ATTENTION TO YOU...

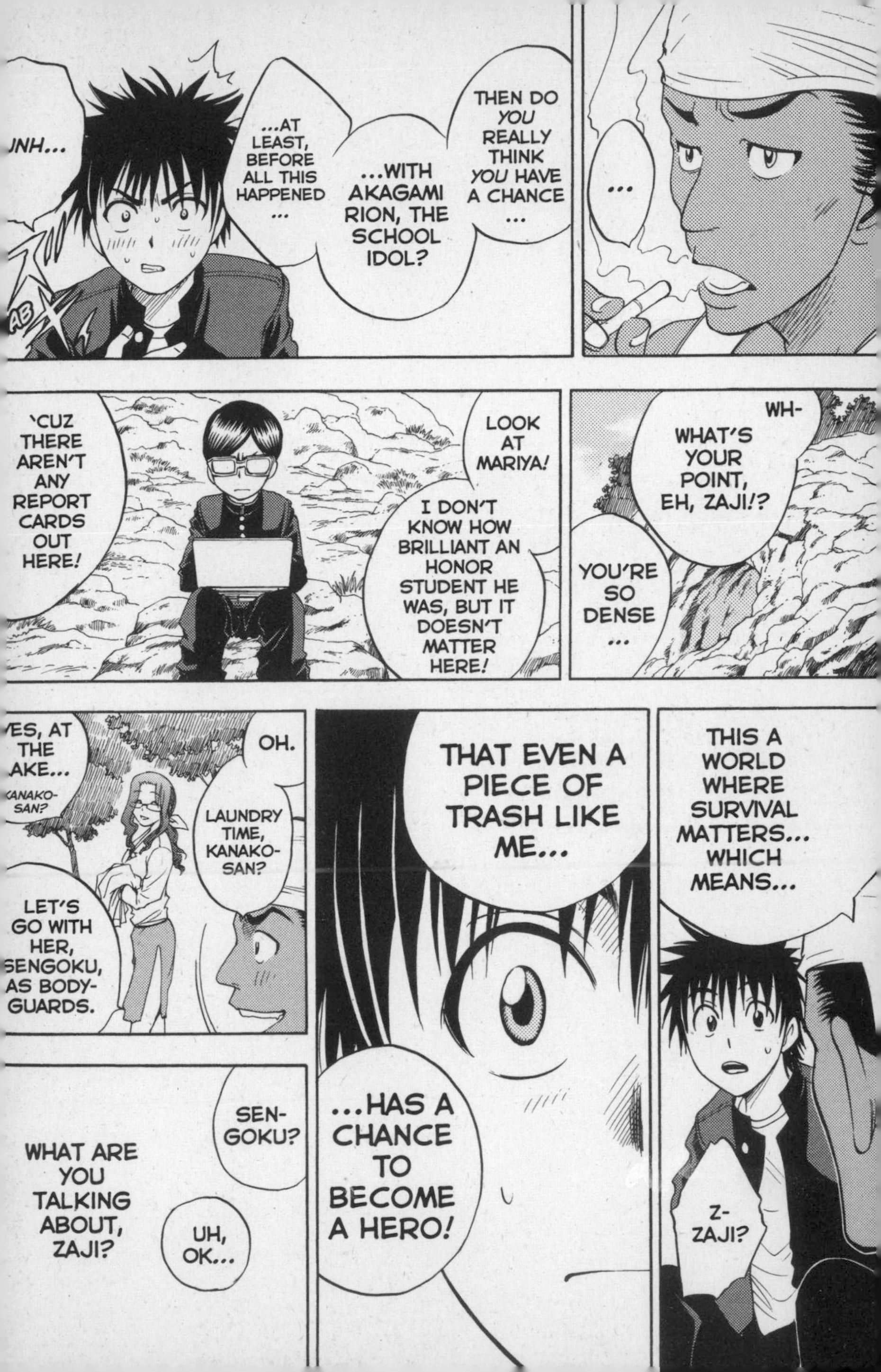
...
THEN DO YOU REALLY THINK YOU HAVE A CHANCE ...
...WITH AKAGAMI RION, THE SCHOOL IDOL?
...AT LEAST, BEFORE ALL THIS HAPPENED ...
UNH...
WH- WHAT'S YOUR POINT, EH, ZAJI!?
YOU'RE SO DENSE ...
LOOK AT MARIYA!
I DON'T KNOW HOW BRILLIANT AN HONOR STUDENT HE WAS, BUT IT DOESN'T MATTER HERE!
'CUZ THERE AREN'T ANY REPORT CARDS OUT HERE!
THIS A WORLD WHERE SURVIVAL MATTERS... WHICH MEANS...
Z- ZAJI?
THAT EVEN A PIECE OF TRASH LIKE ME...
...HAS A CHANCE TO BECOME A HERO!
OH.
LAUNDRY TIME, KANAKO-SAN?
ES, AT THE AKE...
ANAKO-SAN?
LET'S GO WITH HER, SENGOKU, AS BODY-GUARDS.
SEN-GOKU?
WHAT ARE YOU TALKING ABOUT, ZAJI?
UH, OK...

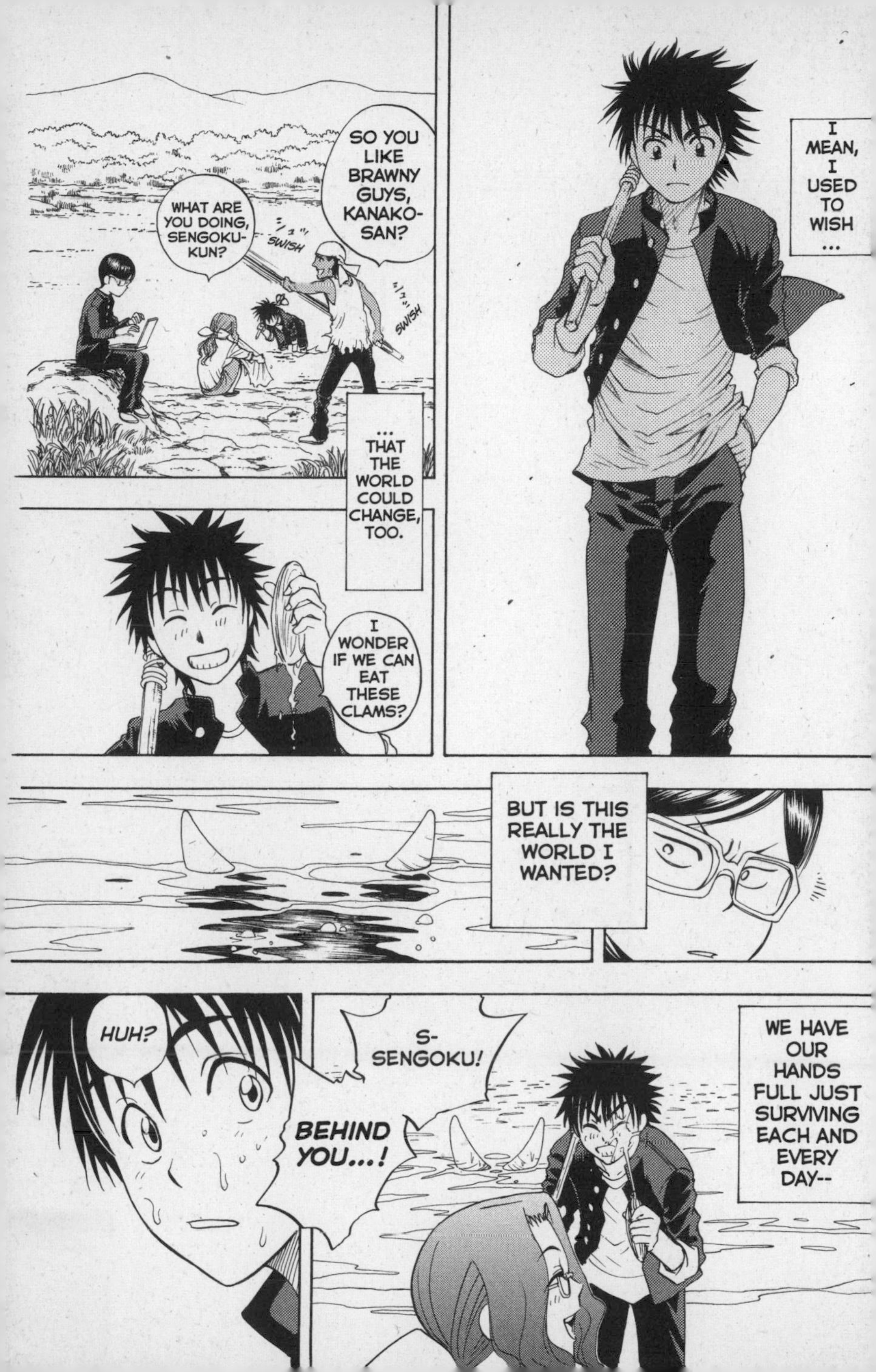
I MEAN, I USED TO WISH ...
SO YOU LIKE BRAWNY GUYS, KANAKO-SAN?
WHAT ARE YOU DOING, SENGOKU-KUN?
SWISH
SWISH
... THAT THE WORLD COULD CHANGE, TOO.
I WONDER IF WE CAN EAT THESE CLAMS?
BUT IS THIS REALLY THE WORLD I WANTED?
WE HAVE OUR HANDS FULL JUST SURVIVING EACH AND EVERY DAY--
S-SENGOKU!
BEHIND YOU...!
HUH?

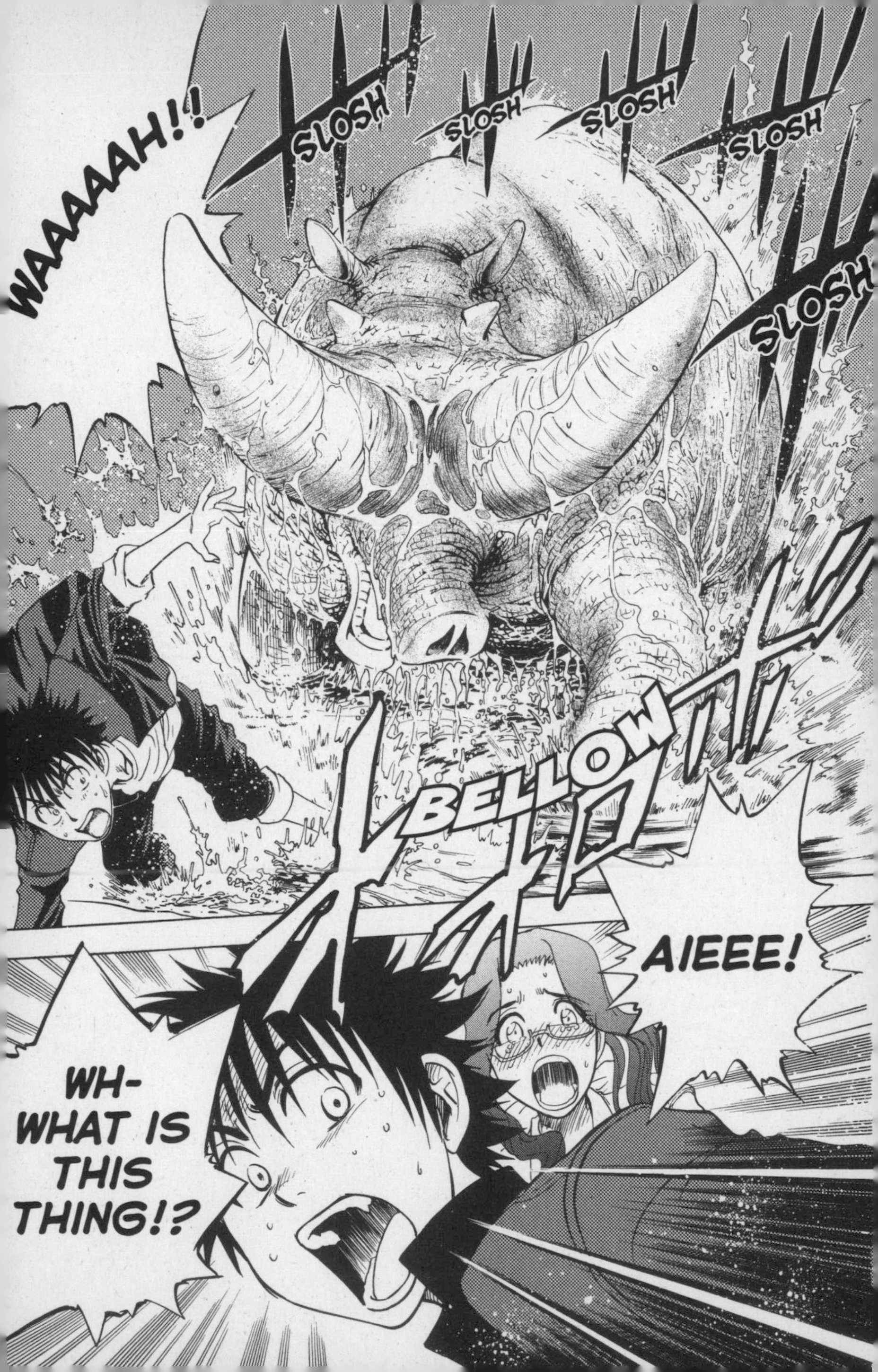
SLOSH
SLOSH
SLOSH
SLOSH
SLOSH
WAAAAAH!!
BELLOW
AIEEE!
WH- WHAT IS THIS THING!?

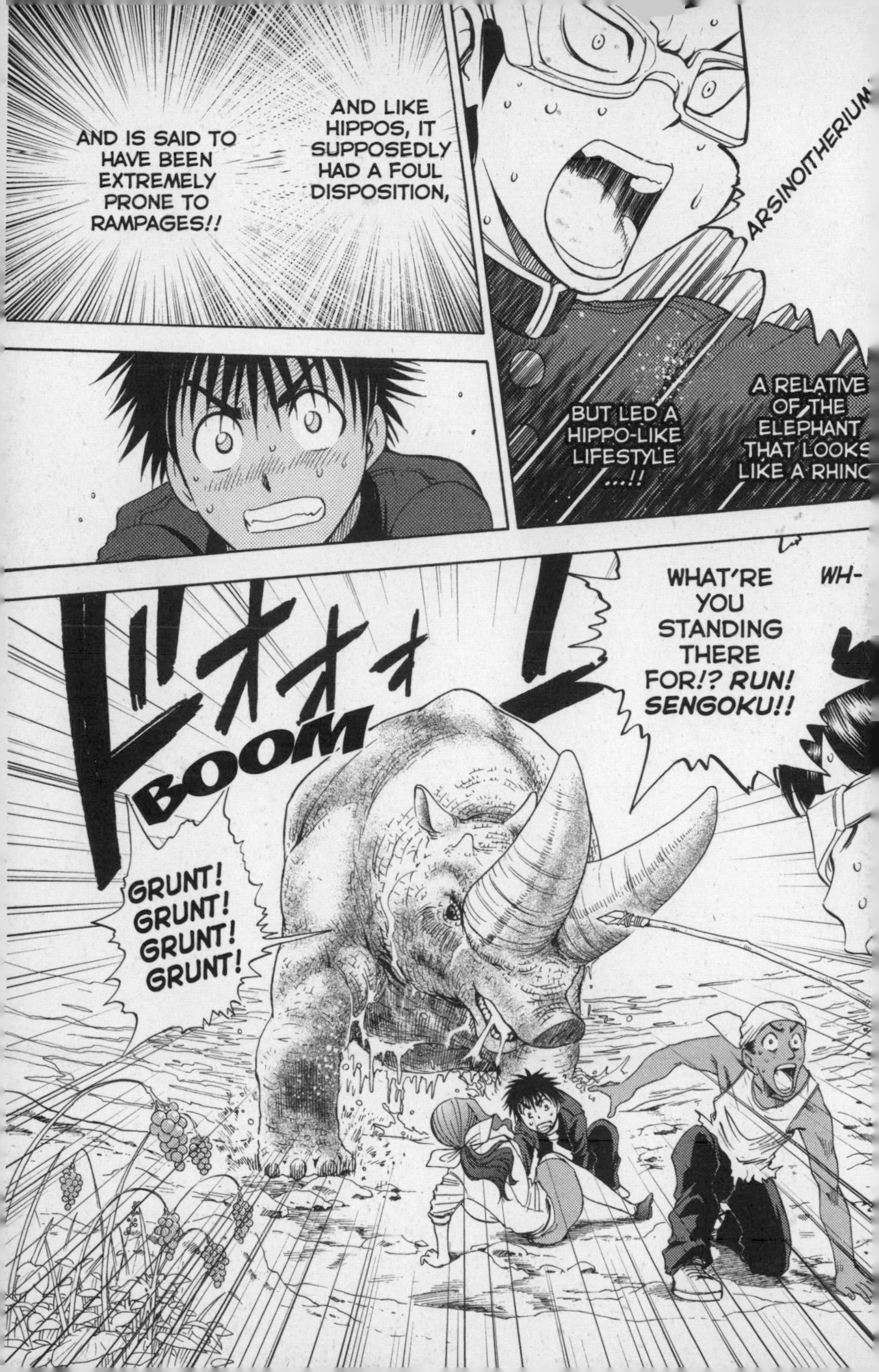
ARSINOITHERIUM
A RELATIVE OF THE ELEPHANT THAT LOOKS LIKE A RHIN
BUT LED A HIPPO-LIKE LIFESTYLE ...!!
AND LIKE HIPPOS, IT SUPPOSEDLY HAD A FOUL DISPOSITION,
AND IS SAID TO HAVE BEEN EXTREMELY PRONE TO RAMPAGES!!
WH-
WHAT'RE YOU STANDING THERE FOR!? RUN! SENGOKU!!
ドオオォー
BOOM
GRUNT! GRUNT! GRUNT! GRUNT!

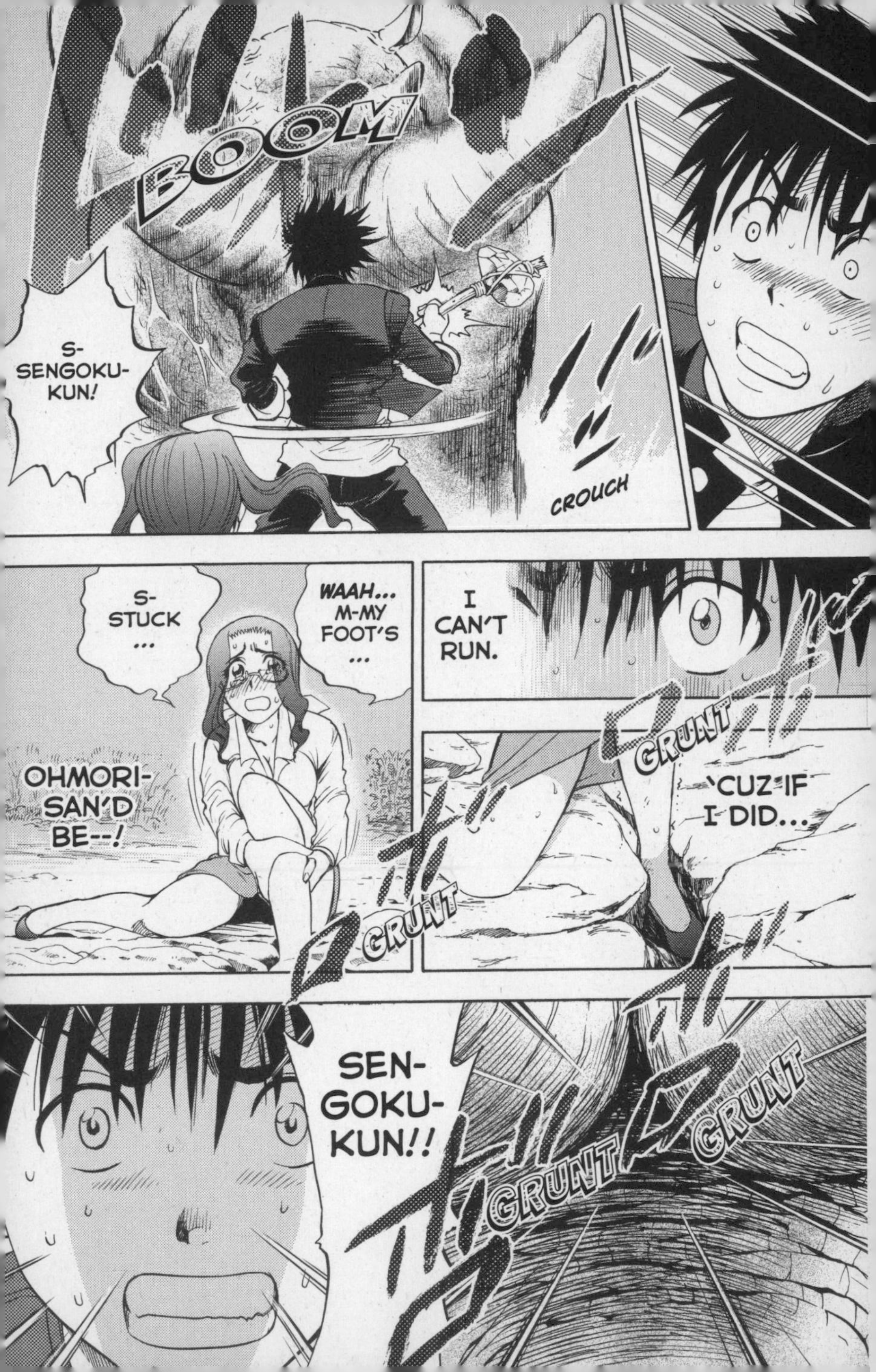
BOOM
S-SENGOKU-KUN!
CROUCH
I CAN'T RUN.
GRUNT
'CUZ IF I DID...
GRUNT
WAAH... M-MY FOOT'S ...
S-STUCK ...
OHMORI-SAN'D BE--!
GRUNT
GRUNT
GRUNT
SEN-GOKU-KUN!!

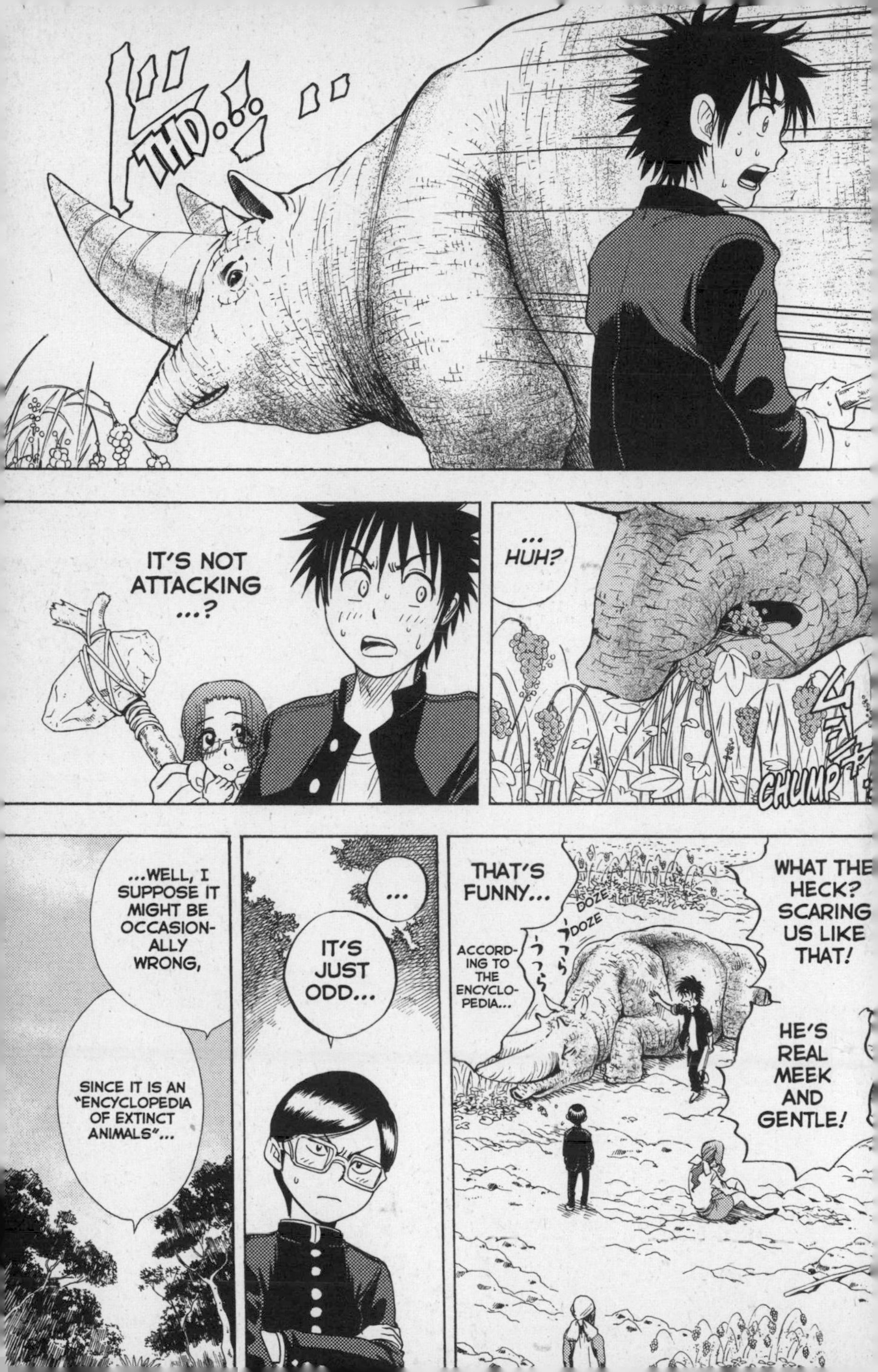
THD...
... HUH?
CHUMP
IT'S NOT ATTACKING ...?
WHAT THE HECK? SCARING US LIKE THAT!
HE'S REAL MEEK AND GENTLE!
DOZE
DOZE
うつら
うつら
THAT'S FUNNY...
ACCORDING TO THE ENCYCLOPEDIA...
...
IT'S JUST ODD...
...WELL, I SUPPOSE IT MIGHT BE OCCASIONALLY WRONG,
SINCE IT IS AN "ENCYCLOPEDIA OF EXTINCT ANIMALS"...

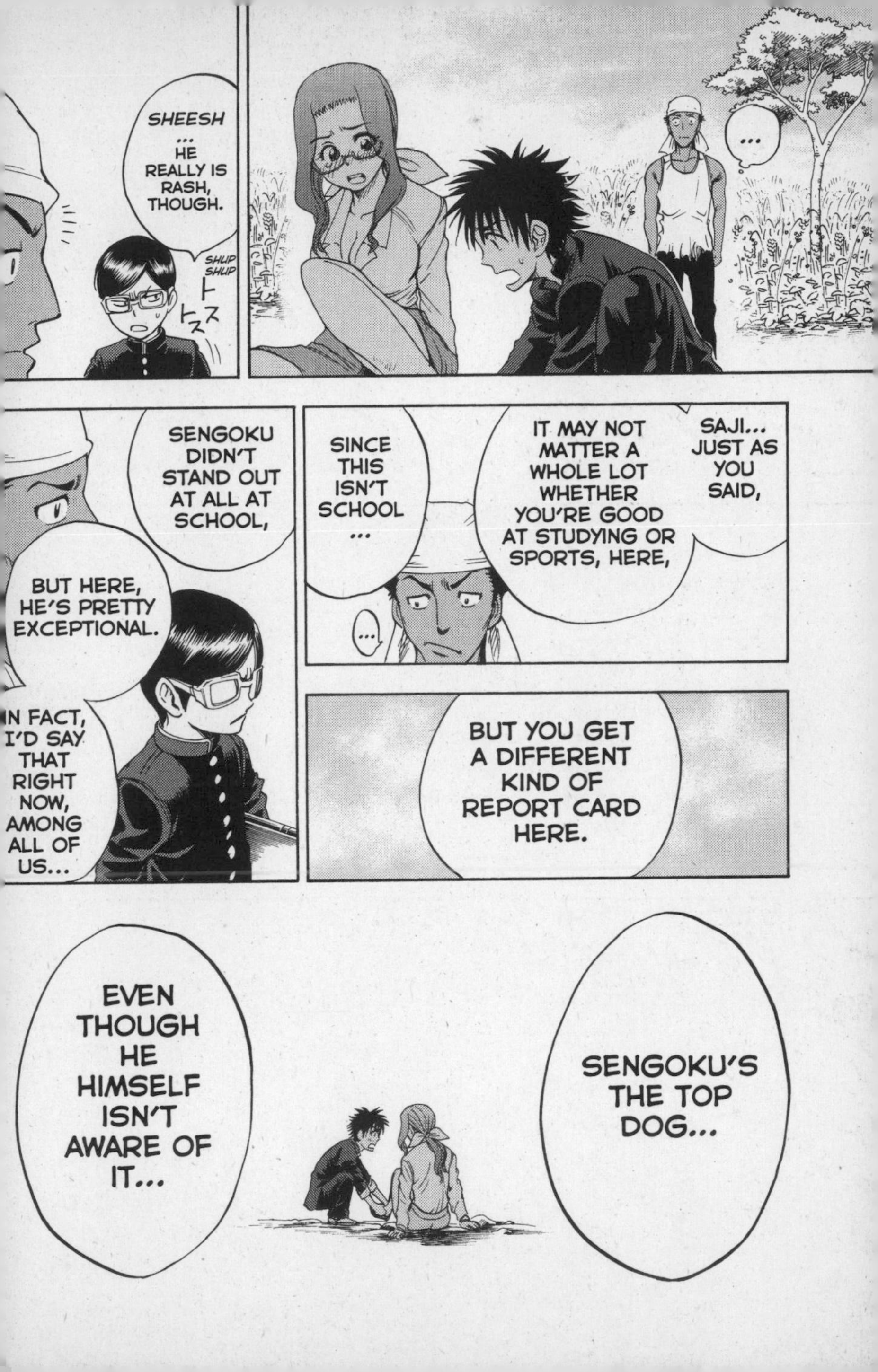
...
SHEESH ... HE REALLY IS RASH, THOUGH.
SHUP SHUP
SAJI... JUST AS YOU SAID,
IT MAY NOT MATTER A WHOLE LOT WHETHER YOU'RE GOOD AT STUDYING OR SPORTS, HERE,
SINCE THIS ISN'T SCHOOL ...
...
BUT YOU GET A DIFFERENT KIND OF REPORT CARD HERE.
SENGOKU DIDN'T STAND OUT AT ALL AT SCHOOL,
BUT HERE, HE'S PRETTY EXCEPTIONAL.
IN FACT, I'D SAY THAT RIGHT NOW, AMONG ALL OF US...
SENGOKU'S THE TOP DOG...
EVEN THOUGH HE HIMSELF ISN'T AWARE OF IT...

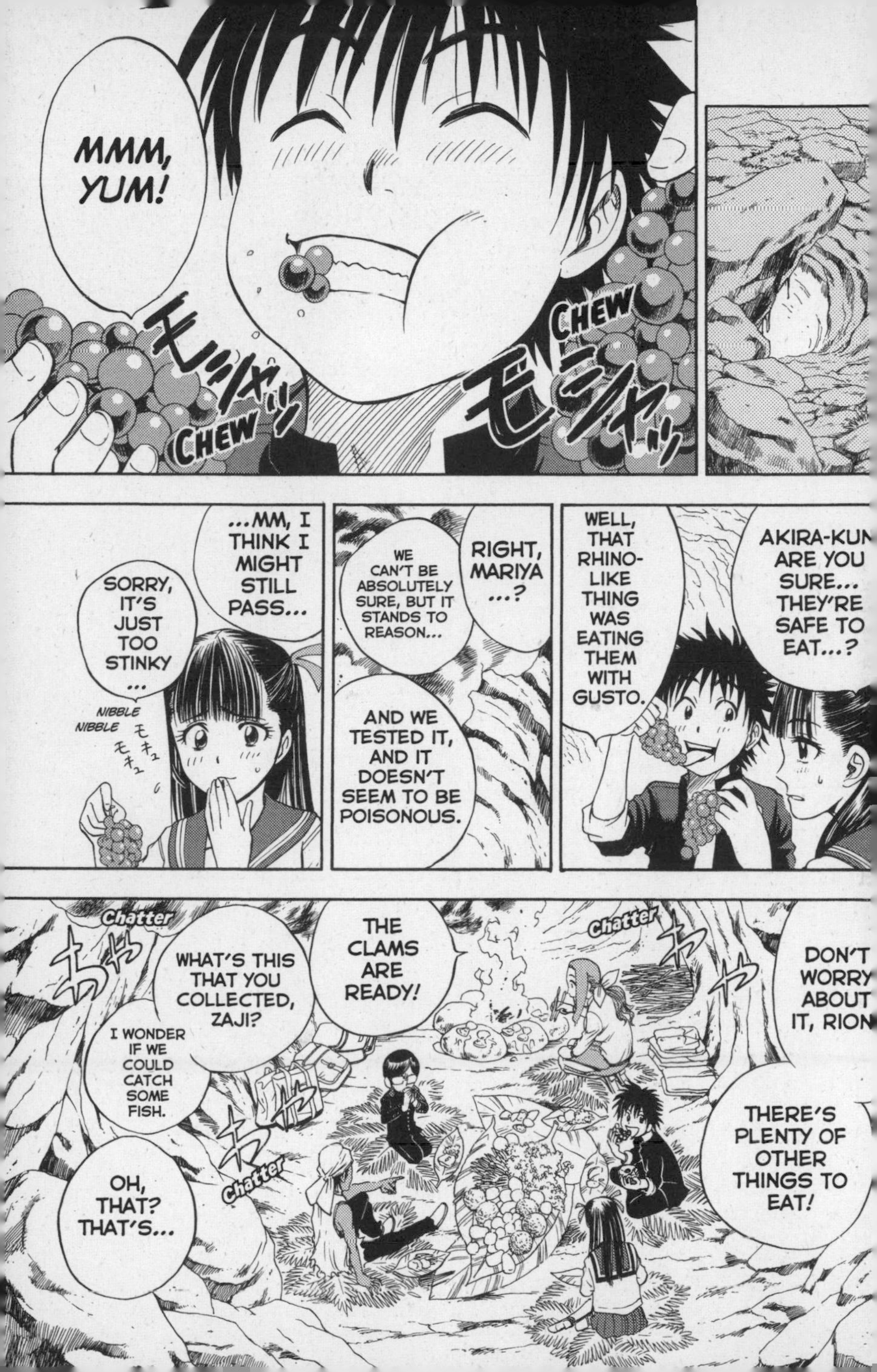
MMM, YUM!
CHEW
モシャッ
CHEW
モシャッ
AKIRA-KUN ARE YOU SURE... THEY'RE SAFE TO EAT...?
WELL, THAT RHINO-LIKE THING WAS EATING THEM WITH GUSTO.
RIGHT, MARIYA...?
WE CAN'T BE ABSOLUTELY SURE, BUT IT STANDS TO REASON...
AND WE TESTED IT, AND IT DOESN'T SEEM TO BE POISONOUS.
...MM, I THINK I MIGHT STILL PASS...
SORRY, IT'S JUST TOO STINKY...
NIBBLE NIBBLE
モキュ モキュ
DON'T WORRY ABOUT IT, RION
THERE'S PLENTY OF OTHER THINGS TO EAT!
Chatter
わや
THE CLAMS ARE READY!
WHAT'S THIS THAT YOU COLLECTED, ZAJI?
I WONDER IF WE COULD CATCH SOME FISH.
OH, THAT? THAT'S...
Chatter
わや
Chatter
わや

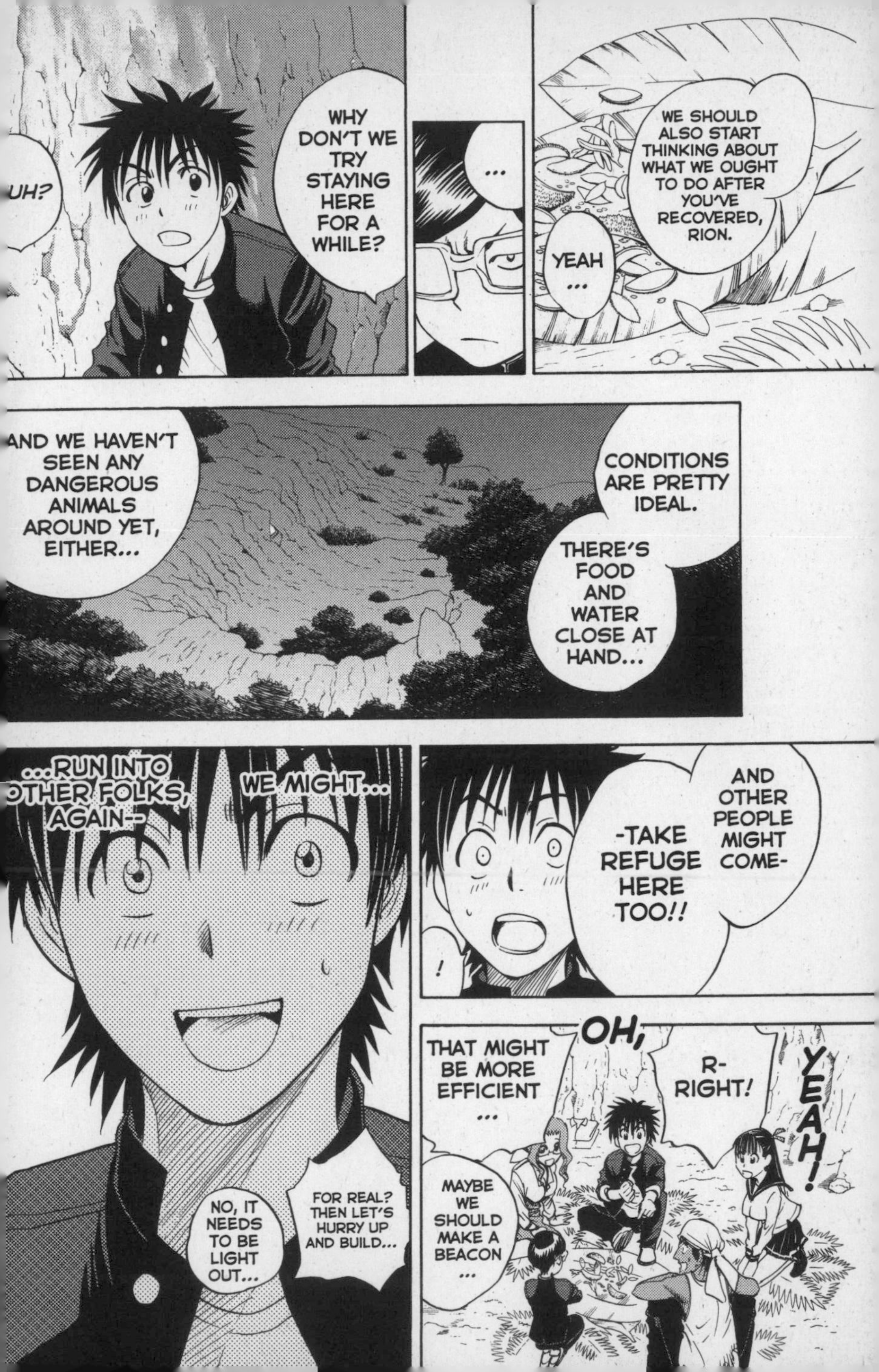
WE SHOULD ALSO START THINKING ABOUT WHAT WE OUGHT TO DO AFTER YOU'VE RECOVERED, RION.
YEAH ...
...
WHY DON'T WE TRY STAYING HERE FOR A WHILE?
UH?
CONDITIONS ARE PRETTY IDEAL.
THERE'S FOOD AND WATER CLOSE AT HAND...
AND WE HAVEN'T SEEN ANY DANGEROUS ANIMALS AROUND YET, EITHER...
AND OTHER PEOPLE MIGHT COME-
-TAKE REFUGE HERE TOO!!
!
YEAH!
R- RIGHT!
OH,
THAT MIGHT BE MORE EFFICIENT ...
MAYBE WE SHOULD MAKE A BEACON ...
WE MIGHT...
...RUN INTO OTHER FOLKS, AGAIN-
FOR REAL? THEN LET'S HURRY UP AND BUILD...
NO, IT NEEDS TO BE LIGHT OUT...

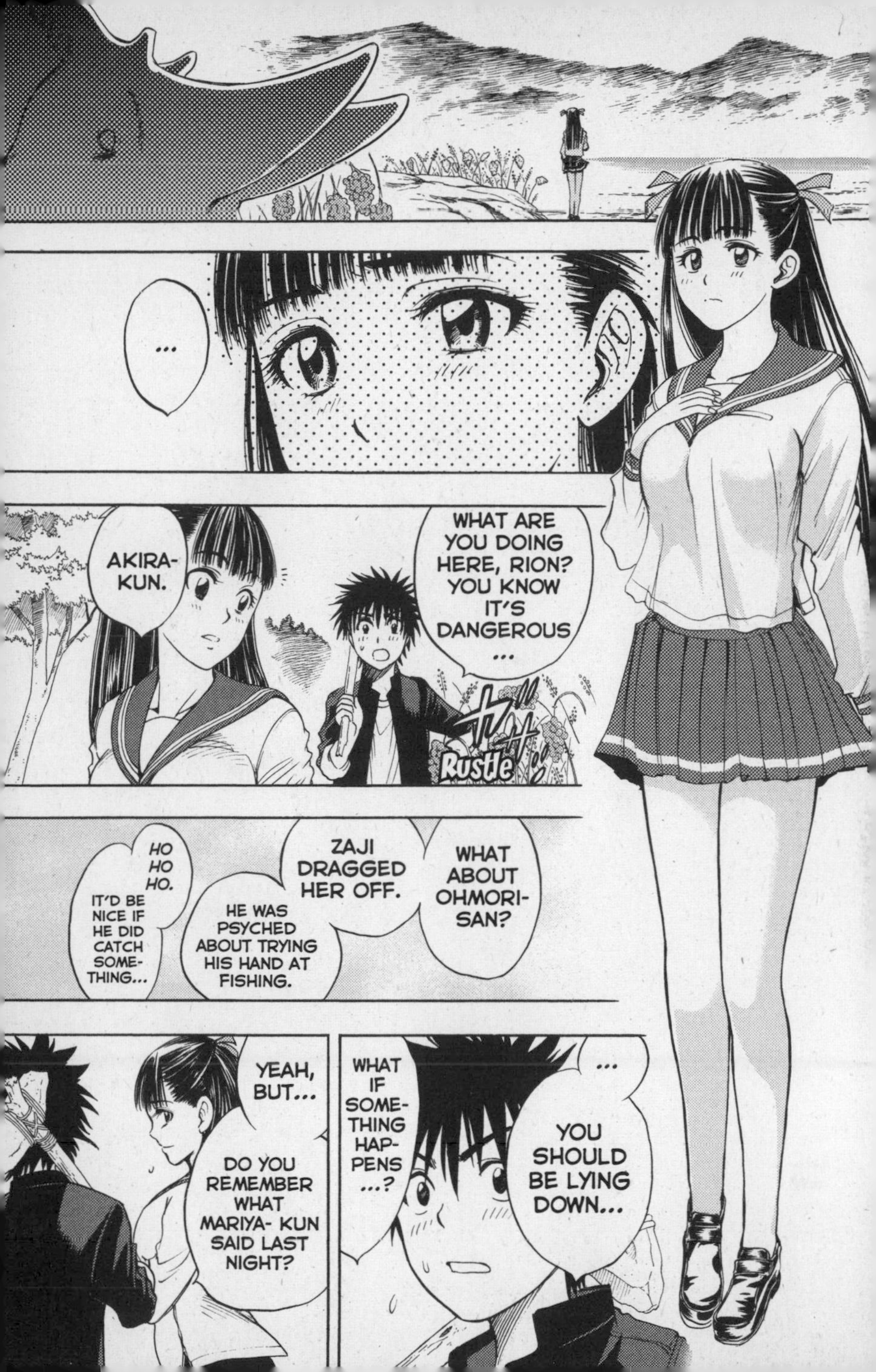
...
WHAT ARE YOU DOING HERE, RION? YOU KNOW IT'S DANGEROUS ...
AKIRA-KUN.
Rustle
WHAT ABOUT OHMORI-SAN?
ZAJI DRAGGED HER OFF.
HE WAS PSYCHED ABOUT TRYING HIS HAND AT FISHING.
HO HO HO.
IT'D BE NICE IF HE DID CATCH SOME-THING...
...
YOU SHOULD BE LYING DOWN...
WHAT IF SOME-THING HAP-PENS ...?
YEAH, BUT...
DO YOU REMEMBER WHAT MARIYA- KUN SAID LAST NIGHT?

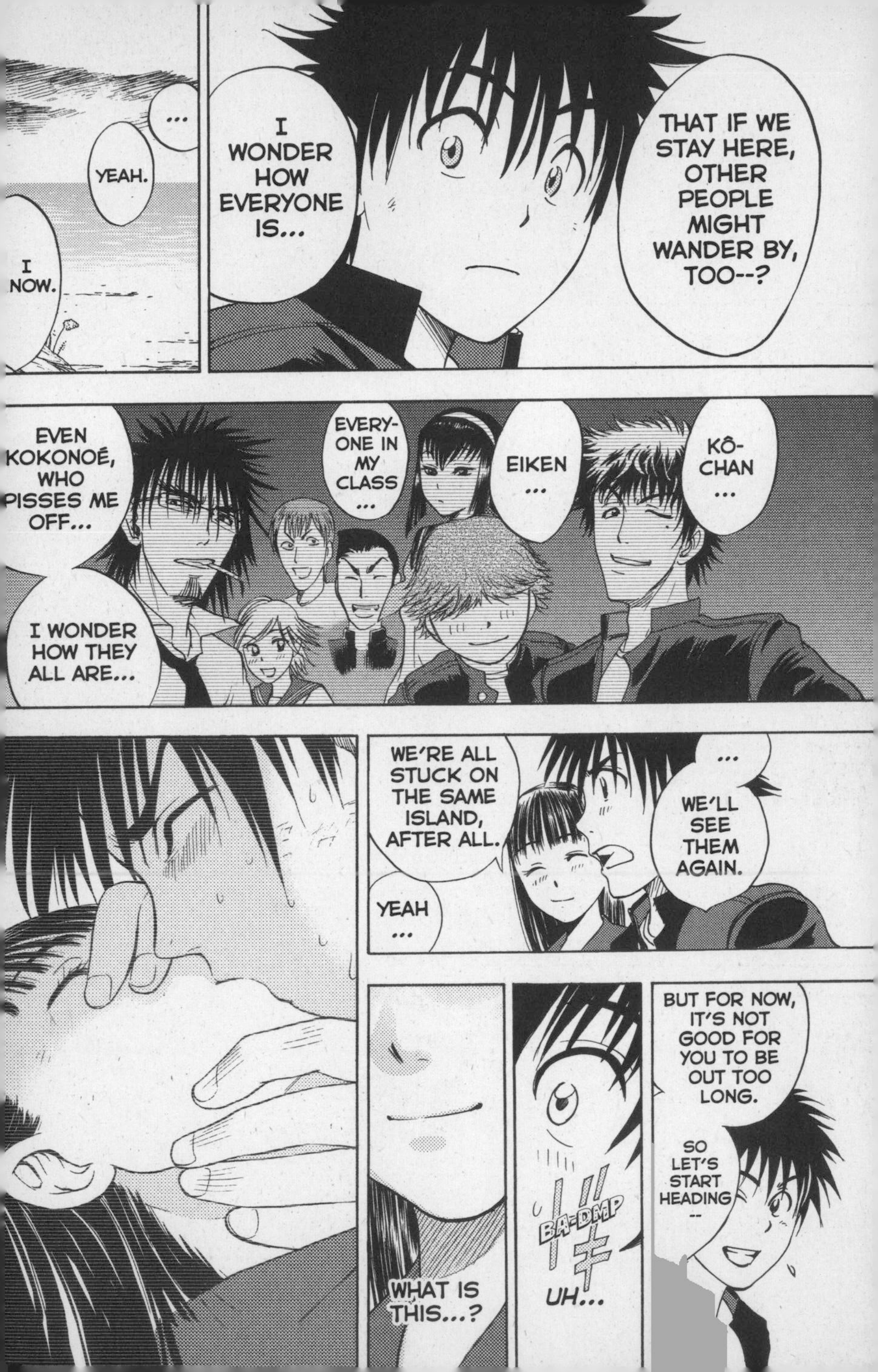
THAT IF WE STAY HERE, OTHER PEOPLE MIGHT WANDER BY, TOO--?
I WONDER HOW EVERYONE IS...
...
YEAH.
I NOW.
KÔ-CHAN ...
EIKEN ...
EVERY-ONE IN MY CLASS ...
EVEN KOKONOÉ, WHO PISSES ME OFF...
I WONDER HOW THEY ALL ARE...
...
WE'LL SEE THEM AGAIN.
WE'RE ALL STUCK ON THE SAME ISLAND, AFTER ALL.
YEAH ...
BUT FOR NOW, IT'S NOT GOOD FOR YOU TO BE OUT TOO LONG.
SO LET'S START HEADING --
BA-DMP
UH...
WHAT IS THIS...?

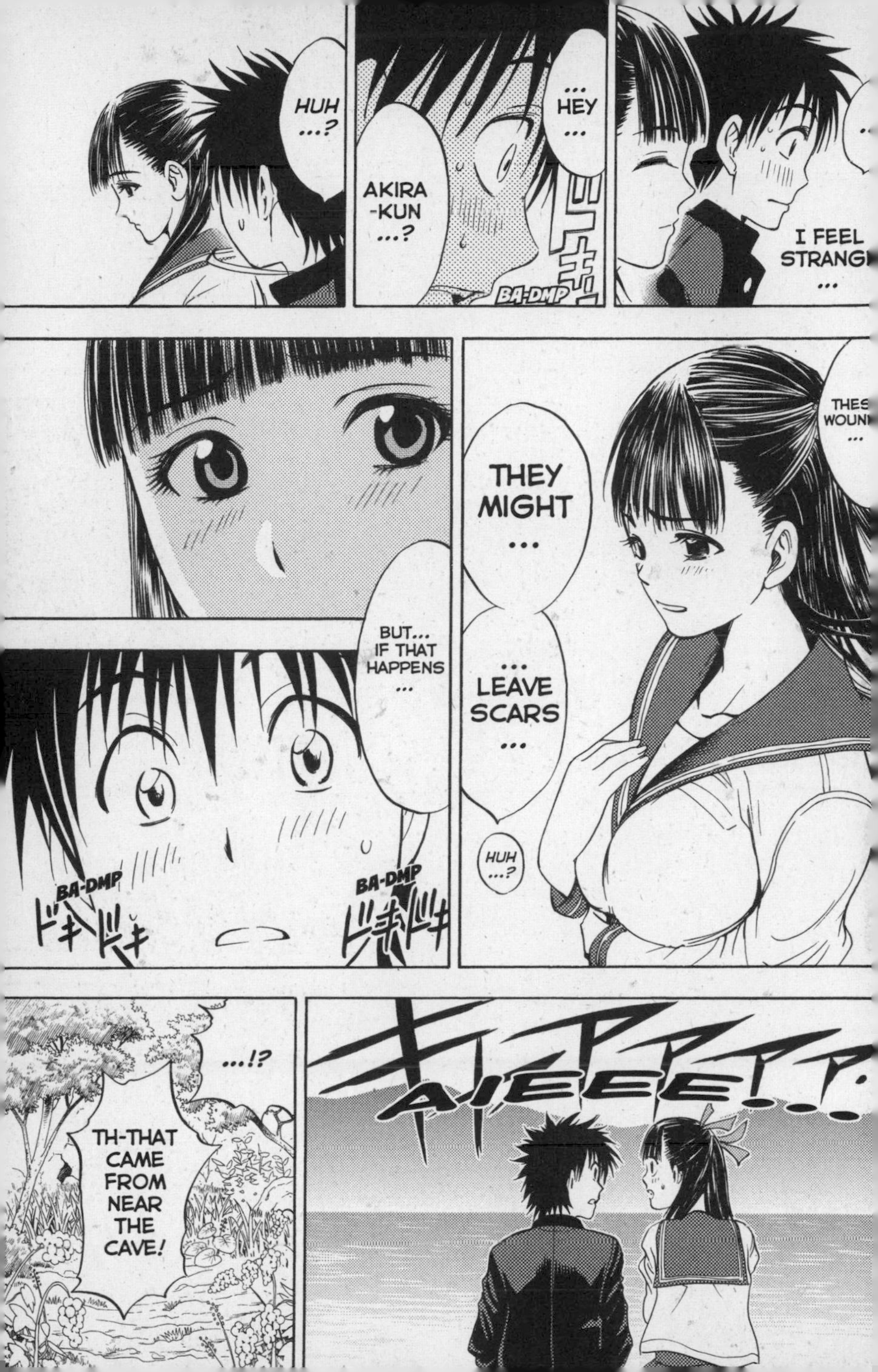

I FEEL STRANG ...
... HEY ...
AKIRA -KUN ...?
BA-DMP
HUH ...?
THES WOUN ...
THEY MIGHT ...
... LEAVE SCARS ...
HUH ...?
BUT... IF THAT HAPPENS ...
BA-DMP
ドキドキ
BA-DMP
ドキドキ
AIEEE!..!..
...!?
TH-THAT CAME FROM NEAR THE CAVE!

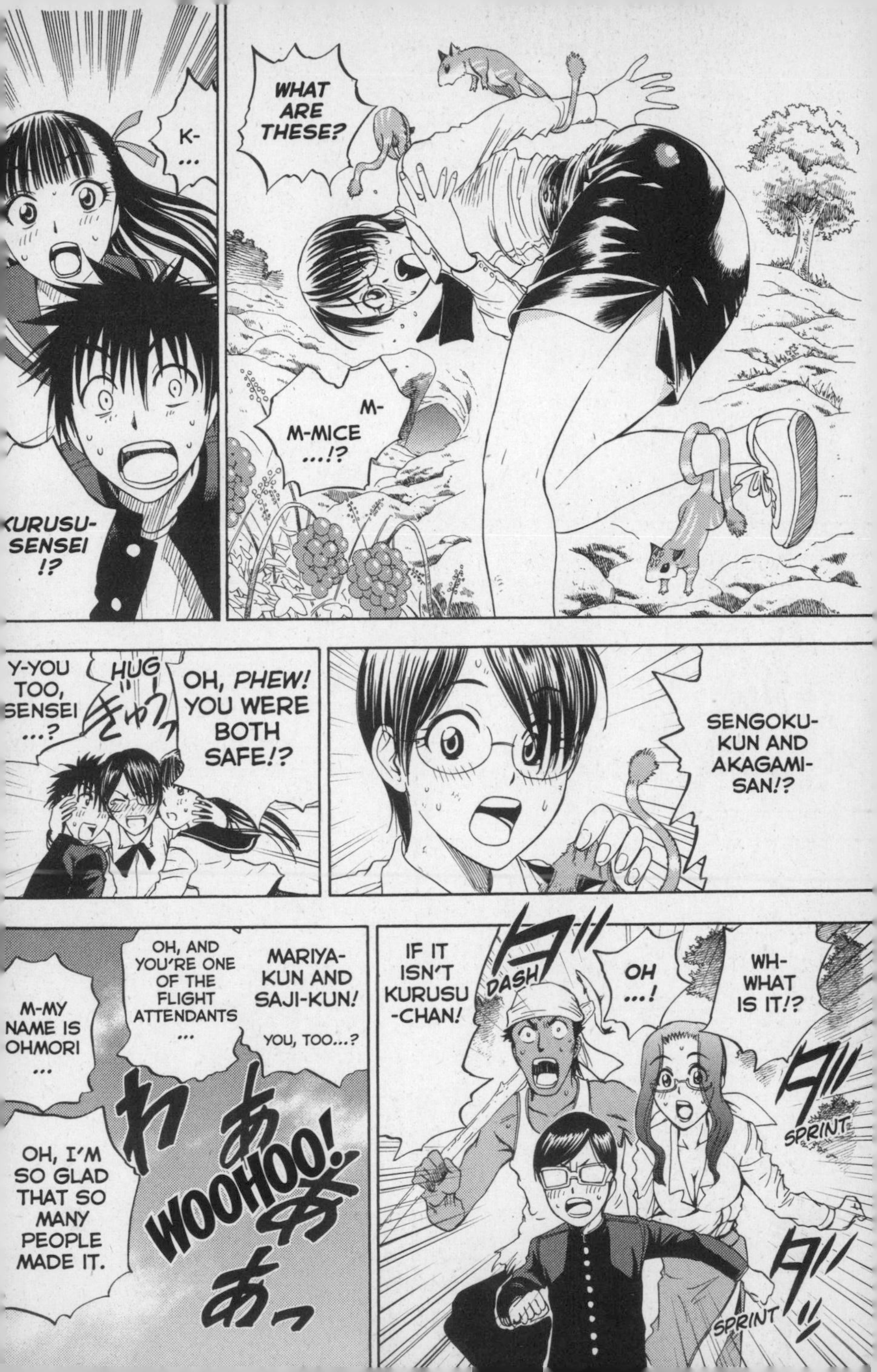
WHAT ARE THESE?
M-
M-MICE ...!?
K-
...
KURUSU-SENSEI !?
SENGOKU-KUN AND AKAGAMI-SAN!?
OH, PHEW! YOU WERE BOTH SAFE!?
HUG
Y-YOU TOO, SENSEI ...?
WH-WHAT IS IT!?
OH ...!
DASH
IF IT ISN'T KURUSU-CHAN!
SPRINT
SPRINT
MARIYA-KUN AND SAJI-KUN!
YOU, TOO...?
OH, AND YOU'RE ONE OF THE FLIGHT ATTENDANTS ...
M-MY NAME IS OHMORI ...
WOOHOO!
OH, I'M SO GLAD THAT SO MANY PEOPLE MADE IT.

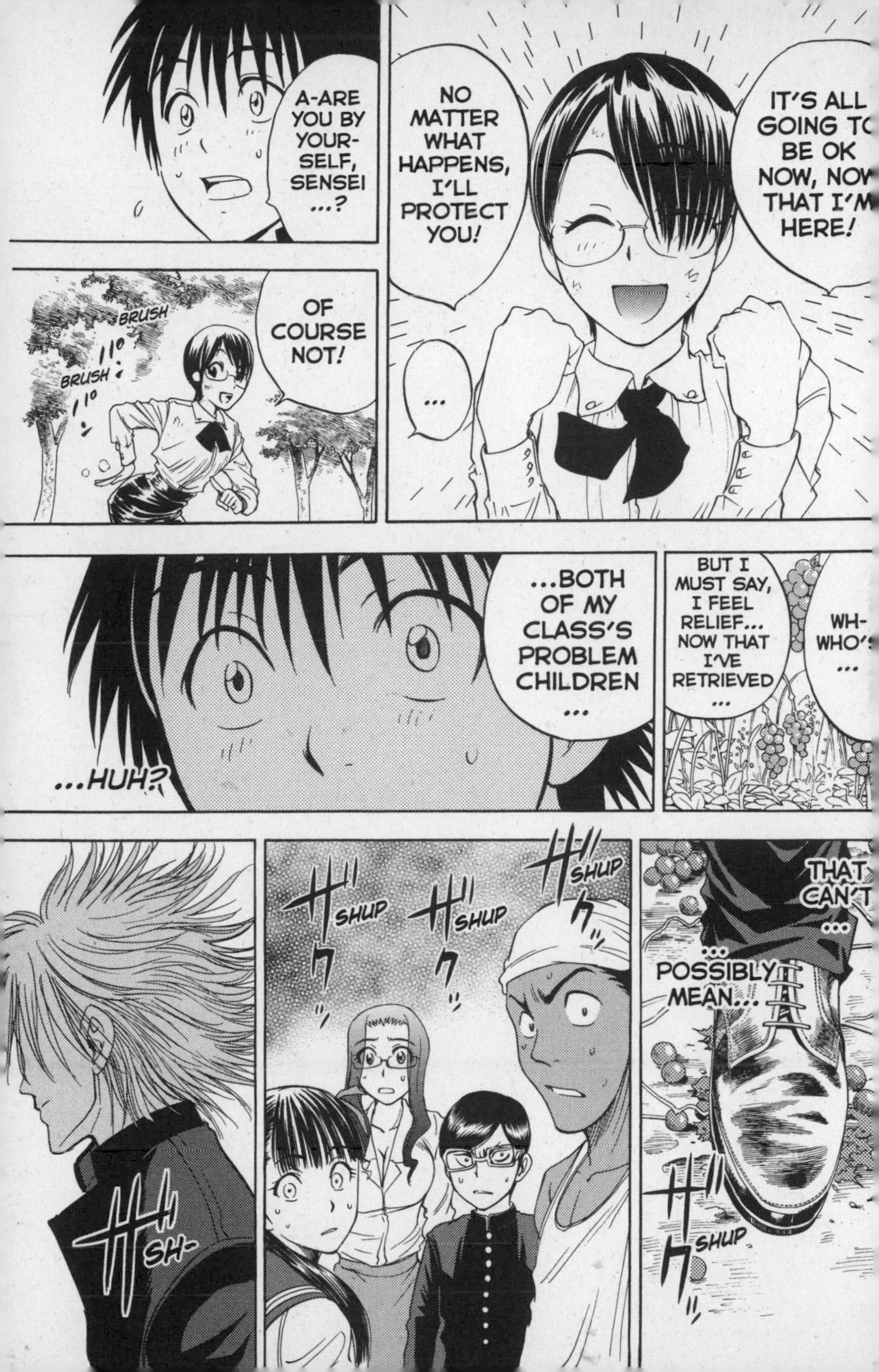
IT'S ALL GOING TO BE OK NOW, NOW THAT I'M HERE!
NO MATTER WHAT HAPPENS, I'LL PROTECT YOU!
...
A-ARE YOU BY YOURSELF, SENSEI ...?
OF COURSE NOT!
BRUSH
BRUSH
WH-WHO'...
BUT I MUST SAY, I FEEL RELIEF... NOW THAT I'VE RETRIEVED ...
...BOTH OF MY CLASS'S PROBLEM CHILDREN ...
...HUH?
THAT CAN'T ...
... POSSIBLY MEAN...
SHUP
SHUP
SHUP
SHUP
SH-

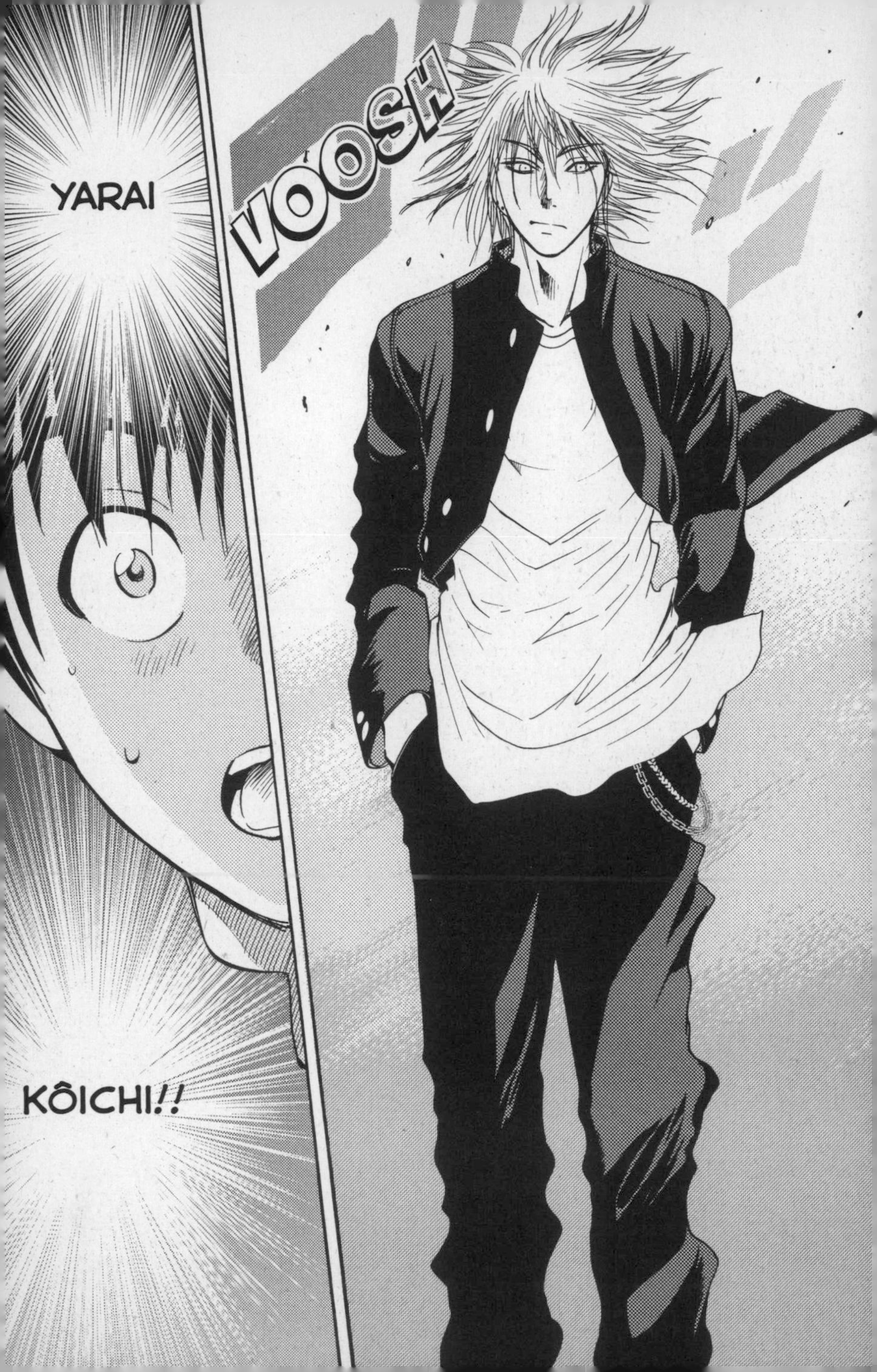
VOOSH
YARAI
KÔICHI!!

To Be Continued...

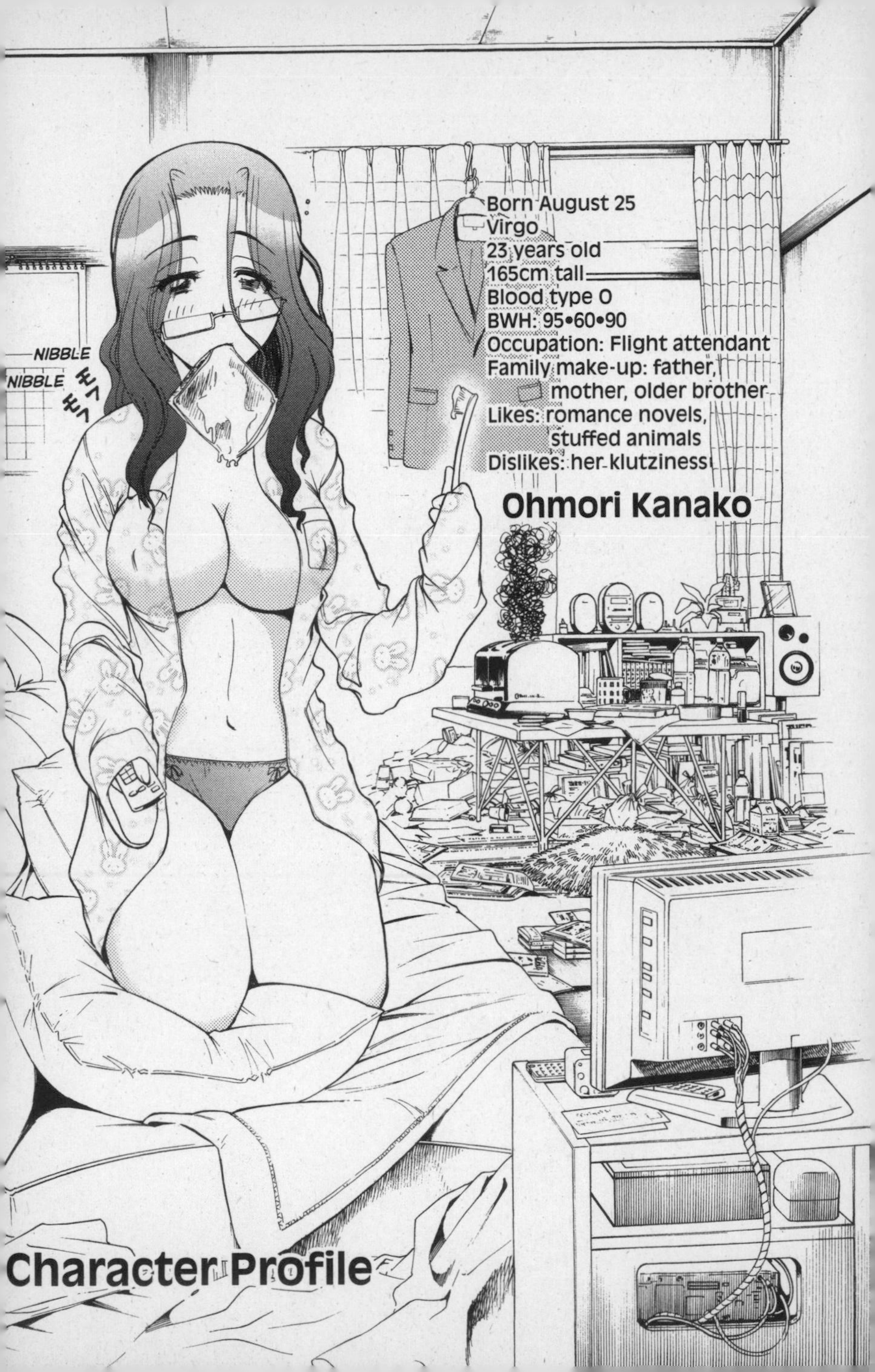

NIBBLE
NIBBLE
Born August 25
Virgo
23 years old
165cm tall
Blood type O
BWH: 95•60•90
Occupation: Flight attendant
Family make-up: father, mother, older brother
Likes: romance novels, stuffed animals
Dislikes: her klutziness
Ohmori Kanako
Character Profile

Character Profile

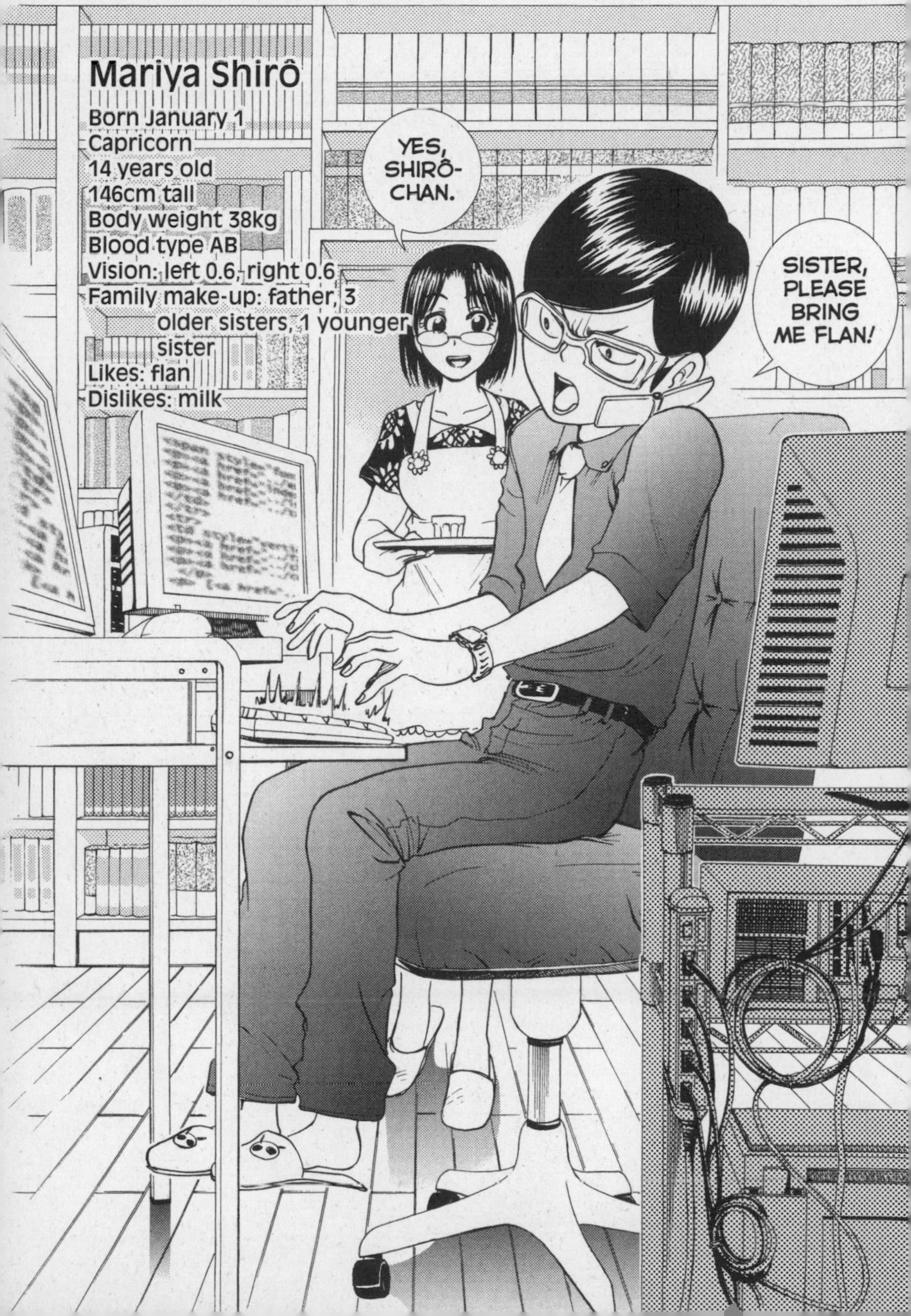
SISTER, PLEASE BRING ME FLAN!
YES, SHIRÔ-CHAN.
Mariya Shirô
Born January 1
Capricorn
14 years old
146cm tall
Body weight 38kg
Blood type AB
Vision: left 0.6, right 0.6
Family make-up: father, 3 older sisters, 1 younger sister
Likes: flan
Dislikes: milk

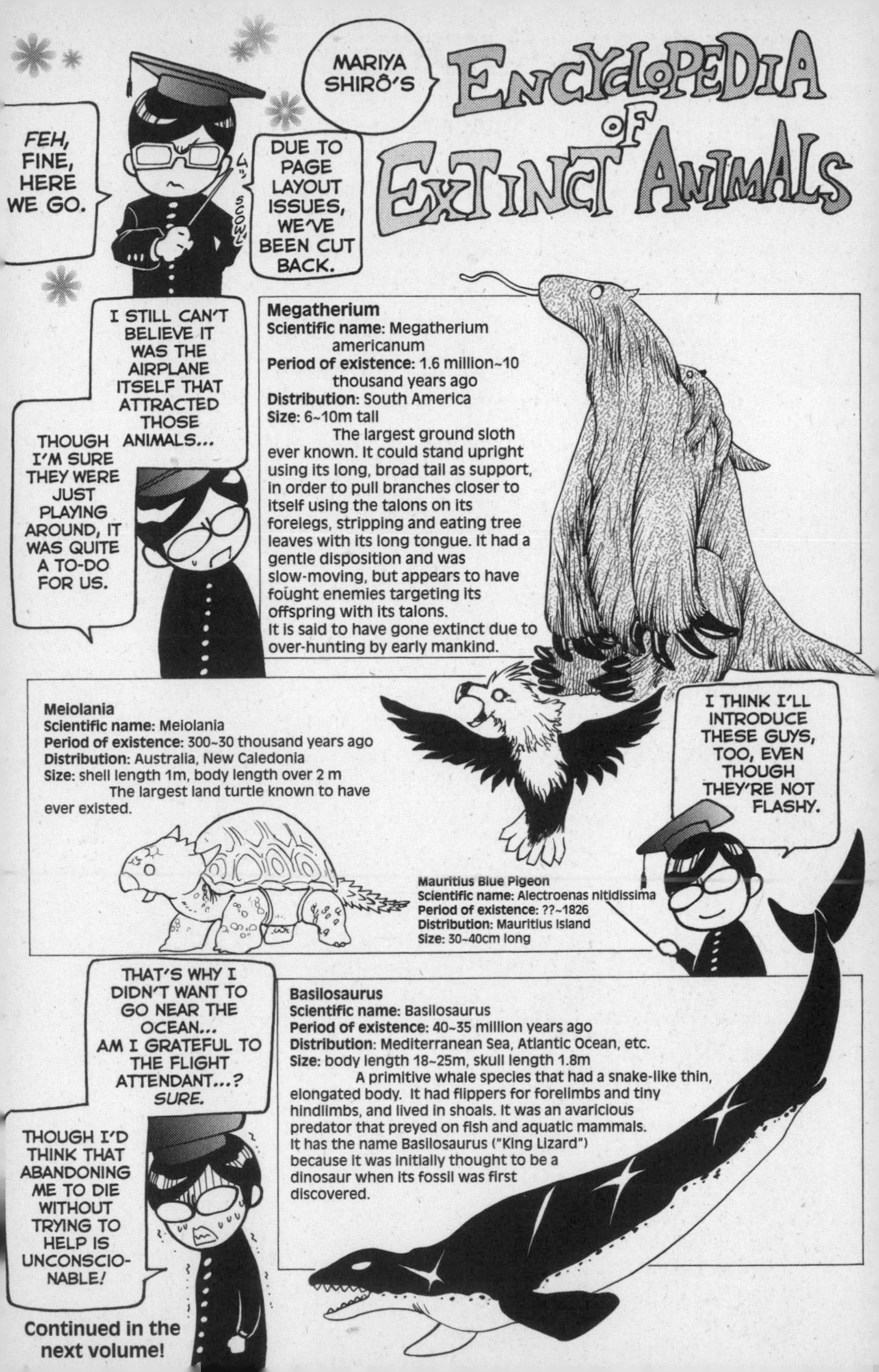
MARIYA SHIRÔ'S
ENCYCLOPEDIA OF EXTINCT ANIMALS
DUE TO PAGE LAYOUT ISSUES, WE'VE BEEN CUT BACK.
SCOWL
FEH, FINE, HERE WE GO.
Megatherium
Scientific name: Megatherium americanum
Period of existence: 1.6 million~10 thousand years ago
Distribution: South America
Size: 6~10m tall
The largest ground sloth ever known. It could stand upright using its long, broad tail as support, in order to pull branches closer to itself using the talons on its forelegs, stripping and eating tree leaves with its long tongue. It had a gentle disposition and was slow-moving, but appears to have fought enemies targeting its offspring with its talons.
It is said to have gone extinct due to over-hunting by early mankind.
I STILL CAN'T BELIEVE IT WAS THE AIRPLANE ITSELF THAT ATTRACTED THOSE ANIMALS...
THOUGH I'M SURE THEY WERE JUST PLAYING AROUND, IT WAS QUITE A TO-DO FOR US.
I THINK I'LL INTRODUCE THESE GUYS, TOO, EVEN THOUGH THEY'RE NOT FLASHY.
Mauritius Blue Pigeon
Scientific name: Alectroenas nitidissima
Period of existence: ??~1826
Distribution: Mauritius Island
Size: 30~40cm long
Meiolania
Scientific name: Meiolania
Period of existence: 300~30 thousand years ago
Distribution: Australia, New Caledonia
Size: shell length 1m, body length over 2 m
The largest land turtle known to have ever existed.
Basilosaurus
Scientific name: Basilosaurus
Period of existence: 40~35 million years ago
Distribution: Mediterranean Sea, Atlantic Ocean, etc.
Size: body length 18~25m, skull length 1.8m
A primitive whale species that had a snake-like thin, elongated body. It had flippers for forelimbs and tiny hindlimbs, and lived in shoals. It was an avaricious predator that preyed on fish and aquatic mammals. It has the name Basilosaurus ("King Lizard") because it was initially thought to be a dinosaur when its fossil was first discovered.
THAT'S WHY I DIDN'T WANT TO GO NEAR THE OCEAN... AM I GRATEFUL TO THE FLIGHT ATTENDANT...? SURE.
THOUGH I'D THINK THAT ABANDONING ME TO DIE WITHOUT TRYING TO HELP IS UNCONSCIONABLE!
Continued in the next volume!

TRANSLATION NOTES

Japanese is a tricky language for most Westerners, and translation is often more art than science. For your edification and reading pleasure, here are notes on some of the places where we could have gone in a different direction with our translation of the work, or where a Japanese cultural reference is used.

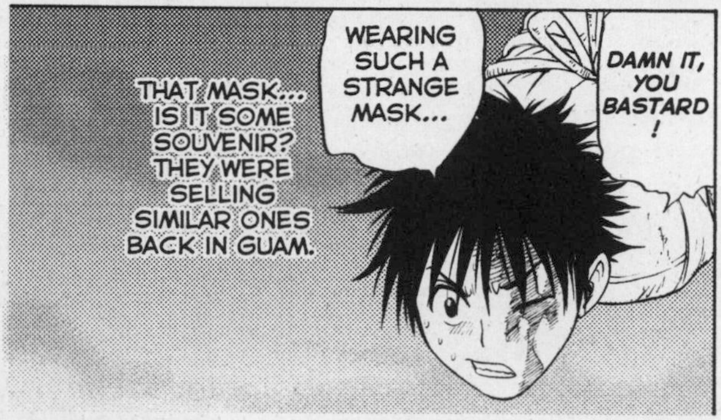
DAMN IT, YOU BASTARD!
WEARING SUCH A STRANGE MASK...
THAT MASK... IS IT SOME SOUVENIR? THEY WERE SELLING SIMILAR ONES BACK IN GUAM.

Souvenir gift, page 9
It is customary in Japan, for those who are traveling, to buy and bring small gifts home for good friends, family, and if of working age, one's co-workers and associates.

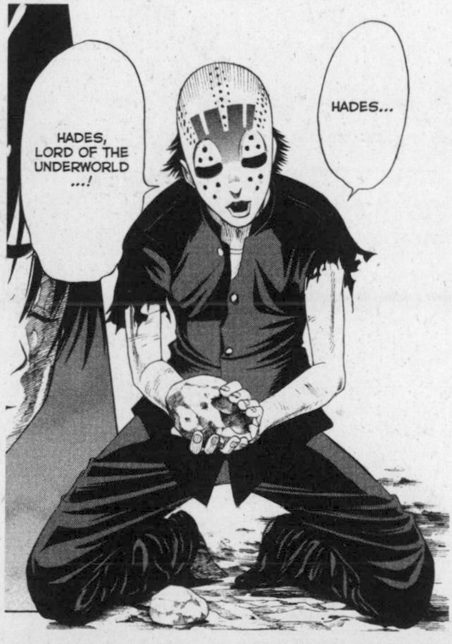
HADES...
HADES, LORD OF THE UNDERWORLD ...!

Hades, page 10
The Ancient Greek god of the underworld and ruler of the dead.

Kitty ears, page 64
An accessory consisting of a headband or hat with stiff cloth cat ears sewn onto it, that helps make one (usually a girl or woman) look like a catgirl. It also identifies one (usually negatively) as a fan of anime or manga. It can be worn by itself or as part of a whole catgirl outfit, which typically also includes a cat's tail, a maid's dress or school uniform, and sometimes even furry paws and/or boots.

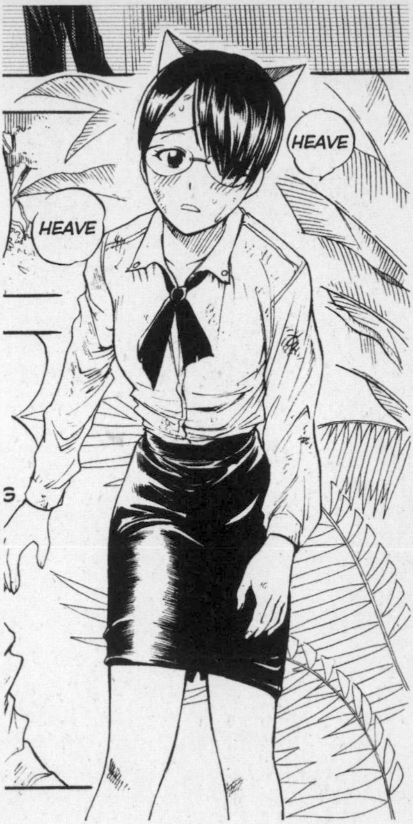
HEAVE
HEAVE

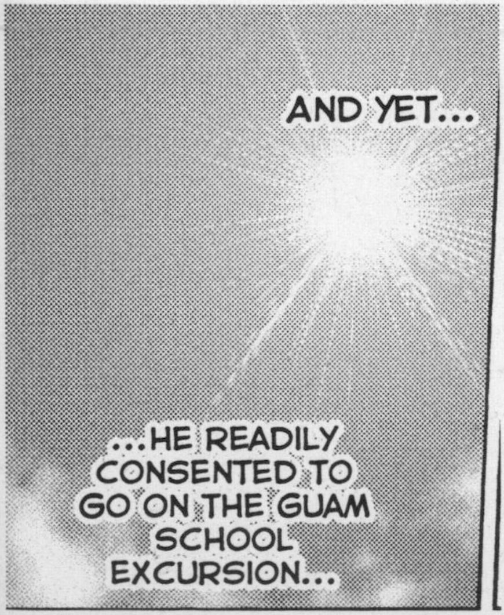
AND YET...
...HE READILY CONSENTED TO GO ON THE GUAM SCHOOL EXCURSION...

School excursion, page 67
A common practice in Japan, where an entire school grade travels together, with teachers as escorts and guardians, during semester or summer breaks. Originally meant as educational experiences and to widen the horizon of those who could not afford to travel much, it is now seen more as opportunities to forge stronger social bonds and foster camaraderie.

WHAT'S UP WITH THIS ISLAND?
WHAT A BADASS SITUATION WE'VE ENDED UP IN.
Class 3-3
Saji "Zaji" Kazuma

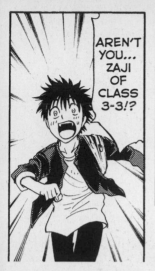

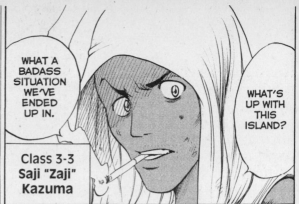

AREN'T YOU... ZAJI OF CLASS 3-3!?

Zaji/Saji, pages 80-81
Zaji is just the nickname this character goes by. His actual name is Saji (family name) Kazuma (given name).

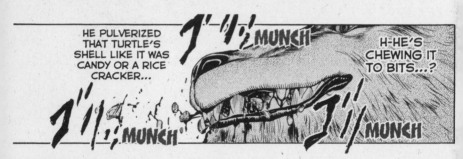

H-HE'S CHEWING IT TO BITS...?
MUNCH
MUNCH
HE PULVERIZED THAT TURTLE'S SHELL LIKE IT WAS CANDY OR A RICE CRACKER...
MUNCH

Rice cracker *(senbei),* page 101
Rice crackers are a type of dry Japanese confection that is made from rice. There are several varieties, such as *senbei* (the term used on page 101), *okaki,* and *arare*, and further subtypes of the previous (such as *norimaki senbei* or seaweed-wrapped *senbei*), that are distinguished by the type

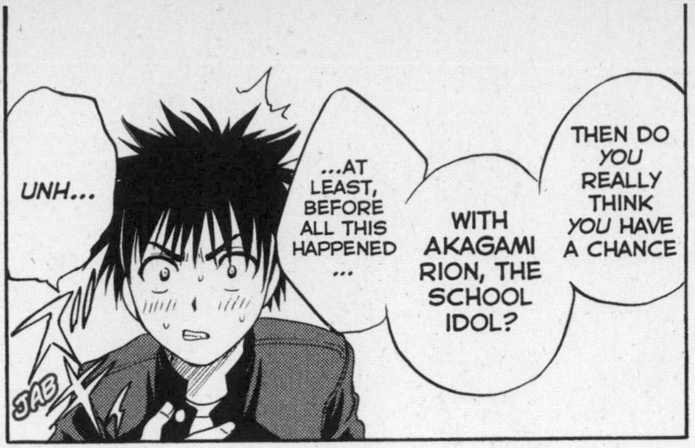
THEN DO YOU REALLY THINK YOU HAVE A CHANCE
WITH AKAGAMI RION, THE SCHOOL IDOL?
...AT LEAST, BEFORE ALL THIS HAPPENED...
UNH...
JAB

Idol, page 170

While most commonly referring to young female media personalities, such as J-pop artists, actresses, and models (but occasionally also foreigners and young male stars), this Japanese phenomenon can extend to civilians as well, i.e. the prettiest student or junior employee.

BWH (3 Sizes), page 186

An abbreviation for bust, waist, and hip, and denotes each respective circumference measurement. Originally intended for the purpose of aiding seamstresses make or fit clothes, it is currently also used by women in their personal ads or profiles to describe their proportions to the viewer.

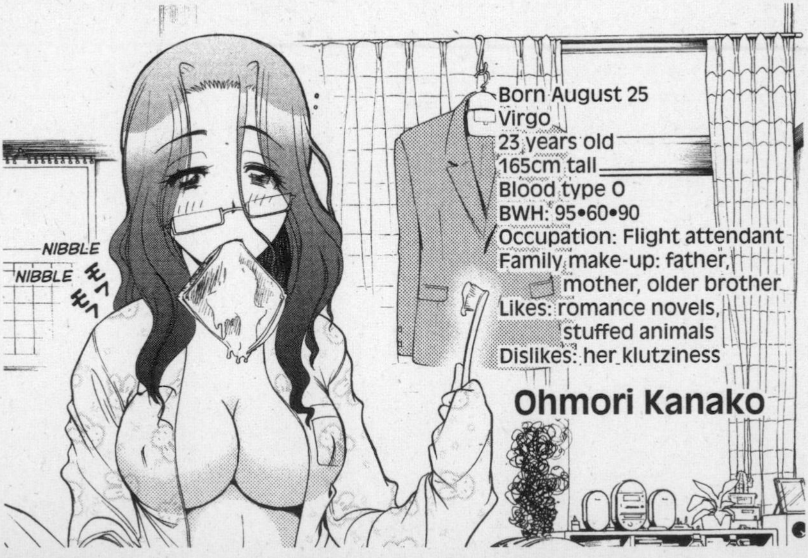
Born August 25
Virgo
23 years old
165cm tall
Blood type O
BWH: 95•60•90
Occupation: Flight attendant
Family make-up: father, mother, older brother
Likes: romance novels, stuffed animals
Dislikes: her klutziness
Ohmori Kanako
NIBBLE
NIBBLE

Preview of

CAGE of EDEN

We're pleased to present you a preview
from Cage of Eden 3.
Please check our website
(www.kodanshacomics.com) to see when
this volume will be available.

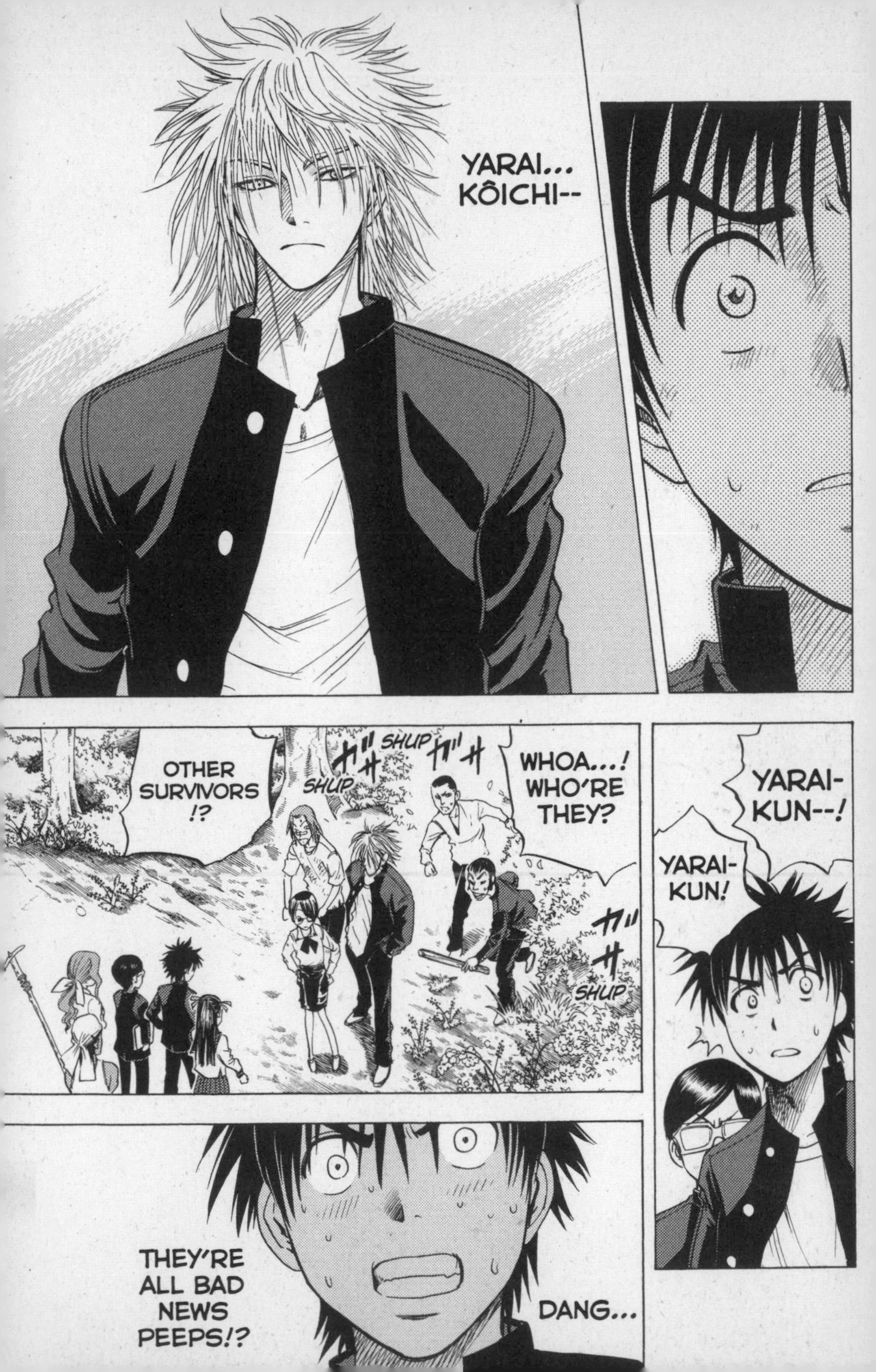
YARAI... KÔICHI--
YARAI-KUN--!
YARAI-KUN!
WHOA...! WHO'RE THEY?
ガサ
SHUP
ガサ
SHUP
ガサ
SHUP
OTHER SURVIVORS !?
DANG...
THEY'RE ALL BAD NEWS PEEPS!?

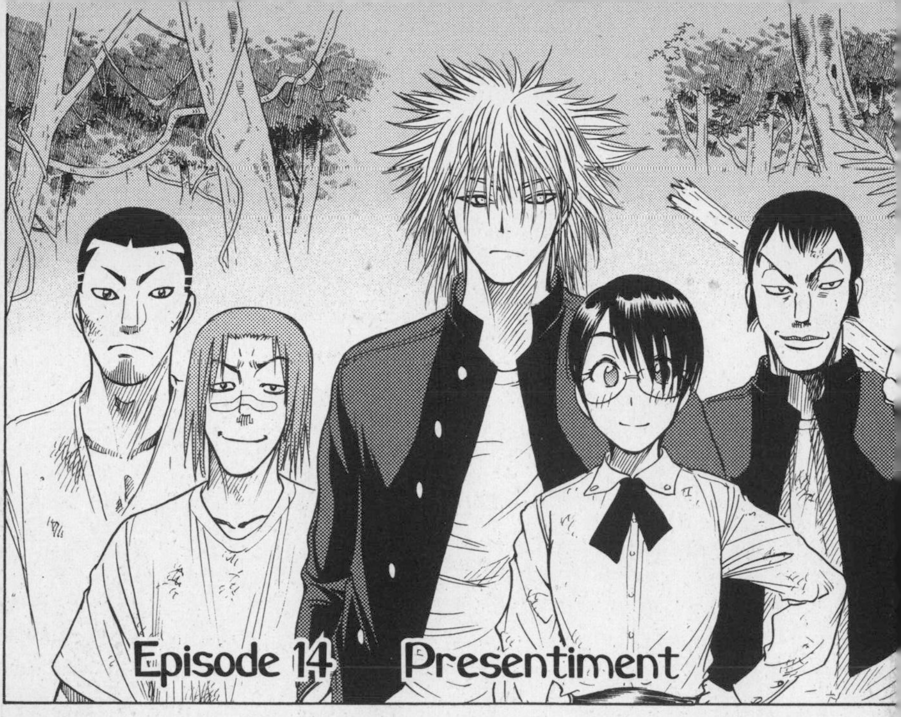
Episode 14 Presentiment
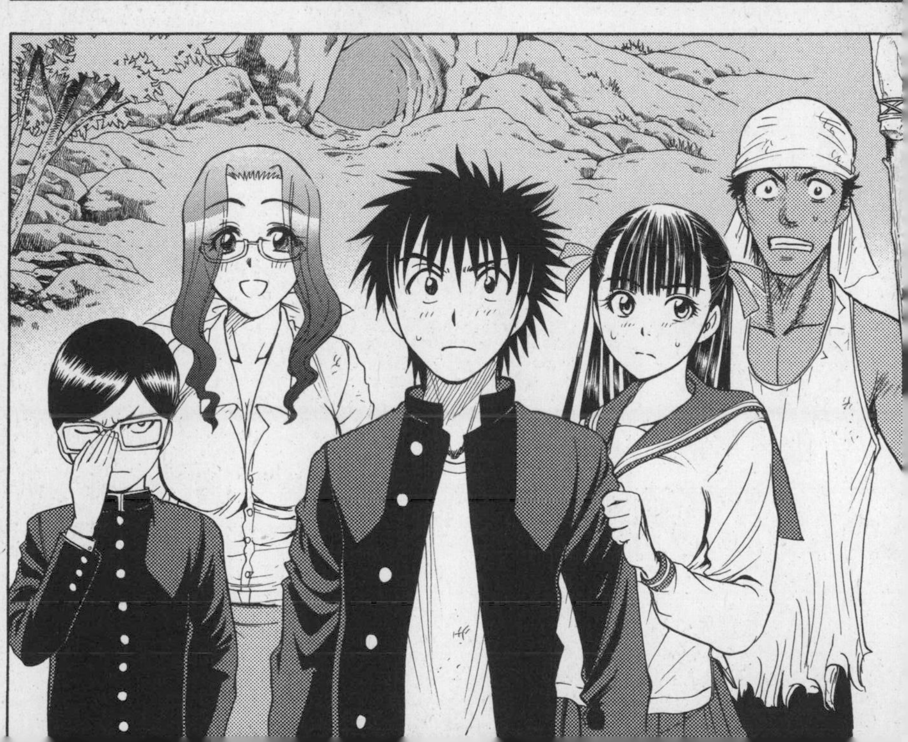

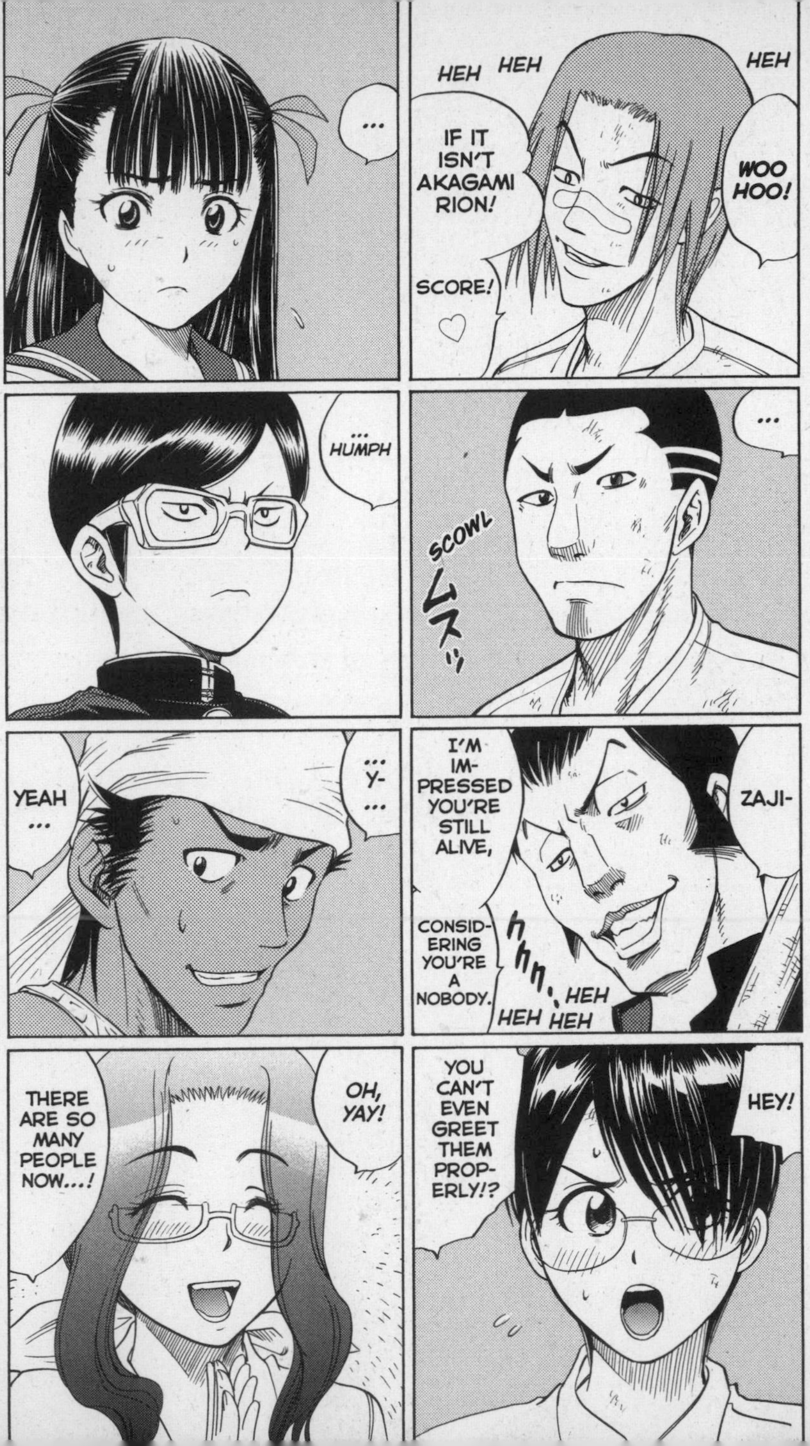
HEH
HEH HEH
WOO HOO!
IF IT ISN'T AKAGAMI RION!
SCORE!
...
...
SCOWL
ムスッ
... HUMPH
ZAJI-
I'M IM-PRESSED YOU'RE STILL ALIVE,
CONSID-ERING YOU'RE A NOBODY.
HEH HEH HEH
... Y- ...
YEAH ...
HEY!
YOU CAN'T EVEN GREET THEM PROP-ERLY!?
OH, YAY!
THERE ARE SO MANY PEOPLE NOW...!

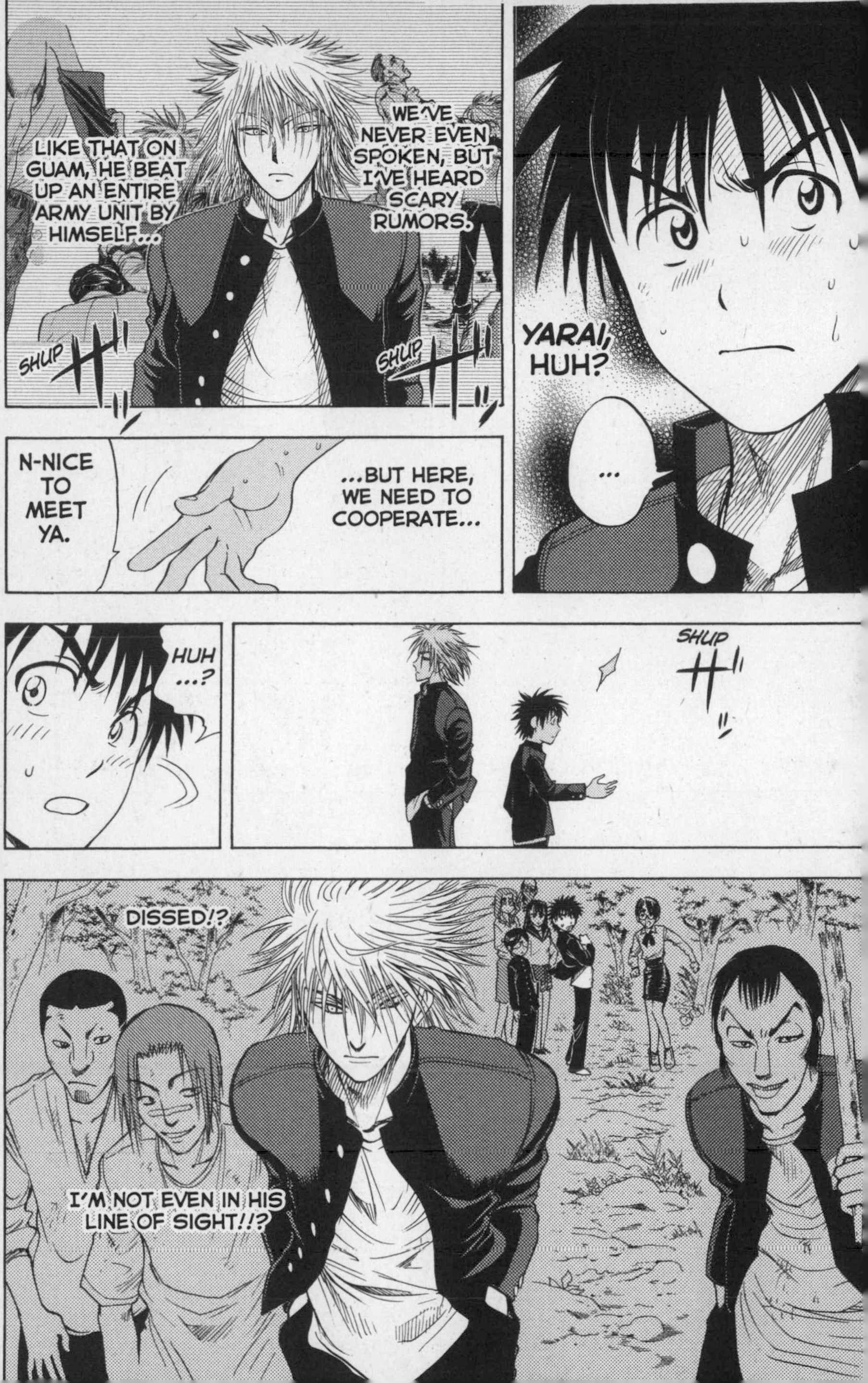
YARAI, HUH?
...
WE'VE NEVER EVEN SPOKEN, BUT I'VE HEARD SCARY RUMORS.
LIKE THAT ON GUAM, HE BEAT UP AN ENTIRE ARMY UNIT BY HIMSELF...
SHUP
SHUP
...BUT HERE, WE NEED TO COOPERATE...
N-NICE TO MEET YA.
SHUP
HUH ...?
DISSED!?
I'M NOT EVEN IN HIS LINE OF SIGHT!!?

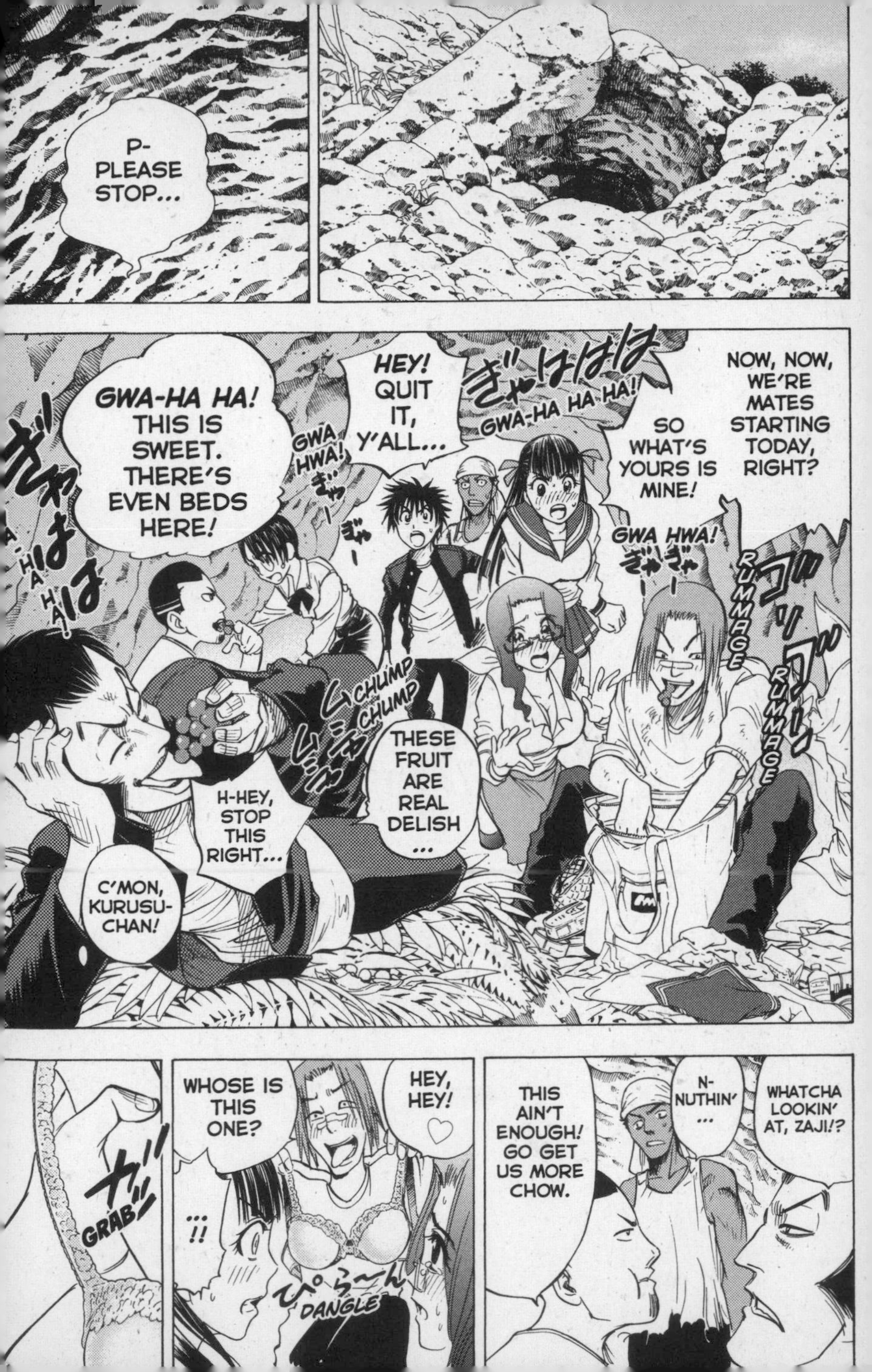
P-PLEASE STOP...
NOW, NOW, WE'RE MATES STARTING TODAY, RIGHT?
SO WHAT'S YOURS IS MINE!
GWA-HA HA HA!
HEY! QUIT IT, Y'ALL...
GWA HWA!
GWA-HA HA! THIS IS SWEET. THERE'S EVEN BEDS HERE!
HA-HA HA!
GWA HWA!
RUMMAGE RUMMAGE
CHUMP CHUMP
THESE FRUIT ARE REAL DELISH ...
H-HEY, STOP THIS RIGHT...
C'MON, KURUSU-CHAN!
WHATCHA LOOKIN' AT, ZAJI!?
N-NUTHIN' ...
THIS AIN'T ENOUGH! GO GET US MORE CHOW.
HEY, HEY!
WHOSE IS THIS ONE?
...!!
DANGLE
GRAB